PEOPLES AND SETTLEMENT
IN
NORTH-WEST ROSS

Edited by

John R. Baldwin

Published in Scotland by:
The Scottish Society for Northern Studies
c/o School of Scottish Studies
University of Edinburgh
27 George Square
Edinburgh EH8 9LD

ISBN 0 9505994 8 4

The Scottish Society for Northern Studies gratefully acknowledges
assistance in the publication of this volume from:

ROYAL COMMISSION ON THE ANCIENT AND HISTORICAL
MONUMENTS OF SCOTLAND
NATIONAL MUSEUMS OF SCOTLAND
HISTORIC SCOTLAND
ROYAL BANK OF SCOTLAND PLC
RJ McLEOD (CONTRACTORS) LTD
KJ MACDONALD ESQ
AM ROSS ESQ (ULLAPOOL ESTATES)
ATF URQUHART (ULLAPOOL) LTD
and from its major sponsors:

 Highland Regional Council
Department of
Libraries and Leisure Services

Rois is Chrombaidh
Leisure Services

 Ross & Cromarty
ENTERPRISE

LETTEREWE ESTATE

Text set throughout in 10 on 11 English Times

Printed by: The Galloway Gazette, Newton Stewart, Scotland

CONTENTS

Illustrations

Cover   : Polglass, Coigach, 1993 (RCAHMS).
Inside Cover : Dornie, Kintail, 1962 (RCAHMS).
p.   v   : Inner Loch Broom, 1992 (RCAHMS).
p. 290   : Badenscallie Burial Ground, 1992 (RCAHMS).
p. 390   : Fish farm, Inverpolly, 1993 (J. R. Baldwin).
Inside Cover : Erected 1889 to the memory of Sir John Fowler of Braemore
               and family. Quay Street, Ullapool, 1992 (RCAHMS).

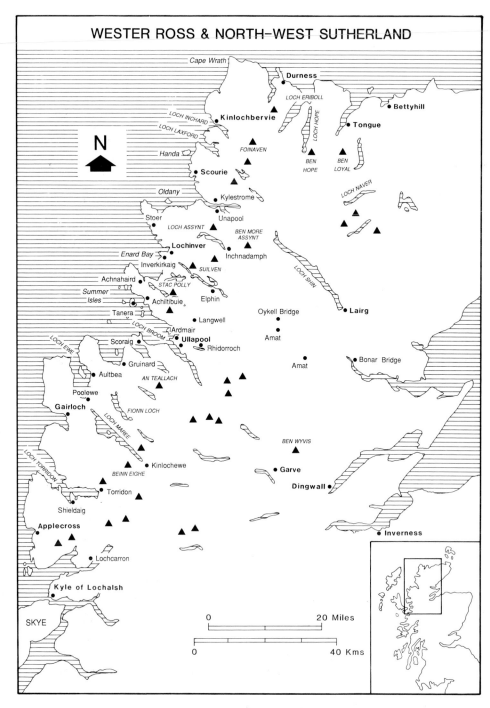

WESTER ROSS & NORTH-WEST SUTHERLAND

Cape Wrath

Durness

LOCH ERIBOLL

Bettyhill

LOCH INCHARD

Kinlochbervie

LOCH HOPE

Tongue

LOCH LAXFORD

N

Handa

FOINAVEN

BEN
HOPE

BEN
LOYAL

● **Scourie**

LOCH NAVER

Oldany

Kylestrome

Stoer

Unapool

LOCH ASSYNT

BEN MORE
ASSYNT

Lochinver

Enard Bay

Inchnadamph

LOCH SHIN

Inverkirkaig

SUILVEN

Achnahaird

STAC POLLY

Summer
Isles

Achiltibuie

Elphin

Lairg

Tanera

Langwell

Oykell Bridge

LOCH BROOM

Ardmair

Ullapool

Amat

LOCH EWE

Scoraig

Rhidorroch

Gruinard

Amat

● Bonar Bridge

Aultbea

AN TEALLACH

Poolewe

Gairloch

FIONN LOCH

LOCH MAREE

BEN WYVIS

BEINN EIGHE

Kinlochewe

Garve

LOCH TORRIDON

Dingwall ●

Torridon

Shieldaig

Applecross

Lochcarron

Inverness

Kyle of Lochalsh

SKYE

0   20 Miles

0   40 Kms

vi

PREFACE

LANDS OF NORTH-WEST ROSS

The lands west of the north-south watershed are referred to popularly as 'Wester Ross'. These are the boggy, rocky, mountainous lands of the northern Highlands, where the potential for settlement is limited to more fertile pockets scattered either coastally or along the bottom of steep-sided straths and glens winding inland from fjord-like sea lochs. These heavily indented coastlines fringe the Northern Minch and mark the Atlantic edge of the great western parishes — from Glenshiel and Kintail in the south, through Lochalsh, Lochcarron and Applecross, to Gairloch and Lochbroom in the north.

These seven parishes contrast strongly with the twenty-two parishes of Easter Ross — essentially Lowland and agriculturally-favoured parishes, some with a Highland hinterland, which have long supported high densities of population attracted by the potential for security and prosperity. The western parishes could offer a richness of salmon, deer and native timber, and at one time played host to herds of wild cattle and horses as well as to wolves and bears. They would long have had substantial value, therefore, as a seasonal (and perhaps recreational) resource. They were, and remain however, a harsh and ungenerous environment for any kind of permanent settlement where access to arable land is both critical and strictly limited. They can support — out of their own resources and in any relative comfort — only a small permanent population.

Coigach and 'North Argyle'

As a term, 'Wester Ross' is insufficiently precise, for neither 'Wester Ross', nor indeed 'North-West Ross', suggests that a part of the area was once distinct from the western lands of Ross. Charters dating back to the 13th and 14th centuries refer to 'North Argyle' — the western coastlands from Kintail northwards to Gairloch and Lochbroom, held by the earls of Ross from 1220 though not as part of the earldom. This 'Argyle' has nothing to do with modern Argyll; rather, as Gaelic *Earra-Ghaidheal*, it suggests a one-time boundary of the Irish-speaking Scots. Just exactly where within the later parish of Lochbroom that boundary lay remains unclear; Coigach, however, looked north rather than south, and in the mid 17th century it was yet recalled as the former fifth part of Assynt (Old Norse *áss endi*, the end of the rocky ridge). Here then is likely evidence for a quite separate Celtic administrative unit stretching north from Loch Broom to Kylesku, not dissimilar perhaps to the 'five quarters' of (Easter) Ross, detailed in 1479 as the confiscated estates of John, last earl of Ross.

During the period of the Scottish monarchy, Coigach continued to be largely 'separate' from the lands to the south. It formed part of the mainland holdings of the MacLeods of Lewis who, in maybe the later 13th century, had supplanted the MacNicols or Nicolsons, owners from perhaps the 10th century. It was the MacLeods who split Coigach off in the 1460s to provide for the second son of the first MacLeod of Assynt; and after the MacKenzies acquired the MacLeod estates in the early years of the 17th century, it was Coigach alone that, by 1686, was consolidated by the first earl of Cromartie and his sons into the area subsequently known as Cromartyshire — a disjoined area that included the east coast Baronies of New Tarbat and Strathpeffer, as well as the west coast Barony of Coigach and the inland upland Fannichs. In 1891 Cromartyshire was assimilated into the County of Ross and Cromarty; in 1975 the County became Ross and Cromarty District. Thus has the orientation of Coigach come to be 'mislaid'!

PEOPLES OF NORTH-WEST ROSS

If these are the lands of North-West Ross, who are the peoples? In all truth they are indistinct and shadowy figures until post-medieval times — prehistoric tribes, Celtic tribes, Picts, 'Irish' Scots, Norse, 'Scottish' Scots, 'Anglo' Scots, English . . . . Over the millenia, the western seaboard has played host to successive waves of peoples who would appear in large part to have come, conquered and settled — and all-too-often left again for kinder pastures elsewhere in the wake of climatic, demographic, economic and/or social hardship and change.

Rarely, however, do conditions bring about a complete abandonment of an area by a people or a culture, for under most kinds of pressure only a proportion of a population would migrate — those who had the means perhaps, and those who were dispossessed. Periodically, and for varying reasons, certain groupings have undoubtedly preferred to stay; and others have had little option but to stay. There has always been considerable scope, therefore, for ethnic and cultural continuity, assimilation and evolution. Nevertheless, these factors alone do not necessarily imply enrichment.

Early Peoples

The modest spread of single standing stones represents one of the earliest traces of man's presence in the landscape — erected perhaps in the 3rd-2nd millenia BC, though we know not why. Equally unclear is the relationship after around 1000 BC and into AD between stone-built brochs and duns and the many small and scattered groups of undefended hut circles — except that these represent an organised society apparently based on local family or tribal groups of farmers who had increasing cause to protect themselves.

How successful they were we cannot tell; by the early centuries AD, however, the 'indigenous' population, whether descendants and/or incomers, appears to have been predominantly Celtic-speaking and with Celtic tribal names. These are Ptolomey's tribes, and from the 4th-9th centuries AD they had coalesced into a people nowadays referred to as Picts.

Whether or not the administrative division of land into 'fifths' and the measurement of farm land in 'davochs' indicate a Pictish presence or later influences, symbol stones in Easter Ross and as far north as Farr on the north coast of Sutherland undoubtedly betray a strong Pictish culture. Placenames too are significant. Names such as Oykell, Achilty and Achilti(buie) may well have emerged around this time. They appear to be of the same origin as Welsh *uchel*, high, and highlight Pictish settlement east-west on this narrowest of necks across mainland Scotland — from Loch Broom to the Kyle of Sutherland and the Dornoch Firth.

However, just as carved symbol stones are at their most common and elaborate on the fertile lowlands of Easter Ross, so also are a host of other names incorporating Pictish elements — whether e.g. *pit*, a place or farmstead (Pitkerrie); *-ais*, a dwelling (Alness); or stream names ending in *-n* or *-ie* (Carron, Conan, Rogie, Grudie, Polly, Runie). Of river names ending in *-ie*, for instance, nine out of twenty-four are found in Wester Ross, fifteen in Easter Ross. Fewer are found to the north, in Sutherland, where Norse influence was strong; and few, if any, are to be found in Dalriada to the south, where Irish Gaelic speakers — the Scots — were settling as early as the 2nd century AD and were well-consolidated by the early 6th century.

The boundaries of 'North Argyle' were likely established by the late 7th century (the monastery at Applecross was founded by the Irish priest, Maelrubha, in 673 AD), but it is a matter for conjecture whether the 'Scots' had effectively colonised the far north-west before the Scandinavians first raided in the 790s AD. Professor W. J. Watson reminds us that the Norse called the Minch *Skotland-fjördr*, the firth of the land of the Scots, and survivals of the name *Annat* indicate the presence of pre-Norse, Gaelic-speaking missionaries from the Irish Celtic church. That these names are to be found off Applecross, beside Loch Torridon, Loch Broom and Loch Laxford, in Skye, Harris, Lewis and on the Shiant Islands does not necessarily confirm that at this time significant numbers of Gaelic speakers were found north from 'North Argyle'. There may have been a mixed population, perhaps bilingual, of Picts and Scots, or maybe they were mainly Picts. Either way, with the coming of the Norsemen, some kind of bilingual or possibly trilingual society emerged along the north-west coast. The more developed Scots would have exercised a superiority over the Picts, but if numbers of Picts and Scots fled eastwards as the more powerful Scandinavians advanced inland from the coast, the latter might well have established their shore bases in a relatively empty land. Around Loch Broom, for example, supported by their longships and established on patches of better land appropriated alongside safe anchorages at Ullapool, Tanera and perhaps Dornie and Reiff, even modest Scandinavian plantations would likely have been little threatened by small clusters of Celts grouped on what nowadays at least are the bleak and windswept slopes around and behind Achiltibuie, home to numerous hut circles and fragmentary field systems. (Bog fir shows that at one time some, at least, of these slopes were well-wooded).

This can only be conjecture. One way or another, the Norsemen and the Gaels, Scandinavians and Scots, assimilated the Picts into their stronger culture; and eventually, as formal ties with Norway weakened and broke, a mixed race of Scandinavians and Scots lost its bilingualism and was absorbed into an essentially Celtic and Scottish world. The formal break is marked by the Battle of Largs and the Treaty of Perth (1266); bilingualism may well have disappeared, however, by the 12th century. And once a language has gone, culture and traditions go too — only fragments surviving the transfer from one language to another.

17th-20th Centuries

By the late 16th century internecine fighting between competing factions within the Lewis MacLeods, descendants of such a mixed race, destroyed the clan and led to the MacKenzie takeover of MacLeod lands. The Mackenzies proved to be a large and extended clan, politically astute (other than for backing the 'wrong' side during the '45), and with a well-developed liking for good living. Whether as earls of Cromartie or as lesser families, they held lands throughout both Wester and Easter Ross and not infrequently fell upon hard times. They survived by speculating abroad, by cattle trading, by selling off such assets as the standing timber and, as fortunes ebbed and flowed, by settling each other's debts through wadsetting, intermarriage and other mechanisms.

But this was not sufficient. Speculative ventures were prone to failure, and growing tastes for expensive south-country life-styles (fine country houses, elegant town houses, 'policy' plantings, servants, life as a Member of Parliament, military responsibilities) all required substantial funding. Increasingly, major and minor landowners sought to extract considerably greater revenue from their estates — whether directly from their tenants in the form of increased rents or by reviewing the uses to which they could put their lands. When leases fell vacant, higher rents could be obtained first from graziers, later from wealthy industrialists — provided that the existing tenantry were relocated and restricted to allow for undisturbed access by sheep, cattle and deer; by shepherds, stalkers and sportsmen. Some sought to diversify into fisheries and kelp, but this was of relatively minor significance. The kelp industry was never as developed as in the islands, and commercial fisheries came into their own only with the establishment of the British Fisheries Society settlement at Ullapool in 1788. In any event, this initiative also proved to be short-lived, the herring becoming remarkably elusive by the 1820s.

The Impact of Development

It is the story of these past 300 or so years that features so strongly in *Peoples and Settlement in North-West Ross*. Early chapters provide an environmental context for settlement and a focus first on the fortifications of early Celtic Scotland, notably brochs, and then on key Norse place-naming elements for farms and for critical geographical features. Analysis ranges widely across the northern and western mainland and islands, revealing a complexity in successive phases of settlement and technology, linguistic and architectural evolution, that will repay continuing study.

The majority of chapters, however, deal with the late medieval and modern periods. They focus on such themes as medieval ecclesiastical sculpture, post-Reformation parish life and structure, and the rise and fall of both the MacLeods and the MacKenzies. Substantial sections examine many and varied aspects of everyday life and work — both the mechanics and economics of land ownership, fisheries, forestry and crofting, as well as their associated buildings and architecture. Churches, country houses, farm houses, crofthouses and such 'industrial' buildings as salmon stations and fishery storehouses all feature in some detail, and an entire chapter is devoted to the planned 'new town' of Ullapool, which celebrated its bi-centenary in 1988. Other contributors explore the evolution of settlement, notably within the context of agricultural improvement, estate management and the Clearances. They examine poverty, famine and the relief of destitution; and they focus on present-day social and cultural change — seeking to determine concepts of identity both for 'locals' and for 'incomers'.

The larger part of the book, therefore, concentrates on land use, life-style, settlement and culture during that lengthy period of instability triggered by the break-up of the clan system and heightened by the social, economic and political aspirations of a new breed of landed proprietor and principal tenant, whether Scottish or English.

The Nature of Change: People and Environment

Change is the all-important factor, the common underlying theme — change and continuity, change and destruction, change and inter-dependence whether between peoples and cultures or between peoples, cultures and their environment. Underlying the concept of ever-present change, however, is the unhappy indication that all-too-often change was engineered by the few, for the few, and at the expense of the many — a view reinforced by not infrequent references in Estate papers to the harassment of timber extractors and commercial sheep farmers by the local tenantry.

Undoubtedly there was, and still is, a need for change. The questions, now as ever, relate rather to the nature of that change: who makes the decisions, on what grounds, how change is carried out and for whose benefit, both short-term and long-term? Change from a pre-industrial peasant economy (still surviving in modified form in the north-west Highlands well into the 19th century, and arguably through until the final demise of traditional crofting in the late 20th century) was perhaps inevitable. But a change to what? And for whom?

Over a period of 200-300 years, 'economic rationalisation' by land-owners and principal tenants faced with a perceived need to generate greater wealth and more substantial cash-flow, all-too-often proved an excuse for the exercise of philosophies somewhat removed from wider concepts of social justice and community well-being. There were honourable exceptions, of course, and the efforts of certain individual and influential families in north-west Ross, particularly the older-established families, ran counter to the prevailing culture. Some were genuinely interested in agricultural and domestic improvement across all levels of society. And on occasion at least, in times of famine, some most certainly contributed to the relief of their starving and impoverished tenants and lost income as a result. They maintained rents at 'uneconomic' levels; they postponed payment of rents; they inaugurated what we would nowadays term 'targeted welfare schemes', building roads in return for meal. But rarely, if ever, do they seem to have stopped to consider whether such hardships and the structural collapse of long-established communities correlated directly with their own underlying activities and aspirations. And the times did not encourage consultation and shared decision-making on the kind of change and development that would have best served the whole community.

How ironic, therefore, that we find so 'pleasing' such surviving landscape features as well-proportioned country houses, fine steadings, well-planted policy woodlands, neat and regular field systems on the (few) substantial farms. And how wretched are the abandoned, rush-infested rigs scratched across the sodden and treeless moorland, the broken-down hill-dykes, the crumbling ruins of tiny crofthouses clustered or in line a little above the shore and frequently beyond all reasonable limits of cultivation.

Nor was poverty felt only by the smaller tenants and cottars; it is echoed in the land. 'Wilderness' the northern and western Highlands may be; but 'natural' this wilderness is not. Hills, moorlands and infields have been largely exhausted; natural forests and native woodlands have all but disappeared through clear-felling, burning, wasting and indiscriminate grazing by sheep and deer. The 'wilderness', both natural and human, is essentially man-made. It is a classic example of short-term profit maximisation by the politically and economically more powerful, and over-use of much-restricted and peripheral lands by a marginalised, impoverished and periodically starving peasantry. The media remind us of environmentally — and culturally — destructive practices by loggers and ranchers in South America, and the over-intensive use of scarce natural resources amongst the increasingly pressurised hill tribes of Nepal; they remind us of the problems that accompany excessive and unsustainable development in these and other localities world-wide. Such have been the practices for two or three centuries in the Scottish Highlands, and the results are plain to see.

Future Directions?

By contrast, traditional and non-intensive Highland economies, based primarily on pastoralism and supported by modest farming, fishing and woodland management, are often recognised nowadays as environmentally as well as culturally sympathetic — role models perhaps for a new era of lower-key, sustainable lifestyles. The old economies and practices had evolved over centuries, through the distillation of generations of observation, experience and knowledge, in such a way that communities understood what was environmentally and socially responsible and what, conversely, would lead to the terminal decline of much-needed resources and to the fragmentation of their society. That so much of this accumulated wisdom has been lost can hardly be laid at the door of today's crofter or fisherman. Rather is it a 'by-product' of the cultural, not simply environmental impoverishment that resulted from continuing exposure to an ascendant culture largely indifferent to non-material and locally-significant values and aspirations.

Such a loss heightens the need to extend environmental, economic and cultural awareness amongst all who live and work both in the Highlands and beyond. 'Education' is insufficient, however, if it does not speedily generate new attitudes, new policies, new ways of looking at distinctive regional cultures, land ownership and land use, new ways of involving communities in determining locally-relevant and sustainable initiatives.

Happily attitudes are changing, and initiatives and investment — albeit often modest — have begun. The emergence of Sabhal Mór Ostaig and Acair; Community Co-operatives; telecottaging and Integrated Rural Development Studies; the Scottish Crofters' Union and Rural Forum; Highlands and Islands Forum; the Assynt Crofters Trust and the Letterewe Accord — these are all pointers to the future. So also are positive contributions from the Local Authorities, Government Departments and Agencies, Conservation Bodies and the European Union. Initiatives such as Integrated/Agricultural Development Projects and Crofter Forestry grants, schemes for Environmentally Sensitive and for Less Favoured Areas, road- and harbour-building projects, green tourism and Gaelic-medium education are all to be welcomed — provided that they genuinely strengthen the long-term interests of local communities and cultures, and encourage stability and reinvestment locally. Although some sectors may still find it difficult to relinquish a 'top down' approach and to agree the significant decentralisation of planning and decision-making powers to knowledgeable locally-elected groups, there is a certain reassurance to be found in the 'grass roots', 'bottom-up' philosophy of much that is emerging.

It is, however, a fragile system — a series of fragile, tentative networks which require careful nurturing. For in the far north-west, it is frequently still a matter of potential rather than of identifiable achievement. And herein lies the paradox. The very nature of environmental and cultural education and of integrated and sustainable development is long-term and low-key; results will not be immediate (though judicious fencing and stock reductions, for instance, can soon be seen to trigger woodland and associated regeneration). In other words, substantial, short-term returns on investment are as unlikely as they are unreasonable — particularly when the true costs of past and future environmental and cultural impact are assessed, accepted and taken properly into account.

Many factors inevitably inter-relate in any consideration of a 'way ahead' for the north-west Highlands. Without continuing commitment to socially, culturally and environmentally sympathetic policies (and regardless of the superficially benign image of retirement homes, tourist facilities, klondykers and palm trees) the future for north-west Ross will be bleak — bleak for its natural landscapes and bleak for its people.

ACKNOWLEDGEMENTS

These fifteen papers do not claim to provide a ready solution to such matters, any more than they would claim to offer a consolidated history of the area. Nonetheless perhaps they can contribute to the debate and to the climate for change. For they can point to past practice, past errors and misjudgements as well as strengths, and hope that — seemingly against all odds and experience elsewhere — society can learn from these mistakes.

Peoples and Settlement in North-West Ross brings together research pioneered over twenty and more years by recognised authorities in their respective fields. That some have begun to explore the potential of archaeological field survey, sociological investigation and oral history in the area, helps provide a counter-balance to surviving estate papers and other administrative, managerial and 'establishment' records.

Such eclecticism reflects the Scottish Society for Northern Studies' multi-disciplinary approach to the study of the Celtic, Scandinavian and other cultures whether within Scotland or across the wider north Atlantic. The skills and strengths of the historian and geographer, the ethnologist, linguist and placename specialist, the archaeologist, sociologist, architectural and oral historian — all are brought to focus on a particular geographical region in the hope and belief that the whole is of greater interest and value than its individual and separate parts.

As always, the views expressed by contributors and editor are not necessarily those of the Society; as always, however, the Society is delighted to recognise its very substantial debt to those who, without exception, have given so freely and voluntarily of their time and expertise. In today's 'free market' climate, where everything supposedly has its price, it is refreshing and reassuring to recognise that higher and more civilised values survive. Likewise, it gives the Society much pleasure to acknowledge the support — both financial and in kind — of a great many organisations and individuals. We could never over-value such local support as that of Ullapool's 'Ceilidh Place' or the Gairloch Museum, or the continuing backing of such national bodies as the Royal Commission on the Ancient and Historical Monuments of Scotland, the National Museums of Scotland, Historic Scotland, the National Library of Scotland, the Scottish Record Office and Edinburgh University's School of Scottish Studies. Moreover, we would want to acknowledge the quite splendid support of Ross and Cromarty District Council, Highland Regional Council, Ross and Cromarty Enterprise and the private sector — notably Letterewe Estate, the Royal Bank of Scotland plc and R. J. McLeod (Contractors) Ltd. Such a blend of public and private support augurs well perhaps for future initiatives in north-west Ross.

We hope that readers will find *Peoples and Settlement in North-West Ross* stimulating and enjoyable. There is a pressing need to record and unravel more of the patterns of culture and settlement in this little-known and superficially-understood part of the Norse, Celtic and latterly Anglo-Scottish worlds — particularly at this time of exceedingly rapid and critical change in population, language, culture, employment and aspirations.

We very much hope that the book will point the way. We hope that it will trigger further research, that it will encourage a stronger sense of community and identity locally, and that it will provide visitors, new residents and in-coming landowners and businesses alike with an attractive and authoritative background to the area's erstwhile cultural and environmental richness and diversity. Above all, we hope it can contribute to the 'new philosophy' so sorely needed to help conserve and reconstruct richness and diversity once more — both in north-west Ross and more generally across the north.

John R. Baldwin
Edinburgh 1994

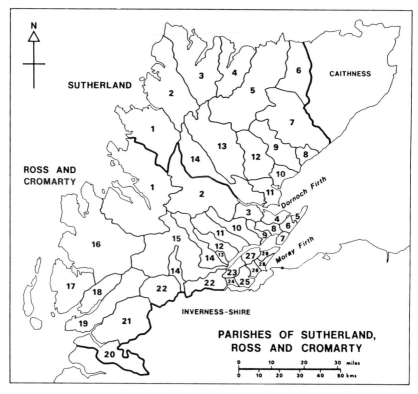

Fig. 1.1   Parishes of Sutherland, Ross & Cromarty.

SUTHERLAND

1. Assynt
2. Eddrachillis
3. Durness
4. Tongue
5. Farr
6. Reay (part of)
7. Kildonan
8. Loth
9. Clyne
10. Golspie
11. Dornoch
12. Rogart
13. Lairg
14. Creich

ROSS AND CROMARTY

1. Lochbroom
2. Kincardine
3. Edderton
4. Tain
5. Tarbat
6. Fearn
7. Nigg
8. Logie Easter
9. Kilmuir Easter
10. Rosskeen
11. Alness
12. Kiltearn
13. Dingwall
14. Fodderty
15. Contin

16. Gairloch
17. Applecross
18. Lochcarron
19. Lochalsh
20. Glenshiel
21. Kintail
22. Urray
23. Urquhart and Logie Wester
24. Killearnan
25. Kilmuir Wester (Knockbain)
26. Avoch
27. Kirkmichael (Resolis)
28. Rosemarkie
29. Cromarty

MAN AND THE LAND: PHYSICAL ENVIRONMENT AND SETTLEMENT IN THE NORTH-WEST HIGHLANDS

Douglas P. Willis

To leave behind the lowlands of the east and travel across country to the North-West Highlands is to experience one of the most complete contrasts in Scottish geography.

The lowland landscape of the east, with its large farms and fertile farmlands, has been moulded in a kindlier environment. Wide expanses of flat land, floored by younger rock and masked by glacial deposits, are coupled with a climate which, because the area lies in the rain shadow of sheltering high ground to the west, is comparatively dry and sunny. The highland landscape of the west, by complete contrast, is one where human settlement of the land has often struggled to maintain a viable presence against the environmental niggardliness of ancient hard rocks, acid and thin soils, and a climatic pattern that is grudgingly cloudy and wet.

In these circumstances, it is hardly surprising that enormous contrasts should exist between the human landscape of the sparsely peopled upland west and that of the more populous lowland east, although both occur within the context of the Scottish Highlands.

ROCK: THE UNDERLYING RESOURCE

The Highlands of the North-West bear the marks of a land that has been long in the making. Even the most cursory glance at a map suggests the enormous contrasts which exist in the relief pattern. Inland from the coast, steep-sided mountains dominate flat-bottomed straths, while along the Atlantic edge, long fingers of sea lochs indent the land. All have been shaped by the erosive power of time, but within a geological context that is the basis of landscape formation.

To understand the geological history of the North-West Highlands is to embark on a long and complex journey through millennia of time. The earliest foundations of the land lie in the grey and dour rock which is the Lewisian gneiss. Bearing the name of the Long Island whose outline can be seen clearly from the mainland on a clear day, this most ancient of Highland rocks is the hard and unyielding basis of much of the human settlement in the west.

1

Fig. 1.2 Ben More Coigach mirrored in a lochan near Drumrunie in Wester Ross. The Torridonian Sandstone massifs of Wester Ross and Sutherland rise steeply from peat moor and dubh lochan. 1990.

Fig. 1.3 Stac Pollaidh, perhaps the most spectacular of all the mountains of Wester Ross with its striking Torridonian Sandstone crags and screes. A negative area for human settlement! 1990.

In fact, the landscape of the Lewisian gneiss may be seen as a fossil landscape from the past, for it bears the marks of having been eroded to a low-lying plain millions of years ago. Where later sediments were deposited on top, they were laid down on a surface which had already been reduced to its roots long before. In much more recent times, powerfully moving ice during the last glacial epoch was to strip and scour the surface of the outcropping rock, resulting in today's sombre landscape of dark peat and dubh lochan.

Above this wild and unpromising surface rears the spectacular sugar loaf peak of Suilven and the impressive outlined forms of Canisp, Ben More Assynt, Stac Pollaidh and the rest. These dominating peaks which contribute so much of the distinctiveness of West Sutherland are the surviving remnants of the once more extensive layer of sedimentary rock termed the Torridonian Sandstone [Figs. 1.2-1.4].

Resembling the younger eastern sandstone only in its reddish colouring, the sandstone of the west is a more ancient rock by far. The character of the North-West Highlands owes much to the presence of the Torridonian Sandstone. Often patterned in extensive lichen growth where it outcrops among the peat, the rock has a grey look, though in places where quarrying has exposed open surfaces, the true colour is revealed.

Fig. 1.4 The distinctive peaks of Cùl Mór (left), Stac Pollaidh, Cùl Beag, Beinn an Eoin and Ben More Coigach provide a dramatic backdrop to Loch Vatachan and the extensive and boggy moorlands of the Aird of Coigach. 1972.

Fig. 1.5   The three caves at Craig nan Uamh lie some 30m above the floor of the valley of the Allt nan Uamh, near Inchnadamph.

Excavated in 1889 and 1926-27, an upper layer of cave earth lying on water-laid deposits of clay or gravel contained animal bones from such extinct Arctic fauna as brown bear, lynx and reindeer. For water to have run into the caves, an ice sheet would have had to have filled the valley to a height of 30m, and such an ice sheet is not now thought to have existed in Assynt later than ca. 11,000 BC.

Human remains, also found in 1926-27, are thought to be of no great age however. No genuine Palaeolithic or Mesolithic flint or stone artefacts were found in the cave earth layers, and the few bone implements and supposed hearths are not closely datable. The case for Palaeolithic man in Scotland remains unproven; the nearest such site is in Cumbria, some 430km to the south (Euan MacKie, 9/4/1988. pers. comm.).

As an enduring building material, the Torridonian Sandstone was once extensively quarried, and until the more recent construction phase, much of Ullapool was fashioned out of small local quarries which today lie disused and overgrown.

The sparkling white quartzite which forms a later geological capping to some of the higher peaks, has been of little significance in the human picture, except as a scenic feature, giving the incongruous impression of a dusting of snow sparkling on the high tops on a fine summer's day.

By contrast, the Cambrian limestone which exists as a narrow band of rock has had considerable impact both in terms of scenery and human value. In a land of acid soils, the presence of outcropping alkaline rock is marked by pockets of better pasture land, such as occur around Elphin. Nearby, at Inchnadamph, solution of the limestone has opened up the rock into caves which have their own attraction these days for visitors keen to have a speleological experience in a Highland setting. But they also once yielded up the bones of an Arctic fauna that included such cold climate beasts as brown bear, lynx and reindeer [Fig. 1.5]. In economic terms, apart from the obvious greater potential for grazing on the limestone-based pastures, the

4

rock continues to be commercially exploited in a large quarry between Ullapool and Rhidorroch as a useful northern source of agricultural lime. And a substantial marble quarry has now opened near Ledbeg, between Elphin and Inchnadamph.

Though many of the geological events that have helped shape the landscape of the North-West Highlands were long and slow in their occurrence, others were far from being so. Throughout the North-West, faulting has produced stress marks that line the face of the land. The straight edge of Loch Broom, so apparent when seen in aerial view from the top of neighbouring hills, is a good example of a feature whose form is strongly fault-guided. Smaller faults may be seen as minor indentations on many hill slopes, where fast-flowing burns have exploited the weaker rock, but sometimes the effects of earth forces were of cataclysmic proportions that left enormous scars on the landscape.

In the most spectacular tectonic happening of all, metamorphic rocks from further to the east were pushed bodily westwards along what geologists term a thrust plane, over-riding the existing rock formations. It was an event whose visible effects were to perplex the generation of early geologists who struggled to interpret them. The view of Murchison of Tarradale, doyen of early British geologists, that the rocks formed a perfectly normal series was strongly challenged by the counter view that earth movements had indeed complicated the sequence.

But, as far as the people who had to gain a living from the land were concerned, such matters were purely academic. In down-to-earth practical terms, the Moine Thrust had been the means of providing a rock type of considerable value. This, the Moine schist, has the distinct value of splitting into layers that may at times resemble thick slate. The potential of such a material as a building medium is obvious, providing a source of well-shaped building stone which could be more easily manipulated than the uneven stones which land or seashore provided. That the value of the schist has long been recognised in this way is apparent in its use for structures as far removed in time as the vitrified Iron Age fortification of Dun Lagaidh in Upper Loch Broom [Figs. 1.6, 1.7], or the walls of recent croft houses and outbuildings with their inset cruck beams [Figs. 1.8]. Indeed, such is the tendency of this rock to split quite naturally into layers and slabs, that its use as doorway and window lintels, and even as stall divisions in old byres, strongly resembles that of the heavy flagstones of Caithness and Orkney (see MacKie, Beaton, this volume).

LANDFORM, SETTLEMENT AND COMMUNICATIONS

Although the landscape continues to be shaped by the powers of weathering and erosion, as the scree-covered slopes of Ben More Coigach or An Teallach amply confirm, it is to the powerful effect of moving ice that so much of the land surface owes its present character. As the climate deteriorated and snowfall accumulated over the higher ground, the great ice

Fig. 1.6   The fort and dun at Dun Lagaidh, looking north to Ullapool, inner Loch Broom. 1984.

Fig. 1.7 Excavation at Dun Lagaidh revealed a fine flight of intra-mural stone steps. 1984.

Fig. 1.8 Cruck-framed house at Cuaig, Applecross. 1972.

Fig. 1.9 The deep U-shaped valley of Strath Broom. Shaped by a glacier during the Ice Age, the valley bottom provides potential for farming in an environment of limited agricultural opportunity. 1990.

Fig. 1.10   Dun Canna on a peninsula at the mouth of Strath Kanaird, Loch Broom. 1974.

tongues of outflowing valley glaciers moved inexorably seawards. On the west side, their erosive power was the greater because of the short distance to be covered by the ice on its powerful downhill journey. The result in today's landscape is the presence of some spectacular scenic features, notably the long and deep sea lochs which parallel the Norwegian fiords in their mode of formation, and the wide glaciated valleys such as Glen Torridon or Strath Broom [Fig. 1.9].

In the human geography of the area, each of these glaciation features has had its own significance throughout time. The wide valley floors have provided flat land in an area where farming has always been influenced by severe relief constraints; and they have given more fertile, alluvial deposits where poor, thin soils have also imposed their limitations upon agriculture.

They have had their value, too, for communications, the flat-bottomed valleys allowing a passage through difficult upland terrain, especially important in providing connecting routes from the east. The sheltered arms of the sea lochs were also a means of communication in an era when travel by sea was easier than by the road transport of the time. However, in this present age, the sea lochs now exist more as a barrier to rapid movement, imposing long detours on communication among lochside communities, a fact which raises its own complications for service provision, such as schooling. On the other hand, the sheltered conditions and previously unspoiled waters of the sea lochs have provided the basis of the sometimes controversial fish farming industry that now has its power base in the west.

Communication up or down the west coast has always been frustrated by the problems of physical geography. Only at Kylesku does a bridge expedite north-south travel across the broken terrain of the North-West; elsewhere, isolation rather than communication has been a recurring feature of west coast communities. In the unsettled times of the past, however, isolation on a local scale could be a positive advantage in strategic terms. Peninsular positions, virtually surrounded by water, assumed a value as defensive sites, as in the Bronze Age fortifications of An Dun at Gairloch and Dun Canna at the mouth of Strath Kanaird [Fig. 1.10], or in later times in the stark fortress of Ardvreck Castle in Loch Assynt [Fig. 1.11]. Sometimes there could be a defensive value also in the kind of rocky outcrop on which the crumbled ruins of Dun Lagaidh now overlook the multinational klondyker invasion of Loch Broom [see Fig. 1.6].

It might be argued that in this most recent economic phase of the North-West Highlands, the very things that frustrated life in the past, such as wild and difficult terrain and isolation (see e.g. Baldwin, Caird, Richards, this volume), have now assumed a positive value in an age when mass communication and a desire to escape into unspoiled, unurbanised areas, have helped consolidate an enormous tourist trade for the area.

For the human generations whose lot it has been to coax a living out of this ungenerous land, nature has both given and taken away. Lack of flat land, paucity of soils and difficulty for communication and social contact present enormous difficulties along the coastal edge. These have been the limiting legacy of the Ice Age.

Fig. 1.11 Ardvreck Castle at the upper end of Loch Assynt. Pen and ink sketch. 1884.

9

Fig. 1.12 Ullapool, established by the British Fisheries Society in 1788, occupies a flat, well-drained site on the raised beach at the mouth of the Ullapool River. Note also the *port* or slipway cleared through the rocky shore, where small boats would be hauled up to safety. 1990.

On the positive side, however, the amelioration of climate and the melting of the ice were to result in the formation of a feature of inestimable value to west coast communities. The immediate effect of the massive return of meltwater was to raise the level of the sea. In time, however, the upward recovery of the land from its depressing cover of ice resulted in the formation of raised beaches; narrow fringes of flat green land to soften the abrupt junction of sea and backing hill slope [Fig 1.12].

All around the western fringe of the land, crofting communities have moulded themselves to fit the physical form of this narrow band of land which has had a value both for farming and settlement. On one side the sea provided a source of food and of fertilising seaware, laboriously hauled up from the shore in creels and dumped in the scattered places where the *cas chrom* and human effort together turned the soil. On the other side was the rising hill slope where stock could be grazed and winter fuel cut in the deep beds of peat. But between these two lay the narrow focus of human settlement, a natural flat site where crofters might construct their homes and grow their rigs of food crops as part of a subsistence economy whose character was fashioned by the contours of the land.

Even the grouped settlements, such as Shieldaig village, sometimes

10

assume a linear form, their houses strung out along the line of the raised beach. Communications could also benefit from this feature, roads and sometimes railway following the flat land of the coastal edge.

Where burns and rivers have deposited their loads of alluvial sediments carried down from the mountains, flat spreads of green croft land stand in striking contrast to the dark colours of the poor grazing land around. The effect in a landscape poor in cultivation potential was strongly to concentrate human activity on such scattered gifts of nature.

The junction of alluvial fan or delta with the hill land behind is made the more noticeable by the presence of the stone dyke dividing the productive land from the grazing land above. This, the head dyke, has been termed a fundamental line in Scottish geography, and in this western context the aptness of that description is often startlingly demonstrated.

The green fan of croftland at Ardmair just to the north of Ullapool, for example, well illustrates this, with its cluster of crofts crowded on to the better land [Fig. 1.13, 1.14]. Ardmair is one of very few townships around Loch Broom where the later, 19th century houses and outbuildings have remained clustered on the site of the earlier multiple-tenant farm buildings,

Fig. 1.13   Crofts once crowded around the head of the alluvial fan at Ardmair in Wester Ross. The unpromising environment of peat-covered moorland behind provided little potential for cultivation and settlement, making the more fertile deposits a focus of human interest. 1990.

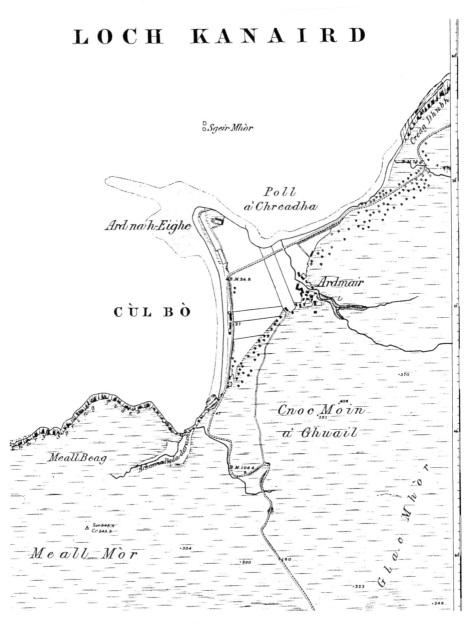

LOCH KANAIRD

ᐤSgeir Mhòr

Poll
a' Chreadha

Ard na h-Eighe

Ardmair

CÙL BÒ

Cnoc Moin
a' Ghwail

Meall Beag

Meall Mòr

Fig. 1.14 The clustered croft buildings of Ardmair are on the site of the earlier multiple-tenant township. O.S. 6 inch Sheet XIII, 1st. edition, surveyed 1875.

rather than re-located, linear fashion, each on its own rectangular allocation of croft land. Yet in that place, as so often elsewhere in the west, the once widespread theme of shortage of suitable land to support a large population is etched still into the face of the land. Among the bracken and heather, outlines of long-abandoned cultivation rigs appear in the most unpromising situations on rocky hill slopes where cultivation would never be countenanced today.

The problem of shortage of cultivable land in the past, and a need to maximise the production from what was available, is also echoed in the presence of shieling remains high above the valleys and coastlands. Such transhumance took the pressure off the better lands by removing the livestock to areas where summer growth was adequate to support them (see Baldwin, this volume).

At the heads of the sea lochs, spreads of alluvial material have long been extending seawards, slowly creating new areas of saltmarsh and increasing the grazing area. But, in human terms, the most striking legacy of this deltaic deposition from the past can be seen at Ullapool itself [Figs. 1.12, 12.1, 12.4]. Today's moderate flow of water down the Ullapool River gives little clue to the vast outpourings which once charged seawards into Loch Broom. Thus the founding fathers of the British Fisheries Society had the fluctuations of post-glacial seas to thank for what was to prove to be a superb site for settlement growth, offering a well-drained area where relief presented no obstacle to the layout of the original settlement and to its more recent expansion (see J. Munro, this volume).

CLIMATE AND CULTIVATION

In climatic, just as in relief terms, nature has provided the North-West Highlands with an environmental mixture of mercies. Incoming Atlantic air, heavily charged with water vapour, loses much of its moisture as rain on meeting the high ground. As a result, rainfall levels are high and sunshine amounts correspondingly reduced by the greater incidence of cloud cover. In the present age this can be an irritation to the tourist on a limited stay, but in times past, an unrelenting wet summer could spell disaster for the harvest of the land and hence for the communities which depended on it.

The waving heads of barley which now so dominate the farmlands of the east find no place in this western environment. Oats, potatoes and hay continue to form the basis of the limited cultivation of the croftlands. Production of the latter crop is not without its difficulties in such a wet climate, requiring a special response to ensure more speedy drying, such as spreading the cut grass over fences to allow the wind to blow through it and hasten both drying and maturation. It is a type of response common along what Professor Estyn Evans succinctly termed 'the Atlantic Ends of Europe.' Sometimes the hay might be heaped up over upturned tree branches for a temporary support, and only when it was reasonably dry could this fodder harvest be safely gathered in.

Although high rainfall may cause problems for drainage, a fact marked everywhere by the ubiquitous sprouting of rushes among the croft lands, in times past it did have the advantage of providing an assured flow down the burns to power the water wheels of mills, as at the mouth of the River Kirkaig at Lochinver and of the Ullapool River.

A positive feature of the climatic environment, however, is the ameliorating influence of the North Atlantic Drift. Since the prevailing winds blow from a south-westerly quarter, they pass over a sea area that is at a higher temperature than it would otherwise be for its northerly latitude, as a result of the constant current of water which has its origins as the Gulf Stream. Although it has lost some of the considerable warmth of its source region, the North Atlantic Drift is nevertheless warm enough to create a situation where the coastal areas of the North-West Highlands enjoy considerably milder temperatures in winter than, say, the exposed landscape of East Anglia which receives the full force of bitter continental air. The result is an extended growing season for pasture, and these generally frost-free conditions were exploited to the full by Osgood Mackenzie when he laid out his gardens on the exposed Inverewe peninsula last century. The secret of success at Inverewe has certainly not been a sub-tropical climate, as so many writers have erroneously suggested, but a combination of shelter from the wind and the critical factor of absence of biting frosts. It is therefore to the generally frost-free conditions of the area that Ullapool and Plockton owe the presence of the cordyline palm trees which lend a slightly exotic air to the villages.

Along this western fringe of our Scottish Highlands, then, the human impress on the land may frequently seem slight and discontinuous compared with that of the lowland east. But where the record of human presence and activity in the past is tangibly expressed in the landscape of the present, the area offers a fascinating commentary on man-land relationships through time.

Acknowledgement

Sincere thanks are due to Dr. J. Close-Brooks for Figs. 1.6, 1.7. These prints, along with Figs. 1.5, 1.9, 1.11 have been kindly provided by the Royal Commission on the Ancient and Historical Monuments of Scotland. Fig. 1.4 is reproduced by permission of the Trustees of the National Library of Scotland; Figs. 1.4, 1.8 were taken by John Baldwin, the latter courtesy of the Scottish Ethnological Archive, National Museums of Scotland. All other photographs are by the author.

References

Evans, E. E. The Atlantic Ends of Europe, in *Advancement of Science*. 1958-59. No. 15: 54-64.
Robertson, I. M. L. The Head Dyke: A Fundamental Line in Scottish Geography, in *Scottish Geographical Magazine*. 1949. Vol. 65 (1): 6-19.

ASPECTS OF THE ORIGIN
OF THE BROCHS
OF ATLANTIC SCOTLAND

Euan W. MacKie

INTRODUCTION

Everyone has doubtless heard of the broch of Mousa in Shetland, the best preserved and most impressive of all those Iron Age drystone towers — between six and seven hundred in number — that have survived in various states of preservation over some two millennia [Fig. 2.1]. It might be thought that after more than two centuries of study, and with such an abundance of architectural data available, the 'problem of the brochs' should long have been solved once and for all. Yet the phenomenon still provokes controversy among archaeologists, in terms not only of the kind of society thought appropriate for the production of such architecturally sophisticated buildings, but of the development of the drystone architecture itself and its origins, and also of the identity of its creators.

There are a number of reasons for this unsettled picture. One is that modern excavation on broch sites began only fairly recently (in 1948), so that the amount of reliable information about the age of the structures, the development of individual sites and the material culture associated with them is still relatively limited. Another is that systematic fieldwork on brochs — both in terms of the study of their architecture and of the relationship of the buildings to the landscape — is still fairly patchy. For example only in Shetland has sophisticated fieldwork of the latter kind been carried out (Fojut 1982), while the author's studies of broch architecture everywhere (begun in 1963 and carried on intermittently ever since) were only the second of their kind and have not been followed up except in restricted areas.

One might also point to the immature nature of some of modern prehistoric archaeology as a scientific discipline, in the sense that each generation seems to want to invent the wheel afresh and not to pay too much attention to what has gone before. The emphasis on the correct theoretical approach compounds the problem since it is easier to change this than to go out and obtain large quantities of fresh information in the field. The result is that the efforts of each generation are not necessarily forming the foundation blocks for those of the next, and a tendency to want to tear down the whole structure and start again is apparent from time to time. This paper is, therefore, partly an attempt at a reminder that existing evidence does not just disappear because some new discoveries have been made or new ideas thought of.

15

Fig. 2.1 Broch of Mousa on its small island off the east coast of Dunrossness, Shetland. This is the best preserved of all brochs and also probably the best built, the highest part of the wall still standing 43.5ft (13.3m) high. 1963.

BROCHS IN GENERAL

The essential features of Mousa, and also of many comparable but less well-preserved sites, are the compact, thick-walled circular ground plan — brochs are rarely more than 10m in diameter — and the unique hollow con-

16

struction of the wall [Figs. 2.2-2.4]. This is built as a double wall, entirely without cement, the two concentric halves forming narrow walkways (when accessible) and being held apart by horizontal rows of flat stone lintels. A stair links the series of superimposed galleries thus formed, and climbs to the top.

One of the many intriguing facts about brochs is that the period during which several hundred of these elaborate stone dwellings were erected in highland and island, or Atlantic Scotland — an area now regarded as a remote and peripheral part of the country — ended a millennium before the earliest mortared stone castles of Medieval times appeared. Moreover it was

Fig. 2.2   Dun Troddan broch, Glen Beag, near Glenelg, western Inverness-shire, 1974. This has a solid base like its neighbour Dun Telve and both are more typical of the brochs of the far north than of the west. The hollow, double wall is clearly visible in cross-section on the left, as are two vertical rows of windows or voids in the interior wallface.

nearly a millennium and a half before the nearest equivalent modern dwellings in Scotland were built — the tower houses of the border country and the earliest single-storeyed, mortared stone houses for the chiefs of the highland zone. In the centuries between the middle Iron Age and Medieval times stone dwellings of any kind were rare, and elaborate, monumental ones almost non-existent. Moreover the period during which these Iron Age structures were built was a short one, probably not more than two or three centuries beginning in the first B.C., although a few plausible prototypes have been traced back to the 7th or even the 8th centuries B.C. in Orkney.

Yet by and large the centuries before the broch period were almost as

Fig. 2.3 Dun Telve broch, Glen Beag, near Glenelg, western Inverness-shire, 1963. This solid-based broch with its high, hollow or galleried wall was almost as well preserved as Mousa when Alexander Gordon saw it in about 1720. Shortly afterwards it was badly damaged by a contractor, presumably he who was building the barracks at Glenelg in 1722.

Fig. 2.4 A general view of Dun Beag broch, Struan, Skye, sitting on its rock knoll. A ground-galleried broch of the type commonly found in the Western Isles, it was visited by Dr Johnson and cleared out about seventy years ago.

barren of small, stone, fortified dwellings — or indeed of stone dwellings of any kind — as those which came after. Thus some basic questions need to be asked, not all of which can be answered here.

BROCH ORIGINS

Why for example did this short but spectacular period of monumental drystone building start when and where it did? More specifically what are the origins of this striking maritime, late prehistoric culture which is distributed throughout the highland and island zone of the west and north of the country and which produced so many of these massive structures?

The latter problem divides into two parts. In the first place there is the question of the material culture associated with the brochs and allied structures (like wheelhouses); this contrasts with the early Iron Age pottery and artefacts found on a few sites like Jarlshof in Shetland and the Orkney roundhouses (below) in being richer, more varied and in having a large number of new elements, including iron-working and rotary querns. To decide whether this new middle Iron Age assemblage is a local development or a foreign import, or a combination of the two, requires a complex analysis beyond the scope of this paper. Some remarks on the subject have recently been made (MacKie 1989).

Broch Prototypes

The other aspect of the problem concerns the architectural origins of the brochs themselves — which can reasonably be regarded as man's greatest achievement in drystone building. A quarter of a century ago a fresh attempt was made by the writer to infer their structural development (MacKie 1965, 1971), it being assumed at that time that such a complex structure could not have sprung into existence from nothing, and that the identification of its immediate forerunners was a worthwhile task.

As early as 1928 it had been pointed out by the Royal Commission on the Ancient and Historical Monuments of Scotland that the greatest variety of comparable buildings, all with various forms of galleried walls, existed in the Western Isles, and that the origin of the broch was likely to have occurred among some of these (RCAHMS 1928. xxvi et seq). However, the class of 'galleried duns' thus identified was clearly not homogeneous. Some were structurally very close to brochs while others were not; in the latter group is Kildonan, a mainly solid-walled dun in Kintyre with only one short stretch of galleried wall (Fairhurst 1939).

Among those diverse 'galleried duns' there exists an homogeneous group of structures with the same high, hollow wall as the brochs (with superimposed, intra-mural galleries) but which are not free-standing, round or oval towers; part of their defensive capability depends on their proximity to a vertical cliff, or at least a very steep slope, to the edge of which these buildings are effectively tied.

Because this specialised form of galleried dun is literally a 'half broch' the term *semibroch* has been used for them (Mackie 1965. 101), and two kinds can be seen. The *D-shaped semibrochs* stand on the straight edge of a cliff, the curved, inland wall straightening out at both ends as it approaches this edge. The open-sided building is likely to have had a low wall along the edge; Dun Ringill and Dun Ardtreck on Skye, and Dun Grugaig, Glenelg are classic instances (Graham 1949. 19) [Figs. 2.5-2.12; 2.20-2.23]. The other group — of which there are only four clear examples (including one hybrid form) — are the *promontory semibrochs,* simple, curved barriers drawn across the neck of a cliff promontory, such as Dun Grugaig (Skye) [Figs. 2.13-2.15].

Fig. 2.5　General view of Dun Ringill semibroch, Strath, Skye, seen from the south with the shore to the right. The half-collapsed mural cell is visible behind the scale, and the trench — probably dug when the site was re-fortified by the MacKinnons in Medieval times — can be seen next to the wallface on the left. 1985.

Fig. 2.6　Ringill D-shaped semibroch, Skye. E.W. Mackie, 1986.

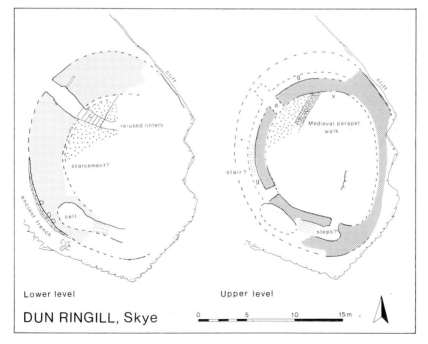

re-used lintels

scarcement?

cell

ancient trench

Lower level

DUN RINGILL, Skye

cliff

g

a

v

Medieval parapet walk

stair?

g

steps?

cliff

Upper level

0　　　5　　　10　　　15 m .

Fig. 2.7 Closer view of the partly-ruined mural cell at Dun Ringill semibroch, 1988. Its original floor has been torn out — probably during the Medieval re-fortification — and the underlying wall core can be seen about level with the top of the lower white stripe on the pole.

Fig. 2.8 The entrance passage of Dun Ringill semibroch, looking out, 1988. The original Iron Age lintels have been re-set over the Medieval inward extension of the passage, the junction of which with the older wall can be seen on the right, forming a door-check. The pole is at one of the door-checks of the unroofed Iron Age passage.

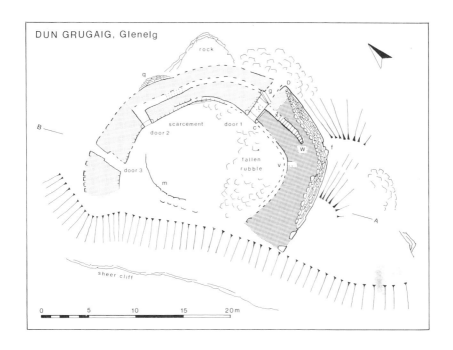

Figs. 2.9 (above), 2.10 (below) Plan and cross section of the D-shaped semibroch Dun Grugaig, Glenelg. E.W. Mackie, 1988.

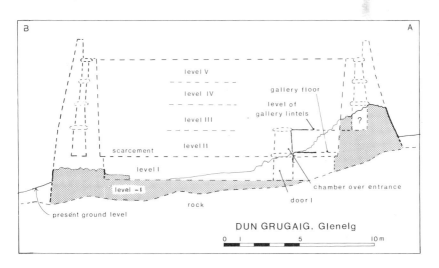

23

Fig. 2.11 Dun Grugaig semibroch, Glen Beag, near Glenelg in western Inverness-shire, showing the outer wallface. The floor of the upper gallery is at the level of the projecting pole. 1985.

Fig. 2.12 General view of Dun Baravat semibroch on a rocky islet in Loch Baravat, Berneray, Lewis, from the north-east, showing the causeway to the shore. The high, galleried part of the wall faces the causeway, the entrance having been at the extreme right, but the rest of the wall is low and apparently solid. 1985.

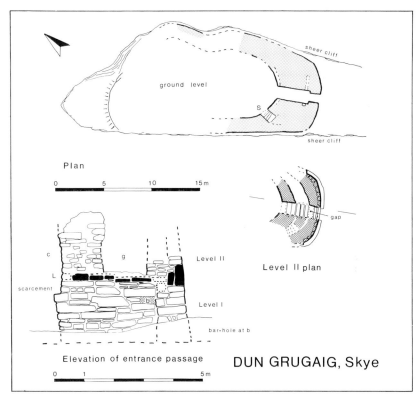

Fig. 2.13   Plan, with reconstructed elevation, of Dun Grugaig promontory semibroch, Skye. E.W. Mackie, 1986.

These semibrochs could be regarded as late, degenerate brochs, built towards the very end of their era when skills were declining and when the builders were perhaps being driven to peripheral lands. Alternatively they might be contemporary variants (Harding 1984. 211-15), or the immediate forerunners from which the free-standing towers developed. Although none had been excavated when the 1965 study was written, their more primitive design and situation, and their distribution, both seemed to make the last view extremely plausible.

Distribution and Development

The distribution of the semibrochs is particularly striking (MacKie 1965. fig. 1), being concentrated in Skye and scattered in adjacent areas, in exactly the same regions as the majority of the ground-galleried brochs are found. This form of broch was deduced, from independent structural evidence, to be typologically the earliest form; the more developed solid-

25

Fig. 2.14 General view of Dun Grugaig semibroch, Strath, Skye, on its cliff promontory, taken in 1963 when the bushes were very much thinner. The high, galleried part of the wall forms a simple cross wall and a fragment of the upper gallery remains.

Fig. 2.15 The entrance passage of Dun Grugaig semibroch, Skye, looking towards the land; the door-checks are clearly visible near the front end. The design of the entrance, and of the galleried wall, is the equal of the brochs although the general defensive design is much inferior. 1963.

based brochs are concentrated in the far north-east mainland and in the Orkney and Shetland islands.

Thus if maps are prepared of the distribution of the two types of semi-brochs and the two types of brochs, they show in a convincing sequence how one kind of architecturally-sophisticated stone building could have evolved over both time and space, in four stages.

The earliest stage [Fig. 2.16] is represented by the four promontory semi-brochs. The second [Fig. 2.17] sees the development of the D-shaped semi-brochs of which at least eight were built over a much wider area. Two have been excavated of which one — the fine example on Loch Broom in Wester Ross, just across the water from Ullapool — enclosed a wooden roundhouse very similar to those usually found inside thoroughly excavated brochs (MacKie 1980. fig 3).

The third stage in this scenario [Fig. 2.18] saw a 'minor technical break-through which had major social implications' (MacKie 1965. 126), namely the emergence of the free-standing ground-galleried broch, an impressive stronghold which could be built close to fields and pastures and which was no longer dependent on the availability of a suitable cliff edge. At this point, it was also argued, the material culture suddenly became more elaborate and some elements of this suggested the arrival of immediately pre-Roman people from Wessex and Brittany; these presumably P-Celtic speaking new-comers could have stimulated the transformation of semibroch into broch. This artefact evidence is at the same time the most important and the most difficult to interpret of all that relevant to our understanding of the origins of the broch cultures, but has to be pursued in another place. It has of course been denied that foreign influences are traceable in the material culture (Lane 1988).

The fourth stage [Fig. 2.19] evidently took place in the far north, probably in Orkney, and consisted of the development of the more advanced solid-based broch. One aspect of this final development has become clearer in the last twenty years. The four definite solid-based brochs in the west are all on the mainland coast — scattered all the way down to Lismore at the mouth of Loch Linnhe — and they dominate small tracts of arable land between vast areas of barren mountains and the western sea. They are strik-ingly absent from the Hebridean islands, and this curious distribution is easily explained in terms of the scenario just outlined.

If broch evolution started in the west and reached its apogee in the far north, the few examples of the latest type built in the west (in a sort of reflux movement) would have to be in those peripheral areas which were not already occupied. This tells us both that the architectural evolution occurred in the way described and also that broch development reached its final stage relatively quickly, while the great majority of the early, ground-galleried forms were still in use.

Thus, or so it seemed in 1965 (and with the exception of the previous two paragraphs), could be explained the genesis, and subsequent rapid develop-ment and spread, of the broch class of what were then called the small stone *forts* (it is now clear that they were fortified dwellings) (MacKie 1989). An

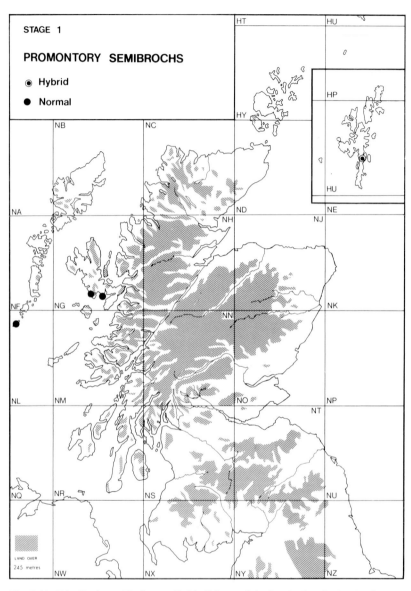

STAGE 1

PROMONTORY SEMIBROCHS

◉ Hybrid

● Normal

HT

HU

HP

HU

NB

NC

HY

NA

ND

NE

NH

NJ

NF

NG

NN

NK

NL

NM

NO

NP

NT

NQ

NR

NS

NU

LAND OVER
245 metres

NW

NX

NY

NZ

Fig. 2.16 Distribution of hollow-walled buildings of the broch class in Scotland. Stage 1: Promontory Semibrochs.

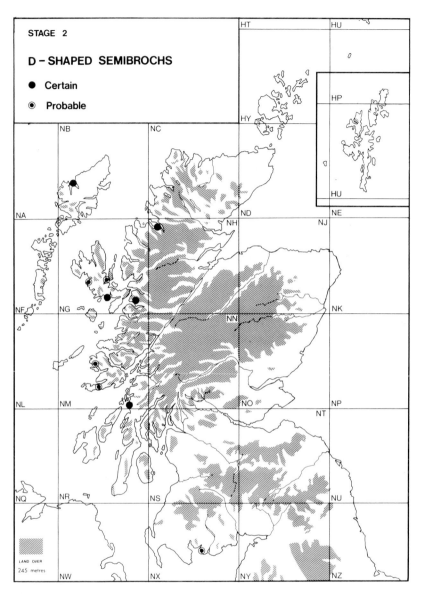

Fig. 2.17 Distribution of hollow-walled buildings of the broch class in Scotland. Stage 2: D-shaped semibrochs.

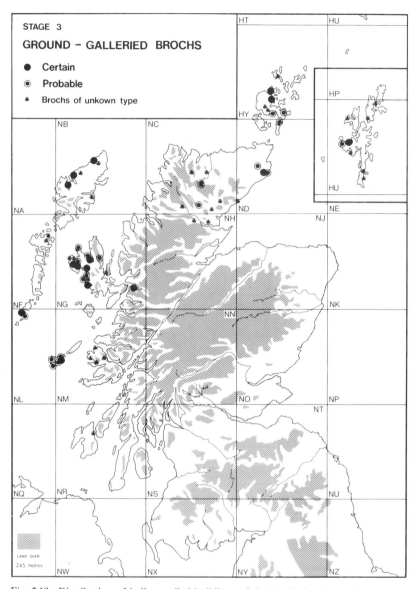

Fig. 2.18 Distribution of hollow-walled buildings of the broch class in Scotland.
Stage 3: Ground-Galleried Brochs.

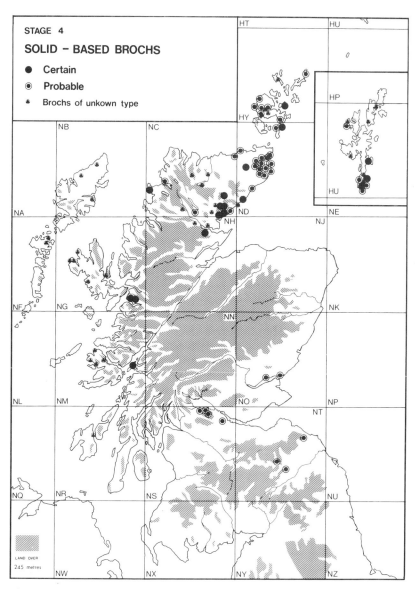

STAGE 4

SOLID – BASED BROCHS

● Certain

◉ Probable

♣ Brochs of unkown type

Fig. 2.19 Distribution of hollow-walled buildings of the broch class in Scotland.
Stage 4: Solid-Based Brochs.

31

important aim of the writer's research in the mid and late 1960s was to find and excavate a semibroch to ascertain whether the group was indeed old enough to be plausible prototype brochs. Two were explored and will be briefly described shortly.

Since that time, however, other forms of possible broch prototypes of a different kind have been found in Orkney and safely dated to the end of the Bronze Age and the early Iron Age, centuries before the period of the classic brochs; these are defined by the characteristic associated artefacts as middle Iron Age in date, and probably not older than the first century B.C. Thus one of the purposes of reviewing this evidence now is to see how well it stands up against the new Orkney data, and whether the criticisms levelled against the 'semibroch hypothesis' are valid. The writer has discussed the whole problem in more detail elsewhere (MacKie 1992).

New Discoveries in Orkney

The Orkney discoveries may be summarised as follows. It has become clear since the early 1970s that large, round drystone buildings with relatively low walls were being put up in those islands from very early times — probably as far back as the late Bronze Age in the 8th or 7th centuries B.C. The Quanterness Neolithic chambered cairn had a stone roundhouse built next to it, and two radiocarbon dates in the 6th and 9th centuries b.c. were obtained for material from the primary occupation layers, while a thermoluminescence date for the associated pottery fell within the 8th century B.C. (Renfrew 1979. 194). One radiocarbon date for the secondary occupation was in the 3rd or 2nd centuries b.c.[1]

The house enclosed an area about 8m in diameter with a wall of uncertain thickness (it was set into older cairn rubble); later the interior was divided by cross-walls into irregular areas. No central hearth was located and the doorway bore no signs of the standardised features seen in broch entrance passages, such as the regular shape with door-checks and a bar-hole and socket. The scanty pottery included a shouldered sherd analogous to the early Iron Age material from Jarlshof, there dated typologically and stratigraphically (but not by radiocarbon which had only just been developed) to about the 5th or 6th centuries B.C. (Hamilton. 1956).

Another late Bronze Age roundhouse was discovered by chance in Orkney a few years later, in a rescue excavation on what was thought at first to be a broch site (Hedges & Bell 1980; Hedges 1987. vol 1). Here at Bu a similar building to the Quanterness house had been subsequenly enlarged by a thickening of the original stone wall to broch-like proportions with less substantial masonry inside and outside; the original wall had an average thickness of only 2.95m (Hedges 1987. fig. 1.3, table 1.1), and the later addition rested on midden material. Two C-14 dates were obtained for deposits laid down at an early stage in the use of the building and fell in the 5th and 6th centuries b.c.; at what stage the wall was thickened is not altogether clear, even from the final report.

In these buildings there were none of the specialised architectural features of the brochs, such as the standardised entrance passage with door-checks and bar-hole, or the intra-mural stair, gallery or cells. The interior of the building was divided up into irregular partitions and lacked a central hearth as well as any signs of a ring of post-holes.

TESTING THE 1965 HYPOTHESIS

As noted in 1965 no semi-broch as here defined had been excavated, and the obvious test for the hypothesis outlined above was to explore one by modern stratigraphical techniques and to date it with radiocarbon measurements. From the evidence of the associated artefacts and from radiocarbon dates from Dun Mor Vaul broch on Tiree (MacKie 1974), the 1st century B.C. seemed the likeliest time of the genesis of the towers, and also for the start of the middle Iron Age period in the artefact sequence (Stages II and III in the sequence as originally described) (MacKie 1971. fig 7). Thus the semibrochs ought to be older than that.

In the light of the discoveries in Orkney just outlined, the evidence for the age and status of the semibrochs clearly must be critically reviewed again (MacKie 1992), since these buildings no longer stand alone as plausible broch prototypes (Hedges & Bell 1980; Hedges 1987).

Fig. 2.20   General view of the interior of Dun Ardtreck at an early stage in the excavations. The 70 ft. (21.3m) cliff is to the right and the entrance out of sight to the left. The inner face of the galleried wall can be seen resting on the rubble platform, and one gallery door has been exposed. It can be seen how the underlying rock slopes downwards from the cliff edge. 1965.

Dun Ardtreck, Skye

Dun Ardtreck was the first semibroch to be excavated, in 1965 (MacKie 1975. 84 et seq.) [Figs. 2.20, 2.21]. It is a D-shaped, drystone fortlet near the end of the Portnalong peninsula, surrounded by an outer wall and sited on the straight edge of a high cliff which forms the upright of the 'D'. The galleried wall straightens as it approaches the edge, and traces of a much narrower wall were found along it. Despite this, it has been claimed that it is the remains of a circular broch, part of which has fallen into the sea (Martlew 1982. 270). Only part of the ground level, intra-mural gallery was preserved and the stair in this had evidently been ripped out; however the wider section of the passage approaching its foot was clear. The structure had undergone destruction by fire, and subsequent partial demolition, before being occupied for a long period as a domestic site; but even so it was clear that it must have had at least two and probably three superimposed wall galleries to have been effective as a defended site [Figs. 2.22, 2.23].

The destruction, and the transition from primary to secondary occupation, was dated by clearly stratified 2nd century Roman pottery which showed that this semibroch was at least as old as the brochs. A rather imprecise C-14 date of 50 ± 105 b.c. (GX 1120) for charcoal from the construction levels showed that it could have been built in the pre-broch era as then defined (MacKie 1975a. 84; in prep.: site NG331). However, the

Fig. 2.21 General view of part of the galleried wall of Dun Ardtreck after excavation, showing the shallowness of the gallery and its rubble floor. Both features are the result of the hollow wall having been built on a rubble platform. 1965.

Fig. 2.22 View of the entrance passage at Dun Ardtreck after excavation, showing the two door-checks (faced with flat stone slabs) and the raised door to the guard cell on the left. At this stage the secondary ramp leading up to the outer end of the passage from the exterior is still in position, in contrast to the situation in Fig. 2.23. An iron door handle was found at the base of the right hand door-check and the passage lintels must have been removed during the secondary occupation of the site. 1965.

Fig. 2.23 View of the outer end of the entrance passage at Dun Ardtreck after the removal of the secondary ramp, revealing the primary paving below. 1965.

associated artefacts were all of standard middle Iron Age type, and a date for the construction of the site *substantially* earlier than the main broch period could not be demonstrated.

Another criticism of the site was that of Fairhurst who surmised that the C-14 date from this site in fact belonged to an earlier building and not to the D-shaped one (Fairhurst 1984. 178.) The point here is the curious construction of the foundations of Dun Ardtreck. The rock surface, thinly covered with turf, slopes downwards and inland from the edge of the cliff, and the builders were evidently unwilling or unable to found the galleried wall directly on this slope. Instead they used the lowest four or five courses of the curved outer face as a revetment for an approximately level rubble platform running backwards from that, until it merged with the rising rock face; the galleried wall was then built on this level foundation and the outer wallface continued upwards with no sign of a break (MacKie 1975. pl. 5f). Neither was there any other sign that the structure was built in two phases; if it had been, the hypothetical earlier one would have had to have rested on exactly the same foundations as the later, gallery-walled one and to have been of exactly the same D-shaped plan!

35

One intriguing object was in the destruction level, and had therefore arrived on the site in its primary phase of occupation. This is a Roman axe-hammer of standard military type (MacKie 1965. fig. 7 no. 2) — the only one so far found outside a Roman military installation in southern Scotland. It is tempting to imagine that it was a present to the chief of Dun Ardtreck by the commander of one of the ships of Agricola's fleet which circumnavigated Scotland from east to west in the mid-80s A.D.

Dun an Ruigh Ruaidh

Dun an Ruigh Ruaidh (or 'Rhiroy') on the south shore of Loch Broom, Ross and Cromarty, was diagnosed as another D-shaped semibroch built on the edge of a low cliff, although it was originally thought to be a broch (Calder & Steer 1949, 72 et seq.) [Fig. 2.24]. It was excavated in 1968 and 1978 and an account of the work has been published (MacKie 1980). Criticisms of the author's interpretation of this site have again concentrated on the dating and the ground plan; it has been maintained that the several radiocarbon measurements do not support a date for the construction of the site as early as the 3rd century B.C. and that the structure is simply another broch, part of which has fallen over the adjacent cliff (Harding 1984. 21).

The site itself stands on the southern shore of Loch Broom, at the cliff edge of a narrow, level terrace which slopes steeply down to the water. The structure has many broch-like features, for example the ledge or scarcement on the inside wallface which is (with one exception) found only in brochs and broch-like buildings. It also has a length of upper gallery preserved on the uphill side with some roofing lintels preserved — another architectural feature which is unknown outside the brochs [Fig. 2.25]. Yet this is relatively crude in construction, having an uneven floor on top of a solid wallbase.

Fig. 2.24 Dun an Ruigh Ruaidh. General view of the site from the north-west. 1978.

Fig. 2.25 Dun an Ruigh Ruaidh. General view of the semibroch in 1978 after excavation. In the foreground is the raised doorway from the interior to the upper part of the intra-mural stair. It was reached from the raised wooden floor resting on the scarcement visible on the inner face. The remaining steps have been re-buried but the flight ran up above the upper gallery visible in the middle of the wall, which therefore ended blind behind the stair.

The intra-mural stair and the standard broch entrance passage also confirm the close links with the brochs.

The site went through two main stages of occupation. At first it had a high, hollow wall and a clean cobbled floor with a massive central paved hearth, and within the interior was a substantial, two-storeyed wooden roundhouse the upper floor of which rested on the scarcement ledge and on a ring of heavy posts set in the floor [Fig. 2.26]. A small midden deposit below the cliff belonged to this stage. The central hearth implies that Dun an Ruigh Ruaidh was built for a single household, presumably that of a chief [Figs. 2.27, 2.28].

There were clear signs that this period of occupation was ended by the substantial demolition of the structure; the wall was lowered, the wooden posts of the roundhouse were pulled out and dark midden material began to accumulate all over the interior, including the fireplace. Three similar C-14 dates suggested that this episode took place in the first century b.c. or a.d. (MacKie 1980. table 1). What the meaning in social terms of this change is is not clear.

Close-Brooks refers to Dun an Ruigh Ruaidh as a broch despite the

Fig. 2.26   General view of the interior excavations at Dun an Ruigh Ruaidh in 1978, showing some of the post holes.

Fig. 2.27   Central primary hearth at Dun an Ruigh Ruaidh partly exposed in 1978.

report, but without giving a specific reason (Close-Brooks 1986. 149); she merely says that there would have been room for the 'missing' part of the wall if about 1.50m of the cliff has fallen away since the Iron Age. Although the structure is oval in plan it was clear from the excavations that the wall along the cliff was narrower and probably lower than elsewhere; the galleried part of the wall clearly did not extend beyond the main entrance which was on the south-east side facing along the cliff; and there just was not room for a wide galleried wall along that edge. A crucial piece of evidence was found by excavating below the cliff; there was no sign of the massive early fall of lumps of cliff followed by tons of rubble which would have occurred if a round broch had partly collapsed.

The question of the nature of the building is also considered by Harding:

> . . . Feachem's view that the missing third had simply fallen over the edge of the rocky bluff on which it stands is certainly not refuted by MacKie's small cuttings beneath the cliff, which were located too close to the cliff edge, and

Fig. 2.28 Section of deposits exposed by trench below cliff on which semibroch stands. The pale subsoil is at the base and the Iron Age midden, underlying much later fallen rubble, is immediately on top of it, the two parts being marked with labels. Dun an Ruigh Ruaidh, 1978.

rather too far south, to expect to find the massive debris which could have tumbled from a very considerable height . . . well down the slope towards the edge of Loch Broom. (Harding 1984. 211).

Yet both the sections show rubble piled highest against the base of the rock face (MacKie 1980. pl. 6a, fig. 11). The general plan (ibid. fig. 2) also shows how much debris is lying strewn down the slope immediately below the cliff, and a large piece of rock was in fact found just in front of its foot, but on the surface (ibid. fig. 11). The idea that debris would have bounded down the hill to the shores of Loch Broom a quarter of a mile away cannot be sustained; the only thing that nearly did that was a Calor gas tank which escaped during the packing up at the end of the 1978 season.

Most of this was obvious before the excavation started and the two trenches below the cliff were dug to find out if this mass of debris was ancient. The southerly of these is in fact immediately below one end of the massive wall and a huge amount of dry rubble debris would have been there if a high broch had collapsed, not to mention large fragments of the rock face. The problem is that the stratigraphy of both trenches under the cliff showed very clearly that most if not all the stone rubble is quite recent; 19th or 20th century objects were found in it, one at a low level, just above the Iron Age midden underneath. The fact is that it was impossible to identify the mass of early dry rubble that the collapse of a broch requires, and neither was there the slightest evidence for the early cliff fall needed to cause it. No amount of special pleading can get round this.

On the other hand, it has to be admitted that the set of radiocarbon dates obtained from excavated and clearly stratified samples of charcoal and buried turf do not form as clear a pattern as one would wish. Harding argues against an early date in the context of a clearly expressed doubt about the existence of the semibrochs as a class. He says that:

> dates . . . afford anything but a consistent sequence and certainly do not demand a third century [b.c.] dating of its initial phase; indeed, if we regard the sixth century date obtained for one of the post-hole samples as probably suspect [as, he might have added, was admitted by the excavator] then it would be hard to sustain a primary occupation, on the basis of the remaining dates, earlier than the first century B.C. (Harding 1984. 211).

The report analyses the difficult chronology of the site in detail, and the problem has been reviewed again recently (MacKie 1992). The only further comment to make here is that, since the dates admittedly do not form as clear a pattern as one would like, one is forced to look for guidance to other types of evidence. Most of the associated artefacts are quite distinct from the standard material culture of the Hebridean middle Iron Age sites and seem not inconsistent with the establishment of the site between the 3rd and 1st centuries B.C. However a rotary quern of middle Iron Age type was found jammed into a post-hole as a packing stone, though this could be secondary. By using the C-14 dates by themselves one could argue, though with less conviction, for a much earlier as well as a slightly later construction date, but the evidence is unfortunately equivocal. The writer tends to think that the date for the top of the old ground surface (approx. 2nd century b.c.) underneath it, is probably the best guide to the date of the erection of the building.

CONCLUSIONS

The results of the two excavations described seemed relatively consistent and satisfactory in the sense that they broadly confirmed the predictions made in 1965 — that the semibrochs existed as a distinct class of buildings closely related to the brochs, that they were very probably broch prototypes and were slightly earlier than the round towers.

Nevertheless, as already explained, persistent criticisms have been levelled at the hypothesis, presumably as a way of challenging what might be called the 'evolutionary' view of broch development — in which the structural evolution and geographical expansion of the buildings is specifically reconstructed — and thereby supporting a vaguer model based on assumptions of purely local development along a variety of paths (Hedges 1987. 1990; Armit 1990).

It has been shown that the doubts expressed about Dun Ardtreck and Dun an Ruigh Ruaidh are hard to sustain convincingly, and further powerful support for the 'semibroch hypothesis' is available from the analysis of the remaining unexcavated sites (MacKie 1992). Of course this does not mean that the remarkable early Orkney roundhouses are irrelevant to the question of how the brochs emerged; the picture must be more complex than the author thought in 1965 and an attempt to review all the available evidence is in progress.

Note

[1] Radiocarbon, or C-14, dates have 'b.c.' or 'a.d.' with them as they do not necessarily refer to calendar years, having to be adjusted — by varying amounts according to the age — by means of the tree ring 'clock'. Thermoluminescence dates on the other hand do relate directly to calendar years, so have 'B.C.' or 'A.D.' with them. In the Iron Age period in Britain, the C-14 dates tend to be a little younger than they should be in terms of calendar years.

References

Armit, I. (ed.) *Beyond the brochs: Changing perspectives in the Scottish Atlantic Iron Age.* 1990.

Calder, C. S. T. & Steer, K.A. Dun Lagaidh and four other prehistoric monuments near Ullapool, Ross and Cromarty, in *Proc. Soc. Antiq. Scot.* 1948-49. vol 83: 68-76.

Close-Brooks, J. *Exploring Scotland's Heritage: The Highlands.* 1986.

Fairhurst, H. The galleried dun at Kildonan Bay, Kintyre, in *Proc. Soc. Antiq. Scot.* 1938-39. vol 73: 185-228.

Hamilton, J. R. C. *Excavations at Jarlshof, Shetland.* 1956.

Harding, D. 1984. The function and classification of brochs and duns, in R. Miket & C.

Burgess (eds.) *Between and beyond the Walls: Essays on the prehistory and history of Northern Britain in honour of George Jobey.* 1984: 206-20.

Hedges, J. W. & Bell, B. That tower of Scottish prehistory: the broch, in *Antiquity.* 1980. vol. 54: 87-94.

Hedges, J. W. *Bu, Gurness and the brochs of Orkney.* BAR. 1987.

Hedges, J. W. Surveying the foundations: Life after 'Brochs', in I. Armit (ed.) *Beyond the brochs: Changing perspectives in the Scottish Atlantic Iron Age.* 1990: 17-31.

Lane, A. English migrants in the Hebrides: 'Atlantic Second B' revisited, in *Proc. Soc. Antiq. Scot.* 1987-88. vol. 117: 47-66.

MacKie, E. W. The origin and development of the broch and wheelhouse building cultures of the Scottish Iron Age, in *Proc. Prehist. Soc.* 1965. vol. 31: 93-146.

MacKie, E. W. English migrants and Scottish brochs, in *Glasgow Archaeol. Journ.* 1971. vol. 2: 39-71.

MacKie, E. W. *Dun Mor Vaul: an Iron Age broch on Tiree.* 1974.

MacKie, E. W. Dun an Ruigh Ruaidh, Loch Broom, Ross and Cromarty; excavations in 1968 and 1978, in *Glasgow Archaeol. Journ.* 1980. vol. 7: 32-79.

MacKie, E. W. Leckie broch — impact on the Scottish Iron Age, in *Glasgow Archaeol. Journ.* 1989. vol. 14: 1-18.

MacKie, E. W. The Iron Age semibrochs of Atlantic Scotland: a case study in the problems of deductive reasoning, in *Archaeol. Journ.* 1992. vol 101: 149-81.

MacKie, E. W. *The Roundhouses, Brochs and Wheelhouses of Atlantic Scotland, c. 700 B.C. to A.D. 300: Architecture and Material Culture.* forthcoming.

Martlew, R. The typological study of the structures of the Scottish brochs, in *Proc. Soc. Antiq. Scot.* 1981-82. vol. 112: 254-76.

Renfrew, C. *Investigations in Orkney.* Rept. Research Comm. Soc. Antiq. London. 1979. no. 38.

RCAHMS. *Ninth Report with Inventory of Monuments and Constructions in the Outer Hebrides, Skye and the Small Isles.* 1928.

DESCENDANTS OF NORSE *BÓLSTAÐR*?: A RE-EXAMINATION OF THE LINEAGE OF *BOST* & CO.

Richard Cox

INTRODUCTION

The account by Nicolaisen in *Scottish Place-Names* of the Norse settlement of Scotland as seen from place-name evidence is a land-mark in the development of our understanding of that largely undocumented process. His analysis of the distribution of selected generic elements clearly plots the gradual but relentless approach of serial settlement, through the Northern and Western Isles, up to and onto the northern mainland and western coastal belt. The chronology proposed for the settlement generic-elements discussed, places them in the following order: 1. *staðr*, 2. *setr* (and/or *sætr*) and 3. *bólstaðr* (Nicolaisen 1976. 87-94).

The remarkable thing about the last of these elements, *bólstaðr*, is that, according to Nicolaisen, it has yielded a large number of different reflexes in modern forms of names. These include orthographic *bist*, *bister*, *bust*, *buster*, *bost*, *pster*, *mster*, *bus*, *boll*, *poll*, *pool* and *bo* (Nicolaisen op.cit. 94). There is general agreement here among earlier commentators, but there are some dissenters concerning one or two individual reflexes (Appendix 2). For instance, not all would agree that *boll*, *poll* or *pool* forms derive from *bólstaðr*. This in itself does not prompt a complete re-examination of the reflexes of *bólstaðr*, but there does seem to be a sufficiently compelling reason to undertake one.

Enquiring into the form and derivation of *shader*-names over the west of Scotland (in Gaelic, *Siadar* ['ʃiadər] ['ʃiədər] or final *-seadar* [ˌʃadər]), the evidence suggested that an early group of these coincided chronologically with name-forms with the reflex *bost*, but that another group of *shader*-names were of a slightly later stratum than *bost*-names (Cox 1990). This did not say that *shader*-names, derived from ON *(-)sætr*, were contemporary with or later than all names with reflexes hitherto deemed to have derived from *bólstaðr*. However, it somewhat weakened the case for the accepted chronology of *staðr* yielding to *setr* (and/or *sætr*) yielding to *bólstaðr*. Unless we choose to ignore this, it begs the question whether it is possible that more than one ON generic element lies behind the variety of reflexes currently ascribed to just the one element *bólstaðr*. If this proved to be the case, we would have quite a different picture before us of the phasing and chronology of Norse settlement.

Our analysis draws upon 105 names, with the benefit of the pronunciations of 85 of these. Of the remainder, although we cannot be at all certain, we may at least be able to make an educated guess at what the pronunciation of some of these may or may not have been. The reason for not having pronunciations for all the names concerned is due to a lack of resources. In part this was a question of time and money, but it was also a question of the availability of pronunciations. This last point needs some clarification. The figure of 105 represents relevant names I was able to trace in what, historically, we may call Gaelic Scotland. Caithness and the Northern Isles are therefore not dealt with here. This was because I did not feel qualified to consider questions of historical phonology there at such notice, and also because the area would deserve separate treatment because of the number of relevant names there. In Gaelic Scotland there were instances where I was simply unable to obtain pronunciations of name-forms as used in a Gaelic nomenclature. For the pronunciations I did obtain, my informants included both local individuals and scholars, and I am much indebted to them. The importance of obtaining Gaelic pronunciations of the name-forms concerned is self-evident, though it cannot be overstated: given the phonological developments of the Gaelic language, we are just one remove from the Norse names themselves, while an approach using English name-forms, themselves borrowed from Gaelic, would place us, at its most simply expressed, at a further remove from the original Norse nomenclature.

The main aim of this paper, then, is to look at Old Norse (ON) generic elements that have traditionally been taken, for the most part at least, as belonging to a category of habitation or settlement-names. We are not looking, therefore, at the derivations of individual ON loan-names, and for this reason I have not made a full sweep of the documentary evidence for individual name-forms. This is macro-onomastics, so to speak, and we can anticipate that some points regarding individual names may escape our notice.

Finally, I should like to point out that in my paper on *shader*-names (*Scottish Gaelic Studies 16.* 1990), I made various suggestions about the origin of some of the reflexes we shall be looking at. Suffice it to say that these were speculative and off-the-cuff remarks made without the benefit of later research carried out for this paper, and in consequence there will be no need to refer to them here.

ON *býli*

The pronunciations of the reflexes under discussion here include [bəl], [bɔst], [bɔ:sta(ɣ)], [bʌsta], [bɔL], [bʌs], [bʌsəɣ], [bɔuLsa], [bɔust], [bɔusta] and [bəL]. In disyllabic forms stress occurs on the initial syllable of the reflex, and in name-final position all forms normally retain a weak stress reflecting the secondary stress of the original ON names.

The first of these, [bəl], we find in only three names, all situated in the Western Isles [Fig. 3.1]. We have *Bayble* in Lewis, and *Paible* which occurs on Taransay, by Harris, and in North Uist. The specific element of the ON reconstructions is *papa* m. a 'cleric, or religious man' as found in

44

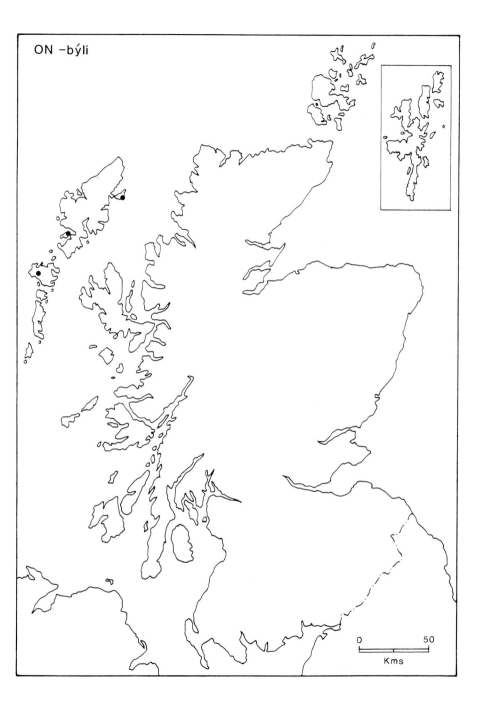

ON −býli

0   50
Kms

Fig. 3.1   Place-names incorporating ON -*býli*.

45

island-names such as *Pabbay*. Our names go back to ON **Papýli*, as found in the Landnámabók (*í Papíli*: Ásmundarson 1891. 26) and in the *Orknøyinga Saga* (*Papuli*: Oftedal 1954. 396). In the Northern Isles we also have survivals, for example in *Papyl* and *Papilwater* in Shetland (Brøgger 1929. 61). ON *Papýli* is a syncopated form of **Papabýli* and the generic here is ON *býli* nt. used in the sense 'domicile, residence'. It is a derivative of ON *ból* nt., to which we shall come later, and was apparently limited in use to compounds (De Vries 1961; Cleasby 1957). Of course the names Bayble and Paible tell us little about Norse settlement since these clerics were Celts. There is really no problem about the origin of final -[bəl] here, and its derivation from ON *býli* is well noted by several eminent scholars, including Oftedal (op.cit. ibid.) and Brøgger (op.cit. ibid.). The names referred to here have quite unjustifiably been included by Nicolaisen in his distribution-map (Nicolaisen op.cit. 93).

ON *bólstaðr* and *bústaðr*

Continuing on the west coast, there are a large number of names which contain orthographic *bosta* or final *-bost*. They are found predominantly in Lewis and Skye but outliers are also found in the Uists and in Coll [Fig. 3.2]. There are two examples of unqualified and 32 of qualified name-forms. The respective pronunciations of the reflexes here are [bɔ:sta] or [bɔ:staɣ], and final -[bɔst]; there was one name here whose pronunciation I failed to get. These undoubtedly derive from ON *bólstaðr* m. which translates variously as 'farm, farmstead, residence', and commentators are unanimous here. The element is a compound of *ból* (a derivative of which we met earlier) and *staðr* m. a 'place, stead', but also 'farmstead'. *Ból* originally applied to a 'lying-place for animals' but was later associated with farm-land and residences. The variants [bɔ:sta] and [bɔ:staɣ] are interesting. Final [ɣ] is not a reflex of ON *ð* but, as is fairly common in the dialects concerned, merely closes an otherwise open final syllable. Compare Gael. *feòil*, gen. ['fjɔ:Ləɣ] besides ['fjɔ:Lə], 'meat'; also *Tairigeadh* [NB 1841] ['thaði,g'aɣ] besides *Taraigea* [NB 2749] ['thari,g'a], names found on the west of Lewis and both from ON *Þaragið* 'ravine of the seaweed'. Final syllable [a] in [bɔ:sta(ɣ)] has developed from an intermediate stage in which the original ON orthographic *a* was lengthened after borrowing to compensate for the loss of the final segment of the stem *bólstað-*. In name-final position the reduction of stress was such that not only was the final syllable lost, but long [ɔ:] shortened to [ɔ], although secondary stress is still discernible today, e.g. *Swanibost* ['sūāN'ə,bɔst] in Lewis, from an acc. ON *Sveinabólstað* '*Sveini*'s farm' (Oftedal 1954. 373).

There are two other names, however, which we can consider here. These are *Boust* [bɔusta] in Skye and *Bousd* [bɔust] in Coll [Fig. 3.3]. Like *Bosta* [bɔ:sta] in Lewis, these are loans from unqualified ON names. [bɔusta] is essentially the same as [bɔ:sta], except that the long stress

46

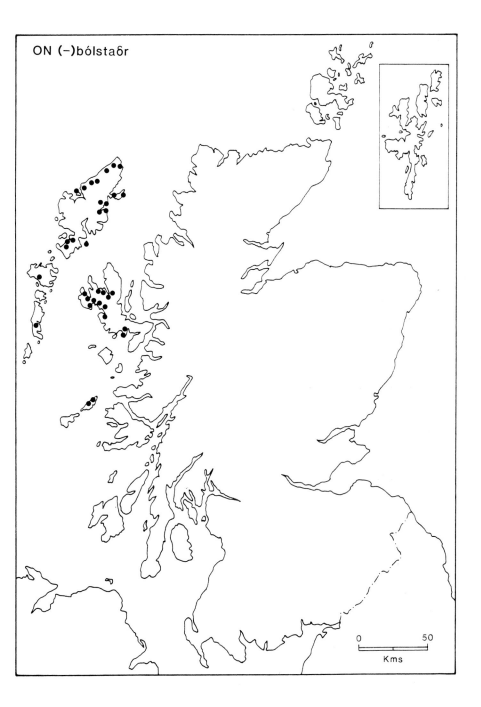

ON (–)bólstaδr

Fig. 3.2 Place-names incorporating ON *(-)bólstaδr*.

47

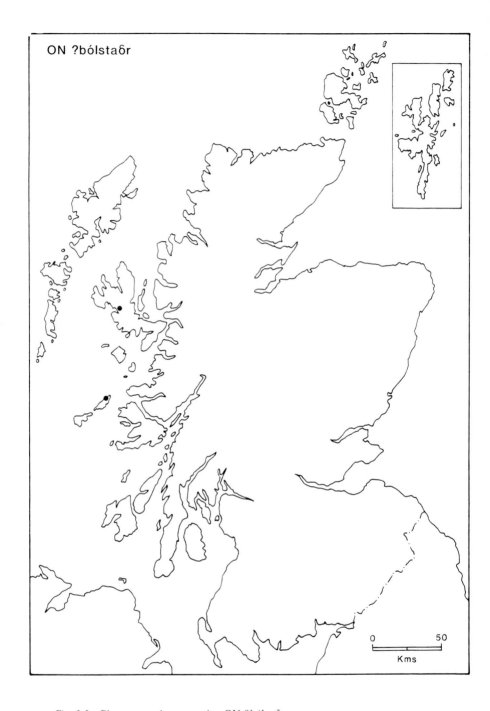

ON ?bólstaðr

Fig. 3.3   Place-names incorporating ON *?bólstaðr*.

48

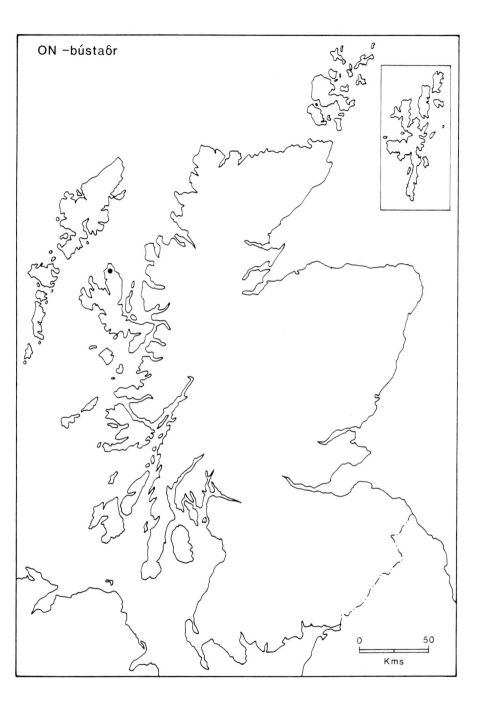

ON −bústaðr

0   50

Kms

Fig. 3.4   Place-names incorporating ON *-bústaðr*.

49

vowel is a diphthong rather than a monothong, suggesting that the lateral survived longer in the south than in the north. The Coll name [bɔust] is different, however, in that we must conclude that it has lost its final syllable. Let us for the moment assume that this was the case.

Now in the north of Skye we also have the name *Heribusta* ['hɛrə,bʌsta], and Forbes (1923. 214) takes this to have included final *-bólstaðr* as well [Fig. 3.4]. However, two points immediately draw our attention: firstly the secondary stress vowel is [ʌ], secondly we have final [a]. Could this be a question of dialectal variation so that here we simply have another reflex of ON *bólstaðr*? I think the evidence in fact points to ON *bústaðr* m., an element with the same range of application as *bólstaðr*. Comparing these elements, it looks as if a final *-bólstaðr* could have undergone a development as follows: final ON acc. *-bólstað* initially yielded Gael. *-[bɔ:Lsta:] compensating for the loss of ð; this gave way to *-[bɔ:Lsta] with shortening of the final syllable; and this became *-[bɔLsta] after shortening of the secondary stress vowel, which in turn yielded *-[bɔ:sta] with temporary lengthening of the secondary stress vowel due to the loss of *l*. Once the final syllable was dropped (due to the retention of secondary stress coupled with the temporary lengthening of the penultimate syllable), we are left with *-[bɔ:st], and this, with eventual reduction of the vowel length, gives us modern -[bɔst]. A final ON acc. *-bústað*, on the other hand, did not need to undergo any further development once the secondary stress vowel was reduced, yielding -[bʌsta], and so the final syllable has survived undisturbed, although its loss would have been of no surprise. Perhaps we also owe something of the survival of this pronunciation to the fact that the location of the name lies well to the north of the cluster of *bost*-names found in Skye. In other words, it may be that there were other *bústaðr*-names in the Western Isles, but which have fallen together in sound with the more predominant *bólstaðr*-names.

ON *ból* and *pollr*

While *bost* name-forms reached Coll, in the vicinity we also have several names with reflexes written *-pol(l)*. We have two in the north of Mull, two in Coll, and six in Tiree [Fig. 3.5]. I have not obtained pronunciations for one of the Mull and two of the Tiree names but the remainder are pronounced -[bɔL]. Gillies in his *Place-Names of Argyll* derives at least two of these names from forms in final ON *-pollr* m. a 'pool, pond': the loan-names in question occur as specifics in the names *Cnoc Bhircepol* and *Loch Bhasapol* in Tiree (Gillies 1906. 236). However, he also sites the use of the ON element *ból* in Argyllshire (Gillies 1906. 223), although he does not say explicitly in which names it occurs. A reflex [bəL] also occurs in the west of Scotland and purely from a phonetic point of view [bɔL] is the more likely candidate for ON *ból*, while [bəL] would formally derive from ON *pollr*. Before considering these Tiree-Coll-Mull [bɔL] forms further, it will be profitable to look at the evidence of [bəL] forms.

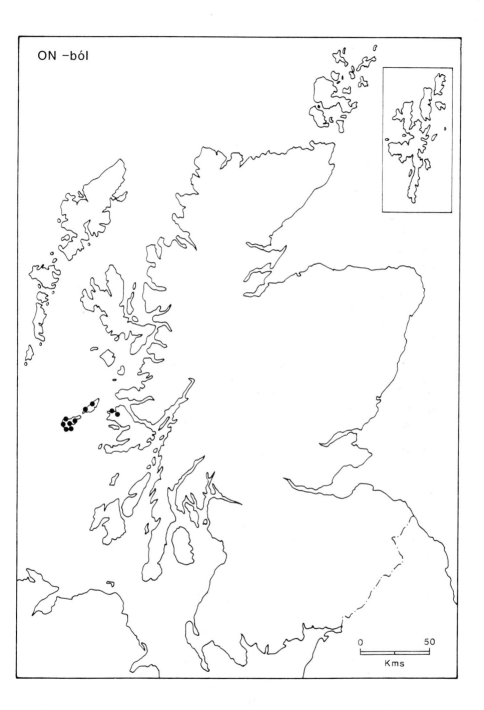

ON −ból

Fig. 3.5 Place-names incorporating ON -*ból* (Tiree, Coll, Mull).

51

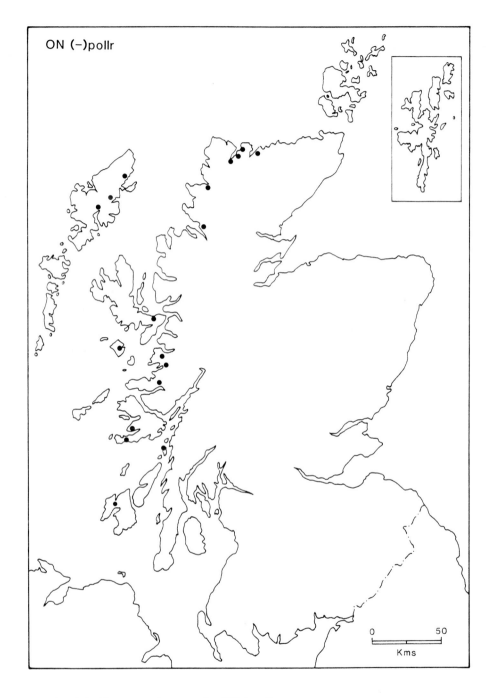

ON (–)pollr

Fig. 3.6 Place-names incorporating ON *(-)pollr*.

52

Of name-forms with a final -[bəL] we find a cluster around the north-west coast and two strings down either side of the Minch [Fig. 3.6]. One name I think we can discount at the outset as having anything to do with *bólstaðr* or any other settlement generic-element, but which was apparently included by Nicolaisen in his distribution maps, is *Noustapal* [NF 8220] in South Uist. The pronunciation of this loan-name is ['Nū:stə‚bəL], and it appears to be a metathesised form of ON *Gnúpsdal* acc. with the gen. sg. of *gnúpr* m. a 'peak, summit', found also, for example, in the loan-name *Nùb* [NB 2643] [Nū̃:b] in the west of Lewis. The generic is ON *dalr* m. a 'valley', and the derivation is certainly acceptable topographically.

On the mainland, in the north, we have *Kirkiboll* by the Kyle of Tongue, *Arnaboll* on Loch Hope, and *Eriboll* on Loch Eriboll. Apart from the pronunciation -[bəL] these names also have in common the fact that they are located by long narrow lochs. The same is true of *Unapool* and *Ullapool* to the west; and to the south we find *Arnabol* on Loch Ailort (but for which I have no pronunciation) and *Reisipol* on Loch Sunart. Coincidence one might think. Shelter-affording sea-lochs (excluding Loch Hope here) are just the place in which settlements would develop. Yet we are, nevertheless, concerned with features to which the ON generic *pollr* would aptly apply. While it had the sense 'pool or pond' as applied to small round lakes or sections of rivers, it is also well attested in place-names in Norway in the sense 'rounded bay or inlet; or the head of a sea-loch, often one with a narrow opening'; and it is especially frequent in this last sense in the west of Norway (Sandnes & Stemshaug 1980. 247).

At the head of Loch Eriboll is the name *Polla*, for which I have heard ['phɔLa] but also ['phɔLə]. Although Gael. *poll* 'pool, hole, mud' is stated by MacBain (1982. 280) to derive from Latin, where we find the sense 'pool, fishing ground', as in the Lewis names *Poll Chràgam* and *Poll an Sgadain* (the former has an ON loan-name as specific, while the latter means 'the pool of the herring'), I think we are in the presence of a loan-word from ON *poll*, acc. of *pollr*. The pronunciation ['phɔLə] of the name at the head of Loch Eriboll seems suspect if we are to consider a derivation from ON *pollr*: [phɔuL] would be expected. If ['phɔLa] is the more authentic form though, the name could represent an ON *Pollǿ* with the stem form of *pollr* and nom. or acc. of *ǿ* f. a 'river', lit. 'lakehead-river'. While the name Polla once applied to the river at the head of Loch Eriboll, the name Eriboll originally applied to the sea-loch itself. Applied to waterways, then, these names in final -[bəL] might be chronologically earlier than any Norse settlements founded beside them.

There are several other -[bəL] name-forms to the south: *Harrapool* in Skye, *Meoble* south of Loch Morar, *Scobull* and *Loch Assopol* in the south-west of Mull, and *Cullipool* in Luing. Scobull lies on the long Loch Scridain and would fall in with Unapool, Ullapool etc. Still in Mull, Loch Assopol could have applied to the sea-loch *Loch na Làthaich*; indeed, it might just be from ON *Hafspoll* acc. (though we would have to accept the development of an intrusive medial schwa), with gen. sg. of *haf* nt. 'sea'. If so, the meaning here would seem to have been 'the bay facing (lit. of) the open sea' (which it does) rather than simply 'bay' (i.e. indentation of the coast) which a term such as *hafsbotn* m. would have done. Like *pollr, botn* was used of the heads of sea-lochs or fiords; it could also apply to valley or lake-heads, and in this sense is found in the Gaelic loan-word *bot*. Harrapool in Skye is also a candidate for a generic with the sense of 'bay'; similarly Cullipool in Luing, where the bay used to be dammed to provide a pond for lobsters awaiting transportation to market (Darling 1969. 84). Meoble, however, if the name has not been transferred away from the loch (which is not impossible), may be an example of ON *pollr* being applied to a pool in a river, in this instance in River Meoble. There are two other names in the Inner Hebrides which are potentially relevant here, though I have no pronunciations for them. The first is *Raonapol* in Rum, and which lies at the head of the deep Loch Scresort on the east of the island. The other is *Corsapool* in Islay. The location here is at the head of Loch Gruinart, a deep sea-loch. The flat land at the head of the lake has long been drained, but it was certainly a very marshy area at one time. Potentially, then, Corsapool referred to the head of this sea-loch, or to a nearby pool or pond.

In the Outer Isles there are three names which appear to concern us here. I have no pronunciation for *Port Grigaspul* which lies in Loch Seaforth on the south-east of Lewis, but were we to be able to derive the generic in the ON loan-name here from *pollr*, we would likely link up the sense of the element here with its use in the names Eriboll, Ullapool etc. *Loch Ulapoll* in east Lewis, though, refers to fresh-water, as does *Loch Chulapuill* in the north of Lewis. While the former, Loch Ulapoll, has final -[bəL], the pronunciation I received for the latter was ['Lɔx'xu:Lə,beN'] along wth the information that the last part derived from Gael. *cùl na beinne* 'the rear of the mountain'. While the folk etymology need not detain us, it would be nice to know whether another and, we may assume, more authentic pronunciation survives.

ON *pollr*, then, survives in quite a large group of names in the west of Scotland, but possibly in three different senses: the head of a sea-loch, or bay; a pool in a river; and a fresh-water pool. *Arnaboll* on Loch Hope in Sutherland, however, does not apparently fit any of these senses, but it may be that its long shape, its north-south alignment and its vicinity to the sea allowed Loch Hope to be considered in terms of the element *pollr*. That this element was used in the Norse onomasticon in three different ways should not surprise us; this is paralleled by the use of the element *vík* in three distinct ways in the Skye names *Uig* [NG 3963] (of a bay), *Uigseadar* [NG 4246] (of a bend in a river), as well as **Uigseadar* [NG 3649] (of a bend in a mountain-range).

That [bəL]-names were not settlement-names makes sense of their wide distribution compared with the more orderly distribution of *bost*-names.[1] Where do the [bɔL]-names of Tiree, Coll and Mull belong here? It has already been stated that Gillies thought ON *pollr* was behind at least some of these names. While it might be argued that [bɔL] was from ON *pollr* and that the occurrence of [ɔ] rather than [ə] was merely a question of

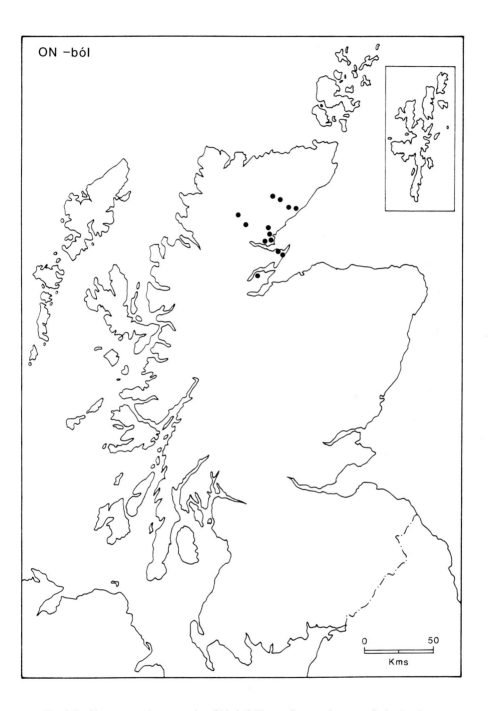

ON −ból

Fig. 3.7 Place-names incorporating ON -ból (Easter Ross and eastern Sutherland).

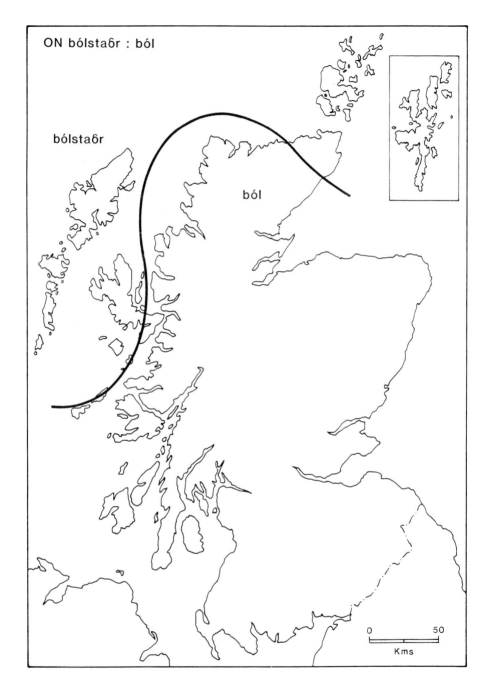

Fig. 3.8 Southern limit of place-names incorporating ON *bólstaðr* — a *bólstaðr/ból* isogloss.

dialect, and while the sense 'pool' could be thought of as being relevant in perhaps two or three instances, the phonetic argument is not convincing. Furthermore, if we accept that *pollr* is behind these names we should not leave much in the way of ON settlement-names in Tiree, although we should not will any into existence just because we wish it so! We have already looked at the semantic development of *ból* and seen that it occurs in the compound *bólstaðr*. Interestingly, on the west of Lewis it is found as a loan-word meaning 'stall', but an earlier application is attested in place-names, for example *Bòl Ruairidh* NB2346 'Ruaraidh's (animal) couch, lying-place'. In Tiree, Coll and Mull, however, it seems to have been used of farmsteads, in the Norse onomasticon at least, and from their location and distribution these [bɔL]-names should be seen as a stage separate from that of *bost*-names.

Distinctions between *bost* and [bɔL]-names may prove significant in terms of chronology and/or demography, or merely in terms of onomasticon. On the east of Scotland, moreover, we have a group of names that may link up chronologically with the [bɔL]-names of Tiree, Coll and Mull.

Unfortunately, it is on the east of Scotland that I fared worst in collecting pronunciations of names. Of 13 that I had noted, I have the pronunciations of just four [Fig. 3.7]. One of these, for *Torboll* in East Sutherland, has final -[bil'] which appears to be an oblique case-form now used as the radical form. The other three have final -[bɔL], although in the case of Easter Ross *Cadboll* the dental lateral has been displaced by an alveolar lateral. Modern English spellings of the reflexes here include *bo*, *ble* and *bol(l)*. Despite the *bo*-forms we can tell from documentary evidence that we are dealing with forms that originally ended in a lateral. Although the vocalism in the few examples I have is [ə], ON *pollr* may have little to do with this group of names. ON final -*ból* would be expected to yield -[bəL] in East Sutherland due to restrictions on the distribution of vowels outside the main stress (Dorian 1978. 56), and this may also be applicable to Easter Ross. It is also notable that few of the names could have been applied in the sense 'lakehead, or bay'. Suffice it to say that it is possible that we have several *ból*-names in the east of Scotland. The evidence from the west would seem to support this view. If we draw a line on a map showing the southern limit of the *bólstaðr*-area, it cuts through Caithness, southern Skye and the tip of Coll, while leaving the north-west mainland untouched [Fig. 3.8]. Both on the west and the east of the country this line can be seen as a *bólstaðr-ból* isogloss. This comparison between what was taking place on the west and what was taking place on the east certainly suggests the distinction between *bólstaðr* and *ból* was more than just a question of lexis: they represent different chronological strata. Whether or not *ból*-names represent internal movement or fresh intake, so to speak, from Norway is harder to judge, but this comparative evidence would favour the latter. But let us now move on.

ON *?*bólshagi*

Heading further south on the west of Scotland we get a very different

57

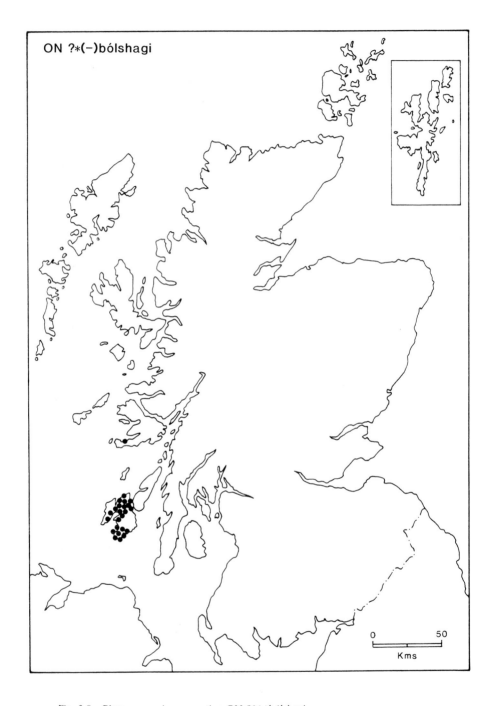

ON ?*(−)bólshagi

Fig. 3.9 Place-names incorporating ON *?*(-)bólshagi.*

58

picture. In Islay, the reflexes [bɔuLsa], [bʌsəɤ] and [bʌs] occur. There is at least one example of [bʌs] in Mull as well [Fig. 3.9]. The first question to be asked concerns the possible relationship between these three reflexes. The first, [bɔuLsa], occurs in the unqualified form *Bolsay*, and probably also in the form *Bolsa* but whose pronunciation I failed to get. The other two reflexes only occur in qualified name-forms. Their distribution is interestingly determined by the number of syllables occurring before the generic. So we have *Grobolls* ['grɔ:ˌbʌsəɤ] and *Robolls* ['Rɔ:ˌbʌsəɤ] where the specific has one or has been reduced to one syllable, but *Coillabus* ['khəL'əˌbʌs] and *Nereabolls* ['N'ɛ:rəˌbʌs] where the specific consists of or has reduced to two syllables. Could the reflexes here be one and the same? Let us view them diagrammatically, with the hypothesis that they do derive from the same ON element:

(1)			b̥	ɔuL	s	a	
(2)		X	b̥	ʌ	s	ə	ɤ
(3)	X	X	b̥	ʌ	s		

In (1) we have full name-stress remaining on the initial syllable of the reflex, and we see a long vowel and lateral surviving before the [s]; the original vowel seems to have been a long ō which was later diphthongised before the lateral. Further we have final [a] which points to an original long vowel or lost consonant. In (2), once the element moves into name-final position, its stress is severely weakened, which affects the vowels of both syllables; final-syllable [a] is reduced to a schwa, and the original stress vowel and lateral have yielded [ʌ]; interestingly, the final syllable is closed by an epenthetic [ɤ]. Finally, the process of reduction continues in (3), where the increased syllable count forces the removal of the final syllable. (Long ON loan-names have almost invariably been pared down to three syllables in their modern Gaelic forms; an exception here is the Skye name Heribusta.) These three reflexes, then, do seem to have arisen from the same ON element. In addition we have documentary evidence which suggests that the forms in question go back to a common source-element.

The form of the element suggested is *bóls*+V̆+C or *bóls*+V̄(+C). All commentators, however, derive these Islay names from *(-)bólstaðr* (e.g. Gillies 1906. 223; Johnston 1934. 41-2; Henderson 1910. 197-98). What has happened to the original *t*? To say that the original medial cluster *-lst-* has lost its *t* in favour of a cluster *-ls-* as a result of dialectal preference is a solution, but by no means conclusive. It would seem more likely for the lateral to be the weakest link in a cluster *-lst-*, as was the case in areas where we can be certain *bólstaðr* occurred; compare Islay [pɔustər] (Holmer 1938. 130) and Kintyre [boˑəsD̥ər] (Holmer 1962. 46), whose etymon gives Eng. *bolster*. In addition to the phonological evidence here, there is the negative evidence of the absence of *bólstaðr*-names, considered in the light of the reflexes looked at so far, in the area of Tiree and Mull: why should the wave of *bólstaðr*-names peter out in Coll only to reappear so strongly in Islay?

Unfortunately, no obvious derivation for [bɔuLsa] etc. springs readily to mind, at least when we make comparisons with the commoner settlement-generics surviving in Norway. Certainly it appears that we have a compound in initial *ból*. Theoretically, the following [s] could be from its genitive form or the initial sound of the second element in a compound-word, as in *bólstaðr*. Could we here be in the presence of a new generic-term, one only marginally in use in Norway, or perhaps one not even pertinent to events in Norway? There is plenty of evidence to show that the Norse nomenclature in the west developed on different lines to the one in Norway itself, and that even within the western area there were distinctive patterns. For example, the absence of *setr* or *sætr* name-forms in Iceland; the high productivity of the stream-element *gróf* in Lewis, e.g. in the name *Allt Alagro* [NB 1939] -['ɑːLə₁gro] fr. ON *Álagróf* 'stream of the eels'; and the use of the early Gaelic loan-word *ærgi* (Gael. *àirigh* a 'shieling') in many Hebridean islands.

Now in the south-west of Norway there is a name *Bolshus* (NG 9, 308). This would appear to give ON *Bólshús* 'the house of the farm', with gen.sg. of *ból*, and *hús* nt. a 'house, or group of buildings on a farm'. We might speculate that [bɔuLsa] etc. derive from a metathesised form of ON **bólshús*, or, perhaps less likely, **ból-hús* with the stem form of *ból*. Altogether better would be an ON compound **bólshagi* with final masc. *hagi*. *Hagi* originally meant an 'enclosed field', but also evolved the more general sense 'pasture'. In modern Scandinavian languages we find the senses 'garden; enclosed pasture; hedge or fence; and meadow'. Reduction of **bólshagi* to [bɔuLsa] is quite straightforward, and although the compound is not attested in Old Norse nor found, to my knowledge, in the modern Scandinavian languages, it is not unfeasible. We can speculate that its sense could have been similar to the use of Gael. *geàrraidh* in Lewis, where it applied to the enclosed land immediately around, often attached to, the dwelling-house and later to the stance of land upon which the dwelling-house stood (Cox 1987. I. 268; II. 18). A modern Norwegian parallel would be *selsbø*, an 'enclosure adjoining a mountain summer farm'.[2]

At this point we can remember that we are looking here at Islay alone, with the exception of one, perhaps two examples in Mull. *Bólstaðr*-names come as far south as Skye and Coll, and in the latter area, as we have seen, *ból* itself then became functional as a settlement generic-element. Once this happened, even if the element had fallen into disuse as regards its other senses, *ból* was again available for re-use in the formation of some other compound-noun. This, I suggest, occurred in Islay.

The south Mull example of -[bʌs] could be seen as an extension of influence or settlement from Islay. Gillies (1906. 232) mentions another apparent [bʌs]-form, but I do not know its location. (An island-name, *Bolsa*, is also cited by Gillies (op.cit. 227) but it is not included here because I do not know its location either.) However, the Mull names could be taken as a link between what happened in the Tiree-Coll-Mull area (the transferral from the use of *bólstaðr* to *ból*) and what occurred in Islay (the employment of another element compounded with *ból*). There may be a geographically closer link though, in the Coll name *Bousd*, but which earlier we attributed to *bólstaðr*. The problem with this name is the loss of the final syllable. It is not as if the generic here were in name-final position, with its stress considerably weakened, which would tend to promote its being dropped. Of course, a general influence from name-forms in final [bɔst] could be cited, although this has not apparently occurred elsewhere. An alternative solution is that [bɔust] is in fact not from *bólstaðr* but from **bólshagi*. An original Coll name, **[bɔuLsa]*, which yielded **[bɔusa]*, would be in a position to be influenced by [st]-forms, but its overall shape could be retained by a simple process of segmental substitution: **[bɔusa]* giving **[bɔust]*.

AN OVERVIEW

While the case for a derivation of Islay name-forms from ON **bólshagi* is not conclusive, because we have no knowledge of such a compound being used elsewhere, the fact that *bólstaðr* is not the only generic element that has contributed to the range of reflexes under discussion here should surely make us wary of making assumptions regarding a derivation from *bólstaðr*. Let us turn and look at the overall picture.

The few names with ON *býli*, as we have seen, do not contribute to our knowledge of Norse settlement patterns. Rather they say something about what Norsemen found already in existence at certain locations when they themselves settled in the vicinity. On a map showing the areal distribution of the generic elements we have been discussing, then, *býli* occurs within the area where *bólstaðr* is found [Fig. 3.10]. This includes Caithness, the Western Isles, and most of Skye and Coll. We are looking at a relatively peripheral penetration of settlement from the north-east and from the north-west. Within this area we also have evidence for the use of the element *bústaðr*, although this was certainly marginal.

Directed inward from this, from Caithness down to the Moray Firth, and in the west within an area including Coll, Tiree and Mull, we find names in *ból* [Fig. 3.8]. That this development is found on both sides of the country suggests, I think, that we are probably not looking at a purely local innovation. *Ból* is found in Norwegian place-names, though its derivative *bøli* nt. is commoner (see Sandnes and Stemshaug 1980. 86; Rygh 1898. 44, 46). And it is also found in Iceland, e.g. *Drápsból*, and *Háaból* (Allee 1973. 48, 50).

The development we next find in the west is not, however, paralleled on the east of Scotland. The generic element here, I suggest, was an innovation and not one we should expect to find necessarily reflected, therefore, in the place-nomenclatures of Norway or Iceland. This was possibly an otherwise unattested **bólshagi*. While the area concerned includes Islay and at least part of Mull, the name *Bousd*, which was discussed earlier in relation to Islay names, may well indicate that part of Coll also lies within this area.

Finally, over the whole area with which we have been dealing (except

61

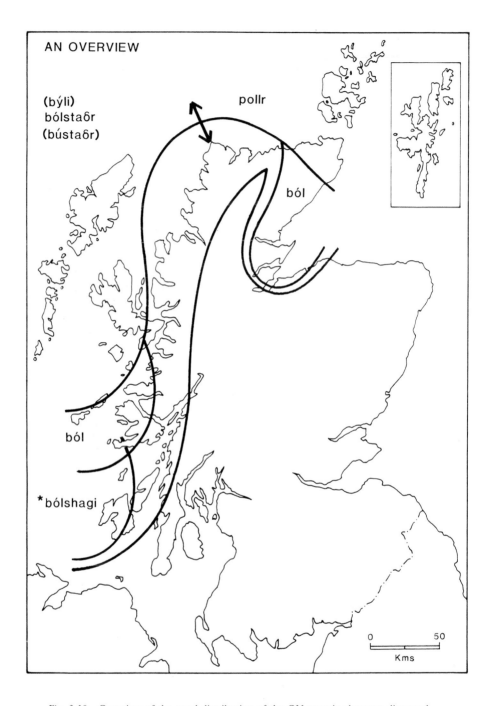

Fig. 3.10 Overview of the areal distribution of the ON generic elements discussed.

perhaps for Caithness, East Sutherland and Easter Ross), we find evidence of *pollr*-names. Since these originally applied to some sort of feature involving water, we cannot view them as settlement-names for our purpose, though they were later transferred to settlements. Of limited occurrence compared to valley-names in ON *(-)dalr*, they nevertheless have a similar significance in showing the distribution of Norse influence as opposed to Norse settlement.

In conclusion, it is submitted that the group of reflexes under discussion here are not all from the one ON element *bólstaðr*, but in fact from six different ON elements: *býli*, *bústaðr*, *bólstaðr*, *ból*, *pollr*, and an unconfirmable form, perhaps an unattested *bólshagi*. Despite the lack of certainty regarding an etymon for the Islay reflexes, the phasing of Norse settlement in Scotland is clearly more serial and more complex than has hitherto been thought, and we must especially review the situation with regard to the west and north-west coast of the mainland. Once a detailed analysis of each individual name has been made, the evidence must be collated with other information about settlement patterns that we already have at our disposal, and, hopefully, new evidence that may yet come to light. In doing so, various tantalising questions of chronology will also have to be addressed. For instance, what had been happening when the abbot quit Iona in 807 AD? This, however, along with other such questions, is not within the remit of this paper.

Notes

[1] Dr Doreen Waugh suggested to me that we might in some cases be dealing with names where *pollr* as an element in the onomasticon was used implicitly of a 'settlement at the head of, or on a fiord'. This is certainly possible, and should be taken into account in making a more detailed examination of the names.

[2] **Bólshagi* could be objected to on the grounds that it is an unlikely compound since it contains the genitive rather than the stem of *ból*. However, the development of a compound as an appellative — one then used in the onomasticon — is plausible.

Appendix 1

The names relevant to this survey are listed here according to island or area, along with grid references and relevant pronunciations. In addition, three names are given whose locations are uncertain. These are unnumbered below and are not accounted for on distribution maps. However, given their likely locations, they do not contradict conclusions drawn above. *Noustapal* should be discounted, and is also unnumbered.

Lewis

1.	Habost	NB5262	-[bɔst]
2.	Swainbost	NB5162	-[bɔst]
3.	Melbost	NB4157	-[bɔst]
4.	Shawbost	NB4625	-[bɔst]
5.	Bosta	NB1841	[bɔːsta(ɤ)]
6.	Bosta	NB1440	[bɔːsta(ɤ)]

7.	Kirkibost	NB1835	-[bɔst]
8.	Loch Chulapuill	NB4843	-[beN']
9.	Garrabost	NB5033	-[bɔst]
10.	Upper Bayble	NB5331	-[bəl]
11.	Melbost	NB4157	-[bɔst]
12.	Crossbost	NB3824	-[bɔst]
13.	Leurbost	NB3725	-[bɔst]
14.	Loch Ulapoll	NB3222	-[bəL]
15.	Habost	NB3219	-[bɔst]
16.	Calbost	NB4117	-[bɔst]
17.	Port Grigaspul	NB2214	?-[bəL]

Harris

18.	Seilebost	NG0696	-[bɔst]
19.	Horgabost	NG0496	-[bɔst]
20.	Tràigh Nisabost	NG0496	-[bɔst]

Taransay

21.	Paible	NG0399	-[bəl]

Scalpay

22.	Meall Challibost	NG2294	-[bɔst]

North Uist

23.	Paible	NF7368	-[bəl]
24.	Claddach Kirkibost	NF7865	-[bɔst]

South Uist

25.	Barp Frobost	NF7525	-[bɔst]
—	Noustapal	NF8220	-[bəL]

Skye

26.	Heribusta	NG4071	-[bʌsta]
27.	Prabost	NG4249	-[bɔst]
28.	Carbost	NG4348	-[bɔst]
29.	Skeabost	NG4248	-[bɔst]
30.	Breabost	NG3653	-[bɔst]
31.	Colbost	NG2149	-[bɔst]
32.	Husabost	NG2051	-[bɔst]
33.	Heribost	NG2745	-[bɔst]
34.	Orbost	NG2543	-[bɔst]
35.	Colbost Point	NG3130	-[bɔst]
36.	Eabost	NG3139	-[bɔst]
37.	Boust	NG3537	[bɔusta]
38.	Carbost	NG3831	-[bɔst]
39.	Ben Meabost	NG5316	-[bɔst]
40.	Kirkibost	NG5517	-[bɔst]
41.	Harrapool	NG6522	-[bəL]

Rum

42.	Raonapol	NM4099	?-[bəL]

Coll

43.	*Bousd*	*NM2563*	*[bɔust]*
44.	Grishipoll	NM1959	-[bəL]
45.	Arnabost	NM2160	-[bɔst]
46.	Crossapol	NM1253	-[bəL]
47.	Mibost	NM2059	?-[bɔst]

Tiree
48. Cnoc Bhircepol   NL9544   ?-[bɔL]
49. Barrapoll   NL9543   -[bɔL]
50. Heylipoll   NL9743   ?-[bɔL]
51. Crossapoll   NL9943   -[bɔL]
52. Kirkapoll   NM0447   -[bɔL]
53. Loch Bhasapol   NL9747   -[bɔL]

Mull
—   Lurabus   ?   (Gillies 1906. 232)
54. Sunipol   NM3753   -[bɔL]
55. Crossapol   NM3853   -[bɔL]
56. Scobull   NM4627   -[bəL]
57. Eorabus   NM3823   -[bʌs]
58. Loch Assopol   NM4020   -[bəL]

Islay
59. Asabus   NR3141   -[bʌs]
60. Kinnabus   NR2942   -[bʌs]
61. Risabus   NR3143   -[bʌs]
62. Coillabus   NR3243   -[bʌs]
63. Lurabus   NR3343   -[bʌs]
64. Upper Cragabus   NR3245   -[bʌs]
65. Cornabus   NR3346   -[bʌs]
66. Cnocan Bhrannabuis NR3447   ?-[bʌs]
67. Grobolls   NR3360   -[bʌsəɣ]
68. West Carrabus   NR3163   -[bʌs]
69. Eallabus   NR3363   -[bʌs]
70. Eorrabus   NR3664   -[bʌs]
71. Coullabus   NR2965   -[bʌs]
72. Lyrabus   NR3065   -[bʌs]
73. Scarrabus   NR3465   -[bʌs]
74. Kepolls   NR3865   -[bʌsəɣ]
75. Dùn Chollabus   NR3567   ?-[bʌs]
76. Robolls Hill   NR3967   -[bʌsəɣ]
77. Persabus   NR4168   -[bʌs]
78. Torrabus   NR4270   -[bʌs]
79. Bolsa   NR3877   ? [bɔuLsa]
80. Nereabolls   NR2255   -[bʌs]
81. Bolsay   NR2257   [bɔuLsa]
—   Tòsabus   ?   (Henderson 1910. 198)
82. Corsapool   NR2966   ?-[bəL]

Luing
83. Cullipool   NM7313   -[bəL]
—   Island of Bolsa   ?   (Gillies 1906. 227)

Moidart
84. Reisipol   NM7264   -[bəL]
85. Meoble   NM7987   -[bəL]
86. Arnabol Hill   NM7584   ?-[bəL]

Wester Ross
87. Ullapool   NH1393   -[bəL]

West Sutherland
88. Unapool   NC2333   -[bəL]

North Sutherland

89. Eriboll	NC4356	-[bəL]
90. Polla	NC3854	['phɔLa] ['phɔLə]
91. Kirkiboll	NC5856	-[bəL]
92. Arnaboll	NC4657	-[bəL]

Easter Ross

93. Arboll	NH8781	?-[bəL]ɬ]
94. Cadboll	NH8777	-[bəɬ]
95. Culbo	NH6360	?-[bəL]ɬ]

East Sutherland

96. Embo	NH8192	-[bəL]
97. Skelbo	NH7895	-[bəL]
98. Skibo	NH7389	?-[bəL]
99. Torboll	NH7599	-[bil']
100. Torroboll	NC5904	?-[bəL]
101. Colaboll	NC5510	?-[bəL]
102. Eldrable	NC9818	?-[bəL]
103. Duible	NC9219	?-[bəL]
104. Learable	NC8923	?-[bəL]
105. Borrobol	NC8726	?-[bəL]

Appendix 2

Exceptions to derivations from ON (-)*bólstaðr* of the names listed in Appendix 1, as given by earlier commentators, are noted below with relevant references, according to source-element.

ON *býli*: Oftedal 1954. 396 (Bayble).
ON *ból*: Forbes 1923. 212 (Harrapool); Gillies 1906. 223 (no examples given); Johnston 1934. 41-42 (no examples given); Henderson 1910. 152-53, 188, 192-93, 355 (names in orthographic -*bol(l)* -*pol(l)* and -*pool*, except Ullapool p. 158); Watson 1976. 40 (Cadboll), 47 (Arboll), 121 (Culbo).
ON *pollr*: Gillies 1906. 236 (Cnoc Bhircepol, Loch Bhasapol).

References

Allee, J.G. Place-Names in Skaftafell, Iceland, in *Onoma*. vol XVII. 1972-73.
Ásmundarson, V. (ed.) *Landnámabók* (Íslendinga Sögur I). 1891.
Brøgger, A.W. *Ancient Emigrants: A History of the Norse Settlements of Scotland*. 1929.
Cleasby, R., Vigfusson, G. & Craigie, W. A. *An Icelandic-English Dictionary*. 1957.
Cox, R.A.V. *Place-names of the Carloway Registry, Isle of Lewis*. Unpublished Ph.D. thesis (University of Glasgow). 1987.
Cox, R.A.V. The Origin and Relative Chronology of Shader-names in the Hebrides, in *Scottish Gaelic Studies*. 1990. vol 16.
Darling, F.F. & Boyd, J.M. *The Highlands and Islands*. 2nd ed. 1969.
De Vries, J. *Altnordisches Etymologisches Wörterbuch*. 1961.
Dorian, N.C. *East Sutherland Gaelic*. 1978.
Forbes, A.R. *Place-names of Skye*. 1923.
Gillies, H.C. *The Place-names of Argyll*. 1906.
Henderson, G. *The Norse Influence on Celtic Scotland*. 1910.
Holmer, N.M. Studies on Argyllshire Gaelic, in *Kunglig Humanistiska Vetenskaps-Samfundet i Uppsala*. 1938. vol 31, 1.
Holmer, N.M. *The Gaelic of Kintyre*. 1962.

Johnston, J.B. *Place-names of Scotland*. 1934.

MacBain, A. *An Etymological Dictionary of the Gaelic Language*. (1896) 1982.

Nicolaisen, W.F.H. *Scottish Place-names, their Study and Significance*. 1976.

Norske Gaardnavne [*NG*]. 1897-1924. vols I-XVIII; 1936. vol XIX.

Oftedal, M. The Village-names of Lewis in the Outer Hebrides, in *Norsk Tidsskrift for Sprogvidenskap*. 1954. vol 17: 363-409.

Rygh, O. *Introductory Volume to Norske Gaardnavne*. 1898.

Sandnes, J. & Stemshaug, O. *Norsk Stadnamnleksikon*. 1980.

Fig. 4.1 At Inverewe, Loch Ewe, 15 October 1905.

WHAT IS A VIK?:
AN INVESTIGATION INTO AN
OLD NORSE COASTAL TOPONYM

Ian A. Fraser

The recent upsurge of interest in Scandinavian contacts with Scotland has prompted a number of questions relating to toponymy which are fundamental to an understanding of the role of the Norse in what was very much a world dominated by maritime activity. The strategic significance of Scotland in the overall framework of Norse conquest and colonisation has been affirmed by an important recent study by Dr. Barbara Crawford (Crawford 1987). The evidence of place-names has been of enormous value in revealing some of the characteristics of Norse settlement, and while many aspects of this settlement have been clarified by an investigation of habitative names (Nicolaisen 1976. ch. 6), there remains a substantial body of Norse placenames which relate to the topograpy and which have yet to be analysed in detail. It is, for example, significant that substantial numbers of Norse topographical names exist on the North-West mainland, yet the number of genuine habitative settlement names is limited to a handful containing the element *bólstaðr,* such as Ullapool, Unapool, Resipole (ibid. 93 map; but see also Cox, this volume).

The significance of these topographical names must therefore be important. Few would deny that there was a Norse presence in the coastal zone north and west of the Great Glen, but the intensity and continuity of that presence has yet to be quantified, and, lacking much in the way of archaeological evidence, the chances of clarification may be slight. If, however, we examine the Norse toponyms in this zone, it may be possible to shed further light on the settlement, its pattern, distribution and intensity.

COASTAL NAMES: Old Norse *fjörðr, vágr, hóp*

Since the Norse activity was coastal in nature, the investigation of coastal names remains the most fruitful aspect of onomastic study. This is not to deny the fact that Norse placenames exist well inland, and the oral tradition relates stories of 'Viking princesses' in such areas as Loch Maree, where there is a traditional account of a Norse burial on Isle Maree, a place of pilgrimage until very recent times (Dixon 1886. 7-10; see also R. W. Munro, this volume).

Such accounts, however, are relatively rare, and are alluded to in this paper only to illustrate the popular, local belief in a rather vague Viking past (see Macdonald 1984. 265-279).

Much of the North-West coast is exposed and dangerous. However, the islands of Skye, Raasay and Rona provide shelter from the prevailing westerly winds for much of the coastline of Wester Ross, and the major sea lochs, such as Loch Ewe, Gruinard Bay, Loch Broom, Enard Bay and Eddrachillis Bay afford locations which have been exploited for safe anchorages by many generations of seafarers. Several of the sea lochs on this coastline have names which contain ON *fjörðr* 'sea loch', as in the case of *Gruinard* and *Enard*. This element is, of course, common in Skye (*Snizort, Ainort, Eyshort* and *Eynort*) and on the adjacent mainland (*Moidart, Knoydart*). Loch Dunvegan is recorded on the Blaeu Map as 'Loch Fallort' (1654).

The Norse place-name terms which have been applied to minor inlet features are relatively few in number. A general term for a broad inlet, ON *vágr* 'bay' can be very difficult to establish as being of genuine Norse origin, since the English *bay* has appeared on maps of the area since at least the 18th century, and the resultant Gaelic *bagh* can conceivably originate from either of the Germanic languages involved. Although there are clear instances of *vágr* being adopted in the Outer Hebrides (e.g. *Carloway, Lemreway* and *Stornoway* in Lewis, and *Finsbay* in Harris), the term is virtually absent on the mainland of Ross. Such examples of *bay* that we find on the modern map are mostly of recent origin, as in the case of *Badcall Bay, Calva Bay, Achmelvich Bay, Slaggan Bay* and many others. *Scourie Bay*, however, is marked as such on the Roy Military Survey of ca. 1750, but the modern *Gruinard Bay* is referred to on the Blaeu map as 'Loch Grunord'.

The ON *hóp* 'bay', 'inlet' is in the same category, since the Gaelic equivalent, *òb*, is found in fresh-water locations as well as on the coast. Normally *òb*-names apply to well-sheltered locations, usually on major sea-lochs, or on large lochs inland. *Òb nam Muc* 'pig-bay' on Loch Maree, *Òb Gorm Beag* 'little green bay' and *Òb Mheallaidh* 'deceitful bay' on Loch Torridon and *Òb an Dreallaire* 'idler's bay' on South Rona are good examples. The latter was a bay in which fishermen rested during bad weather.

COASTAL NAMES: Old Norse *vík*

The most interesting Old Norse element from the point of view of this paper, however, is ON *vík* 'bay'. Most of the locations where we find the term have attracted settlements, some of which are substantial and of seemingly long standing. These inlets demand further investigation, especially as regards their physical characteristics. The availability of sheltered water, with a measure of protection from westerly and north-westerly winds, is an obvious requirement. A reasonable depth of water close inshore, together with a smooth stretch of beach of gravel or sand are other factors. Boats would require to be beached for repair, and the presence of a natural rock quay which would ease mooring and loading of vessels would add to the attraction of the site.

Such good harbours and anchorages attract permanent settlement, so the availability of arable land close to the *vík*, for the purposes of grain-growing, grazing and hay-making, would seem obvious as a local resource. A maritime economy always requires timber, so the *vík* should ideally be within range of good forest land. However, good timber for house-building and boat-building was, in some cases, relatively scarce, especially in the islands, and the mainland areas of Ross and Argyll must have been exploited for timber even in pre-Norse times.

When we look at the distribution of names in *vík* for West Sutherland, Ross and Skye, we find that individual sites vary a great deal. On the modern map, they are often prefixed by Gaelic elements, such as *loch*, or compounded with English terms like *River* or *Bay*. Thus a name like *Kirkaig* in Sutherland (O.N. *Kirkju-vík* 'church inlet': McBain 1922. 17) appears on the map as *Inverkirkaig* 'the confluence of the Kirkaig River', from Gaelic *inbhir* 'confluence'; so we find also *River Kirkaig* and *Loch Kirkaig*. The Gaelic forms would be *Ciorcaig, Inbhir-chiorcaig, Abhainn Chiorcaig* (the river) and *Loch Chiorcaig* (the inlet). Such developments reflect not only the amount of contact between Old Norse and Gaelic, but also the importance of an Englishing process which originated primarily with documentary forms in the 16th century, and with map-makers after this period.

Those names which had Norse origins led themselves easily to Anglicisation, and in some instances this must be one of the reasons for the survival of many Norse place-names. Gaelic speech, however, has preserved many Norse names particularly well, so that the pronunciation record is often vital in the understanding of the Norse elements involved. As Watson puts it, 'the modern Gaelic pronunciation is extremely conservative in resisting corruption' (Watson 1904. iv).

Vík Names in Wester Ross

I will now examine a few of these *vík*-names, and try to make an assessment of the site and situation qualities involved. The coastline from Enard Bay to Loch Duich contains some eighteen examples which ostensibly come into the category, viz., *Inverkirkaig,* in Sutherland; in Ross, *Scorraig, Miotag, Tournaig, Camastrolvaig, Melvaig, Shieldaig* (Gairloch), *Diabaig, Shieldaig* (Applecross), *Ardheslaig, Cuaig, Tausamhaig* (marked on the O.S. 6" map as *Allt Sabhsach,* but suggested as Norse by Watson), *Reraig* (Loch Carron), *Fernaig, Erbusaig, Pladaig, Reraig* (Loch Alsh) and *Totaig*. Of these, it is probably safe to exclude *Fernaig,* which Watson supposes to be from Gaelic *fearnaig* 'place of alders' (ibid. 205, 184) [Fig. 4.2].

Scorraig, at the mouth of Little Loch Broom is in some ways untypical of the *vík* situation.[1] There is no inlet as such, and this otherwise level stretch of south-facing coast-line is interrupted only by a low promontory, *Corran Sgoraig,* in the lee of which lies the landing-place and the present pier. This is, in fact, probably the only site on the north shore of Little Loch

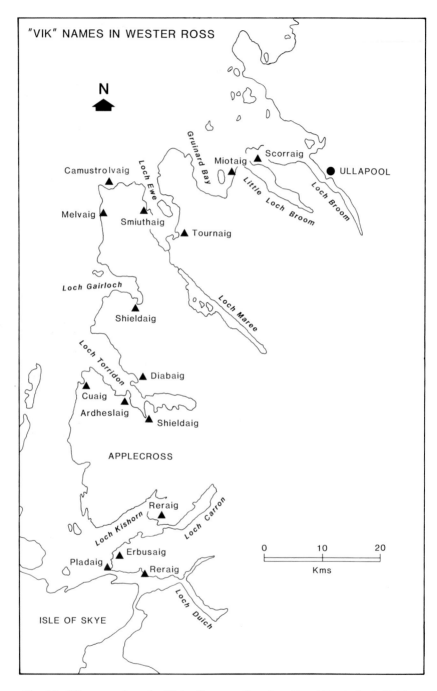

Fig. 4.2 Vik-names along the Wester Ross coastline, from Enard Bay to Loch Duich.

Broom which affords sufficient shelter for boats, so the *corran* (literally Gaelic for sickle, but in topographic terms meaning a sand or gravel spit or the horn of a small bay) assumes an importance on an otherwise difficult coastline. It is the hinterland of this *vík*, however, that is the crucial factor here. The interior is difficult of access from the settlement itself. But the coastal paths — to Rhireavach and Badrallach on Little Loch Broom, and that by Badacrain at the mouth of Loch Broom — skirt the massif of Beinn Ghobhlach, which straddles the peninsula. These paths are rough and narrow, making Scorraig almost as inaccessible as an island. It would therefore have been a useful base for a Norse settlement, especially as there is workable arable land close to the *corran,* which commands the entrance to the loch, and therefore, passage to the interior. Watson (ibid. 249) quotes a Gaelic couplet:

Sgoraig sgreagach, 's dona beag i,
Aite gun dìon gun fhasgadh, gun phreas na coille.

Scraggy Scorraig, bad and little,
A place without protection or shelter, bush or wood.

Yet despite its exposed position, this township flourished in the latter part of the last century, with a thriving fishing industry, a good merchant's shop (which dealt direct with Glasgow!), a school, post office and church, which served a vigorous population. And Annat, on the north side of the peninsula would have been an ideal situation for an early ecclesiastical site — difficult of access by land, but of considerably easier access from Loch Broom.

Camastrolvaig is another headland site a few miles west of the mouth of Loch Ewe. It has been deserted for several generations, partly because of its isolation on the extreme north of the peninsula which divides Gairloch from Loch Ewe. Watson gives as its derivation ON *troll-vík* 'goblin bay' with the prefixed Gaelic *camas* 'inlet'. This hybridised form, where *camas* and *vík* occur in the same name, is to be found in instances like *Camastianavaig,* Skye. According to Watson (ibid. 228), it was 'counted a most uncanny place', and although Dixon does not refer to it, he has several accounts of unnatural happenings occurring at the nearby settlement of Loch an Draing (Dixon 1886. 161 et seq.). Open to the force of north and north-west winds, Camastrolvaig could only have served as a safe anchorage in conditions where the wind was from south of due west.

A few miles south of this lies the township of Melvaig, on a sloping shelf in an exposed position. We first record the name in a Retour of 1566 where it is spelt 'Malefage', and another document of 1638 records it as 'Mailfog'. This corresponds closely to the Gaelic rendering, *Mealabhaig.* Watson gives the derivation as ON *melar-vík,* 'bent grass bay' (Watson 1904). Although Dixon claimed that Melvaig 'is placed at the top of a rocky cliff, of no great height but so steep that the shore below can only be safely reached by those who are acquainted with the place and have a ladder'

(Dixon 1886. 330), there is a site at the mouth of Allt Mealabhaig where boats can be drawn up. It is still, however, a most dangerous stretch of coast, bare and treeless, and it is puzzling that the *vík* element should have been used for this location.

In the south-east corner of Gairloch lies the inlet of Shieldaig (ON *síld-vík,* 'herring bay'). This contrasts strongly with the other *vík* sites we have examined so far, in that it is almost completely enclosed, with a deep water anchorage and reasonable arable land at the head of the inlet, together with a considerable amount of natural timber. There is, in addition, good access to the interior, where hunting, a favourite Viking pastime, could be had in abundance.

Shieldaig (not to be confused with the place of the same name in Applecross parish some 20 miles, 32 kms, further south) has long been used as a safe anchorage for quite large vessels. The sea-loch of Gairloch is open to the west, and, together with the bay of Badachro, the best anchorages are on the south shore. Shieldaig is protected by two small islets, *Eilean an t-Sabhail,* 'shed island' and *Eilean Shìldeig,* 'Shieldaig Island', while Badachro to the west lies behind *Isle Horrisdale* (from ON *Thorir's dalr*). Both sites are still extensively used by commercial fishing boats, yachts and other small craft.

Another site which fulfils most of the requirements present at Shieldaig is the settlement of *Diabaig* at the mouth of Loch Torridon, which lies partly in Gairloch and partly in Applecross. The boundary, in fact, runs through the township lands, formed partly by a stream, *Allt a' Chladha.* Watson (1904. 212) quotes a delightful local couplet which amply indicates its remoteness and security:

'S fhada bho 'n lagh Diabaig,
's fhaida na sin sios Mealabhaig.

Far from the law is Diabaig,
Yet farther is Melvaig.

The bay is deep, surrounded by rocks and backed by mountains [Fig. 4.3]. It faces almost due west, protected from the south-west by *Meall na h-Araird,* a promontory of 400 ft. (122m) to the west, and by the off-shore skerries of *Sgeir Ghorm* and *Sgeir Dughaill.*

The shelving rock called *Sgeir Ghlas* serves as a natural breakwater, and it is here that the stone pier, built in the last century, provides mooring for substantial fishing boats. In the lee of this, boats of all sizes may be drawn up on a shingle beach. The arable land, apart from a narrow strip behind Sgeir Ghlas, consists of steeply-sloping crofts which rise from sea-level to over 500 ft (152m). The two lochs, *Loch a' Mhullaich* and *Loch Diabaig's Airde* are fringed by arable land, thus giving the hinterland of the *vík* a considerable amount of potential for arable and grazing. The small settlement of Araird (now Aird), (Gael. *air-aird,* fore-headland) lies to the south of the bay. The township has a long history of seafaring associations. Diabaig men

Fig. 4.3 Diabaig, 'deep bay', a substantial and safe anchorage on the north shore of outer Loch Torridon. It is a classic *vík*-site, with a natural breakwater (now a stone-built pier), extensive shingle beach (for drawing up boats and drying fish), arable land (albeit steep) and woodland. Diabaig has a long history of seafaring and fishing. 1972.

were notable fishermen, often venturing out in conditions which defied many of their neighbours along the coast. The anchorage was regarded as one of the safest havens in the area, and is still a most impressive example of coastal settlement based on a fishing economy.

The inner part of Loch Torridon, known as *Upper Loch Torridon* affords relatively sheltered conditions compared to the outer part. On its indented south shore, several inlet names contain the element *òb* 'pool', alluded to earlier. The Upper Loch opens into Loch *Shieldaig* on its seaward side, both fed by substantial rivers which form the northern drainage of the Ben Damph and Applecross forests. The loch of Shieldaig is considerably larger and more open than Diabaig. The name is likely to be a secondary form, although it is marked as 'Loch Sheildaig' on Roy (1750). The Blaeu map of 1654 is so inaccurate for this area that, although *Shilkag* clearly refers to Shieldaig itself, the loch is not marked. It is therefore difficult to decide the key topographic feature which is involved in the coining of the name. If *vík* is to be applied to the whole of Loch Shieldaig, it is uncharacteristic compared with those we have already examined. It is much more likely that the *vík* involved is at the extreme head of the loch, marked on the Ordnance Survey map as *Ceann-locha* 'head of the loch'. The village of Shieldaig itself lies on the lee of a rocky, wooded island, known as *Eilean Shìldeag,* giving reasonable protection from westerlies, but the only suitable place for beaching boats lies to the south of the village, where a small headland offers some shelter.

Reraig, at the northern entrance to Lochcarron has been suggested as ON *reyr-vík* 'reed-bay' by Watson (1904. 188). This is one of two such names in our area, the other being on Loch Alsh, near Balmacara. The Lochcarron example is a settlement lying at the head of a shallow, muddy bay, while the Loch Alsh Reraig (for which we have a 1548 form 'Rowrag') lies on an indentation in the loch which is also shallow-bottomed and, ostensibly, unsuitable as an anchorge. Both sites, however, have good arable land close to the shore, and must have been quite pleasant settlement areas.

Erbusaig, cited as 'Arbesak' 1554 and 'Erbissok' 1633, is said by Watson (ibid. 188) to be from the Pictish personal name *Erc*, borrowed into Norse as *Erp*. Again, this bay is exposed to the west, has a shallow, muddy bottom, and the southern approaches are a maze of dangerous skerries, islets and reefs. There is, however, a reasonable amount of arable land round the shores of the bay, and good access to the interior.

Criteria for Establishing *Vík* Names

An analysis of these *víks* must of necessity be conjectural. There must have been considerable silting at the mouths of the major streams at the two Reraigs, and perhaps Erbusaig also. Few of the other sites are likely to have been affected by silting, with the possible exception of Shieldaig in Applecross, where the Shieldaig River enters the loch. Studies investigating dominant wave and wind direction might also be carried out to establish the quality of shelter in such sites (see Morrison 1985. 62-4, fig. 4.1). Much of the data, of course, will relate to present-day conditions, but such could hardly have changed dramatically since the Norse period.

Other factors involve the availability of land suitable for cultivation in close proximity to the *vík*. All the examples studied have reasonable areas of such land, at least with the potential for cultivation [Fig. 4.4].

When we compare the Wester Ross examples with *víks* in other areas, we find a similar, wide-ranging set of physical characteristics. The Skye examples (for a good account of Norse Settlement in Skye, see Small 1976. 29-37), range from *Uig* in the north, which has all the requirements for a good haven and anchorage, to *Fiskavaig* at the mouth of Loch Harport, another enclosed inlet, and *Ramasaig* in Duirinish which is very exposed to westerly winds.

Names in Harris and Lewis in this category include *Crulivig, Miavaig* and *Islivig*, all of which are sheltered inlets; *Loch Meavaig* in North Harris ON (*mjó-vík* 'narrow bay') is also typical, as is *Maaruig* on Loch Seaforth.

In summary, we can point to a number of physical features which combine to produce the conditions necessary for the establishing of a *vik* place-name:

*The availability of shelter, anchorage or beaching
*The availability of potentially arable land

*Supplies of fresh water, timber and game (if possible)
*Access to sea-routes.

On mainland sites, protection by isolation from the interior is an additional, and perhaps vital, factor. Many of these sites may have been occupied only on a seasonal basis, and for specific purposes, such as timber-felling, fishing or hunting.

A SAMPLE OF WESTER ROSS '*VIKS*'

	Anchorage	Beaching Facilities	Shelter from West	Arable
Scorraig	good	good	good	√
Camastrolvaig	poor	fair	poor	√
Melvaig	poor	poor	poor	√
Shieldaig (**Gairloch**)	excellent	excellent	excellent	√
Diabaig	excellent	good	excellent	√
Shieldaig (**Applecross**)	good	good	good	√
Reraig (**Lochcarron**)	?	doubtful	fair	√
Erbusaig	fair	?	fair	√
Reraig (**Loch Alsh**)	poor	good?	fair	√

Fig. 4.4 Geographical characteristics of a sample of Wester Ross 'viks'.

Such considerations, of course, would not be valid for those *vík* sites in the islands, but we can well imagine that *Scorraig* or *Diabaig* might qualify as seasonal dwelling-sites, in view of the fact that Lewis and Skye are within easy reach. We are speculating here, of course, lacking as we do even the most limited of historical sources, so the place-name record has to work overtime in this area of Scotland. It is, of necessity, a record that has to be treated with caution, but it affords us clues which are of inestimable value in the reconstruction of the Viking past.

Note

[1]At the outer extremity of Little Loch Broom, on the south side, lies *Stattic Point*. *Stad* ('statt') in western Norway (Sogn og Fjordane) signifies an exposed promontory; and *Start Point* on Sanday, Orkney, would once have been a promontory, rather than the tidal islet it is today. In both latter cases it is difficult to round the promontory/point safely in bad weather. Little Loch Broom too is notoriously difficult to enter by sea in many weathers. *Stattic Point*, Gael. *Stàdaig*, would appear therefore to refer to a short stretch of coast *(Stad-vík)* in the lee of the promontory, where it might even have been possible to seek shelter if caught out by weather and tides (c.f. Watson 1904. 245). As at Scorraig, there is no inlet as such; *stad* as a naming element seems to be associated with difficult and exposed headlands which it was nonetheless necessary for small boats to pass (Editor).

Acknowledgement

I am grateful to Jim Ford, Geography Department, Dundee University, for re-drawing Fig. 4.2. Fig. 4.3 was taken by John Baldwin and, with Fig. 4.1, is reproduced by kind permission of the Scottish Ethnological Archive, National Museums of Scotland.

References

Blaeu 1654.
Crawford, B. E. *Scandinavian Scotland.* 1987.
Dixon, J. H. *Gairloch and Guide to Loch Maree.* 1886.
McBain, A. *Place-names . . . Highlands and Islands of Scotland.* 1922.
Macdonald, D.A. The Vikings in Gaelic Oral Tradition, in A. Fenton and H. Palsson. (eds.), *The Northern and Western Isles in the Viking World.* 1984.
Morrison, I. A. *Landscape with Lake Dwellings: The Crannogs of Scotland.* 1985.
Nicolaisen, W.F.H. *Scottish Place-Names.* 1976.
Retours. 1566.
Roy's Military Survey. 1750.
Small, A. Norse Settlement in Skye, in R. Boyer (ed.), *Les Vikings et leur Civilisation; problèmes actuels.* Bibliothèque Arctique et Antarctique V. 1976.
Watson, W. J. Place-names of Ross and Cromarty. 1904.

MACKENZIE FAMILIES
OF THE
BARONY OF LOCHBROOM

Malcolm Bangor-Jones

Between the early 17th and mid 19th century the Highlands underwent a
profound social and economic transformation. All sectors of society were
affected but the landlords played a crucial role in this process. This study is
concerned with the history of landownership in a small area in the north
west Highlands, an area which includes much of the parish of Lochbroom
and a good proportion of the parish of Gairloch. The area largely coincides
with the old lands or barony of Lochbroom, but with the addition of
Inverlael [Fig. 5.1]. To the north was the district of Coigach, owned by the
Mackenzies of Coigach/Cromartie since the early 17th century and the
subject of various papers in this book, and to the east was the estate of
Gairloch, which had belonged since about 1500 to the Mackenzies of
Gairloch. The two main themes which dominate the earlier history of landownership in this area are the acquisition of the lands or barony of Lochbroom by the Mackenzies of Kintail and its subsequent parcelling out
amongst a number of Mackenzie lairds, some of whom were members of
the leading families in Ross and Cromarty, others of whom were only of
local prominence [Fig. 5.2]. By focussing on such an area it is thus possible
to compare the histories of a range of families of varying status.[1] This is
particularly important in view of the fact that a preliminary analysis of
landownership in Ross and Cromarty indicates that, between ca. 1650 and
ca. 1850, there was a definite trend towards larger estates; as the number of
small landowners declined so the greater landlords came to own an increasing proportion of the county.[2]

THE DOCUMENTARY SOURCES:
AN INTRODUCTION TO LANDED RIGHTS

The works of Alexander Mackenzie, clan historian and activist for the
crofters' cause during the 1880s, are a common starting point for studies of
Highland families. But although his *History and Genealogies of the
Mackenzies* covers many of the Mackenzie landowners of Gairloch and
Lochbroom, it cannot be relied upon.[3] Duncan Warrand's study, *Some
Mackenzie Pedigrees,* is far more trustworthy and there is also a very useful
work on the Mackenzies of Ballone.[4] However, Warrand's work only deals
with a limited number of families and is more concerned with genealogy
than landownership. For comprehensive information on the ownership of
land it is necessary to consult a variety of documentary sources.[5]

Although valuation rolls can suggest the main trends in landownership, they do not, given the very wide incidence of credit agreements secured on land, always identify the actual owners. In this study extensive use has been made of the deeds relating to property rights, particularly those recorded in the Registers of Sasines. The Register of Deeds, records of the Court of Session and various manuscript collections have also been consulted. Family papers have not survived for any of the Mackenzie families featured here; this study therefore serves in part as an evaluation of what can be achieved by a systematic search of a diverse range of sources.

Even using deeds it is not always a straightforward task to establish the facts of landownership. The first point to bear in mind is that while according to the feudal system all land belonged ultimately to the Crown, there was no limit on the number of superiors who might come between the sovereign and the owner or vassal. Some landowners held directly of the Crown but many more were vassals of a subject superior. For instance, the Earls of Cromartie were superiors of the lands of Kildonan on Little Lochbroom and the actual owners, the Mackenzies of Keppoch and Kildonan, were their vassals. Secondly, it was very common for landowners to create rights in land by granting liferents to their wives (to commence at the onset of widowhood) or by raising money on the security of their estates. The usual means employed to achieve the latter was by creating one of three now obsolete heritable securities:

(a) **Wadsets:** Early wadsets consisted of an outright disposition of land by a debtor in return for a letter of reversion whereby the creditor promised to hand the lands back when the debt had been repaid. During the 17th century these deeds were combined in a single contract of wadset involving both parties;

(b) **Annualrent Rights:** which were created by the debtor giving the creditor not land, but right to a sum or rent to be levied from specified lands equivalent to the annual interest on the debt or loan. Annualrent rights were often known as *localities;*

(c) **Heritable Bonds:** which gave the creditor right to both lands and an annualrent.

All these rights were redeemable by the debtor when the loan was repaid but only a wadset right gave the creditor actual possession of the lands until redemption and the power to let the lands to tenants. If a landlord failed to repay a debt a creditor could initiate a process to obtain complete ownership of his lands by an *apprising;* from 1672 known as an *adjudication.* While the acquisition of such rights could give a creditor possession of an estate, it did not confer immediate ownership as the debtor could redeem the estate by paying the debt within a certain number of years. Apprisings or adjudications were transferable and any number could be led against a landowner.

Up until about the mid 18th century most transactions were made in merks or £ Scots (1 merk was equivalent to 13sh 4d Scots and during this period £12 Scots were equivalent to £1 sterling). In this study, £s are expressed in sterling unless otherwise indicated.

Fig. 5.1   The lands or barony of Lochbroom in the 16th century.

The precise boundaries of Achnasheen (a part of the lands of Lochbroom situated in the parish of Contin) and of Kinlochewe are not known. Furthermore, it is as yet unclear how the Forest of Fannich, here included within the lands of Lochbroom, relates to the Forest of Ned, acquired by the Mackenzies of Kintail in 1542.

BEFORE THE MACKENZIES: THE MEDIEVAL PERIOD

In the 14th century the lands of Lochbroom appear to have included much of the parish of Lochbroom, a good deal of the parish of Gairloch and a small corner of the parish of Contin. Like the neighbouring lands of Gairloch, which formed a major part of the parish of Gairloch, the lands of Lochbroom probably formed a part of the territory known as North Argyll, held by the earls of Ross.

If Lochbroom was not an integral part of the earldom in the early 14th century, it appears to have become one by 1370. With the exception of Inverlael, the district of Lochbroom was contained within the earldom of Ross inherited by Alexander, Lord of the Isles, in 1437.[6] The lands of Lochalsh, Lochcarron, Lochbroom and others in Wester Ross appear to have been given by Alexander to his son, Celestine, otherwise known as Gillespic or Archibald, who took the designation 'of Lochalsh'. In 1463, his half brother, John, fourth Lord of the Isles, confirmed the grant. The lands continued in the Lochalsh family until 1519 when, on the death of Donald Gallda of Lochalsh, they were divided between his two sisters: Margaret, married to Alexander MacDonald of Glengarry; and Janet, married secondly to William Dingwall of Kildun. By these marriages, Lochbroom became shared between the Dingwalls and the Glengarry families.[7] It was this area, the lands or, as they were later termed, the barony of Lochbroom, which was eventually acquired by the Mackenzies of Kintail.

On the other hand Inverlael, which included Ardcharnich, did not form part of the lands of Lochbroom and was therefore not among the lands acquired by Mackenzie of Kintail (although it may, like Kinlochewe, have originally been part of a greater territory of Lochbroom). This was because Inverlael had been disposed of by the Earl of Ross and in 1370 had been granted by Elizabeth de Berclay, heiress of one Robert Lytyll, to Hugh Munro of Foulis; the grant was confirmed the following year by William, Earl of Ross.[8] Inverlael continued in the possession of the Munros of Foulis until Robert Munro, who succeeded in 1603, ran into debt on account of his extravagant lifestyle including his 'prodigal spending in his travels in France'.[9] In 1617 Foulis came to an arrangement with Simon Fraser, Lord Lovat, whereby Lovat provided security for Foulis in £19,900 Scots of debts, and in return was assigned the estate, including Inverlael, redeemable on payment of the various debts. In effect Lovat acted as a trustee albeit with the advice of Foulis and the leading Munro families. In 1623 Lovat granted a wadset of Inverlael to Hector Munro of Pitfuir for 10,000 merks. Five years later Lovat, with the consent of Foulis, Hector Munro of Clyne and John Munro of Obsdale, sold Inverlael to John Mackenzie, archdean of Ross and first of the Mackenzies of Inverlael.[10]

THE MACKENZIES OF KINTAIL

The Mackenzies of Kintail were the chiefs of the clan Mackenzie. As Sellar

MACKENZIE FAMILIES OF THE BARONY OF LOCHBROOM:
Showing their descent from the Mackenzies of Kintail

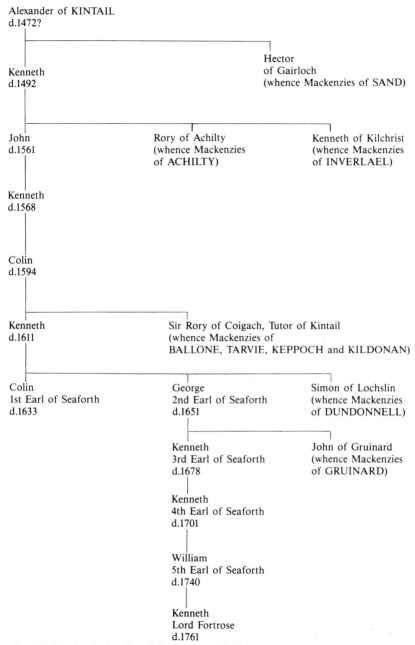

Fig. 5.2 Mackenzie families of the barony of Lochbroom.

N

COIGACH

SCORAIG
LOGGIE
BADRALLACH
KILDONAN
DURNAMUCK
LECKMELM
5
KEPPOCH
MELLON
2
SAND
CRAIGOUR
AUCHTASCAILT
INVERLAEL
3
7
INVERIANVIE
4
DUNDONNELL
6
TOURNAIG
BEINN A'
EILEAN A' CHIP
CHAISGEIN
KIRKTOWN
LARACHANTIVORE
AUCHLUNACHAN
KERNSARY
ACHNEIGIE
AUCHINDREAN

LOCH MAREE

LETTEREWE
KINLOCHNID

FANNICH

| 0 | 10 |

Kms.

KINLOCHEWE

1 MEIKLE GRUINARD
2 GLENARIGOLACH
3 BADENLELEOD
4 BAD AN DUCHARAICH
5 MUNGASDALE
6 FEABEG
7 KIRKTOWN

Fig. 5.3 Ownership units within the lands or barony of Lochbroom in the 17th and 18th centuries.

has recently argued, they may be descended from a junior branch of the family of del Ard, from the Aird, a district to the west of Inverness.[11] By the mid 15th century, however, the Mackenzies were established in Ross-shire.[12] They then rose through service to the Crown and advantageous marriages to become one of the foremost clans in the Highlands. In particular they took full advantage of the opportunities to acquire land which followed the forfeitures of the Douglas family in 1455 and of the earldom of Ross in 1476, and the subsequent feuing of crown lands during the 16th century.[13] The earliest document relating to the family upon which any reliance can be placed is the grant in 1464 by John, Lord of the Isles and Earl of Ross to Alexander Mackenzie of Kintail of the lands of Strathgarve, Strathbran and Kinlochewe which was, according to a clan historian 'to defray expences in making peace between the king and the earl'.[14] Alexander's son was fostered by a family living in Kinlochewe and served heir to his father in the lands of Kintail, Kinlochewe, Strathbran, Strathgarve and Strathconan on 2 September 1488.[15] All of these lands were included within the barony of Eilean Donan granted to Kenneth's son John in 1509.[16]

The lands of Lochbroom, it will be recalled, had been split between Dingwall of Kildun and Macdonald of Glengarry. In 1543 Thomas Dingwall sold his half (a half share of each township) to John Mackenzie of Kintail in return for the lands of Fodderty and a sum of money.[17] The acquisition of the share belonging to Macdonald was rather more complex. During a feud between Clanranald of Moidart and the Frasers in 1544, Glengarry and Locheil raided the Grants' lands of Urquhart and Glenmoriston. The Grants brought an action against the perpetrators for the spoil and loss suffered by them for which Glengarry's lands were apprised in 1547 and the following year James Grant of Freuchie was granted a charter of Glengarry's share of Lochbroom, subject to Glengarry's right to redeem it within seven years. The lands were not redeemed but neither was Grant able to take possession, even though the Queen ordered her officers to assist. Eventually the lands were obtained by Colin Mackenzie of Kintail in 1572 upon his marriage to John Grant of Freuchie's daughter. Colin appears to have taken possession of Lochbroom without much difficulty but it was only after a long and bloody feud with Glengarry that he was able to gain possession of Lochcarron and Lochalsh.[18] The Mackenzies had already in 1542 acquired the forest of 'lie Ned' (Fannich) and they also gained by the secularisation of church lands at the time of the Reformation; in 1567 they obtained a feu disposition from John, bishop of Ross, of the 'kirklands of Lochebroome' with the fishing rights — a grant confirmed by the Crown in 1587.[19]

It is during this period that one comes across references to the barony of Lochbroom — later to be subsumed within the larger barony of Eilean Donan. Little is known, however, about the initial impact of the Mackenzies on Lochbroom, although it is likely that most of the barony would have been placed under the control of Mackenzie tacksmen. In 1590 Colin Mackenzie of Kintail granted a wadset of Leckmelm to his 'officer', John MacIver, who appears to have possessed the lands previously and who was to be the founder of the MacIvers of Leckmelm.[20] Similar grants may have been made to members of leading Mackenzie families.

Colin's successor Kenneth did much to further the fortunes of the Mackenzies of Kintail, taking an active role in national affairs and acquiring more lands including Lewis and Coigach belonging to the MacLeods of Lewis. In 1609 Kenneth was created Lord Mackenzie of Kintail while his son Colin, who was also prominent in national life, was created Earl of Seaforth in 1623 in recognition of the family's territorial importance and power. Colin, however, found the court expensive, although some of his activities in the Highlands, such as the building of the castle of Brahan, must have also been a drain on his finances. As a result, Colin's half brother George inherited a considerable financial burden when he succeeded in 1633. Colin's advice to his brother, written two years earlier, had been to dispose of the family's lands in Lochbroom first of all, though not on a scale to threaten the route to Lewis.[21] Colin had already wadsetted various lands, including half of Auchlunachan, to Alexander Mackenzie, fourth son of Sir Rorie Mackenzie of Coigach and first of the Mackenzies of Ballone,[22] and George continued the process. In 1633 Letterewe was wadsetted to Alexander Mackenzie of Kilcoy (Seaforth's uncle) for 10,000 merks[23] and a wadset of Kinlochewe and a half share of the saw mill of Bianasdail was granted the following year to Alexander Mackenzie of Coul (an illegitimate uncle).[24] In 1637 Durnamuck, including Badluachrach, was wadset to Donald Mackenzie of Logie (Logiereich in the parish of Logie Wester, not Loggie in Lochbroom); and two years later he was given a wadset of the neighbouring lands of Auchtascailt and the shieling of Feabeg.[25] In 1639 Meikle Gruinard, excepting the salmon fishing, was wadsetted to the resident possessor, one Hugh Mackenzie, for £1,000 Scots.[26] Seaforth's uncle, Thomas Mackenzie of Pluscarden, was given a liferent tack of Loggie,[27] while other lands were wadsetted to relations such as Colin Mackenzie of Kinnock, a younger son of Colin Mackenzie of Kintail. By 1644 only 16% of the barony of Lochbroom was in Seaforth's direct possession: he was still owner of the remainder but was not in receipt of the rents.[28]

As with many landed families, the period of the Scottish Revolution was particularly costly for the Mackenzies of Seaforth. There was the expense of maintaining troops in the field, fines imposed by the Cromwellian government and, perhaps most important of all, the disruption to agriculture and trade through military operations. In 1654, for instance, much of the estate, including lands in Lochbroom, was burnt by General Monck.[29] After Earl George went into exile on the continent, his creditors began legal proceedings to take possession of the estate. His son Kenneth, who succeeded in 1651, continued to support the Royalist cause but, despite suffering forfeiture and occasional imprisonment, he was able — largely through the assistance of some of the leading Mackenzie families — to evade his creditors. It was even found possible to come to an arrangement with Patrick Smith of Braco who had been awarded Earl George's moveable goods, though not until after Smith had sold the family furnishings, clothes and silverware at Fortrose.[30] Simon Mackenzie of Lochslin who had acted as factor and had paid many of his brother, Earl George's debts, continued to assist the family; in 1658 he was given a 10-year tack of Seaforth's lands in Lochbroom on the understanding that the rents were to be paid directly to some of Earl Kenneth's creditors.[31]

The Restoration did much to restore Kenneth's power and influence. He became a 'great Coirt favourite' who, it was later alleged, 'did by Violence and Threats . . . for several Years debarr the poor creditors from all access to the estate'.[32] However, it soon became difficult to borrow on the security of a heavily burdened estate and in 1664, for instance, Kenneth was forced to pledge an 'inameld gold picture case sett with diamonds to the number of three score' to obtain a loan from an Edinburgh merchant.[33] Drastic steps were necessary and Sir George Mackenzie of Tarbat, Alexander Mackenzie younger of Coul, Colin Mackenzie of Redcastle and Sir John Urquhart of Cromarty (Seaforth's brother-in-law) began to buy up the debts affecting the estate. This clever and complex scheme, which was doubtlessly the product of Tarbat's fertile brain, involved the four, variously described as Seaforth's 'friends' or 'trustees', mobilising the support of a large number of Mackenzie landholders, including all of the landowners and wadsetters in the Lochbroom area.[34] Between 1667 and 1675 nine apprisings were acquired which, as the larger and more preferable debts affecting the estate, gave the trustees a sufficient right to claim ownership. Urquhart was forced to drop out but the remaining three obtained a charter from the Crown which they had ratifed by Act of Parliament in 1681. This title was subsequently passed to the Countess Dowager Isabel, widow of Kenneth who had died in 1678.[35]

This did not mean that debts could be left unpaid, and the trustees were forced to grant certain creditors rights over parts of the estate which were to subsist until their claims had been satisfied. A good deal of land was also sold, particularly in the Lochbroom area [Fig. 5.4], primarily to reimburse those Mackenzies, including the trustees, who had assisted in the task of buying up Seaforth's debts. In 1690 the Countess-Dowager sold various lands to Mackenzie of Fairburn.[36] However, neither the Mackenzies of Redcastle, who had bought Achtadonnell in 1673[37], nor the Mackenzies of Fairburn, were to retain their lands in the Lochbroom area for very long. Redcastle sold up in 1690,[38] while Fairburn was forfeited for his part in the Jacobite Rebellion of 1715 and was forced to sacrifice his lands in Wester Ross to enable him to buy back the remainder of his estate.[39]

The Countess Dowager Isobel continued as owner of the Seaforth estate after the death of her son Kenneth in 1701. However, in 1706 the Countess Dowager Francis seized possession of the estate for payment of her annuity, accumulating at the rate of £1,000 per annum, thereby forcing her mother-in-law, the Countess Dowager Isobel, to take refuge in the sanctuary of the Abbey of Holyrood. Frances continued to uplift the rents until 1715 when, as a result of her son's involvement in the first Jacobite Rebellion, the estate and title were forfeited. None of the wadset lands in the Lochbroom area were discovered by the Commissioners who had been given powers to sell the estate as soon as the claims of creditors had been determined. Two

DISPOSITIONS OF SEAFORTH LANDS IN THE LOCHBROOM AREA: 1666-1749

1666	Achlunachan (half)	Mackenzie of Ballone
1668	Sand	
	Udrigill	
	Drumchork	
1669	Mellan	Mackenzie of Gairloch
1669	Auchindrean	Mackenzie of Kilcoy
1669	Glenarigolach	Mackenzie of Tarbat
1671	Fannich	Mackenzie of Tarbat
1671	Auchtascailt	Mackenzie of Tarbat
1671	Achneigie	Mackenzie of Tarbat
1672?	Kildonan	Mackenzie of Tarbat
	Keppoch	
1672?	Auchlunachan (quarter)	Mackenzie of Tarbat
1672?	Inverewe	Mackenzie of Coul
	Kernsary	
	Tournaig	
1673?	Auchlunachan (quarter)	Mackenzie of Achilty
1673	Meikle Gruinard	Mackenzie of Tarbat
	Isle of Gruinard (part)	
1673	Achtadonnell (Dundonnell)	Mackenzie of Redcastle
	Bracklach	
1690	Mungasdale	Mackenzie of Fairburn
	Inverianvie	
	Beinn a' Chaisgein	
	Isle of Gruinard (part)	
1743	Kinlochewe	Mackenzie of Gairloch
1743	Durnamuck	Mackenzie of Dundonnell
1745	Loggie	Mackenzie of Dundonnell
1749	Leckmelm	Mackenzie of Achilty
?	Letterewe	Mackenzie of Letterewe

Fig. 5.4 This table is based mainly on *SRO* Registers of Sasines and *SRO* GD 305. For disposals made between 1666 and 1673 it is not always possible to establish precisely when purchasers entered into possession, since they often received dispositions both from the Earl himself and also from his trustees.

exceptions, however, were made to the forfeiture — one by Kenneth, the second son of John Mackenzie of Gruinard, who had received a disposition from the Countess Dowager Isobel in 1713 and had married the Countess Dowager Frances; and the other by Kenneth Mackenzie of Assynt who was cousin to Seaforth, had been served heir to the Countess Dowager Isobel after her death in 1715, and who was now put forward as the Protestant heir to the Seaforth estate in terms of the 1700 Act for preventing the growth of

Popery. Neither claim was successful, but when the Commissioners tried to take possession of the estate they met with strong resistance which continued until Major-General George Wade was sent to pacify the Highlands. Proceedings, however, were then delayed by litigation amongst the creditors, a situation which Seaforth exploited as part of his scheme to regain ownership. By playing one group of creditors off against the other and promising to 'procure a preference' from the Court for whichever group offered him the most favourable terms, Seaforth was able to bid down the claims against the estate. He then employed third parties to purchase the estate when it was eventually put up for sale in 1730; and by persuading his mother, the Countess Dowager Frances, to convey to him her right to the large sum which she was to receive out of the estate, he was able to reduce considerably the financial burden.[40] In 1741, after Seaforth's death the previous year, the estate was formally conveyed to his son, Lord Fortrose. The estate was now in the actual ownership and possession of the head of the family for the first time in almost one hundred years, although the financial difficulties of the family were not yet over.

During the 1740s and 1750s a good deal of property was disposed of, including the remaining Seaforth lands in the parishes of Lochbroom and Gairloch, all of which had been held on wadset. Kinlochewe, which the Mackenzies of Coul had held as wadsetters since 1634, was redeemed in 1743 and sold to Mackenzie of Gairloch.[41] The same year Durnamuck was sold to Mackenzie of Dundonnell. Daniel Mackenzie of Logie (Logiereich, Logie Wester), the wadsetter, had run into debt in the late 1660s and had lost most of his estate to his creditors although his widow, Agnes Morrison, continued to possess Durnamuck until her death.[42] The lands of Loggie [sic] including Annat, Achmore and Ardindrean were sold to Mackenzie of Dundonnell in 1745,[43] and in 1749 the lands of Leckmelm were sold to Murdoch Mackenzie of Achilty who had acquired a right to the property. Leckmelm had remained in the hands of the original wadsetters, the MacIvers of Leckmelm, from 1590 until well into the 18th century. However, when Murdoch MacIver succeeded to an already burdened inheritance as a minor, his neighbours took advantage and effectively deprived him of any right to the lands.[44] Finally, Letterewe may have been sold to its possessors, the Mackenzies of Letterewe, at about this time.[45]

This was not quite the end of the Seaforth interest in the area. The later Mackenzie of Seaforth, James Alexander Stewart (who took the name of Mackenzie on his marriage to Mary Frederica Elizabeth and who had succeeded to the estate on the death of her father in 1815), acquired several properties in Ross-shire, including in 1825 the small estate of Kernsary, of old a part of Inverewe. It was not long, however, before the Seaforths were in financial difficulty, and in 1829 the estate was placed under the management of trustees. Kernsary was eventually sold in 1844.[46]

THE MACKENZIES OF INVERLAEL

The Mackenzies of Inverlael were a relatively distant branch of the

89

Mackenzies of Kintail who flourished in the 17th century and whose interests spanned the width of Ross-shire.

The founder of the family was John, the second son of Alexander Mackenzie of Kilchrist, who may be assumed to have been a grandson of Kenneth Mackenzie of Kintail. Both his father and grandfather appear to have served the church and John followed suit, obtaining a degree from Aberdeen University and then becoming Archdeacon of the diocese of Ross and minister of Killearnan.[47] He then proceeded to acquire various lands in Easter Ross: in 1607 the mill lands of Avoch (previously held by his father) and a feu charter of the lands of Balmaduthie from Kenneth Mackenzie of Kintail (John and his father assisted Kintail to complete the purchase of Balmaduthie the following year); in 1614 the neighbouring churchlands of Arcanduich.[48] In 1628 he bought the lands of Inverlael in Lochbroom from Simon Lord Lovat, who was acting as a trustee for Munro of Foulis. It then took two years for John to redeem a wadset over Inverlael from the descendants of Hector Munro of Pitfuir.[49] After his eldest son, Kenneth, died without male issue John settled the estate on his second son Thomas. The settlement, which was in favour of Thomas's male heirs and assignees bearing the surname and arms of Mackenzie, was confirmed by Charles II in July 1642 — a form of reward for the family's support for the King's cause.[50]

Thomas had gone to University, become minister of Tarbat in 1633 and five years later had succeeded his father as minister of Killearnan and Archdeacon of Ross. He appeared at the General Assembly in November 1638 with a commission from the Chanonry of Ross. But when Sir John Mackenzie of Tarbat had protested against the commission, Thomas made a counter protest against the election of ruling elders and as a result was then formally accused of 'Fornication, Drunkenness and Marrying of Adulterers'. Although he wrote a vindication against this 'Scandalous Libel', he was deprived of his living and forced to leave the country. However, after remaining for a few years in Ireland, he returned to live quietly on his estates to which he had succeeded on the death of father.[51] He sold Balmaduthie in 1645 but later acquired, mostly through apprisings, various rights to lands in Easter Ross, including parts of Cadboll and Rarichies.[52] He styled himself 'Mackenzie of Inverlael' but continued to live in Easter Ross, probably at Hilton of Cadboll.

Like many he became caught up in the events of these turbulent times. In 1649 he refused to comply with an order of Parliament to give an assurance for keeping of the peace. When hauled up before the Commissioners of Ross he declared that he had not been involved in any act of rebellion, particularly 'the first ingagement nor in the insurectione & disturbance of Inverness', and was 'most willing to find security for himself, his men tennents and servants wtin the Incountrie of Ross be east the brig of Alness'. At the same time he was confident that 'he sall not be troubled not put in questione for the behaviour of his men in Lochbroome raised at all occasiones be my Lord Seaforts doers against his expresse comand'.[53] In 1654, however, Thomas apparently took part in Glencairn's Rising against

the Cromwellian Government. In July, Thomas, along with other Mackenzies under Seaforth, their tenants and servants and a part of Middleton's
'broken army', invaded the lands of Assynt. Three months later the Mac-
Leods of Assynt retaliated by raiding the lands of Inverlael 'under silence
and cloud of night' and made off with 47 horses with foals and 40 cows.[54]

After the Restoration, Thomas was restored to his church and dignities.
He died in 1665 and was buried at Fearn. In a contemporary court case it
was claimed that 'Mr Thomas mckenzie was a comone agent & doer for
many gentlemen in the north and receaved liberallie from them for his
paines'. However, an early 18th century clan historian described him as: 'A
man of good Learning and Parts but of a very Litigious temper which
involved him in a great many Law Suites with his Neighbours which was
not only Unbecomeing his Character as a Minister of the Gospel of Peace
but likewise was very prejudicial to himself and his Family.'[55]

For whatever reasons, it is apparent that from the late 1650s his debts
began to grow and extensive borrowings were made on the security of the
estate.[56] In 1657 one Kenneth Mackenzie was granted, in return for a loan
of 3,000 merks, a heritable bond over the lands of Inverlael which gave him
an annualrent of 180 merks; and the following year, William Mackenzie in
Fadoch of Kintail, was given an annualrent over the quarter of Inverlael
called Balblair in security for a loan of £1,000 Scots.[57] In 1662 Thomas
Mackenzie borrowed 1,200 merks from his second cousin John Mackenzie
and granted a bond over Ardcharnich, another quarter of Inverlael.[58]

These burdens did not prevent Thomas's eldest son John from becoming
involved in the plan to save the Seaforth estate.[59] In 1662 he was MP for
Ross-shire. It was not long, however, before John's own creditors took steps
to safeguard their interests and a number of apprisings, or adjudications,
were led against him between 1671 and 1676, including one by the well-
known money lender, Smith of Braco. John's creditors also attempted to
recover funds from his cautioners, particularly the Mackenzies of Coul. Sir
Kenneth Mackenzie of Coul had married, as his second wife, a daughter of
Thomas Mackenzie of Inverlael and Sir Kenneth and his son, Alexander,
were both creditors and engaged as security for the Inverlael family 'in
diverse considerable debtes and obleidgments'. In 1673 an advocate,
William Moir, led an apprising against Inverlael in 1671 and proceeded to
obtain an adjudication against Coul. Sir Alexander, who had by then succeeded his father, was forced not only to purchase this adjudication but also
to acquire several other adjudications led against the Mackenzies of
Inverlael, apparently 'for sumes far exceeding the value' of their estate. He
himself obtained an adjudication against Inverlael and was eventually able
to claim ownership in the 1680s, although he was to face various legal
actions by other creditors for many years.[60] In 1693 Kenneth, the eldest son
of John Mackenzie of Inverlael, renounced all right to his father's estate as
Sir Alexander had paid him various sums towards his 'better subsistence'.
John's younger brother John, a lawyer in Edinburgh, had died in 1677.
Kenneth died a 'Gentleman' of the Horse Guards, his two younger brothers
died while serving in Flanders.[61]

THE MACKENZIES OF BALLONE

The Mackenzies of Ballone were a cadet family of the Mackenzies of Cromartie who were prominent in the Lochbroom area between the 1630s and 1770s.

Alexander, the founder of the family, was the fourth son of the redoubtable Sir Rorie Mackenzie of Coigach, and therefore the immediate younger brother of Colin Mackenzie of Tarvie (qv). In 1633 Alexander received a wadset worth £10,000 Scots from Colin Earl of Seaforth for the lands of half of Auchlunachan, Auchtascailt, the shielings and grazings of Craigour and half of Glenarigolach and Strathnashalag (Larachantivore and Eilean a' Chip) — all of which were then possessed by Sir Rorie Mackenzie.[62] Four years later Alexander assigned his wadset and various other debts to his elder brother, Sir John Mackenzie of Tarbat, to be held in trust while he was out of the country. In 1640 Sir John transferred to Alexander a new wadset of the original lands which he had obtained from the Earl of Seaforth for 19,000 merks. Alexander, who also possessed lands in the parish of Avoch on the Black Isle, settled in Lochbroom and appears to have given the name of Ballone to his half of Auchlunachan — his father owned the lands and castle of Ballone on the Tarbat peninsula in Easter Ross. Alexander, however, was wounded at the battle of Auldearn in May 1645 and died shortly afterwards, leaving his son Alexander to succeed as a minor under the tutorship of Kenneth Mackenzie of Scatwell.[63]

In 1666, the Earl of Seaforth, who was in no position to redeem the wadset, granted Alexander the right of reversion to his lands in Lochbroom and a charter ratifying the transaction. The superiority of the lands was retained by Seaforth but was subsequently acquired by Sir George Mackenzie of Tarbat who granted Alexander a feu disposition of his lands in 1673. In 1686 the same Alexander obtained from Kenneth Mackenzie of Davochmaluag the quarter of Auchlunachan in Lochbroom known as Kerrowmore, which stretched from Foich to Braemore; and two years later he bought the lands of Knockbaxter near Dingwall from Roderick Mackenzie, chanter of Ross. Alexander, described as a 'bulky, big man', died in 1714 aged 80; his tomb may be seen in Lochbroom churchyard.[64]

He was succeeded by his eldest son Alexander who continued to maintain the family ties with the Earls of Cromartie. In 1732 Alexander lent the Earl 3,000 merks in return for which, together with 1,000 merks due on a earlier bond, he was given a wadset of Auchtascailt. His son, also Alexander, who succeeded in 1737, was loth to part with this wadset since his mother was in possession of 'the principal dwelling house and mains and best sheallings' and he had already been at a 'Considerable Expence' with the 'bigging' of Auchtascailt. Alexander offered Cromartie an additional 2,000 merks, claiming that 'There is none desended of your family hade greater Dependence on you than I'. Cromartie, however, was swayed more by financial considerations. The wadset was transferred to Mackenzie of Dundonnell for an even greater increase and Alexander was forced to build himself a new house 'on the East side of ye Closs of his house of

Hilton', the family residence then occupied by his mother.[65] Alexander's younger brother, Colin, was a captain in the Earl of Cromartie's Regiment in the Jacobite Army during the '45 Rebellion. Colin was captured but was one of those released through the intervention of the Rev. James Robertson, minister of Lochbroom. It was a costly episode for Alexander and probably contributed to his financial difficulties.[66]

When Alexander V succeeded on the death of his father in 1752 the estate was said to be 'greatly burdened and embarassed'. The debts secured on the estate amounted to about £1,400 and while the free rent was about £100, £36 fell to be deducted in annuities [Fig. 5.5].

INCUMBRANCES AFFECTING THE BALLONE ESTATE IN 1752

Contracted by	Nature of debt	Annuities	Principal
Alexander 1645-1714	bond of provision to his second son		£167
Alexander 1714-1737	liferent right to his widow	£20	
	bonds of provision to his younger children		£361
Alexander 1737-1752	bond of provision to his widow	£16	
	bonds and bills		£872
		£36	£1,400
Principal of annuities (£36 x 20)			£720
Total			£2,120

Fig. 5.5 Incumbrances affecting the Ballone Estate, 1752, from Mackenzie, H.H. *The Mackenzies of Ballone.* 1941. 146-148.

Apparently 'Some well disposed Gentlemen who are near Relations to the family and who have it at heart that the family Should subsist' were prepared to lend about £1,111 to pay off the creditors, most of whom were 'near Relations and well disposed, from whom with good grounds Compositions are expected'.[67] In the event, Alexander's curator, Kenneth

Mackenzie of Dundonnell, appears to have provided financial assistance and Alexander entered upon an army career, eventually becoming a captain in the 77th regiment. He was killed in 1762 and was succeeded by his brother John, who retired from his captaincy in the 78th regiment to attend to the estate.[68]

Colin Mackenzie, a merchant in London who was originally from near Strathpeffer and was related to Ballone, decided to help John 'with a Loan of as much money as will discharge such of his Creditors as are not willing to give him time also as much as will enable him to put a proper Stock of Cattle &c on such part of his Estate as he shall be advised to keep in his own hands'. At first John refused the offer, thinking to sell a part of the estate. However, in July 1765 he borrowed £200 from the widow of Kenneth Mackenzie, a merchant in Inverness. This was the first heritable bond over the estate. His other debts, which consisted of personal bonds, then amounted to £1,224 including £426 to Dundonnell. Some creditors, especially Mackenzie of Achilty, were pressing for repayment and in September John borrowed £600 on a heritable bond from Colin Mackenzie.[69]

John attempted to make money in the cattle trade. But in 1769 he lost on the droving and ended up borrowing £400 from another drover, Alexander Mackenzie of Hilton. Unfortunately he was no more successful the following year. In October, the minister of Gairloch reported that John had returned from Creiff unable to pay his creditors and 'All this part of the coast depends upon Ballone'. According to another account John was 'ruin'd' and his brother-in-law, William Crichton, a merchant in Stornoway, was 'proceeding against him with great severity'. However, Crichton accepted a heritable bond for £500.[70] John had now borrowed £1,700 on the security of his estate in Lochbroom and also owed £1,720 to Mackenzie of Dundonnell (confirmed by bond of corroboration in January 1773).[71]

Rather than allow his creditors take possession, John decided to sell up. He sold his lands of Knockbaxter near Dingwall for £500 to the Rev. Colin Mackenzie acting on behalf of the Earl of Seaforth in May 1772. Ballone was advertised in the Scottish newspapers in June, and was eventually sold in November 1773 to Henry Davidson of Tulloch for £3,500 plus an annuity of £28 to John's mother.[72] John thought of emigrating to America, but instead remained as a tacksman farmer in the Lochbroom area; he was joint tacksman of Auchtascailt 1773-1776, tacksman of Mellon in the parish of Gairloch 1781-1800 and tenant of Island Ristol 1805-1813. He died in 1829 aged 91.[73]

THE MACKENZIES OF GRUINARD

The Mackenzies of Gruinard were one of a number of families who owned little if any land outside the Lochbroom area but who were still quite substantial lairds.

John, the first of the family, was an illegitimate son of George, second

Earl of Seaforth.[74] In about 1668 he obtained the right to a wadset of the lands of Gruinard, known as Meikle Gruinard, in the parish of Lochbroom and half of the isle of Gruinard which had been apprised from Mackenzie of Tarvie in 1657.[75] In December 1668 John acquired from the Earl of Seaforth the lands of Udrigle and Sand, including Little Gruinard (though without the fishing of Little Gruinard) in the parish of Gairloch — apparently as part repayment for 'settling some of Seaforth's debts'.[76] Seaforth's trustees confirmed the grant two years later (the confirmation specifically mentions the lands of Drumchork and Tighnafiline which had probably been included in the grant of 1668).[77] In 1685 John, prior to being succeeded by his son George, gave a liferent right of half of Sand and half of Little Gruinard to his wife Christian Mackenzie.[78] In 1694 the wadset of Gruinard was redeemed from George by Mackenzie of Tarbat who had acquired the lands in 1673.[79]

In the meantime, however, George was in the process of obtaining possession of Inverianvie (excluding Cambusgannich) and Beinn a' Chaisgein from Mackenzie of Fairburn. He had lent Fairburn 2,500 merks in 1693 for which he obtained a heritable bond followed by a tack (a combination which was effectively a wadset) in 1697.[80] In 1709 George obtained right to a wadset of Cammis of Inverewe.[81] He was now owner of Udrigle, Drumchork and Sand (George built or repaired the chapel at Sand) as well as wadsetter of adjoining or neighbouring lands belonging to the Mackenzies of Fairburn and Coul. Despite residing at Udrigle, the family continued to style themselves 'of Gruinard'.[82]

In 1696 George had provided his wife Margaret, the eldest daughter of Alexander Mackenzie of Ballone, with a liferent right to the lands of Sand and Little Gruinard, together with the lands of Tighnafiline; a much more generous provision than his father had given to his wife.[83] George also provided for younger members of the family. In 1690 he had been hard put to raise money for his brother Kenneth, then in London, 'but all to litle purpose since we can gett nothing for our Cows'. George was prepared, however, to send Kenneth 40 to 50 dollars; although 'but verie litle q[uhe]r he is, yet it has taken a considerable number of C[ows] from me' — a very revealing comment both on the importance of cattle as a source of wealth and the effort it took to earn a relatively small sum of money. He probably also assisted another brother, Alexander, to become a surgeon.[84]

George was to be the father of an extraordinarily large family. When his first wife died after bearing 23 children he married Elizabeth, an illegitimate daughter of Duncan Forbes of Culloden, Lord President of the Court of Session, who bore George a further 10 children. The financial burden must have been considerable, especially if, as Alexander Mackenzie claimed, all of his offspring were well provided for. His son, Colin, for instance, was apprenticed to an Inverness goldsmith.[85]

In 1715 George unsuccessfully applied to the Earl of Cromartie for the purchase of 'some litle thing to the value of four or five thousand marks' in the 'InCountry' or Easter Ross. However, in 1717 he was given a wadset over Ridorch, a part of the lands of Glenarigolach, probably as security for a debt.[86] George's own finances appear to have been under strain and his eldest son, John, took a voluntary reduction in his allowance. When, in 1713, John had married Katherine, the second daughter of Alexander Mackenzie of Balmaduthie, his father had provided him with a yearly annuity of 660 merks to be drawn out of the lands of Tighnafiline, Drumchork and Cammis of Inverewe. In 1718 John, who had also been given possession of Tighnafiline and Drumchork, agreed to restrict his annuity to 550 merks in return for possession of Cammis and 'Durigarty' then possessed by his father.[87] The next step was for George to borrow, and in 1721 he raised 3,000 merks by granting a heritable bond over his wadset of Cammis.[88] More enterprising was the family's involvement in the local herring fishing; George supplied Inverness merchants with fish caught not only by his own tenants but also by the tenants of neighbouring estates as well — the merchants provided salt and casks for preserving the fish, and tobacco, brandy, whisky and cash to pay the fishermen. A storehouse was maintained at Tighnafiline.[89]

As was sometimes the case when landowners remarried, the provision George made for his second wife appears to have been prejudicial to the children of his first marriage. In 1727 George sold the 3,000 merks wadset over Cammis; but rather than apply this money to the advantage of the children of his first marriage, he obtained a wadset of Meikle Gruinard and Auchtascailt for 6,000 merks from the Earl of Cromartie and then proceeded to assign this right along with the lands of Ridorch to his second wife and her children. Athough this was in satisfaction of the terms of the marriage contract with his second wife, it had been made, as George's grandson William later complained, at 'my Expence, and forgetting his prior obligations in the Contract for my Father'.[90] For George, it was very inconvenient when in 1738 Cromartie tried to redeem the wadset (which still had 11 years to run) and he could not persuade his wife to dispense of her jointure without advising with her father, the Lord President, who had custody of the deeds. Even if the wadset were redeemed, his wife would occupy the lands under a 5-year lease 'Seing she not any oyr place to retyr her to were I once sett in my Greave which of necessity will be in a very short time, for my sight is allready failing me'.[91]

George's son John does not appear to have possessed the estate for more than a few years before his death, in early January 1742. John was succeeded by his son William who was for several years plagued by his grandfather's creditors, even though he claimed not to be liable for any of the debts contracted by his grandfather after his father's marriage.[92] With his step-grandmother living at Meikle Gruinard (she was still alive in 1762), William had to provide his wife with a liferent right to the lands of Drumchork and Tighnafiline with the house of Tighnafiline 'principally design'd for her use'.[93]

In 1745 William built a small but very fine mansion house at Udrigle (see Beaton, this volume).[94] That year he also bought the lands of Beinn a' Chaisgein from Mackenzie of Dundonnell, a purchase which was made to strengthen the Mackenzie political interest in Ross-shire. These lands brought his total holding in the valuation roll to £401 Scots, just sufficient to entitle him to a vote.[95] A dispute over some salmon fishing rights with Mackenzie of Gairloch, a 'powerfull Tyranicall Neibour the reall Successor of Lovate' (Simon Lord Fraser of Lovat), was settled amicably in 1757 by William paying 20 guineas for a heritable title to the 'salmon fishing of one coble upon the seaside opposite to' Drumchork, Mellon and Tighnafiline.[96] William was a very active drover, taking cows to markets in Easter Ross, often to Crieff or Falkirk and down into England as far south as Leicester. He also traded in salmon, cod and ling and, almost certainly, herring; and he was probably involved in smuggling goods into Easter Ross and Sutherland.[97]

William's enterprises, legal or otherwise, appear to have been matched by high spending. Strong evidence is hard to come by although he is, for instance, recorded as purchasing a 'black durant Negligee' gown for his daughter Katherine in 1761.[98] Eventually the family indebtedness reached a critical level and in 1774 Colin Mackenzie, minister of Fodderty and a well-known money lender, obtained an adjudication against the estate for the large sum of £6,099, a sum which probably represents an accumulation of unsecured debt which had built up over the years. Colin Mackenzie made the adjudication over to William and was given a bond for £1,200 secured over the estate — a transaction which suggests that the adjudication was arranged to defend the estate against other creditors.[99] A few years later William borrowed further sums from Colin Mackenzie followed by a small loan from his nephew, Roderick Morrison, tacksman of Mellon Udrigle, a merchant and shipowner in Stornaway and soon to be involved in establishing the fishing station on the Isle of Tanera (see J. Munro, this volume). By 1782 the accumulated debt secured on the estate amounted to £2,840, almost ten times the free rent.[100]

William died in about 1782[101] and was succeeded by his third son John, a Lieutenant with the 73rd Regiment. William's eldest son Simon had received a disposition of the estate from his father in 1778 but had died while returning from service as an officer with the 78th Regiment in India; and George, the son next in line, had died from a fall in Jamaica.[102] John failed to attend to the loans affecting the estate, and by 1788 Colin Mackenzie was owed about £500 in unpaid interest and the other creditors were in a similar position. A process of ranking and sale had already been commenced but when John announced that he had decided to sell, Colin Mackenzie, who 'wished to show every indulgence', suspended further proceedings. John, however, put a price on the estate 'far exceeding its value and accordingly no offer was made upon the day of the sale'. Legal action was recommenced and on 4 March 1788 a judicial factor was appointed to safeguard the creditors' interests.[103] This achieved the desired effect and on 26 March John sold the estate to Murdoch MacIver, minister of Lochalsh, for £6,600.

John was still keen to retain part of his inheritance and managed to persuade MacIver — who was finding it difficult to come up with the purchase price because money which he had hoped to obtain from his brothers abroad had failed to materialise — not only to restrict his purchase to two-thirds of the estate but also to give John a pre-emption of buying the estate back if he ever wished to sell. MacIver was sold the lands of Udrigle, Sand and Little Gruinard, John held on to Drumchork and Tighnafiline and the mill of Aultbea, and the fishing and kelp rights were shared in proportion. John remained in occupation of the mains of Tighnafiline, mansion-house, farm buildings and garden.[104] The £4,400 proceeds from the sale enabled him to clear the loans secured on the estate, and a formal disposition of the estate to MacIver was signed in February 1790 when John also gave his mother a life-rent annuity of £30 over the remainder of the estate.[105]

John's army career gave him little opportunity to manage his small estate and his debts once more increased. In July 1791 Davidson of Tulloch, who had obtained an adjudication against the estate the previous year, agreed to lend John £1,000. Tulloch was to be secured by a heritable bond and was also to receive a conveyance of John's right of pre-emption. John regretted making the agreement, fell out with Tulloch and sold the right of pre-emption to Rose, minister of Dingwall for £100.[106] In 1792 John successfully obtained a loan of £1,000 from John Morrison, the tacksman of Drumchork and brother of the now deceased Roderick Morrison. Three years later he borrowed £600 from Simon Fraser of Bruiach.[107]

The level of debt secured on the estate had once again reached critical levels and there was little scope for increasing the estate rental in the short term. A shepherd had offered £100 for the farm of Drumchork but the lands were let on a long lease to Morrison for £38. Furthermore John had also taken on the tack of Meikle Gruinard after the death of his cousin, Captain John Mackenzie of Avoch.[108] Crisis point had been reached, and John made a last attempt to save the estate by assigning it to George Mackenzie of Avoch. Then it became evident that the latter was unable to pay the creditors, the estate was sequestrated in June 1797 and sold by judicial sale the following year. A disposition by Avoch to the purchaser, Duncan Davidson of Tulloch, in January 1799 completed the transaction (see Caird, this volume).[109]

THE MACKENZIES OF TARVIE

The Mackenzies of Tarvie were a minor landowning family whose influence in the Lochbroom area extended to little more than fifty years.

Colin, the first of the Mackenzies of Tarvie, was the third son of Sir Rorie Mackenzie of Coigach and an elder brother of Alexander Mackenzie of Ballone. In 1621, while still a boy, he was provided in the sum of £6,666 13sh 4d Scots by way of a wadset right over the lands of Culloden in Inverness-shire.

The contract, made between Sir Rorie and Colin on the one hand and Lachlan Mackintosh of Torcastle on the other, probably reserved a liferent right to Sir Rorie. After the death of Sir Rorie, steps were taken to have the loan repaid and Colin obtained a decreet of apprising in 1629 for £10,467 Scots, a sum which suggests that neither Colin nor his father had ever received any rent or interest on the loan. Colin renounced his right to the lands in 1634,[110] and three years later reinvested his money in a wadset right to the lands of Tarvie, Comrie and Glenvaich in the parish of Contin. The wadset was later converted into full ownership, and in 1640 Colin and his wife Isobel obtained from the Earl of Seaforth a lifetime tack of part of the lands of Kinellan at an annual rent of £230 Scots. Two years later Seaforth granted a wadset right over Kinellan in return for a loan of 4,000 merks. The wadset confirmed Colin's liferent possession while his sons were each given right to an annualrent of £213 6sh 8d Scots (equivalent to the interest on the wadset), thus leaving Colin and his successors to pay an annual superplus of £26 13sh 4d Scots.[111]

In 1648 Colin, at Seaforth's request, obtained an assignment to a wadset right of the lands of Meikle Gruinard in the parish of Lochbroom and half of the Isle of Gruinard by paying off the previous wadsetter, Hugh Mackenzie. Seaforth ratified the assignation and gave Colin a lease of the lands to endure for Colin's lifetime and 19 years thereafter.[112] In the meantime Colin had been acting as factor for his mother, 'Lady Cogeach', in uplifting the rents from the lands in her possession in virtue of her second marriage to Thomas Fraser of Strichen.[113]

After Colin's death, a considerable portion of his small estate was possessed by his widow, Isobel, the 'goodwife' of Tarvie who later married Murdoch Mackenzie of Achilty. She, however, gave a lease of Kinellan to her eldest son, Alexander in 1663, reserving to herself the house and isle of Kinellan (still visible site of an old stronghold of the Mackenzies of Kintail, just west of present-day Strathpeffer). Three years later Seaforth discharged Alexander for any arrears of superplus and suspended the redemption of the wadset during his mother's lifetime.[114]

There were soon indications of financial strain; in 1657, Alexander's uncle, Kenneth Mackenzie of Scatwell, obtained an apprising of the wadset of Gruinard (Scatwell had been cautioner to Colin of Tarvie in a bond made in 1648).[115] Alexander eventually reached his credit limit and in the spring of 1667 Sir George Mackenzie of Tarbat brought proceedings against him for three debts, including one outstanding since 1647, amounting in total to 7,260 merks excluding interest. The following year Tarbat acquired an apprising against the whole estate, and two years later he completed his title by obtaining a charter of confirmation.[116] In April 1671 an agreement was made whereby Alexander gave Tarbat his possessions in the parish of Contin in exchange for lands in the parish of Lochbroom and bonds to the extent of 9,000 merks. In February 1672, after further negotiations, Tarbat sold Alexander the lands of Kildonan, Keppoch, Glenarigolach and Auchtascailt in Lochbroom.[117] These lands were rented at over 1,000 merks per year but Alexander was only allowed to uplift 420 merks during his mother's lifetime.[118] Alexander does not appear to have taken up residence in Lochbroom and indeed his mother granted him a lease of that part of Tarvie which she still possessed in virtue of her liferent right.[119]

Alexander's own problems did not prevent him appearing as one of the many relations and friends to offer security for Seaforth.[120] In the meantime he had lost possession of Gruinard; he had been unable to redeem the lands after they had been apprised, despite in 1672 bringing a process of removing against John Mackenzie of Gruinard who appears to have been in possession since 1668. Five years later he assigned any right he had to Gruinard to Tarbat.[121]

Alexander died between 1677 and 1682 and was succeeded by his son John. In 1683 Colin Mackenzie, a brother of Alexander Mackenzie of Ballone, obtained an apprising against John which he transferred to Tarbat the following year. This may have been to protect John, who was apparently still a minor, from other creditors.[122] John looked to retrieve his fortunes through military service and joined one of the Scottish Regiments on the continent. He returned and landed in Harwich in December 1693, expecting his regiment to move to Scotland. The Government, however, was notoriously slow in paying the army, and by February the following year John was stuck in York and could not stir for want of money. In a letter to Tarbat, whom he claimed had 'alwise been ye greatest instrument of my encouragement and preferrment', John referred to 'our misfortunes since wee came from Flanders, both at sea and since', and requested a small sum of money as it was 'verie expensive living in this place'.[123] It was at this point that John probably took up residence in Lochbroom. His financial affairs were in considerable disorder and by 1696 he owed Tarbat £8,000 Scots. Tarbat agreed to write off one half, but took the lands of Auchtascailt and any right Tarvie had to the wadset of Meikle Gruinard as payment for the other half. John also agreed to pay both an increased feu duty for his remaining lands in Lochbroom and, from the time of his mother's death, the 'annualrent' on a debt of 2,000 merks to his uncle Kenneth who had been in possession of lands in Strathkanaird at a very reduced rent.[124]

With his small estate only producing a yearly rental of 600 merks, John's situation gradually became more and more desperate. In 1714 Kenneth Mackenzie of Dundonnell advised the Earl of Cromartie that if he had 'any thoughts of preserveing any thing for Tarvie's poor family' then John should be restricted by legal means from burdening his estate any further, 'for now hie has allmost don with all that he has on this side Contacting, which he must do or his familie starve, and allwise threatens to brake upon his stock now that he has no oyr way'.[125] In 1716 it was found that John had not paid any feu duty since 1700. He settled his arrears by giving Cromartie a 'locality' or right to the rents of the lands of Kildonan, then possessed by Tarvie's brother George 'and severall others small tennents'.[126] The following year he granted a wadset over the lands of Ridorch, a part of Glenarigolach.[127] His health was not good; indeed in February 1717 it was reported that he had been 'beadfast near this halfe year'.[128] Eventually in 1727 John sold his lands of Kildonan and Keppoch to James Mackenzie of Achindrean, also descended from the Mackenzies of Coigach and to whom he owed 1,430 merks. John was dead by July 1729 leaving a son Alexander of whom nothing is known. His brother George, who at the time was living in Auldnahinin, a part of Keppoch, was one of the elders of Lochbroom in 1742 when he was styled 'broyr to ye late Tarvie'.[129]

THE MACKENZIES OF ACHILTY

The Mackenzies of Achilty were an old cadet family descended from Rory, the third son of Kenneth Mackenzie of Kintail, who received a charter of Achilty and other lands in the parish of Contin in 1529. The family maintained close links with the Mackenzies of Kintail and Rory's grandson Murdoch appears in several of Kintail's charters, including some relating to land transactions with the MacLeods of Lewis. Both Murdoch and his father are said to have died in Lochbroom. His son, Alexander, served in the clan wars against Macdonald of Glengarry and then took part in the colonisation of Lewis by the Mackenzies, later acting as chamberlain or factor for the Earls of Seaforth. The lands of Achilty appear to have been disposed of by the mid 17th century and the family had taken up residence on the Isle of Lewis, although they continued to style themselves of Achilty. Both Alexander and his son Murdoch, who was a substantial cattle drover, were Gaelic poets familiar with classical Gaelic poetry.[130]

In 1673 Murdoch bought a quarter of Auchlunachan in Lochbroom and in the early 18th century his son Alexander acquired an apprising over half of MacIver's wadset of Leckmelm.[131] Alexander continued to lease extensive lands in Lewis and also acted as chamberlain. However, on the appointment of a new factor in 1740, the family lost all of their lands on the island and Alexander took a tack of the lands of Dornie in Coigach and various grazings on the Cromartie estate in Lochbroom.[132] After Alexander's death in 1742 his son Murdoch, who had also possessed lands in Lewis, took over some of the lands on the Cromartie estate. In 1747 Murdoch obtained, after paying off some of Mackenzie of Coul's debts, a 10-year lease of the lands of Inverlael and took up residence there.[133] Two years later he took a lease of the whole of Coigach, introduced tenants from Lewis and made a fair profit until 1756 when allegations of oppression were made against him by the tenants.[134] The factor, however, found him a very honest person and thought that the Commissioners for the Forfeited Estates were being hard on a 'Gentleman that has been so useful to ye Government'.[135] Murdoch, who had for many years been a JP, later served as baron baillie of Coigach.[136] In the meantime he had, in 1749, bought the lands of Leckmelm from Mackenzie of Seaforth and taken over an extensive wadset on the estate of Assynt.[137] When his possession of Inverlael terminated he obtained a tack of Corrie, where he took up residence, and Dalvraid in Coigach which he later claimed to have considerably improved.[138] He acquired Mungasdale and Glenarigolach in 1767.[139] He died in 1770 after a prosperous career as a merchant, farmer and drover.[140]

On Murdoch's death, without heirs, the bulk of his estate passed to his nephew Colin, except the quarter of Auchlunachan which Murdoch had settled on his youngest brother Roderick, tacksman of Glenarigolach.[141]

Colin's father Donald had been a merchant in Stornoway, trading in fish and kelp who, after his involvement in a scandalous divorce case, eventually became tacksman of lands in Coigach and self-appointed baron baillie to the herring fishery for which he extracted dues from the fishing vessels.[142] Donald died in 1760 when Colin was only twelve. Colin built a substantial house at Keanchrine but after succeeding to his uncle's small estate, took the farm of Corrie where he made further improvements.[143]

Colin, however, did not have his uncle's business ability and became involved in an unsuccessful scheme to organise emigration. As the minister of Gairloch, the Rev. John Downie predicted, 'a part of old Murdo's money will find wings before the remainder is settled on the Banks of the Ohio'.[144] Indeed it was not long before his fortunes went into decline. In 1774 Colin sold Mungasdale and Glenarigolach, and the following year he raised money on Leckmelm.[145] His uncle Roderick, who may also have been involved in the emigration scheme, had sold Auchlunachan in 1773.[146] A few years later Colin embarked on an army career. After serving as a Lieutenant in the 73rd Foot, he took a lease of the mansion and farm of Kinkell beloning to the Mackenzies of Gairloch on the Black Isle. He joined the 78th Highlanders in 1793, retiring as a captain two years later after being badly wounded at the Battle of Nimeguen.[147] No doubt encouraged by the development of Ullapool, in 1807 he had plots measured out for fishermen at Leckmelm.[148] Nothing appears to have come of this initiative and the following year he sold Leckmelm for £7,200 and placed his affairs under the management of trustees.[149] He died in 1813 with his affairs greatly involved.[150]

THE MACKENZIES OF DUNDONNELL

The Mackenzies of Dundonnell were a well-connected family who built up an extensive estate in Lochbroom and became the leading resident landowners.

Kenneth, the first of the family, was the only son of Simon Mackenzie of Lochslin by his second marriage, and was thus half brother to the celebrated advocate, Sir George Mackenzie of Rosehaugh.[151] Kenneth had almost certainly received some legal training which enabled him to act as a man of business for the foremost Mackenzie families. In 1680, for example, Sir George Mackenzie of Tarbat appointed Kenneth Deputy Master of the Game, with the task of upholding the laws relating to game and muirburn between the 'March of Cogach to Edderakilis and Strathokell'. This appointment was probably connected with the Mackenzie take-over of Assynt organised by Sir George, and a few years later Kenneth was made factor over that estate.[152]

In 1681 Kenneth obtained the lands of Meikle Scatwell, 'Auchyeir' and Strath Chromouill in the parish of Contin, and for a time styled himself Mackenzie of Glenmarksie.[153] In 1690 he exchanged these lands for those of Achtadonnell, including Badrallach and Kinlochnid, in Lochbroom, then owned by Mackenzie of Redcastle.[154] Eight years later he bought the lands of Auchindrean from Roderick Mackenzie of Kilcoy.[155] Kenneth appears to have decided to establish his family in Lochbroom, for in 1703 he executed a deed of entail settling his estate on his eldest son Kenneth and a number of substitutes, reserving the liferent to himself.[156] He also changed the name of Achtadonnell to Dundonnell, although he appears to have continued to reside for several years in Assynt, probably in Ardvreck Castle.[157] In the meantime, he had in 1714 been appointed baron bailie over the Seaforth lands in Lochbroom, and between 1725 and 1730 he acted as Deputy Receiver General to the well-known Edmund Burt over the forfeited estate of Seaforth.[158] In 1726 he bought the lands of Mungasdale, Inverianvie, part of the Island of Gruinard and Beinn a' Chaisgein, which had belonged to the Mackenzies of Fairburn.[159] Mungasdale was sold in 1730,[160] probably to enable Kenneth to assist the Mackenzies of Assynt by taking an assignation to a wadset right to a number of farms in Assynt which the wadsetter was anxious to redeem. However Kenneth was not only 'doer and agent' to the Mackenzies of Assynt, but also appears to have been having an affair with 'Lady Assynt'.[161]

Kenneth died in 1730 and was succeeded by his eldest son, Kenneth, who had already begun to make his mark.[162] As a young man, Kenneth had looked to the Earls of Cromartie for advancement and had written obsequious letters with the aim of securing posts such as Forester of Fannich. In 1715 Kenneth had lent the Earl 1,000 merks and had been granted what amounted to a wadset right to the lands of Achneigie. He was evicted from these lands by Colin Mackenzie of Kincraig who held an 'ancient' wadset right, but in 1723 was given a similar right over part of Auchtascailt. By 1726 Kenneth apparently had some involvement in Cromartie's exercise of his right of Admiralty and the herring assise. In return for this and other services, he asked the Earl to grant him 'an attollerance for some 2 or 3 yeares of taking up the Quirns of Achteskailt & Gruinort To oblige them to come in to my new miln which I have built upon a very small sucken' — effectively asking Cromartie to order his tenants in Auchtascailt and Gruinard to grind their corn at Kenneth's new mill for several years.[163]

When he succeeded to the Dundonnell estate Kenneth was fortunate in that there were no debts or provisions burdening the estate apart from a £100 life-rent right held by his mother. After he married in 1737 he gave his wife a liferent disposition to Auchindrean and Bracklach, to take effect from the time of his death.[164] He had acquired a heritable bond for 3,000 merks over Auchtascailt and entered into a contract with the Earl of Cromartie to take over Mackenzie of Ballone's wadset right of 4,000 merks. Ballone eventually relinquished the wadset in 1742, and two years later Cromartie gave Kenneth a wadset right not redeemable until 1760 — to allow Kenneth to recoup his additional investment.[165] In the meantime Kenneth had begun buying up lands surrounding his estate as the opportunity arose; he bought Keppoch in 1742, Durnamuck in 1743 and Loggie in 1745 .[166] The latter purchase was probably financed by the sale of Beinn a' Chaisgein and also the lands of Glenarigolach, bought in 1744.[167] In 1748 he disposed of his wadset in Assynt in exchange for a wadset over Achneigie.[168]

Kenneth's ability to sustain this momentum was probably reduced by the effects of the '45 Rebellion when several of his relatives served as officers in the Earl of Cromartie's Regiment.[169] The Mackenzies of Dundonnell were not Jacobites, but Cromartie held the feudal superiority of some of their lands and so was able to call upon their services. Very sensibly neither Kenneth nor his eldest son participated, but Kenneth was, however, put to a good deal of expence in trying to obtain the release of several prisoners. Indeed it was Kenneth and Mackenzie of Ballone who paid for the Minister of Lochbroom, the Rev James Robertson's successful journey to London to free some of the 'Unhappy people'.[170]

Kenneth was also faced with providing for the family. He assisted his brother Thomas's attempt to become a surgeon in the armed forces, paying for Thomas to spend a winter studying under Professor Munro in Edinburgh and also contributing £100 towards his equipment. By some 'Unlucky Miscariage', Thomas ran into financial difficulties which necessitated the remittance of a further £50, although Kenneth was determined to 'risk no more for him at least till he show himself to be a better Manager'.[171] Kenneth's own numerous offspring had also become a greater priority for as he wrote in 1770 'as my family is now come to some Maturity it's my duty to do for them while they deserve it'.[172] His second son, for instance, was apprenticed for three years to a lawyer in Tain, and served in a similar position in Edinburgh before eventually managing through family influence to gain a post with the Board of Customs.[173] By 1774 Kenneth could boast that of his 7 sons there was 'one in Virginia, one in Holland one at London one at Edin[bu]r[gh] one at home and two at schools'. He complained with some justification, however, that there was 'neither Chief or Leader in this Country, particularly in our Name, to take any Concern with the growing generation'.[174] To a large extent it was the Edinburgh lawyer, Mackenzie of Delvine, who acted the all important role of broker between families in the north and the world of patronage and favour in the south.

Although we know little of how the estate was managed during this period, it is clear that while Kenneth did not take part in the droving of cattle, he was extensively involved in commercial cattle farming. He was also involved in the herring fishing; he used to hire a cooper to supervise the packing of herring caught by tenants on the estate, and contracted with a skipper to ship the barrelled herrings to market.[175] In addition Kenneth took the lead in various local matters. For instance, in 1758 he made a joint application for assistance from the Forfeited Estates Commissioners to make a road to Lochbroom, and in the early 1770s he organised the repair of the church and manse of Lochbroom.[176] With the purchase of Kildonan and Scoraig in 1775 he achieved complete ownership of the peninsula between Little Lochbroom and Big Lochbroom.[177] This final acquisition and the almost permanent tenure of various lands on the Cromartie estate, including Auchtascailt, established Kenneth as the foremost landowner in Lochbroom and one well respected in the county. The most visible sign of the family's status was the new mansion house which Kenneth had built at

Dundonnell in 1767 (see Beaton, this volume).[178] The last word, however, should be given to a contemporary, Sir Alexander Mackenzie of Coul, who described Kenneth as 'a man of real worth', who appeared 'among his Neighbours as the full moon among the stars in a frosty night'.[179]

His son George, who is said to have succeeded in 1789, was also a careful manager; he preferred to hold to the traditional ways of a Highland laird, dressing very plainly in a 'kelt-coat and trousers' and enjoying the services of a numerous tenantry, rather than turning his estate over to sheep to support a more extravagant lifestyle. By the turn of the 19th century he was the only resident landlord in the parish of Lochbroom. Some thought him 'stingy' but when he died in 1816 he left the estate free from debt, personal property valued at £5,176 and his family well provided for.[180]

Unfortunately his eldest son, Alexander — who had been a 'young man of great promise', had gone to university and had then been apprenticed to an Edinburgh lawyer — had died in 1813. His life was celebrated by an elegy composed by John MacLennan, a local Gaelic poet.[181] George was succeeded by his second son, Kenneth, who was rather stupid and a bit eccentric. He had made little progress with his schooling, despite intensive drilling by private tutors at home and in Aberdeen, and had then served, after a fashion, for six years as an officer, firstly in the Ross-shire Militia and afterwards in the Inverness Militia. It was during this period that he began to acquire those habits — including a passion for all sorts of hens, an evident enjoyment of the company of wandering idiots and a firm belief in the supernatural — which were to remain with him for the rest of his life. He was also, much to his father's concern, very extravagant and, largely through his partiality for 'beef steaks and his favourite drink cream', becoming very obese.[182]

No sooner had Kenneth succeeded to the estate than he had to flee to France to escape from his creditors. A loan of £6,000 from Davidson of Tulloch[183] enabled him to return to Scotland and in 1817 he married Isabella, daughter of James Roy, surgeon at Fort George. She was provided with a generous annuity of £500 per year.[184] It was only after Kenneth's own finances had been restored and a series of disputes relating to the property settled (disputes involving Kenneth, his younger brother Thomas, his sister Jean — married to the Rev. Dr Thomas Ross, minister of Lochbroom — and his father's executors), that Kenneth and his wife were able to come to Dundonnell. However, while Kenneth did take some interest in his inheritance, the management of the estate, the running of the Mains Farm and the house with its substantial number of servants largely rested with his wife, who 'managed all the laird's affairs and the laird into the bargain'.[185]

The financial condition of the estate was steadily deteriorating and further loans were obtained. In 1824 it became necessary to place the estate in the hands of a trustee, James Scott, an accountant from Edinburgh who immediately raised an additional loan bringing the total debt secured on the estate to £18,500.[186] This, however, was merely the prelude to the sale of land to existing creditors; Auchindrean was sold to Davidson of Tulloch in

1825 for £7,500, and the following year Inverianvie (Fisherfield) was sold to Thomas Fraser of Balnain for £8,500.[187] The trustee was able to pay off £12,500 of debt;[188] but further progress was prevented by the death of Kenneth in April 1826 and the discovery that in 1821 Kenneth had settled the estate on his brother-in-law, Robert Roy, a lawyer, and others of his wife's relations to the total exclusion of his brother, Thomas.[189]

This settlement produced a good deal of ill-feeling both within the family and throughout Ross-shire. In Lochbroom resentment against the Roys led to a series of lawless outrages (1826-28) which later became known as the Dundonnell Atrocities. Shots were fired at Dundonnell House, buildings were fired, Roy's carriage horses were killed and cattle were maimed. Identifying the perpetrators proved to be impossible — threats were allegedly made against anyone who supported the 'Sassenachs' — and no-one was ever brought to trial.[190] The Atrocities were the subject of extensive correspondence in Scottish newspapers following the Lochbroom yair riot in 1832, after the Rev. Dr. Ross wrote a number of grossly exaggerated accounts.[191]

Thomas, who had become bankrupt in 1822 through an unsuccessful attempt at sheepfarming, did not have the money to challenge the settlement.[192] However, after 'many of the country Gentlemen of Ross-shire' had subscribed to a fund, he was enabled to begin legal proceedings to have the settlement overturned on the grounds that his brother had been either incapable or that his incapacity had been acted on by fraud. The case eventually came before the Jury Court of the Court of Session in May 1830 and attracted considerable public interest. Although a huge amount of evidence was produced relating to Kenneth's life and the circumstances under which the deeds had been executed, the jury was unable to reach a verdict.[193] However Thomas was successful at the retrial which took place in January 1831, when it was convincingly argued that the deeds had been 'concocted' by Roy and his 'confidential agent' while other papers had been forged by Kenneth's wife. An even greater quantity of evidence was produced relating to the state of Kenneth's mind, but it was Roy's dual role as lawyer and beneficiary which swayed the jury.[194]

With the fraudulent settlement set aside, Thomas's succession to the estate was regulated by the settlement made in 1817. In the meantime, the estate had remained under the management of the trustees for Kenneth's creditors. In 1827 the stocking of the Mains was sold off after the farm had been let to Davidson of Tulloch, who had also become tenant of Dundonnell House.[195] After taking account of the public burdens, provisions for widows and the interest on the debts, the trust made a small loss every year. A valuation made in January 1831 put the net rental at £900, the heritable debts at £8,000 (after a further loan of £2,000 had been obtained in 1829), the legacies at £8,000 and the value of the annuities at £7,772. The total amount of debts and other burdens affecting the estate was put at upwards of £23,000, and it was estimated that if the estate were sold there would only be about £500 left to the owner after all the debts had been paid.[196] Efforts were made to increase estate revenues by reorganising some of the farms, but Thomas decided not to claim his inheritance and the estate was eventually sequestrated. It was found that Kenneth's trust took precedence and the trustee chose to bring the estate to a sale. Dundonnell was sold for £22,000 in April 1834 to Murdoch Mackenzie, formerly of Ardross and founder of the second family of Mackenzies to own Dundonnell.[197]

THE MACKENZIES OF KEPPOCH AND KILDONAN

The Mackenzies of Keppoch and Kildonan were one of the minor cadet families of the house of Cromartie whose status was more that of substantial tacksmen farmers than landlords.

James, the first of the family, was a younger son of Alexander Mackenzie of Ardloch, a wadsetter in Coigach and later Assynt, and was therefore a nephew of the George, 1st Earl of Cromartie grandson of Sir Rorie Mackenzie of Coigach. He was a Catholic or, in the words of the presbytery a 'profest papist', possibly because he grew up under the influence of the Mackenzies of Assynt. He was almost certainly the only Catholic in the parish of Lochbroom.[198] In the early 1720s James appears to have collected the rents of Coigach for the Earl of Cromartie.[199] In 1721 he acquired a wadset of Achindrean in Strathkanaird from Sir James Mackenzie of Royston. He gave this up in 1730 having the previous year bought the lands of Keppoch, Kildonan, Scoraig and Glenarigolach from his relative, John Mackenzie of Tarvie. These lands were bought in satisfaction of a bond of corroboration which Tarvie had granted James three years earlier. James was granted a feu charter by his superior, the Earl of Cromartie.[200]

The family were also tacksmen of several farms in Coigach. In 1725 James, styled 'of Achindrean', paid 650 merks grassum (entry money) for Inverpolly and Dalpolly. His eldest son Alexander succeeded him in these farms while another son, Roderick, was a tenant in Dalcanloch.[201] James appears to have been a successful farmer, the Earl's factor described some of his milk cows as 'much the largest and best I see in Coigach', and he was also involved in the cattle trade. In 1734 James, styled 'of Keppoch', sold 550 merks worth of 'Blacke Cattle' to drovers from Assynt. The following year, he and his partner, Alexander Mackenzie of Corrie, bought 1,300 merks worth of cattle from a tacksman in Assynt.[202]

Despite, or perhaps because of his dealings in cattle, James did not prosper. He made Keppoch over to his eldest son Alexander in 1741 but then sold the lands the following year. Glenarigolach was sold in 1744, having been placed under wadset in 1741.[203] Alexander took part in the '45 Rebellion as an officer in the Earl of Cromartie's Regiment and, it was later claimed, forced men to enlist. His brother, Roderick, also served in the Regiment but despite being taken prisoner was later acquitted. Alexander on the other hand escaped capture, returned to Lochbroom and assisted various attempts by French ships to find the Prince.[204]

James died in about 1748 and was succeeded by Simon, the eldest son of his second marriage, who was usually styled 'of Kildonan' but sometimes 'of Scoraig' in reflection of the fact that James's widow Anne continued in possession of Kildonan in virtue of her liferent right.[205] One of the family, probably Simon's brother Colin, borrowed money from Peter Mackenzie, a younger son of the Earl of Cromartie and therefore a distant relative, 'to Outrigg him for Jamaica'. According to Mackenzie of Dundonnell it appeared 'very plain that the young Man was much straitened for money for his voyage' for his father 'left no Subject or funds that ever I heard of'.[206] Simon died in about 1765 when his family were still quite young. Kildonan was still in the hands of his mother and Scoraig in the possession of his widow Frances, who later married George Mackenzie, tacksman of Scoraig. Simon's creditors continued to pursue his widow for payment until Alexander, who succeeded his father on the death of his elder brother James, sold his lands to Mackenzie of Dundonnell in 1775.[207] A Mrs (Anne?) Mackenzie of Kildonan died in 1805 aged 106.[208]

THE MACKENZIES OF SAND

The Mackenzies of Sand were a minor landowning family descended from Murdoch Mackenzie, a younger son of Alexander Mackenzie of Gairloch who died in 1638.

There has in the past been a good deal of confusion over the origins of this family and, in an article published in 1887, Sir Kenneth Mackenzie of Gairloch inclined to the view that Murdoch was descended from one Duncan Mackenzie of Sand who died of the cat's bite in 1635.[209] However new evidence has come to light which establishes Murdoch's descent beyond doubt. In August 1638 Kenneth Mackenzie of Gairloch granted to his brother Murdoch a liferent right to the lands of 'Mikle' or Big Sand in the barony of Gairloch. There is also a statement in the Gairloch family papers to the effect that Murdoch Mackenzie of Sand, 'the first of that family', was the second son of Alexander of Gairloch (he was therefore the Murdoch Mackenzie who was accused in 1633 of taking part in the mutilation and dismembering of one Elspeth Smith). In 1639, Murdoch, with the consent of his elder brother Kenneth, entered into a marriage contract with Mary, daughter of John Mackenzie of Fairburn.[210] He was also cautioner for his brother in various borrowings. An indication of his worth is revealed by a bond associated with the marriage contract of his eldest daughter Margaret in 1657, whereby Murdoch was bound to deliver 'fyftie good and sufficient kowes with calffe to be milk kowes that year at the feast of Beltan', or £16 Scots for each undelivered cow, towards payment of 1,000 merks, and another 1,000 merks in 'sufficient gold and money' by Whitsunday 1659.[211]

It appears that Murdoch, who was still alive in 1669, was succeeded by another Murdoch, probably his grandson (family traditions of the late 19th century plausibly state that the first Murdoch is believed to have had a son Alexander who in turn was succeeded by his son Murdoch).[212] In 1702 Murdoch lent 5,000 merks to Murdoch Mackenzie of Fairburn, in return for an annualrent right over Inverianvie and other lands in the parish of Lochbroom. In addition, Murdoch's possession of the lands was secured by a lease. This arrangement was confirmed in 1707 and continued for a further three years by Roderick Mackenzie of Fairburn by a heritable bond of corroboration. Under a contract, which took in both the original loan and a further bond for 1,000 merks dating from 1705 (tocher or dowry promised to Murdoch's eldest son Alexander on his marriage to Fairburn's sister), and a lease drawn up in 1711, repayment of the loan was suspended until 1717. This new arrangement, later referred to as a wadset, specified that Murdoch was to pay 384 merks tack duty but was allowed to retain the interest on 6,000 merks.[213] These lands were additional to Murdoch's holdings on the Gairloch estate; rentals of 1706 and 1721 state that the family paid a rent of £276 11sh 8d for the two Sands (Big and Little), Longa Island and 'Lochadrink'. In the meantime, his son Alexander had leased the salmon fishings on the River Gruinard from the Earl of Cromartie, although this did not turn out to be a profitable venture.[214]

Murdoch's wadset right became a claim against the forfeited estate of Fairburn and in 1723 it was found to be a just debt affecting the estate, although Alexander (who by now had succeeded his father) was to account for the superplus rent for all years remaining unpaid. In 1724 Alexander made an agreement with Alexander Mackenzie of Gairloch whereby he became bound to resign his interest in Fairburn's estate in return for an infeftment of annualrent in the lands of Sand and others on the Gairloch estate, then possessed by him and his subtenants. The arrangement was never put into effect, however, for while Sand assigned his claim against the Fairburn estate to Mackenzie of Allangrange, he relinquished his Gairloch possessions. At about this time he took a 5-year lease of Gruinard, a detached part of the Cromartie estate.[215]

In 1730 Alexander bought Mungasdale in the parish of Lochbroom from Dundonnell for 3,000 merks.[216] The family had now severed all connection with Sand and were proprietors of a small estate in Lochbroom. Alexander died leaving his eldest son Alexander, then a minor, under the care of John Mackenzie of Lochend, also descended from the Mackenzies of Gairloch. In 1741 a wadset for 4,000 merks was obtained for Alexander over the lands of Glenarigolach. In 1744 Alexander came of age and married Janet, the eldest daughter of Murdoch Mackenzie of Letterewe. He gave her a right to an annuity of £200 Scots and possession of the 'Mansion House Garden & Office houses of Mungasdale' (the 'mansion house' was probably a one-and-a-half storey house of stone and lime and not necessarily with a slated roof).

The following year Alexander became the outright proprietor of Glenarigolach.[217] But this prosperity was not to last. In 1762 Alexander was forced to grant an annualrent right to a creditor, Alexander Mackenzie, a merchant from Dingwall. This measure only served to postpone the inevitable: three years later Alexander (with the approval of his eldest son Alexander) sold his small estate to Alexander Mackenzie, by then provost of Dingwall.[218] With no landed estate to support them, the family returned to Gairloch; and in 1770 Alexander Mackenzie, still styled 'of Sand', was tenant of Inveraspidale and 'Ballachnehimrich' of Kinlochewe.[219]

CONCLUSION

While in many respects the rise of the Mackenzies of Kintail parallels the rise of other major families such as the Campbells, it is clear that the establishment of junior branches in areas such as Lochbroom was largely determined by the financial difficulties of the Mackenzies of Kintail/Earls of Seaforth. The Mackenzie take-over of the Island of Lewis, by contrast, was achieved in the face of determined opposition and the Earls of Seaforth subsequently attached a good deal of importance to the island; hence the greater emphasis on the role of the Mackenzie tacksmen. There was a much greater readiness to dispose of land in Lochbroom, provided it still remained within overall Mackenzie ownership, and the phase of tacksman control was relatively short-lived.

On the other hand it is worth emphasising that many of the greater landowners in Scotland were facing financial difficulties in the early 17th century, and that the Earls of Seaforth were not unique in having to cope with a growing burden of debt. Furthermore, it appears that no matter how much the disasters, military or otherwise, of the years of the Scottish Revolution contributed to this indebtedness, they were not necessarily the cause of it. In drawing on the resources of the junior branches of the clan to escape from financial crisis, the Seaforths were typical of many leading families in the Highlands.

It is not altogether surprising that, during the 17th and 18th centuries, landownership within the Lochbroom area was largely confined to the ranks of the existing families and that a significant number of land transactions were tied to credit arrangements. Hence the importance of the wadset, not only as a means of borrowing but also as a stepping stone to full ownership. Some wadsets endured for such a long time that they should be treated as a form of ownership.

It was debt rather than demographic crisis — the failure of families to provide heirs — which accounted for the vast majority of land transactions. Financial difficulty was clearly related to rising standards of living, including the building of new houses and the provision for wives and children. While rental income rose in line with the general trends, evidence for agricultural improvement is sparse. This is attributable to the fact, however, that the documentary material has not survived, rather than a low interest in improvement. For there is no doubting the enterprise of landlords, particularly in connection with the fishing industry or the cattle trade, even though neither activity was without risk.

The tendency of smaller landowners to succumb to their indebtedness should be judged against their general failure to live within their means, and in particular against the effects of having a high proportion of their income tied up either in family provisions or in interest payments. With little room for manoeuvre, their ability to survive business failure was limited.

Notes

[1] Devine's comment that 'little has been published on the mass of middling and smaller proprietors' is as applicable to the 17th and 18th centuries as the 19th. Devine, T. M. The Emergence of the New Elite in the Western Highlands and Islands, 1800-60, in T. M. Devine (ed.) *Improvement and Enlightenment.* 1989.

[2] This analysis is based on a series of valuation rolls from 1644 to 1856. Comparable data for Aberdeenshire is presented in Callander, R. A. *A Pattern of Landownership in Scotland.* 1987.

[3] Mackenzie, A. *History and Genealogies of the Mackenzies* (2nd edition). 1894.

[4] Warrand, D. *Some Mackenzie Pedigrees.* 1965; Mackenzie, H. H. *The Mackenzies of Ballone.* 1941.

[5] Examples and further information on most of the deeds mentioned here can be found in Gouldesbrough, P. *Formulary of Old Scots Legal Documents* (The Stair Society). 1985. Useful background is provided by Dunlop, J. (Dr. J. Munro) Gunpowder and sealing wax: some Highland charter chests, in *Transactions of the Gaelic Society of Inverness.* XLIV. 1964-66. .

[6] Munro, J. The Earldom of Ross and The Lordship of the Isles, in J. R. Baldwin (ed.) *Firthlands of Ross and Sutherland.* 1986; C. T. McInnes (ed.) *Calendar of Writs of Munro of Foulis, 1299-1833* (Scottish Record Society). 1940. The Munro writs provide evidence that Lochbroom was incorporated into the earldom earlier than is suggested by Munro.

[7] *RMS* II No. 806; Gregory, D. *History of the Western Highlands and Isles.* (1881) 1975. 59-60, 218; Munro, J. The Clan Period in D. Omand (ed.) *The Ross and Cromarty Book.* 1984. 134-135; J. & R.W. Munro (eds.) *Acts of the Lords of the Isles* (Scottish History Society). 1986. 117-119, 303-307.

[8] C. T. McInnes (ed.). 1940.

[9] R. W. Munro (ed.) *The Munro Tree.* 1978. 19; Mackenzie, A. *History of the Monros of Fowlis.* 1898. 76-77.

[10] SRO GD242/57/3/1.

[11] Sellar, D. Highland family origins — pedigree making and pedigree faking, in L. MacLean of Dochgarroch (ed.) *The Middle Ages in the Highlands.* 1981. 110-113.

[12] Munro, J. 1984. 131-32.

[13] Stell, G. Architecture and Society in Easter Ross before 1707, in J. R. Baldwin (ed.) *Firthlands of Ross and Sutherland.* 1986.

[14] Although the charter is lost, its terms are known from several sources. Excerpts from manuscript histories of the Mackenzies by the first Earl of Cromartie and Dr. George Mackenzie, are quoted in J. & R. W. Munro (eds.) *Acts of the Lords of the Isles* (Scottish History Society). 1986. 129-30, and a 17th century inventory of the Seaforth charters has been discovered by the author in the Cromartie Papers SRO GD305/1/166/7. According to the latter, the charter, which is the earliest Mackenzie charter in the inventory, included the lands of Killin, Garve, Corrimoillie, Kinlochluichart, Garbat, 'Dalnatua', 'Auchlusk' and 'Taag', all later included in the barony of Eilean Donan. Dalnatua has not been located but Auchlusk and Taag can be identified as the two parts of Kinlochewe, an identification which is suggested by the Earl of Cromartie's version of the charter. Each part, according to a later charter (*RMS* IX no. 2140), consisted of a davoch of land, and this corresponded to the two davochs of Kinlochewe. It is also worth noting that Kenneth Mackenzie of Kintail was fostered in 'ye Taaks of Kinlochu' (J.R.N. MacPhail (ed.) *Highland Papers.* vol. II (Scottish History Society). 1916. 31) and the name still survives in the place-name Taagan.

[15] SRO GD305/1/166/7.

[16] *RMS* II no. 3313.

[17] *RMS* III nos. 1957, 3005.

111

[18] SRO GD46/20/6/3/3, 4; RMS IV no. 2273; Gregory, D. *History of the Western Highlands and Isles of Scotland.* (1881) 1975. 157-59; Mackay, W. *Urquhart and Glenmoriston.* 1893. 104-111; Warrand, D. 1965. 11.

[19] RMS III no. 2817; SRO GD305/1/166/7 (The confirmation of 1587 was not registered).

[20] SRO GD305/1/1/4; GD46/20/6/3/5.

[21] British Library Add MSS 39187 f.2.

[22] SRO GD46/20/6/3/6.

[23] SRO GD305/1/163/4; RS38/6 ff.94-95.

[24] SRO RS37/5 ff.310-11.

[25] SRO RS37/6 ff.68-69, 229-30.

[26] SRO RS37/6 ff.312-13.

[27] SRO RD4/28 pp.645-51; Dundee District Archives, Wharncliffe Papers, Box 1, 'The true start of Sir George Mackenzies affairs Octr 1673'.

[28] Fraser-Mackintosh, C. *Antiquarian Notes* (2nd ed). 1913. 358. No title appears to have been registered for Kinnock.

[29] Firth, C. E. *Scotland and the Protectorate.* 1899. 236; Dow, F. D. *Cromwellian Scotland 1651-l660.* 1979. 127, 129-30.

[30] SRO GD190/2/210.

[31] SRO RD3/9 pp.425-38.

[32] SRO Forfeited Estates Papers (1715), Mackenzie of Seaforth.

[33] SRO RD2/21 p.108.

[34] SRO RD2/37 pp.80-95; RD3/37 pp.66-88.

[35] *APS* VIII. 382-84; SRO Forfeited Estates Papers (1715), Mackenzie of Seaforth.

[36] SRO RS38/5 ff.520-21.

[37] SRO RS38/4 f.236.

[38] SRO RS38/5 ff.542-43.

[39] SRO Forfeited Estates Papers (1715), Mackenzie of Fairburn.

[40] SRO Forfeited Estates Papers (1715), Mackenzie of Seaforth.

[41] SRO RS38/9 ff.377-78.

[42] SRO CH1/2/70 ff.351, 357-8; RS38/3 ff.131-2, 463-7; RD3/20 p.341-44; Gairloch Papers, bundle 8/1, 2; RS3/178 ff.332-35.

[43] SRO RS38/9 ff.460-61.

[44] SRO CHl/2/70 ff.349, 351; RD4/176/1 ff.277-79; RS38/10. 139-40.

[45] No deed has been found transforming Letterewe's wadset to full ownership.

[46] *RAS* 2/292, 618; 4/218.

[47] Warrand D. 1965. 105-107; SRO GD46/14/1 pp.l40-1, 148; Scott, H. *Fasti.* 1928. vol. 7. 10-11.

[48] *RMS.* VII. nos. 395 1094; SRO GD242/57/3/8.

[49] SRO GD242/57/3.

[50] *RMS.* IX. no. 1181.

[51] Scott, H. 1928. vol. 7. 11; SRO GD46/14/1 pp.149-150; Baillie, R. *The Letters and Journals of Robert Baillie, A. M.* 1841. 135, 168, 426; Peterkin, A. *Records of the Kirk of Scotland.* 1838. 111, 137-138, 181.

[52] SRO RD4/31 pp.81-89; *RMS.* X. nos. 24, 25, 272, 286.

[53] *APS.* VI: 2. 734-35, 739.

[54] SRO PA7/9/2/128/1-9; Firth, C. H. *Scotland and the Protectorate.* 1899. 236.

[55] SRO CS15/324 27 February 1663, Balnagown v Mackenzie; GD 46/14/1 pp.149-50.

[56] The Register of Deeds contains a great number of bonds granted by the family.

[57] SRO RD2/10 pp.74-76; RD4/12 pp.773-77.

[58] SRO RS38/1 ff.65-7; GD46/14/1 p.141.

[59] SRO RD2/37 pp.66-88.

[60] SRO CSll9/49; RD 4/65 pp. 1073-79 for the disposition of John's escheat and liferent obtained by Moir in 1670 and purchased by Coul in 1674; GD242/57/3, 6; Forfeited Estates Papers (1715), Mackenzie of Seaforth, 'Double Wryts Taken from the records of the Comissariat of Ross'; NLS MS1116 ff.7-8. In 1687 Sir Alexander redeemed the lands of Ardcharnich from John Mackenzie, ancestor of the Mackenzie wadsetters and tacksmen of

Langwell in Coigach SRO RS38/5 f.419.

[61] SRO RH15/44/161; Forfeited Estates Papers (1715), Mackenzie of Seaforth 'Double Wryts Taken from the records of the Commissariat of Ross'; GD46/14/1 p.150.

[62] SRO GD46/20/6/3/6. George Earl of Seaforth confirmed the wadset in 1635, SRO RS37/5 ff.256-57; GD403/54/1; Mackenzie H. H. 1941. 23, 114-18.

[63] SRO GD305/1/18/5; GD305/1/37/1-3; RS37/6 f.324; Mackenzie, H. H. 1941. 23-25, 119-23. Some sources put the wadset at 19,500 merks.

[64] SRO GD403/54/25 27; Mackenzie H. H. 1941. The 1724 inscription on his gravestone is incorrect.

[65] SRO RS38/8 ff.612-613; RS38/9 f.321; E746/1 p.144; GD305/1/37/7 GD305 Letters bundle XIX, Alexander Mackenzie 23 April, 9 November 1737.

[66] A. Livingstone, C.W.H. Aikman and B. S. Hart (eds.) *Muster Roll of Prince Charles Edward Stuart's Army 1745-46.* 1984; A famous Highland minister of the Forty-Five, in *The Celtic Magazine.* 1878. III. 261-69; NLS MS1341 ff.23-25.

[67] Mackenzie, H. H. 1941. 148.

[68] SRO E746/70 p.112; Mackenzie H.H. 1941. 39.

[69] NLS MS1367 ff.94-97, 102; SRO GD403/56/23; RS38/11 ff.481-85, RS38/12 ff.25-30.

[70] NLS MS1367 f.166; SRO GD427/216/5, 6; RS38/10 ff.378-81; J RS38/12 ff. 423-25.

[71] SRO RS38/13 ff.56-57.

[72] NLS MS1368 f.37; SRO D197/4 ff.377-78; SRO RS38/13 ff.116-117; *Caledonian Mercury.* 17 June 1772.

[73] NLS MS1368 f.112; SRO E746/113/106; E721/19 p.61; SRO 25/22/2 Execution Mrs MacLeod a Lieut MacKenzie; Gairloch Papers, bundle 46/19; Gairloch Papers, Rental Book of Gairloch 1788; SRO SC25/22/25 Summons Magnus Adams Agt Lieut John Mackenzie and others; SRO SC25/22/45 Lybd. Summons of Removing the British Society and Agent Agt Mr Thomas McKenzie and others; Mackenzie, H. H. 1941. 62.

[74] He was not related to Hugh Mackenzie who received a wadset of Meikle Gruinard from Colin Earl of Seaforth in 1639.

[75] SRO GD305/1/70/28, 30, 31, 34, 35-37.

[76] John had been named as security in a bond his brother, Kenneth Earl of Seaforth, had given to Patrick Smith of Braco in 1656; and in 1668 John had granted a large bond to Braco who had in turn witnessed Seaforth's disposition to John: SRO RD2/17 pp.299-302, RD2/27 pp.331-32; RS38/3 ff.366-68.

[77] SRO RS38/4 f.19.

[78] SRO RS38/5 ff.327-28.

[79] SRO GD305/1/70/37; RS38/6 f.2.

[80] SRO Forfeited Estates Papers (1715), Mackenzie of Fairburn; RS38/6 ff.55-56.

[81] SRO RS38/9 ff.397-98.

[82] NLS MS1343; Dixon, J.H. *Gairloch.* 1886. 70, 100.

[83] SRO RS38/6 f.56.

[84] NLS MS1343 f.2. Presumably George's brother Kenneth who had been or was to be a schoolmaster in Fortrose; MacGill, W. *Old Ross-shire and Scotland.* 1909. No. 158; SRO RS38/8 ff.344-46.

[85] Mackenzie, J. D. *Genealogical tables of the Clan Mackenzie.* 1879. Sheet 12; SRO RD2/127 12 February 1730.

[86] SRO G305 Letters, bundle XIII, George Mackenzie 7 June 1715; RS38/8 f.436.

[87] SRO G403/60/1.

[88] SRO RS38/8 ff.113-14.

[89] SRO GD23/6/45.

[90] NLS MS1343 ff.141, 152; SRO E746/1 pp.183-84; RS38/8 ff.437-40; RS38/9 ff.397-98; CS29 24 July 1762 Claim of John Mackenzie on Cromartie.

[91] SRO GD305 Letters, bundle XIX, George Mackenzie 3 January 1738.

[92] NLS MS1343 ff.141, 152, 153.

[93] Although William appears to have possessed the lands of Meikle Gruinard as tacksman to his step-grandmother, her eldest son Captain John Mackenzie of Avoch was subsequently in possession. SRO E746/1 pp.183-84; E746/70 pp.114-15; E787/23/2; RS38/9 ff.319-20.

[94] Beaton, E. *Ross and Cromarty, An Illustrated Architectural Guide.* 1992. 91. The new house, which stands to this day, although in need of urgent restoration, was presumably on the site of an older family house. See also Beaton, this volume.

[95] NLS MS1343 f.156; SRO RS38/9 f.461.

[96] NLS MS1343 ff.l57-61; *RAS* 1/543.

[97] NLS MS1343 ff.l52-55 171 174; SRO GD347/48/2.

[98] SRO GD128/24/7/51.

[99] SRO RS38/13 ff.225-28.

[100] SRO GD427/26/4, 5; RS38/13 ff.418-19, 483; *RAS* 1/61.

[101] He was alive in April 1782, but in 1788 it was stated that he had died 'some years ago'. SRO CS111/389; *RAS* 1/61.

[102] *RAS* 1/542 but not 1/202; Mackenzie A. 1894.

[103] SRO CSlll/389.

[104] Session Papers, Campbell Collection.

[105] *RAS* 1/244, 245, 289 and 448.

[106] Session Papers, Campbell Collection.

[107] *RAS* 1/369 and 469.

[108] SRO GD305/1/163/177 and 200; GD403/60/12.

[109] *RAS* 1/514 and 585; *Edinburgh Gazette.* 27 June 1797, 30 March and 8 June 1798.

[110] SRO GD176/329/1, 5; GD176/335-336; GD23/4/5.

[111] SRO GD305/1/103/271; GD305/1/162/263; GD305/1/166/254; GD242/57/6/3.

[112] SRO GD305/1/157/19; RS37/7 ff.51-52.

[113] NLS Dep.327/164.

[114] SRO GD305/1/162/272; GD305/1/103/272.

[115] SRO GD305/1/155/63 & 68; RD2/40 pp.608-609.

[116] SRO Gl)305/1/166/24; GD305/1/155/72 & 73; GD242/58/1/21.

[117] SRO GD305/1/18/4; RS38/4 ff.162-63; GD242/58/1/21.

[118] SRO GD305/1/164/25.

[119] SRO GD305/1/162/271.

[120] SRO RD2/37 pp.87-88.

[121] SRO GD305/1/70; GD305/1/145/15; GD305/1/154/126; GD305/1/155/80.

[122] SRO GD305/1/154/84 & 85; GD305/1/157/38 & 39.

[123] NLS MS1351 ff.141, 143; SRO GD305 Letters, bundle V, 1 February 1694, John Mackenzie.

[124] SRO GD305/1/18/9; GD305/1/153/8; GD305/1/162/297; RS38/6 f.119.

[125] SRO TE19/9 Lochbroom; GD305 Letters, bundle XIV, 21 December 1714, Kenneth Mackenzie.

[126] SRO GD305/1/71/39.

[127] SRO RS38/5 f.436.

[128] SRO GD305 Letters, bundle XIV, 15 February 1717, Kenneth Mackenzie.

[129] SRO RS38/8 ff.346, 416; CH1/2/81 f.53.

[130] Warrand, D. 1965. 130-33; SRO GD305/1/1/2, 4; GD305/1/7/2; NLS Acc. 9711 Box 8.

[131] SRO E746/70 p.77; TE19/9 Lochbroom; CH1/2/70 f.351.

[132] NLS Acc.9711 Box 8; MS1315 f.8; SRO GD305/1/163/64.

[133] NLS MS1315 ff.5, 9; SRO RD2/181 18 March 1757.

[134] SRO E721/1 pp.31-33, 64; E746/70 pp.78-81; E746/152/1-6.

[135] SRO E746/74/8; E787/9/33.

[136] SRO E721/4 pp.170-72, 185-86; E721/9 p.104.

[137] SRO RD4/176/1 ff.277-79; RS38/10 ff.139-40.

[138] SRO E721/4 p.251; E721/8 p.168; E746/74/13; E746/113/11,20. There are many references to his farming activities in Coigach.

[139] SRO RS38/12 ff.168-70.

[140] NLS Acc.9711 Box 8.

[141] SRO RS38/12 ff.389-90, 455-56.

[142] SRO CC8/6/14 Mackenzie v Mackenzie; E746/70 pp.99-100; E787/9/12.

[143] SRO E721/19 p.39; E746/113/27, 86 109.

[144] SRO GD427/216/17.

[145] SRO RS38/13 ff.267-69 337-39.

[146] SRO RD4/215 pp.310-312.

[147] Gairloch Papers 45/71; Warrand, D. 1965. 135.

[148] SRO SC25/22/42 Summons of removing Mackenzie v MacLennan.

[149] SRO RD5/145 pp.165-172.

[150] NLS Acc.9711 Box 8.

[151] Warrand, D. 1965. 60.

[152] SRO GD128/32a/6/5; GD128/66/12/1-3; *Register of the Privy Council.* 3rd ser., XVI. 341-342; Warrand, D. 1965. 60.

[153] SRO RS38/5 ff.100-101.

[154] SRO RS38/5 ff.542-43.

[155] SRO RS38/6 ff.177-78.

[156] SRO RS38/6 ff.381-82; RT1/6 ff.90-95.

[157] SRO GD128/32a/6/1.

[158] SRO Forfeited Estates Papers (1715) Mackenzie of Seaforth; GD128/23/1/12.

[159] SRO RS38/8 ff.281-83; GD46/18/29, 31.

[160] SRO RS38/8 f.479.

[161] SRO RS38/10 f.70; CH2/508/1 p.107.

[162] SRO RS38/8 ff.281-83 but CH2/508/1 p.139 suggests 1732.

[163] SRO GD305 Letters, bundle XIV, Kenneth Mackenzie 21 December 1714, 15 February 1715, bundle XVIII, Kenneth Mackenzie 5 December 1726; GD305/1/162/321.

[164] SRO RS38/9 f.411.

[165] SRO E746/1 pp.144-45; CS29 24 July 1762 Claim of Mackenzie of Dundonnell (I am grateful to John Ballantyne for this reference).

[166] SRO RS38/9, ff.408-409, 460-61; SRO RS3/178 ff.332-35.

[167] SRO RS38/9 ff.409-410, 461-62.

[168] SRO RS38/10 f.70; NLS MS1341 f.52.

[169] A. Livingstone, C.W.H. Aikman and B. S. Hart (eds.). 1984; Warrand, D. 1965. Kenneth's uncle Colin, his brother Alexander and son Murdoch are known to have taken part.

[170] NLS MS1341 ff.23-25.

[171] NLS MS1341 ff.28, 30, 34, 36.

[172] NLS MS1341 f.56.

[173] NLS MS1341 ff.53, 56, 63; Warrand, D. 1965. 62.

[174] NLS MS1341 f.62.

[175] NLS MS1341 ff.32, 37-38; SRO E746/113/94.

[176] SRO E721/4 pp.142, 154; DI97/4 ff.363-64.

[177] SRO RS38/13 ff.237-238.

[178] Stell, G. & Beaton, E. Local Building Traditions, in D. Omand (ed.) *The Ross and Cromarty Book.* 1984. 208. There appears to have been quite a substantial house there previously SRO RHP3478.

[179] NLS MS1336 f.188.

[180] Hogg, J. A. *Tour in the Highlands in 1803.* (1888) 1986. 91; *Old Statistical Account, Lochbroom; Dundonnell Cause.* 1830. 6; *Dundonnell Cause, Second Trial.* 1831. 97; SRO RD5/99 ff.428-39; *Session Papers.* new ser., V. 151.

[181] *Dundonnell Cause, Second Trial.* 1831. 2, 96; Mackenzie, W. Leaves from my Celtic Portfolio, in *Transactions of the Gaelic Society of Inverness.* 1877. VII. 104-109.

[182] *Dundonnell Cause, Second Trial.* 1831.

[183] *RAS* 1/1299.

[184] SRO RD5/119 pp.507-527.

[185] *Dundonnell Cause, Second Trial.* 1831. 9.

[186] *RAS* 1/1483, 1544, 2/118, 235; *Dundonnell Cause, Second Trial.* 1831.

[187] *RAS* 2/401, 478; Private Act of Parliament 5 & 6 Vict c.21.

[188] *RAS* 2/462-5, 468.

[189] SRO CS232/M/60/1 Summons of Reduction.

[190] SRO AD14/28/392 precognitions and other papers.

[191] See, for instance, *Caledonian Mercury* 24 June 1833; Bangor-Jones, M. The Lochbroom yair riot of 1832, in *Ross-shire Journal.* 1989.
[192] SRO CS313/2156; *Dundonnell Cause, Second Trial.* 1831. 70, 72.
[193] *Dundonnell Cause.* 1830. The proceedings were also extensively reported in the Scottish newspapers.
[194] *Dundonnell Cause, Second Trial.* 1831.
[195] SRO CS46/1831/No 41/Dec.
[196] *Dundonnell Cause, Second Trial.* 1831. 109; *RAS* 2/632.
[197] *Session Cases XII.* 266-68; *Session Cases.* new ser. III. 31^; *RAS* 3/281.
[198] SRO CH1/2/83 ff.269-270.
[199] SRO GD305/1/163/125; GD305/1/167/142.
[200] SRO RS38/8 ff.346, 416, 449-50; E746/70 pp.109-110.
[201] SRO GD305/1/163/64, 126-29, 131.
[202] SRO GD305 Letters, bundle XIX, 2 Jan 1730 MacLeod; RD4/157 12 March 1735 Mackenzie v Mackenzie, RD2/139 2 Feb 1736 Mackenzie v Mackenzie.
[203] SRO RS38/9 ff.276, 408-10.
[204] SRO E746/74/4(2); A. Livingstone, C.W.H. Aikman and B. S. Hart (eds.). 1984; Gibson, J. S. *Ships of the '45.* 1967.
[205] SRO RD2/217/1 pp.1042-46; RS38/13 ff.237-38; E746/1 p.186; *Service of Heirs* 9 August 1749.
[206] NLS MS1341 f.49; Mackenzie, J. D. 1879. Sheet I.
[207] SRO E746/72/3; DI 97/4 f363-64; RS38/13 ff.236-38; Macgill, W. *Old Ross-shire and Scotland.* 1909. nos. 236 & 805.
[208] *Caledonian Mercury* 28 December 1805. The George Mackenzie of Kildonan, living at Inverlael in 1805, enjoyed a courtesy title through his marriage to Simon's widow, SRO SC25/22/25 Summons Magnus Adams Agt Lieut John Mackenzie and others.
[209] Mackenzie, K. S. Notice of marriage contract of 1657, with notes, in *Transactions of the Gaelic Society of Inverness.* 1887. See also Gairloch Papers, bundle 30/5.
[210] SRO RS37/6 f.161; DI62/8 f.256; Gairloch Papers, bundles 41, 54/1.
[211] Gairloch Papers, bundles 30/5, 33/2, 3.
[212] SRO RS38/3 ff.366-68; Gairloch Papers, notes on the Mackenzies of Sand. These notes appear to have been used by Mackenzie: Mackenzie, A. 1894.
[213] SRO Forfeited Estates Papers (1715), Mackenzie of Fairburn.
[214] Gairloch Papers, bundle 48; SRO GD305, Letters, bundle XII, 20 December 1708, Norman MacLeod.
[215] SRO Forfeited Estates Papers (1715), Mackenzie of Fairburn; Gairloch Papers, bundle 34/2; SRO GD305/1/163/126, 128, 129. The family tradition - which states that Murdoch's eldest son, Hector, was killed in America and was succeeded by his younger brother Alexander — may well refer to a later generation: Gairloch Papers, notes on the Mackenzies of Sand.
[216] SRO RS38/8 f.479.
[217] SRO 2S38/9 ff.276, 412-13, 461-62.
[218] SRO RS38/11 ff.303-305; RS38/12 ff.168-70.
[219] Gairloch Papers, bundle 46/7, 12.

Acknowledgement

I would like to thank John Mackenzie of Gairloch for assistance and permission to consult the Gairloch Papers, Dr. Annette Smith for help with the Forfeited Estates Papers (1715) and Dr William Matheson for permission to copy his papers. I am also indebted to the staff of the Scottish Record Office and National Library of Scotland for their assistance and forbearance over many years.

Abbreviations

ERECTED
BY
John MacDonald to the me
mory of his Father William
MacDonald late tenant Cou
lags Who departed this life
on the 24th June 1838 Aged
90

Gravestone in Old Lochcarron Churchyard. Drawing by John Hume.

THE CHURCH IN THE
WESTERN PARISHES:
KINTAIL TO LOCHBROOM

R. W. Munro

In any discussion of life in Ross-shire, past or present, the great geographical contrast between East and West has to be borne in mind. In ecclesiastical affairs that contrast is seen in the thick cluster of parish churches found in the fertile and populous lowlands of the east coast, while on the other side of the watershed lie the huge parishes of the western seaboard [Fig. 6.1].

What we loosely call Wester Ross today first appears on record as 'North Argyll'. So it was named in King Robert's charter to Thomas Randolph as Earl of Moray, even though it was distinctly stated then to belong to the Earl of Ross. At various early periods the lands of Kintail, Lochalsh and Gairloch are all shown as lying in North Argyll. In history as well as geography, this is a place apart, worth studying for itself (*RRS*. V. 633, VI. 505; *OPS*. II(ii). 395; *RMS*. I. 437).

THE EARLY CHURCH

In trying to give some idea of how the church operated in these western parishes, I leave the story of the medieval church in Ross to be read in Dr. Ronald Cant's paper in *Firthlands of Ross and Sutherland* (1986. 47-58).

By way of prelude, however, something must be said, albeit briefly, of the place held by Applecross in the early Christian community [Figs. 6.2, 6.3]. We really know very little of the monastery of 'Apurcrossan' or of its founder, the missionary from Ireland named Maolrubha. According to the Irish annals, he founded his church in the year 673, and died there in 722 in his eightieth year. The Norsemen (or Danes) are blamed in the *Aberdeen Breviary* for his death, for the violation of the sanctuary and the robbing of priests — but their ships were sunk within sight of land with no storm blowing. The parish of Applecross is spoken of in Gaelic as 'The Sanctuary', *A' Chomraich,* and as we shall see some strange rites were performed in his name at Loch Maree even up to the 17th century (*OPS*. II(ii). 402-3; Watson 1904. 201).

The influence of various missionaries, and perhaps their actual wanderings, are recalled by the church dedications and associated names — *Clachan Mulruy* at Lochcarron (and perhaps also at Gairloch), *Killilan* and *Kilduich* in Kintail, *Cill-Chaointeort* and *Cill-Fhearchair* in Glenshiel, *Kilchaon* in Lochalsh, *Kildonan* on Little Loch Broom. Such names incor-

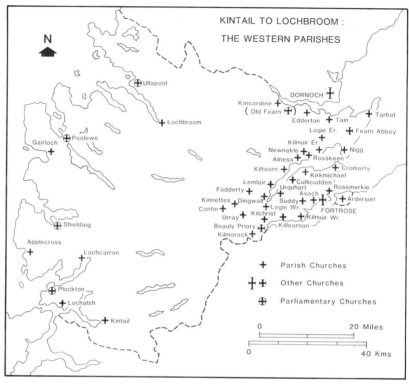

Fig. 6.1 The map of the former Diocese of Ross shows how few and extended are the parishes along the western seaboard (once 'North Argyll'), in contrast to the close cluster in the east. The frontier between 'highland' and 'lowland' Ross-shire more-or-less coincides with the north-south watershed, and some of the eastern parishes extend up to the headwaters of the longer rivers which flow eastward — e.g. Kincardine, Contin, Urray, Fodderty and Kilmorack. (Adapted from Fig. 4.8. in Cant 1986. 54).

porate Gael. *cill* (church) and *clachan* (stone church). Along with names incorporating Gael. *annaid* (church), *cléireach* (priest) and Old Norse *múnkr* (monk), and the many burying grounds scattered through these parishes, they point to a wide variety of church sites used in days gone by to the glory of God.

There are two periods of church life in Wester Ross on which I propose to concentrate — (1) Post Reformation and pre-Revolution, ca. 1560 to 1690, and (2) Post-Revolution, 1690 to modern times. These dates will be blurred because the catholic, episcopal and presbyterian periods and systems of church government inevitably overlapped. This was likely to be especially true in a rural and relatively remote area, and changes in both doctrine and organisation were bound to be slow to take effect in the Highlands, particularly in the north-west (Murchison 1962. 63; Craven 1886. 78).

Fig. 6.2 The parish church at Applecross, 1966.

Fig. 6.3 Part of an
Early Christian cross-
slab, Applecross church.

121

THE POST-REFORMATION CHURCH: ca. 1560-1690

Dr. Cant's paper left us with a picture of parish churches appropriated to the cathedral and its services . . . and other parish churches fobbed off with vicars (or deputies of the non-resident rectors) drawing only a pittance from the parish teinds. Evidence is thin or completely lacking for most of the western parishes, but it seems that the churches of Lochalsh and Lochcarron at least were served by a vicar (Haws 1972. 164, 165).

The Reformers inherited a parochial system whose boundaries can still be identified today, though there have been changes in detail. The diocese of Ross had six 'common kirks', whose revenues belonged to the canons or chaplains of the cathedral at Fortrose. Kintail, Lochalsh, Lochcarron, Gairloch, Applecross and Lochbroom were so listed in the Register of the Privy Seal in 1567. The 'haill commoun kirkis of the realm' having come into the sovereigns' hands, these six in Ross were in that year granted by Queen Mary and her husband to their new bishop, the famous John Leslie. In the accounts of ecclesiastical revenues to be devoted to the church, the 'common kirks' of Kintail and Lochbroom both figure, with the added words 'McKenzie intromitter' (Donaldson 1949. 4) — perhaps some 'sticky fingers' in Kintail may have seen that the proceeds got no further on their way to the cathedral, fifty miles off the east!

Highland parishes were — some of them still are — inordinately large. The biggest in Wester Ross was Lochbroom (273,000 acres: 110,483 ha), the third largest in Scotland, and Gairloch was not far behind (227,000 acres: 91,867 ha). It used to be thought that the Highlanders were at first untouched by the religious movement of the Reformation; but a closer study of the national records, led by the late Professor Gordon Donaldson, suggests that the apparent dearth of reformed clergy in parts of the Highlands, including the north and west, may have been largely illusory. Dr. James Kirk has found that in the diocese of Ross church appointments were made 'relatively promptly' in the east, and in the west by 1574 only the parish of Gairloch was without at least a resident 'reader' (Groome 1901. 625, 1092; Kirk 1986. 1-2, 10, 12).

The presbyterian system of church government was slow to emerge, and many years in growing. How far it commanded the support of the people when it was introduced is hard to judge. By 1618 episcopacy, with its dioceses and church hierarchy, had been fully restored, only to be temporarily overthrown in 1638 and revived again after the Restoration (1662 to 1689) — one of the 'outed' bishops was John Maxwell of Ross, the 'greatest Scottish prelate of the reign of Charles I' (Craven 1886. 62). The minutes of the Presbytery of Dingwall, which have survived for the years 1649-87, offer a detailed account of the changing church life in 17th century Ross-shire.

'Wise Men From The East' : Presbyterial Visitations

The presbytery of Dingwall was acutely aware of the difference between its

122

eastern and western parishes — the 'low country' and 'the hielands' as they are called in the record. Meetings were nearly always held in Dingwall or nearby, sometimes two or three a month, which meant for the 'hieland brethren' a journey on horseback of 50 or even 70 miles over rough tracks and unbridged rivers. It was the Presbytery's duty to carry out periodic 'visitations' of every parish within its bounds, and when a three-day round of Kintail, Lochalsh and Lochcarron had been completed in August 1649, a planned extension to Gairloch and Lochbroom had to be postponed to the following year 'the way long, not rydable, and inabilitie of brethren to goe afoot' (Mackay 1896. xxvi, 147-52, 191, 192, 194-8).

What the Presbytery clerk noted on these 'visitations' gives some idea of what the brethren found — and what they thought should be done. These were troubled times, as the wise men from the east were more than once reminded. This was largely Mackenzie country, or at least Mackenzie-dominated. We are told by Mackenzie of Applecross that in the days before the two Covenants, Colin, first earl of Seaforth, lord of Kintail from 1611-33, 'caused build a church in everie baronie of his Highlands, and left a donatione to ilk church to maintain a minister' (HP. II. 65). But his successor had been excommunicated by the General Assembly in 1646 for producing his own 'humble remonstrance' against the Covenants, and raising men in defiance of the Government (Peterkin 1838. 445-6).

The ministers of the four parishes visited in 1649-50 were a varied lot, and it is worth noting that two of them had been more than 30 years in the same parish, and the other two over a dozen (*Fasti.* VII. 152, 155, 157, 160; Mackay 1896. 253):

Kintail — Farquhar Macrae, a son of Seaforth's constable of Eilean Donan, educated at Perth Grammar School and Edinburgh University (Bishop Maxwell called him 'a man of great gifts *but unfortunately lost in the Highlands*'), transferred to Kintail in 1618 after ten years as minister of Gairloch, succeeded his father as constable and founded a dynasty of Macrae ministers of Kintail which lasted until 1716;

Lochalsh — Donald Clark, MA of Edinburgh University, parish minister here by 1614, up to 1653 at least;

Lochcarron — Alexander Mackenzie, son of Seaforth's chamberlain of Lochcarron, here by 1636 (when he was made JP), followed as minister by his son who died in 1721;

Lochbroom — Donald Ross (presumably from the east?), minister and JP 1636, suspended 1649 on accusation of immorality, drinking wine on the Sabbath, and other 'unministerial carriage' (sentence rescinded 1650).

Before a presbyterial visitation, ministers were supposed to intimate the date to their people, who were expected to attend along with their elders. In

Lochalsh and Lochcarron, it was found that all the elders were 'incapacitate' for office 'be reason of malignancie' (i.e. opposition to the Solemn League and Covenant of 1643 and thereby opposed to Government policy); at Lochcarron the 'late elders' declared that their minister had urged them to subscribe this Covenant, but they refused 'for fear of their superiors'. At Lochbroom there were seven elders present, but few people. One minister didn't know why his people were absent, and another had heard that *his* were in pursuit of stolen goods 'taken from several corners of the country'. When the Presbytery visited Lochbroom they carried out the full procedure of examining the minister and elders separately and then together, and also the people ('being few'). As well as cases of discipline, stress was laid on Sabbath observance, catechising on the essentials of the Christian faith, baptism and marriage, family worship, attendance at the kirk, and collections for the poor (Mackay 1896. 147-52, 194-8).

Fig. 6.4 Medieval cross-slabs on *Eilean Ma-rui'*, Isle Maree. The stones have never been dressed or squared; they lie flat, next to each other and roughly east-west, and are traditionally said to mark the graves of a local Norwegian prince, Olaf, and his wife (*P.S.A.S.* vol. IV, 251 et seq.; Dixon 1886. 10).

The church at Kintail was found to be without 'thacking', and there was no pulpit nor precentor's desk; at Lochalsh 'nothing found in this kirk but the bare walls'; Lochcarron had a stool of repentence, but neither puplit nor desks. Orders were given for remedying these deficiencies, with help from the parishioners. The General Assembly's order forbidding burials within kirks was emphasised, and a Lochbroom elder was deposed for 'presumptuously avowing' his own resolve to ignore the ban (Mackay 1896. 147, 150, 195).

Strange Rites At Loch Maree

The Presbytery's most startling 'excursion' to the west was made in 1656 to investigate reports of superstitious rites at Loch Maree — 'the most extraordinary story of idolatry which we know in connection with the Highlands', it has been called [Figs. 6.4, 6.5]. The loch and its islands are in Gairloch parish, but some of the ringleaders seem to have come from Achnashellach in Lochcarron, whose minister (Alexander Mackenzie) also served the parish of Applecross in the absence of a settled minister.

Next best thing to the actual words of the clerk's minute of the visit is the summary by Dr. William Mackay (of Inverness) who edited the Dingwall Presbytery's records:

> The Presbytery found that the Protestant inhabitants of Applecross, Lochcarron, Lochalsh, Kintail, Contin, Fodderty, Gairloch and Lochbroom, were in the habit of sacrificing bulls to the saint (Maolrubha) on his annual festival day, 25th August; of giving the sacrificed meat and other offerings to those poor, mentally deranged persons who were known as St. Mourie's afflicted ones — *derilans* — and who owned his special protection; of making pilgrimages to his monuments of idolatry in various places, including Isle Maree, to which as well as to Loch Maree he gave his name; of visiting and 'circulating' ruinous chapels associated with his memory — marching round them sunwise, no doubt; of learning of the future, 'in reference especialie to lyf and death in taking of jurneys' by trying to put their heads into 'a holl of a round stone', which, if they 'could doe, to witt, be able to put in thaire heade, they expect thair returneing to that place; and faileing, they conceived it ominous'; and of adoring 'wells and other superstitious monuments and stones, tedious to rehearse' (Mackay 1896. xxxviii, 279-83).

As it turned out, none of the eleven men accused seems ever to have been brought to book. All were summoned to appear before a special meeting of the Presbytery at Applecross on 5 September, with Mr Alexander as their accuser. None appearing, they were summoned to Dingwall in October, along with two more men from Torridon and Applecross. The Presbytery decided that anyone found guilty of such 'abhominations', especially sacrifices 'of ony kynd', must appear in sackcloth in six of the churches within the bounds on successive Sundays, and also be rebuked before the Presbytery. But again they failed to appear; and the records of the Synod of

Fig. 6.5 The 'wishing tree' on Isle Maree is now dead — killed perhaps by copper poisoning Patients visiting the island to seek a cure drove in nails and attached pieces of their clothing. Countless 'old' pennies and half-pennies have also been wedged into the wood, many of them now concealed by the once-growing bark.

Other elements in the hoped-for cure of 'lunatics' required them first to be rowed several times around the island, plunged three times into the loch, made to kneel before an altar and then to drink some of the holy well water. Only then did they attach an offering to the oak tree. It was a process to be repeated every day for several weeks. By the 17th century the sacrifice of a bull (formerly quite unconnected with the cure) came to be seen as an essential preliminary (*P.S.A.S.* vol. IV. 253 et seq.; Dixon 1886. 150-153).

Ross (to whom they were referred) have not survived, so we do not know the sequel — if there was one. But future generations are surely indebted to the presbytery clerk for recording so much detail 'with the relish of an antiquary', as well as with 'indications of horror at the darkness of superstition' (Mackay 1896. xxxvii, 280-2, 287).

The Return (Again) Of Episocacy

After Cromwell's usurpation (which incidentally brought General Monck with an army into the fastnesses of Kintail), episcopacy was re-established at the Restoration of Charles II. The bishop, archdeacon and others figure in the presbytery records, but there is little other sign of change, at least in the west. Of one minister (Roderick Mackenzie, son of a small laird near Dingwall), a parish historian once wrote: 'When he came to Gairloch, Presbyterianism ruled; when Episcopacy was established in 1660, he conformed; and when the Revolution put an end to Episcopacy, he became a Presbyterian again' (Dixon 1886. 65; *Fasti*. VII. 146).

References to the western parishes are fewer after the Restoration. In 1665 the minister of Lochbroom (Murdoch Mackenzie, younger brother of Gairloch's 'vicar of Bray'), feels 'constrained to leave his ministry, for want of maintenance' — his kirk is unthatched, and he has nowhere convenient to preach. On both counts he is referred to the Bishop and Synod — and as he is still here in 1681 we can only hope that conditions had improved. The old practice of bull-sacrifice in Loch Maree emerges again in 1678, when a Gairloch family tried to cure an ailing wife and mother; but the accused failed again and again to appear. Ministers from 'highland' parishes were sometimes excused from attending Presbyterian meetings at Dingwall, and some form of ecclesiastical devolution seems to have been tried out; but such expedients were soon overtaken by much wider changes (Mackay 1896. 292, 309, 323, 326; Craven 1886. 64, 66).

AFTER THE REVOLUTION: 1690 TO MODERN TIMES

The End of Episcopacy

Following the Revolution of 1688-89, when James VII abdicated and forfeited the throne and William and Mary reigned in his stead, episcopacy was finally dis-established by the Scots Parliament. Prelacy and all superiority of office in the Church were abolished, as being 'contrary to the inclinations of the generality of the people', and in its place Presbyterian church government by kirk sessions, presbyteries, provincial synods and general assemblies was 'by law established' in 1690 (*APS*. IX. 40, 133-4).

Many of the episcopalian clergy were deposed, not always on very solid grounds, but a considerable number of the old incumbents remained as *de facto* parish ministers. As well as those who were prepared to take the new oaths and accept the presbyterian system, many retained their parishes simply because it proved impossible to dispossess them. Whether you read a presbyterian evangelical source like Dr. Kennedy's *Days of the Fathers in Ross-shire*, or Archdeacon Craven's history of the diocese prefaced to the *Journals . . . of Bishop Forbes*, the facts speak for themselves — the five great Wester Ross parishes still had the former episcopalian incumbents as their ministers, and no doubt the people remained loyal to them.

In *Gairloch* Roderick Mackenzie, over 60 years a minister, died 'Father of the Church' in 1710; *Lochalsh*'s Finlay Macrae was deposed in 1717; in *Kintail* Donald Macrae, admitted in 1681, refused to conform and survived the Jacobite 'attempt' of 1719; *Lochcarron*'s second Alexander Mackenzie died in 1721; and finally, in *Lochbroom*, the last survivor of the old incumbents (John Mackenzie) died in 1723, more than 30 years after the Revolution settlement (Dickinson & Donaldson 1954. 217-19; *Fasti*. VII. 146, 152, 155, 157, 160; VIII. 680-1).

Seaforth had supported King James, and Jacobite and episcopalian sympathies were strong in his 'country'. Mackenzie influence extended from Kintail to Lochbroom, and the chief was active in the cause. Both title and estates were forfeited after 1715, and with failure at Glenshiel there was a possibility that Wester Ross could be opened up to presbyterian influence and loyalty to King George. As has been said, the conflict was not so much between the 'old faith' and the 'new faith', as between two kinds of Protestantism, with political overtones and clan loyalties thrown in. According to Lord Tarbat 'The Presbyterians are the more zealous and hotter; the other [of which he was one] the more numerous and powerful' (MacInnes 1951. 36; Murchison 1967. 113; Dunlop 1967. 69).

A revived system of presbyteries was gradually set up in the North by the 'zealous few' from 1693 onwards. As the old ones died off, attempts were made to settle a new generation of ministers in Wester Ross — at first from an eastern base at Fortrose or Dingwall. In 1711, it was decided to appoint Mr John Morrison, former minister of Boleskine beside Loch Ness, to Gairloch; but when a brother minister was sent to prepare the way for him, he was forcibly prevented from reaching the parish church and kept prisoner at Kinlochewe (where he read the presbyterial edict 'before six or seven persons'). So the formal admission took place in the 'sure presbyterian refuge' of Kiltearn — but when Morrison went to his new parish he too was seized and kept under guard, and Sir John Mackenzie of Coul declared that 'no presbyterian should be settled in any place where his influence extended, unless His Majesty's forces did it by the strong hand'. The minister discreetly withdrew to Sutherland (Craven 1886. 76-7; *Fasti*. VII. 146; Dixon 1886. 65-6).

For the parish of Lochalsh, vacant since 1717, the Presbytery chose Mr John McKilligan of Alness, son of a redoubtable Covenanter. For convenience if not for safety, he was ordained at Dingall, but was never able to live in his parish 'by reason of the troubles in this country', as he told the Presbytery in 1719; he thought Seaforth's old factor (Donald Murchison) had something to do in turning the people against him. Any further attempt to fill the vacancies by 'dictation' from the east was now abandoned, and replaced by a more localised approach (*Fasti* VII. 155; Craven 1886. 105).

The 18th Century Presbytery of Gairloch

In 1724 four new presbyteries were set up by the General Assembly in the north-west. One, comprising all our six parishes, was to be called the Presbytery of Gairloch; its minutes have survived and were the subject of two long papers by the late Dr. T. M. Murchison, former minister of Glenelg, published by the Gaelic Society of Inverness. On hearing about McKilligan's problems, they decided to go to Lochalsh and see for themselves. But no meeting there was possible, for — as the clerk minuted — 'the Presbytery had been *rabbled* at Lochalsh the 16th of September, being the day appointed for a visitation of the said parish'. They sent McKilligan and another minister to the next General Assembly, with instructions to report their failure 'because of the violent opposition given by the enemies of the present establishment' (Murchison 1967. 11-16).

Ministers from other presbyteries were now brought in to preach, visit, baptise and catechise, with probationers acting as itinerant missionaries. Some were rudely treated, and one 'episcopal intruder' (Alexander Maclennan) arrived to 'divert the people of Lochalsh and Kintail from hearing the brethren sent to supply these parishes'. The Presbytery complained to the factor responsible for uplifting rents on Seaforth's forfeited estate (Edmund Burt), to the sheriff-principal of Ross (Sir Robert Munro of Foulis), and even to General Wade, commander of the forces in Scotland — but I don't know of any action having been taken in Wester Ross by the civil authorities (ibid. 117-18; Craven 1886. 110).

By persistence and unflagging zeal, however, in a matter of eight years from its inception, the Presbytery was able to 'plant' all its parishes with ministers — mostly young men in their 30s. There were some stalwarts (still remembered) among them. Besides Gairloch and Lochalsh, the following were settled:

Lochcarron	Aeneas Sage (1726)	minister 43 years
Lochbroom	Archibald Bannatyne (1726)	minister 4 years
Kintail	John Maclean (1730)	minister 44 years
Glenshiel	John Beaton (1730)	minister 51 years
Applecross	Aeneas Macaulay (1731)	minister 29 years

It would be tiresome to recount the difficulties they met with and survived. Two ministers pled with the Presbytery in 1731, after four or five years at their posts, to be allowed to accept calls to other parishes; but Sage (who was one of them) stuck it out for a further 38 years — and an average of over 40 years for four out of these five pioneers says something for their staying powers once planted in Wester Ross (Murchison 1967. 118-32). The first invitation to a minister from within the parish itself came in 1732 from 'the heritors and elders of Gairloch', and was backed by a local Mackenzie elder — a sign of growing acceptance, whereas the previous appointments had all been made by the Presbytery itself (ibid. 125).

Coigach apart, Wester Ross was spared some of the worst 'troubles and confusions' of 1745-6. William earl of Seaforth had learnt caution since 1715 and 1719, and was released in 1736; his son took no part in the Rising of 1745, and most of the Mackenzies in the west stayed at home (including the lame laird of Gairloch, who had just built himself a new house there) (*SP*. VII. 512; Warrand 1923-30. IV. 111-12; Mackenzie 1949. 34).

Kintail tradition recalls the quaint story of how John Maclean, dressed in the homely garb of a Highland minister, shielded his loyal Macrae flock from the insults of Lord George Sackville's government troops: to prove his status, Mr John was ordered to appear before Lord George 'with his library', and a successor tells how, by producing a copy of Matthew Poole's *Annotations upon the Holy Bible*, the minister 'convinced his lordship that the want of pontifical robes in the Highlands was no obstacle to veracity'. In Lochbroom James Robertson from Atholl — remembered as 'the strong minister' (*am ministeir laidir*) — early in 1746 received two notable visitors in his manse, Lord President Forbes and the Earl of Loudon, who had escaped from Inverness when it was taken by the Jacobites and were on their way to Skye. (Robertson earned his *soubriquet* from his tough way with difficult parishioners, and from having saved many lives by putting his shoulder to a weak lintel stone when the roof of the church at Fearn fell (1742) killing 44 worshippers). The minister later went himself to London to plead the cause of some of his 'deluded' flock after the Rising had been suppressed (*OSA*. 522n; *NSA*. 78-82; *Fasti*. VII. 157-8).

Contributions to Sinclair's first *Statistical Account* show us some of these parish ministers at work, from the perspective of the 1790s. When Sage went to Lochcarron in 1726, he had to carry arms for his own defence, and after five years admitted that only one family regularly attended his ministry. But he had courage as well as faith and earned the respect, loyalty and affection of his people. His like-minded successor, Lachlan Mackenzie, described by Sage's grandson as the only minister in the presbytery who 'preached the gospel with purity and effect', has a firm place in the evangelical folklore of the Highlands. At a time when drunkenness was all too common at Highland funerals, his people signed a pledge that they would take only one glass at the house of mourning, and none at all in the churchyard (in bad weather another was admissable 'at a seemly distance'). 'The people seem to have a strong attachment to religion', wrote Mr Lachlan, 'and yet they would be the better for a little more'. He comments on the belief in his and other parishes that a 'popish priest' could cast out devils and cure madness, while presbyterian clergy had no such power (*OSA*. 573-5; Murchison 1967. 131; Sage (1840) 1975. ch. 2).

The belief that baptism was necessary for salvation long persisted in the Highlands, and even some who did not grudge paying the shilling registration fee imposed by the presbytery in 1778, might seek baptism for their children from the nearest priest. A Catholic mission had been established at

Dornie by Alexander Macrae (son of the last episcopal minister of Dingwall), and this is said to be one reason for a 'landslide to Rome' in Kintail, where several hundred converts were reported (*Fasti*. VII. 34; *OSA*. 528-9n; Maclean 1931. 232; Ritchie 1927. 236).

Emigration, Education and Communications

The ministers of this far-flung presbytery were not concerned solely with the spiritual welfare of their people, however.

Some deplored the tide of emigration which was beginning to strip the glens; a minister of Applecross was released in 1774 to go to America to fix a place for his emigrating parishioners to settle in; his successor complained in his published account of 'landlord oppression', and called for a stop to the 'sheep traffic' and the introduction of manufactures. Where hundreds of people could formerly be seen, he wrote, 'no human faces are now to be met with, except a shepherd attended by his dog'. The Kintail and Glenshiel folk might be 'extravagant' in their attachment to Seaforth, who ruled his restored estates from Brahan (when not in London as MP, or in Barbados as governor); but they were confident that he at least would 'never prefer sheep to men' (*OSA*. 408, 409, 524, 562; *Fasti*. VII. 144-5).

On the matter of communications, Kintail's minister noted that 'till of late' the maxim 'the more inaccessible, the more secure' had led to a strong aversion to roads. But now there was a demand for them, and the building of a good road from Dingwall to Ullapool led to a suggestion from Lochbroom that 'perhaps a few cross roads would also be proper' — for instance, if one from Ullapool to Poolewe were extended to Lochcarron 'an easy communication would be opened from one parish to another' (a minister of Lochalsh had been drowned in 1790 going by sea from his parish to Gruinard). Nor was travel within the parishes easy — a paper of 1709 giving a graphic account of the associated difficulties. The minister of Applecross officiated once a quarter in the districts of Lochs and Torridon and once a month at Kishorn, and there were six burial places apart from the parish churchyard; Gairloch had three additional places of worship (at Kinlochewe, chapel of Sand (Udrigil), and the croft of Tollie at Poolewe); and in Lochbroom Dr. Thomas Ross has seven public burying grounds in his parish in addition to eight places where he thought it his duty to preach, though not obliged to do so (*OSA*. 292, 402, 521, 558, 566-8; *NSA*. 73; *Fasti*. VII. 155; Dixon 1886. 70).

It should be noted, moreover, that the church's work in the western parishes included the difficult task of establishing schools in the area. To do justice to the subject would unduly lengthen this paper, but it is only right to refer to the importance that church courts attached to the spread of education, and to the efforts made to provide for it by the parish ministers.

The 'Parliamentary' or 'Telford' Churches

Wester Ross, with its large parishes, was helped very much by an important government step taken 'for the advancement of religion in the Highlands of Scotland'. Whilst several old parish churches were replaced in the first half of the 19th century — for instance Lochbroom 1817, Applecross 1817, Lochcarron ca. 1840 — in 1823 a grant of £50,000 was voted by parliament for building 42 new churches and paying for their ministers, in most cases also providing a manse. Four of these were in Wester Ross — Plockton (in Lochalsh parish) and Shieldaig (Applecross) both built in 1827, Poolewe (Gairloch) in 1828, and Ullapool (Lochbroom) in 1829 [Fig. 6.1] (see also Beaton, this volume). They are known as 'parliamentary' churches, or sometimes 'Telford churches'. The basic plans and specifications, although actually drawn up by the Inverness architect James Smith, were approved by Telford, and the work carried out under the supervision of men like Joseph Mitchell, who had worked for Telford on the Highland roads and bridges. How useful these churches were is illustrated by the fact that exactly half the population of Gairloch parish was connected with the new church at Poolewe (Maclean 1889; *NSA*. 98, 104; Groome 1901. 1093, 1337, 1595).

Disruption and Reunion

The Disruption of 1843, which split the Church of Scotland in two, affected the religious life of Ross-shire deeply. The conflicting rights of patrons and congregations in the appointment of ministers led to controversy and litigation in the civil courts. In Wester Ross, it is true, the only parish minister to leave 'the Establishment' and join the new Free Church was the scholarly Dr. Thomas Ross of Lochbroom (and formerly of Rotterdam); but in three out of four of the parliamentary churches the minister 'came out' (the exception being Ullapool). Dr. Ross had foreseen the inevitable well in advance, and was followed by his people 'almost to a man' (he died soon afterwards); and the whole or most of the *congregations* of Applecross, Gairloch and Lochcarron also joined the Free Church. A young man from Lochcarron, Alexander MacColl, took charge of three parishes until new ministers were settled (he ended his days as Free Church minister of Lochalsh) (Brown 1893. 105; Ewing 1914. I. 217, II. 228-9).

New churches and meeting-houses were built wherever sites could be obtained — the laird and his family in Gairloch joined the Free Church, so there would be no problem there; but the Mackenzie proprietor of Shieldaig, though a near relative of the minister, refused a site and forbade his tenants to give lodging to any Free Church minister — presumably the kind of circumstance which produced the 'preaching caves' of Wester Ross (such as those between First Coast and Sand). In 1893, however, a substantial number of members from Lochbroom, Shieldaig and Lochcarron left the Free Church to join the Free Presbyterians (Mackenzie 1949. 156; Ewing 1914. I. 237, II. 228-9; Barnett 1930. 124-7) [Figs. 6.6, 6.8].

Though seriously weakened, the 'auld kirk' maintained its ministry in the parishes. When attempts to heal the old divisions were made, in the

Fig. 6.6 Free Church of Scotland, Achiltibuie, 1992. The slate roof was replaced with blue corregated asbestos ca. 1990, when other repairs were made.

Fig. 6.7 The former Free Church Manse, Achiltibuie, 1992. A modern bungalow adjacent to the Church, now serves as a manse.

Fig. 6.8   The former Free Presbyterian Church of Scotland, Achiltibuie, built of corrugated iron in the 1890s. Latterly a craft workshop, gallery and hay store. 1992.

Highlands particularly many congregations felt obliged to decline entering the union between the Free Church and the United Presbyterian Church in 1900, and also the larger union of the Church of Scotland and United Free Church in 1929. Thus there are still three distinct presbyterian denominations represented in Wester Ross (Church of Scotland, Free Church, and Free Presbyterian). In addition, there are Scottish Episcopal Church congregations and services by resident or visiting clergy, and a Roman Catholic priest and chapel at Dornie in Kintail.

The civil parish has for long been superseded as a unit of local government, and its boundaries have disappeared from official maps. And so also, it may be said, as each branch of the Christian Church tries to meet the needs of a shifting population and the changing ways of life which mark the later years of the 20th century, the ecclesiastical parish is not always seen as the key to current church history, as it was in the past.

Acknowledgement

Figs. 6.2, 6.3, 6.6, 6.7, 6.8 are reproduced by permission of the Royal Commission on the Ancient and Historical Monuments of Scotland. Elizabeth Beaton kindly provided Fig. 6.5. James Ford kindly drew Fig. 6.1; John Hume the Old Lochcarron gravestone.

References

APS: The Acts of the Parliament of Scotland. 1814-75.
Barnett, T. R. *Autumns in Skye, Ross and Sutherland.* 1930.

134

Brown, T. *Annals of the Disruption*. New Edition. 1893.

Cant, R. G. The Medieval Church in the North: Contrasting Influences in the Dioceses of Ross and Caithness, in J. R. Baldwin (ed.) *Firthlands of Ross and Sutherland*. 1986.

Craven, J. B. History of the Episcopal Church in the Diocese of Ross, chiefly during the 18th century, in *Journals of the Episcopal Visitations of Bishop Robert Forbes*. 1886.

Dickinson, W. C. & Donaldson, G. *A Source Book of Scottish History*. 1954. vol. III.

Dixon, J. H. *Gairloch*. 1886.

Donaldson, G. *Accounts of the Collectors of Thirds of Benefices*. 1949.

Dunlop, A. I. *William Carstares*. 1967.

Ewing. W. (ed.) *Annals of the Free Church of Scotland*. 1914. 2 vols.

Fasti: Fasti Ecclesiae Scoticanae. New Edition. 1928. vol. VII.

Groome, F. H. *Ordnance Gazetter of Scotland*. New Edition. 1901. 1 vol.

HP: Highlands Papers, ed. J.R.N. Macphail. 1914-34. 4 vols.

Haws, C. H. *Scottish Parish Clergy at the Reformation*. 1972.

Kennedy, J. *The Days of the Fathers in Ross-shire*. 1861.

Kirk, J. The Kirk and the Highlands at the Reformation, in *Northern Scotland*. 1986. vol. 7.

MacInnes, John. *The Evangelical Movement in the Highlands of Scotland, 1688-1800*. 1951.

Mackay, W. (ed.) *Records of the Presbyteries of Inverness and Dingwall, 1643-1688*. 1896.

Mackenzie, A. *History of the Mackenzie*. New Edition. 1894.

Mackenzie, O. H. *A Hundred Years in the Highlands* (1921). New Edition. 1949.

Maclean, A. *Telford's Highland Churches*. 1989.

Maclean, D. *The Counter-Reformation in Scotland, 1560-1930*. (1931).

Maclean, D. The Presbytery of Ross and Sutherland, 1693-1700, in *Records of the Scottish Church History Society*. 1935. vol. V.

MacNaughton, C. *Church Life in Ross and Sutherland from the Revolution (1688) to the present time*, compiled chiefly from the Tain Presbytery records. 1915.

Murchison, T. M. The Synod of Glenelg, 1725-1821: notes from the records, in *Transactions of the Gaelic Society of Inverness*. 1962. vol. XXXVIII.

Murchison, T. M. The Presbytery of Gairloch, 1724-1750, in *TGSI*. 1967. vol. XLIV.

Murchison, T. M. The Presbytery of Gairloch, 1751-1827, in *TGSI*. 1972. vol. XLVII.

NSA: The [New] Statistical Account of Ross and Cromarty Shires. 1841.

OPS: Origines Parochiales Scotiae (Bannatyne Club). 1851-55.

OSA: The [Old] Statistical Account of Scotland. (1791-99); (Inverness-shire, Ross and Cromarty). New Edition. 1981. vol. XVII.

Peterkin, A. (ed.) *Records of the Kirk of Scotland, containing the Acts and Proceedings of the General Assemblies*. 1838.

Ritchie, J. *Reflections on Scottish Church History*. 1927.

RMS: Registrum Magni Sigilli Regum Scotorum.

RPC: The Register of the Privy Council of Scotland.

RRS: Regesta Regum Scottorum.

RSS: Registrum Secreti Sigilli Regum Scotorum.

Sage, D. *Memorabilia Domestica* (1840). New Edition. 1975.

SP: The Scots Peerage, ed. Sir J. B. Paul.

Warrand, D. (ed.) *More Culloden Papers*. 1923-30. 5 vols.

Watson, W. J. *Place-Names of Ross and Cromarty*. 1904.

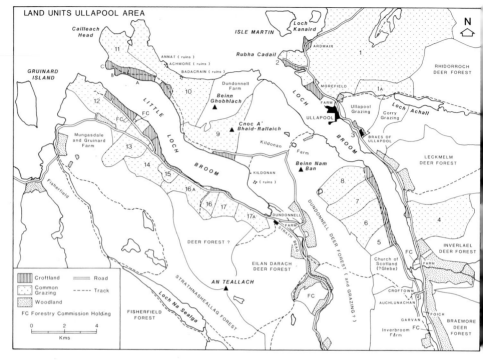

Fig. 7.1 Land units around Loch Broom and Little Loch Broom, 1980.

As well as the crofting townships with their common grazings, there are several larger farms and estates, deer forests and Forestry Commission plantations. (1 acre = 0.4047 hectacres).

TOWNSHIP		No. of CROFTS	COMMON GRAZING (Area in Hectares)
1	Ardmair	9	
	Rhue & Morefield	22	1619
1A	(Enlargement 1902/11)	—	566
2	Rhue	6	?
3	Braes of Ullapool	2	?
4	Ardcharnich	8	545
5	Letters (Small Holdings)	11	—
6	Ardindrean	7	454
7	Rhiroy	3	193
8	Loggie	10	425
9	Badrallach	11	648
10	Rhireavach	8	1898
11A	Carnach	3	?
11B	Scoraig	4	?
11C	Lots of Scoraig	14	?
12	Badluchrach	24	535
13	Durnamuck	10	490
14	Badcaul	?	355
15	Badbea	1	78
16	Ardessie	3	102
16A	(Enlargement)	—	283
17	Camusnagaul	4	117
17A	(Enlargement)	—	228

THE MAKING OF THE GAIRLOCH CROFTING LANDSCAPE

J. B. Caird

In the last two centuries kelp and fisheries, sheep farms, crofts, clearances, emigration and deer forests are the main developments which have contributed to the cultural landscape of the Highlands and Islands. The creation of crofts from Kintyre in Argyllshire to Unst in Shetland resulted in the formation of a distinctive landscape, settlement pattern and distribution of population, with the crofting population occupying small lots almost exclusively round the coast, except in the eastern parts of Inverness-shire, Ross and Cromarty and Sutherland and in Caithness and Orkney where the Old Red Sandstone provides potential arable land beyond the coastal fringe. Such crofts as there are in the straths are almost exclusively 20th century creations, the result of settlement schemes recommended by the *Report of the Royal Commission of Inquiry into the Condition of Crofters and Cottars in the Highlands and Islands of Scotland* of 1884, which resulted in most of the cleared land being restored to small tenant holdings (Caird 1979. 7-25).

The pattern of settlement around Loch Broom and Little Loch Broom is typical of what emerged in the North-West Highlands during the 19th century [Fig. 7.1]. This paper, however, concerns the creation of the crofting system in Gairloch, which was distinctly unusual. The resultant landscape on the Gairloch Estate is one of squares rather than rectangles and the associated settlement pattern is scattered rather than linear.

ESTATES IN THE PARISH OF GAIRLOCH

The Gruinard Estate, in the northern part of Gairloch, extends from Drumchork, immediately south-east of Aultbea, northwards and eastwards to the Little Gruinard River which forms the parish boundary with Lochbroom [Fig. 7.2]. It was in the possession of the Mackenzies of Gruinard before 1655 but was bought by Henry Davidson of Tulloch, near Dingwall, in 1795 (see Bangor-Jones, this volume), and the crofts were created during Davidson's ownership. In 1835, it was sold to a wealthy Englishman, Meyrick Bankes (Dixon [1886] 1974. 60), whose family held it till the first decade of the 20th century, expanding the estate by the purchase of Letterewe also in 1835. Bankes cleared Little Gruinard and Badantsluig (NG 935906) after 1835 to form a sheep farm and reduced the

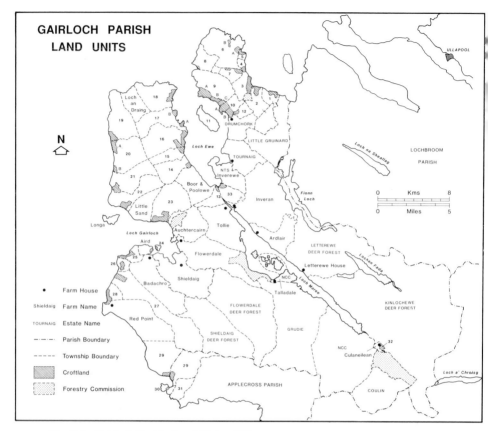

GAIRLOCH PARISH LAND UNITS

N

- ● Farm House
- Shieldaig Farm Name
- TOURNAIG Estate Name
- —·—·— Parish Boundary
- — — — — Township Boundary
- Croftland
- Forestry Commission

Fig. 7.2 Gairloch Parish, Land Units, 1981.

The crofting townships (with crofts shaded and common grazings given in hectares) are the dominant agricultural units numerically. Five farms are also worked, two small estates are mostly used for sporting purposes, there are Forestry Commission plantations, four deer forests and the National Trust area which includes Inverewe Gardens. (1 acre = 0.4047 hectares).

TOWNSHIP		No. OF CROFTS	COMMON GRAZING (Area in Hectares)
1	First and Second Coast	7	169
2	Sand	11	293
3	Laide	15	279
4	Udrigle	3	98
5	North Udrigle	1	51
6A	Mellon Udrigle	8	
6B	Opinan	7	1036
7	Achgarve	8	295
8	Slaggan	1	406
9A	Mellon Charles	44	
9B	Ormiscaig	15	
9C	Buailnaluib, Aird	9	988
10A	Culconich, Tignafiline	9	
10B	Aultbea	9	250

138

11	Isle Ewe	11	?
12	Badfearn	4	109
13	Pool Crofts	10	299
14	Naust	11	575
15	Braes	8	458
16	Midtown	28	891
17A	Coast of Inverasdale	18	
17B	Mellangaun	7	868
18	Cove	15	1014
19	Melvaig	28	1295
20A	Aultgrishan	23	
20B	Allt am Phadruig	5	1189
21	North Erradale	22	944
22	Big Sand	33	741
23	Strath	47	1065
24	Eilean Horrisdale	5	?
25	Port Henderson	21	87
26	Opinan	13	129
27	South Erradale	17	2285
28	Red Point	7	195
29	Lower Diabeg	23	1214
30	Arrat	2	?
31	Upper Diabeg	?	277
32	Incheril	7	?
33	Londubh	14	118

number of crofters in Sand by increasing the number of crofts in First and Second Coast but also added Beinn a' Chaisgein (NG 965822), the sheiling ground of Sand and First and Second Coast, to the sheep farm (*Royal Comm.* 1884. para. 1861). Crofters at Drumchork, where he built his lodge in 1881 were also evicted: Drumchork had a farm of 100 acres as early as 1851 sharing the land with crofters, but the crofters were cleared and their land 'added to a sheep farm' (*Census* 1861; *Royal Comm.* 1884. paras 1862, 1881). In North Gairloch in 1888, there were 91 crofts whose rents were reduced by 37 per cent, and 78 per cent of the rent arrears were cancelled during the Fair Rents exercise, not uncommon percentages (*Northern Chronicle* 13 June 1888). Bankes did, however, make the crofters drain their land and built piers to assist the fishermen (*Royal Comm.* 1884. para 1862).

The remainder or the parish, with an exclave north-west of Aultbea consisting of the present crofting townships of Buailnaluib, Ormiscaig and Mellon Charles and Isle Ewe, has been held by the Mackenzies of Gairloch for some five centuries, though death duties have forced sales of land since the 1950s. Their title to Gairloch goes back to a protocol of 1494 (Dixon ibid. 60), which granted 'the landis of Gerloch lyande betwix the watteris callyde Innerew and Torvedene within the Shireffdom of Innerness' — from the River Ewe and Loch Maree to Loch Torridon — to which was added Mellon, half of Isle Ewe and fishing rights on the left bank of the River Ewe in 1671. The Kinlochewe Estate, at the eastern end of the parish, was purchased in 1743 (ibid.). The Kernsary estate, mainly a sheep farm,

SHEEP RACKS.

SHEEP RACKS.

A SPECIALITY.

GARDNER'S TURNIP CUTTERS.

LEVER BALL TURNIP CUTTERS.

BRUISERS. CHAFF CUTTERS.

RICK AND CART COVERS.

WIRE NETTING FOR SHEEP in any width.

Special quotations for large quantities.

PRICE LISTS ON APPLICATION.

Ben. Reid & Co.,

BON-ACCORD WORKS, Aberdeen.

From *List of Sheep Marks for the Counties of Aberdeen . . . and Inverness.* 1897.

140

was purchased from Mackenzie of Seaforth in 1844, partly to add the fishing rights on the right bank of the River Ewe. Inverewe and Tournaig were bought from Mackenzie of Coul in 1862 for Osgood Mackenzie, later the creator of Inverewe Gardens and half-brother of Sir Kenneth Mackenzie of Gairloch, from whom the part of Kernsary adjacent to Inverewe was purchased (also for Osgood Mackenzie) in 1862; Kernsary was cleared of sheep a few years later. Letterewe on the north side of Loch Maree was a wadset acquired by the Mackenzies of Gairloch in 1696 and exchanged in the same year for Wester Logie or Conon in Easter Ross with an uncle, the first Mackenzie of Letterewe: this excambion gave the Mackenzies of Gairloch a base in Easter Ross which became their principal residence (ibid. 62). The Gairloch Estate now consists of the area from Strath township (immediately north-west of Gairloch village), to Talladale on the south side of Loch Maree and southwards to the Torridon-Gairloch boundary north of Diabeg. The only other Highland estates which have retained substantial lands for such a long period are the estates of the Duke of Argyll and those of Lord Macdonald of Sleat and MacLeod of Dunvegan in Skye.

CROFTING ON THE GAIRLOCH ESTATE

In addition to ancestral ownership, the circumstances in which the crofts were created on the Mackenzies of Gairloch Estate and the ideas on which they were established were decidedly unusual: the aim was not specifically to retain labour for kelp-making or fishing as on most other crofting estates, but to improve agriculture and housing. This was quite unlike the creation of the Argyll crofts, where the crofting system was first developed in Iona and Tiree in 1801 and 1802, under clear instructions from the Duke that crofts were to be created for the accommodation of people 'who are to derive their subsistence from sources other than the produce of the land' (Cregeen 1964. 48, 51, 136-7, 199). Furthermore, the creation of the crofts in Gairloch was carried out in 1845, later than elsewhere in most of the Highlands and Islands.

The Beginnings of Agricultural Change

The *Military Survey,* or Roy's Map, provides a view of the landscape of Gairloch ca. 1750, with clustered settlements at the edge of unenclosed parcels of arable land on farms held by tacksmen or leaseholders and their sub-tenants in a sparsely settled area. The only sign of improvement is in the area immediately surrounding Flowerdale House, the present mansion of the Mackenzies of Gairloch, where building was begun in 1738 by Sir Alexander Mackenzie, the second baronet, close by the site of the earlier Tigh Dige or moated house. He also built Conon House in 1758 (Dixon ibid. 102; Byam Shaw 1988. 64). During Sir Hector Mackenzie, the fourth baronet's tenure, the first sheep farm in Gairloch parish was created before 1810 on the Seaforth Letterewe Estate, and others followed around Kinlochewe (Dixon ibid. 137). In this period, the *Old Statistical Account* states that the oat crop only provided meal for seven to eight months of the year, but emphasised thè role of the cod and herring fisheries with 30,000 to 40,000 cod annually exported (McIntosh 1792. 89-93). In 1815, portions of the lands of South Erradale and Ardrisaig were cut off from these farms and let to 22 tenants to form a fishing village at Port Henderson, which later became a crofting township. In the same year, small tenants replaced tacksmen at Mellon Charles and cottars were added: on some of the farms, tenants were bound to have subtenants, in reality cottars, to complete the crews of the cod fishing boats (Mackenzie 1885. 1-11).

The fifth baronet, Sir Francis Mackenzie, who succeeded to the estate in 1826, had previously improved Isle Ewe after the small tenants had been removed — apparently the first attempt at agricultural improvement on the estate (Byam Shaw 1988. 216, 226). The author of the *New Statistical Account* pointed out the urgent need for road construction to facilitate agricultural improvement: 'without public roads, no regular improvement can be carried out in this part of the Highlands' (Russell 1836. 99). But Sir Francis was also the author of *Hints for the use of Highland Tenants and Cottagers: by a Proprietor,* published in 1838 in Gaelic and English. In the introduction, he explains:

> that this treatise . . . is chiefly intended for the benefit of you, my Cottar Tenants . . . it would be well were you supplied with a small book of reference to which recourse could be had in your domestic economy and agricultural occupations . . . Considering the wretched hovels which many of you inhabit, it would be absurd to hope for substituting at once the beautiful Swiss or English cottages or require from you the delightful cleanliness of a Dutch Boor. All I recommend for the present is some little improvement on the present system. In a dwellinghouse, the porch comes first under consideration; for I must protest against human beings and cattle entering together, in your present fashion at the same doorway.

He also refers to 'smocky dens with a hole in the roof with sometimes an old creel stuck in it in imitation of a chimney'. Besides a new house with a porch, kitchen and bedroom, he recommended a garden of a quarter of an acre, with fruit trees, the reduction of the barley crop (used for distilling) and the substitution of oats, clover and turnips : draining and trenching the land with the spade, but also the use of ploughs and carts and of liquid manure (Mackenzie 1838. 29, 33, 50, 51-8, 118-20) [Fig. 7.3a/b].

Sir Francis also urged consideration before entering early into marriage, 'bringing labourers into a world already overstocked, taking employment and food from those who already have not enough'. Here he was referring to existing congestion on the estate, for the population of Gairloch had increased from 1,437 in 1801 to 4,445 in 1831, an increase of 309 per cent.

He continued by saying: 'I confess that you, my countrymen, are in almost everything . . . behind the inhabitants of those countries which I am acquainted . . . I wish to see a change for the better' (ibid. 268-70). He had travelled in England, Holland, Switzerland and Brittany, where his son by a second marriage, Osgood Mackenzie, later of Inverewe, was born in 1842. Sir Francis died in 1843, having in 1841 given the management of the Gairloch estate to his younger brother, Dr John Mackenzie, Doctor of Medicine, who was factor for the estates of Redcastle and Tarradale in Easter Ross and tenant of the farm of Kinellan, on the western edge of Strathpeffer and thus an experienced factor and farmer (Byam Shaw 1988. 192-3 et seq.).

It seems likely that these ideas broadly formed the basis for the subsequent plan for the conversion of the Gairloch small tenant farms into crofts, but in 1835 Dr Mackenzie had investigated a system of small-holder cultivation in Belgium. He published his findings in 1842 in a sixteen-page pamphlet entitled *The Improvement of Highland Crofts* in which 'the necessity of improving the cultivation by crofters by the adoption of Flemish husbandry' was urged: the keystone of this type of husbandry 'being feeding the cows indoors during the whole year and collecting the liquid manure in proper vessels and applying it immediately to the land wherever it is most required'. Dr Mackenzie had also visited an estate on the South Downs near Eastbourne where some 400 tenants practised the system, cultivating holdings of three to six acres solely by the spade on thin, poor soils. In this pamphlet, he also gave his views on ' the advantages offered by the spade husbandry over the present Highland cottar system' adding that Highland estate proprietors should ' think no more of clearing their properties of those unfortunate neglected, poor and ignorant, yet warm hearted creatures than if they were a drove of sheep ordered off to the Falkirk Market' (Mackenzie 1842. 3). This last advice was diametrically opposed to the conclusions of the author of the *New Statistical Account* of Gairloch, 1838, who stated that 'a government grant to convey one-third of the people to Upper Canada would be most desirable': some 150 persons had already emigrated from the parish between 1831 and 1841 (Russell 1836. 99; *Census* 1841).

Dr Mackenzie also cited a 'more rational plan' practised by Mr Blacker of Armagh in Ulster who used 'agricultural teachers' to instruct the small tenants and claimed this method was successful in increasing the yield of the land. Referring in the pamphlet to his brother's book *Hints for the Use of Highland Tenants and Cottagers,* he clearly doubted whether 'one single individual has altered his course a hairbreadth' and reckoned that 'a tenant who is to live by his land should only have as much as he can cultivate with the spade . . . and enable them not only to live well by the land, but also to pay their rents punctually and without difficulty' (Mackenzie 1842. 5-6).

Planning for a Crofting Economy

He then set out his plan for the Gairloch estate: *firstly*, to create crofts of approximately four to five acres 'which a man and his family, if industrious, can properly cultivate with the spade alone without aid from a horse, but

The old Highland Dwelling House

OLD TIMES
SEANN THIMEAN

Fig. 7.3 (a) Seann Thimean, Old Times. The illustrations in Sir Francis MacKenzie's *Hints . . . for Tenants . . .* reflect his view of what was no longer acceptable. Out would go the cas-chrom, the back creel, the solid-wheeled cart, unprotected stacks, open fields, outdoor milking; also the single-entrance, reeking and crumbling byre-dwelling with a midden outside the door, 1838.

with occasional aid from his cows in carting out dung and carting home crop'; *secondly* 'to appoint a well-educated agriculturalist, whose whole time will be devoted to instructing a certain number of cottars in the most approved methods of growing all kinds of produce' . . . and *thirdly*, he 'was quite aware that there are difficulties to overcome' . . . but thought that 'they were by no means so serious as they appear at a distance' (ibid. 6).

The Trustees and Tutors Nominate for the heir to the estate, Sir Kenneth Mackenzie, were his stepmother, Dame Mary Hanbury or Mackenzie and Thomas Mackenzie of Ord; and the estate was under entail. Dr John

House and Steading of Plan 1. J.F.'91

NEW TIMES
UIR THIMEAN

Fig. 7.3 (b)   Uir Thimean, New Times. Improvement to the old Highland house would bring a separate dwelling and byre, an implement store, enclosed garden, stackyard and stockyard, (partly-) enclosed fields, trees, a new horse-drawn plough, spoke-wheeled carts, and hens industriously pecking around the steading. Figs 7.3 (a) + (b) are from Sir Francis MacKenzie's *Hints for the use of Highland Tenants and Cottagers by a Proprietor,* 1838.

Mackenzie, as Factor, and because he was the next substitute heir after his nephews, the children of his deceased brother, declined to accept appointment as a trustee. In order to grant leases of the farms, nearly all of which were due to expire in 1846, as the heir was a pupil and would not succeed until 1853, the Trustees had to petition the Court of Session on 25th June, 1844 for authority to grant new leases (*Petition: CS/235/M/64/8*). Whereas the heir in possession could grant leases of nineteen years duration in terms of the entail, the Tutors could not grant leases beyond the extent of their office. Not only did the trustees request authority to deal with farms and cottar lots or small tenants' holdings but they stated that 'the estate contained a very large cottar population, occupying land from year to year in "runrig" and in other terms equally adverse to the interests of both landlord and tenant'.

Dr Mackenzie advised that leases of ten years were required for what he called the 'cottar lots', that is, the new crofts about to be created: it is certain that Dr Mackenzie had a fairly free hand in running the estate during the minority, as his sister-in-law was English and not fully conversant with estate conditions, and the other trustee never visited Gairloch.

In a *Report to the Tutors* presented as an Appendix to the Petition, George Campbell Smith of Banff, an experienced land surveyor who carried out surveys of estates in the Northern Highlands from 1828-1862, including a survey and sub-division of a portion of the Gairloch estate near Flowerdale in 1840, stated that:

> many hundreds of acres of fine soil, now lying waste, might profitably be reclaimed and made available to the wants of the poor cottar population . . . The condition of these poor people would be very much improved were they to obtain leases of their crofts, on condition of building better houses, and draining, liming, and cultivating the whole in a proper manner.

Leases were required to encourage them to improve their lots. The previous Laird had built one or two 'good houses' in different parts of the estate: granting of leases would encourage completion of his plan. At present, the proprietor obtains 'almost nothing; and often he gives rather than receives': urgent action was required to create crofts. Regarding the larger grazings and sheep walks, Campbell Smith advocated the granting of improving leases of seven to ten years. Dr Mackenzie entirely concurred (*Report: CS/235/M/64/8 —* Appendix). Campbell Smith had previously been engaged to make a full survey of the small tenant farms which he began in March 1844: the final cost was £537.4.9 (Byam Shaw 1988. 259).

Implementation: Joint-Tenant Farms to Individual Crofts

Campbell Smith's manuscript plans [Fig. 7.4] bound as T*he Atlas of the Townships of Gairloch, 1848,* show the existing arable land in runrig and the houses, outbuildings and stockyards of the tenants. Superimposed on the existing tenant farms, they also show the new lots or crofts within straightened township boundaries, with the acreages of 'old arable' and pasture inscribed on each numbered croft. The plans are in colour and are quite the finest plans of any crofting estate. The cottars' houses are also recognisable without stack yards or outbuildings. The surveyor appears to have laid out the crofts, but Dr Mackenzie may well have chosen the tenants for he states that 'a lot of from two to five acres [was] given to every family in the rental book, and to many others I found jammed in with their parents, unnoticed as tenants' . . . He also states that 'first choice was given sometimes to the crofters who had for years been most punctual in paying rent, and when

146

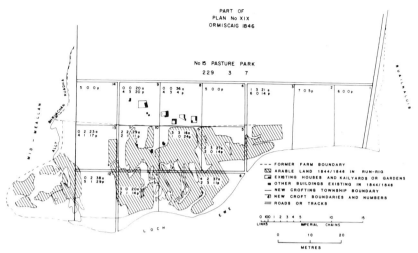

Fig. 7.4 Part of Plan No. XIX, Ormiscaig, Gairloch.

This illustration, redrawn from George Campbell-Smith's estate plan, clearly shows an example of the transition from small tenant farm to crofting township. The existing small tenant farm had irregular boundaries and the five small tenants (with houses, outbuildings and stackyards in the linear cluster) shared the arable land in scattered plots or rigs in equal proportions as each paid one-fifth of the rent of the farm.

The new crofts are superimposed on the existing layout and the plan gives both the extent of arable land (e.g. for Croft 7: 3 acres, 3 roods and 16 poles) and the extent of pasture (1 acre and 24 poles). Six crofters had no arable land on their new holding and would have to reclaim it, but sub-tenants and sons of tenants were probably thankful to be allocated a croft, even if it was on pasture land. The new crofters were bound to build a new house on these crofts [see Fig. 7.11]. From Cambell Smith, G. *Atlas of the Townships of Gairloch* 1848. Gairloch and Conon Archives.

these [few] were served, the others drew lots for their choice' (Byam Shaw 1988. 246-48). In fact, at Ormiscaig, a comparison of Fig. 7.4 and Fig. 7.5 shows that all the existing five tenants, four of them in arrears, were allocated the best five new crofts on which there was over 50 per cent of existing arable land. One of the four cottars was allocated croft number 8 in Ormiscaig, a moorland croft with no arable land on it and another obtained a croft in the adjacent township of Buailnaluib.

Fourteen crofts were created in Ormiscaig, six on improvable moorland with no existing arable land. Fig. 7.5 shows where the new tenants came from: in the rent ledger for the years 1845-1853, under the croft number, is a pencil note in Dr Mackenzie's handwriting giving the previous location and status of the new tenant. For example, in Ormiscaig, tenant number 2 in the pre-crofting rental (*Rental 1843: SRO* SC 25/44/4, Appendix 2, 54) received croft number 6 and the new tenant of croft number 2 is entered as s/t Altgrishan, sub-tenant or more properly cottar, Altgrishan (NG 743855). Fig. 7.6 shows the spatial moves made by the tenants of the three townships of Mellon Charles, Ormiscaig and Buailnaluib some of whom moved considerable distances. Of the 364 small tenants on the farms of the Gairloch

147

ORMISCAIG, GAIRLOCH:
TENANTS 1843 AND CROFTERS 1845

TENANT 1843	CROFT NUMBER AND TENANT 1845 (Nov 15)	PREVIOUS LOCATIONS
	1. Mo McLennan	Isle of Ewe*
	2. Ken Urquhart	Altgrishan*
	3. Murdo McKenzie	Melvaig*
	4. [Vacant]	
John McIver (deceased before Nov 15 1845)	5. Widow McIver	Ormiscaig
John MacGregor	6. John McGregor	Ormiscaig
Hector McGregor	7. Hector McGregor	Ormiscaig
	8. Ken McDonald	Ormiscaig*
	9. Alex McPherson	Cove
Alex Cameron	10. Alex Cameron	Ormiscaig
Rodk Chisholm	11. Rodk Chisholm	Ormiscaig
	12. Dun McDonald	Cove*
	13. Hector McKenzie (1846)	Loch an Draing
	14. [Vacant]	
		(*Subtenant)

Fig. 7.5   From *Rental of the Estate of Gairloch and Conon, for Crop and year Eighteen Hundred and forty three, Testament Dative and Inventory Sir Alexander MacKenzie*, registered 20 March 1844, Dingwall Sheriff Court Commissary Record, SRO SC 25/44/4. Appendix II. 54; Ledger: Rental of Gairloch, 15 November 1845 to 24 May 1853. Gairloch and Conon Archives.

Estate in 1843, 74% were allocated crofts on the farm where they had previously resided and 94 (or 26%) moved to crofts on other farms. An additional 98 tenants were added to the rental, 34 of whom were sons of small tenants, 30 were cottars who remained on the same farm and 34 were cottars who obtained crofts in other townships. Thus, of 462 new crofters, 72% were allocated crofts on the farm where they had previously resided, and 28% had to move to new locations on other farms (Caird 1987. 73).

The reason why some tenants of the new crofts had to move is not documented, but all the new crofting townships had a larger number of crofting tenants than the number of small tenants on the pre-existing farms, some of which were very overcrowded, so some movement was inevitable. But this scheme of creating crofts meant that Campbell Smith's 'many hundreds of acres of *fine* soil, now lying waste' (the non-arable parts of the new crofts), could be reclaimed. Cottars and sons of tenants in the overcrowded small tenant farms would have been glad to obtain a croft anywhere, even if it was on unimproved land.

The new crofting townships were mostly created out of former small tenant farms, but three additional townships were also laid out [Fig. 7.2]: Altanphadruig (NG 742832) and Upper Diabeg (NG 812601), both

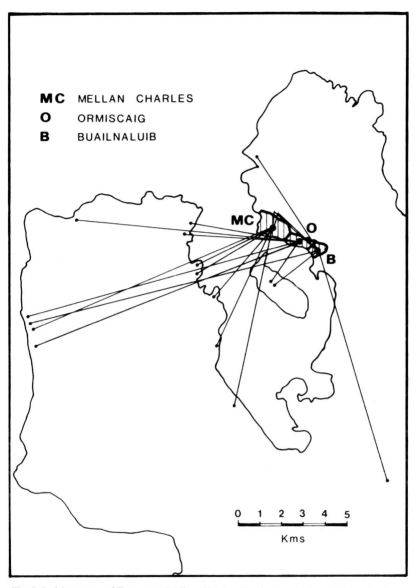

MC   MELLAN CHARLES
O   ORMISCAIG
B   BUAILNALUIB

0 1 2 3 4 5

Kms

Fig. 7.6   Movement of Tenants to Mellon Charles, Ormiscaig and Buailnaluib, Gairloch.

In Gairloch there was considerable movement of tenants and their families to new crofting townships where crofts were created to absorb sub-tenants or cottars and sons of tenants. This diagram shows the pattern of movement to three crofting townships. From *Rental of the Estate of Gairloch and Conon, for Crop and year Eighteen Hundred and forty three* SRO SC 25/44/4: Ledger, Rental of Gairloch, 15 November 1845 to 24 May 1853. Gairloch and Conon Archives.

149

moorland settlements on former grazing land, and Opinan (NG 745725) on part of the former arable land of South Erradale. In this process of reorganising the estate, Port Lair (NG 801577) was made into a small farm and the Tollie crofts with seven families (NG 865786) were cleared, as were six crofters from Kernsary (NG 893794) in 1848 when their crofts were added to Inveran Farm (NG 873787), which was subsequently merged with the farm of Kernsary in 1852 (*Rental* 1845-52).

Improving the Land

After the crofts were allocated, according to Alexander Mackenzie, author of *The Highland Clearances* and a native of Gairloch, the crofters were obliged to trench and drain their new holdings and Dr Mackenzie insisted that they followed 'specified rotations of crops and sown grasses, clover and rye grass, turnips, cabbages and carrots, Jerusalem artichokes and numerous other vegetables of which they had never heard before so as to enable them to feed their cattle indoors and to have plenty of green vegetables for their own consumption' (*Royal Comm. Report* 1893. 153). They were also obliged to build houses on their new crofts. But the agricultural instructor was not appointed, probably because the trustees felt that the estate could not afford to make the appointment: the late Sir Francis had died heavily in debt (Byam Shaw 1988. 229, 248-9, 262-4).

In 1847, after the crofts were created, the potato blight struck Gairloch. The estate borrowed £10,000 under the Drainage Act, part of which was used 'to guarantee that no one on the estate would be allowed to starve' (Mackenzie [1921] 1950. 37), but most of it was used to pay the new crofters to drain and reclaim their own holdings. Alexander Mackenzie stated that he was obliged to work on his father's croft at North Erradale digging drains and removing stones: he was probably nine or ten years old at the time (*Royal Comm. Report* 1893. 152). At Ormiscaig £222.14.5$^1/_2$ was paid out to the crofter tenants for drainage and probably also for reclamation work, sums ranging from £3.2.1 to the tenant of croft 3, to £32.2.14 to the tenant of 14 who had been allocated a bare moor croft. Over the whole estate, the maximum sum paid to a crofter was £33.17.0 in one of the new moorland crofts at Altgrishan and the minimum sum of 8s 2d to a crofter in Strath. In all, £5,590.6.6 was expended, and the total expenditure on the combined estate of Gairloch and Conon was £8,693 (*Drainage Act* 1850). The tenants who had received payments were charged 6.5% interest on the sum which was added to their rent and was still being charged in 1885. In 1850, work was made available for the completion of the Loch Maree road, partly funded by the Government, and earnings from employment on the road helped the new crofters to recover from the famine. The impact of reclamation was reflected in the rents: when the crofts at Ormiscaig were let in 1845, the total rental increased from £32 to £35.11.0, was slightly reduced to £35.7.10 in 1864, and increased again to £44.18.0 by 1883. On the other hand, the Fair Rents Commissioners reduced the total rent to

£32.19.0 in 1888 to less than the rents charged in 1845 when the crofts were created; and they cancelled 71% of the accumulated arrears of £125.1.1, or almost three years' rents, including those of two more crofts which were added to Ormiscaig before 1875 (*Northern Chronicle,* 13 June 1888).

Expansion, Regression and Amalgamation

What then was the effect of the plan for the creation of crofts in order to improve the small-holders conditions in Gairloch? On 30th October 1844, the *Inverness Courier* reported that 'Dr. Mackenzie is about to confer on the tenants of Gairloch the benefits of the allotment system with crofts of from 2 to 4 acres', and that he had visited the Eastbourne estate where the system had been adopted. The reporter doubted that 'our inferior soils and climate will suit as well as the rich lands of Sussex', but thought the experiment was 'at least worth a trial' (*Inverness Courier Index,* 30 October 1844). On 19 September 1850, a representative of the same newspaper who visited Gairloch, thought it 'little less than an entire failure, but the housing had improved' and neither 'profitable to the estate — nor the crofters' (ibid. 19 September 1850; Byam Shaw 1988. 267-70). Evander MacIver, the Scourie Division factor of the Sutherland estate agreed, and added that there was much dissatisfaction among the crofters. 'They don't go along with Dr McKenzie in his views . . . The published accounts by Dr Mackenzie's partisans have been grossly exaggerated' (*Sutherland Papers: NLS* Dep. 313/1392).

Yet a comparison of Figs. 7.7-7.10 shows that the arable land increased from the 20.8 acres recorded on Campbell Smith's plan of Ormiscaig in 1844, to 50 acres in 1875 (*Ordnance Survey Book of Reference:* Cameron 1876); and it was further increased by 1902. From the map of land use in 1981 [Fig. 7.11], it is evident that some areas which were moorland in 1844 [Fig. 7.7], and reclaimed after the crofts were laid out, are still cultivated — although much less overall of the crofting township lands are now cultivated than was the case in 1844. On the other hand, Figs. 7.11 and 7.12 also show that only three of the 16 tenants of Ormiscaig worked their crofts in 1981, although one of them, a part-time crofter, had a unit comprising four crofts. Indeed, most of the land in Ormiscaig is used by tenants of neighbouring townships. Clearly, a township of 16 crofts with 15 tenants and only three effective units worked within the township does not accord with the *Report and Recommendations of the Commissioners of Enquiry into the Condition of Crofters and Cottars in the Highlands and Islands of Scotland* of 1884. Nor, within the wider context of all the crofting townships of North Gairloch in 1981, do 197 crofts with 148 tenants and only 53 effective units (35 with cereal or hay crops, 23 with cattle and sheep, 25 with sheep only) — where in addition, there are but 60 active crofters, only 7 of them full-time and 27 over 65 years of age, out of a total male population over 14 years of age of 137 (total population, 298) [Fig. 7.12].

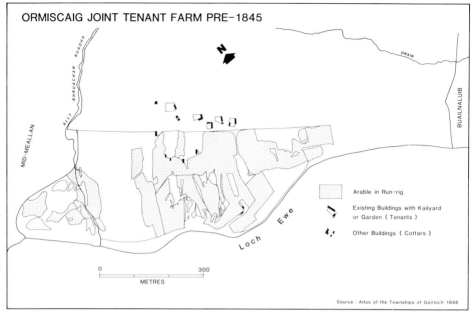

ORMISCAIG JOINT TENANT FARM PRE-1845

N

Arable in Run-rig

Existing Buildings with Kailyard
or Garden (Tenants)

Other Buildings (Cottars)

0   300
METRES

Source : Atlas of the Townships of Gairloch 1848

Fig. 7.7

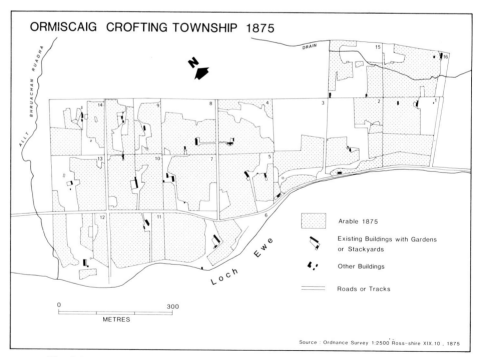

ORMISCAIG CROFTING TOWNSHIP 1875

N

Arable 1875

Existing Buildings with Gardens
or Stackyards

Other Buildings

Roads or Tracks

0   300
METRES

Source : Ordnance Survey 1:2500 Ross-shire XIX.10 , 1875

Fig. 7.9

152

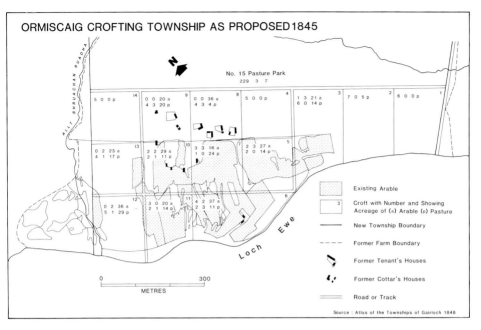

ORMISCAIG CROFTING TOWNSHIP AS PROPOSED 1845

No. 15 Pasture Park
229 3 7

| 14 | 9 | 8 | 4 | 3 | 2 | 1 |
| 5 0 0 p | 0 0 20 a / 4 3 20 p | 0 0 36 a / 4 3 4 p | 5 0 0 p | 1 3 21 a / 6 0 14 p | 7 0 5 p | 6 0 0 p |

| 13 | 10 | 7 | 5 |
| 0 2 23 a / 4 1 17 p | 2 2 29 a / 2 1 11 p | 3 3 16 a / 1 0 24 p | 2 3 27 a / 2 0 14 p |

| 12 | 11 | 6 |
| 0 2 36 a / 5 1 29 p | 3 0 20 a / 2 1 14 p | 4 2 37 a / 2 3 11 p |

Loch Ewe

| 0 | 300 |
METRES

Existing Arable

| 3 | Croft with Number and Showing Acreage of (a) Arable (p) Pasture

——— New Township Boundary

– – – Former Farm Boundary

Former Tenant's Houses

Former Cottar's Houses

═══ Road or Track

Source : Atlas of the Townships of Gairloch 1848

Fig. 7.8

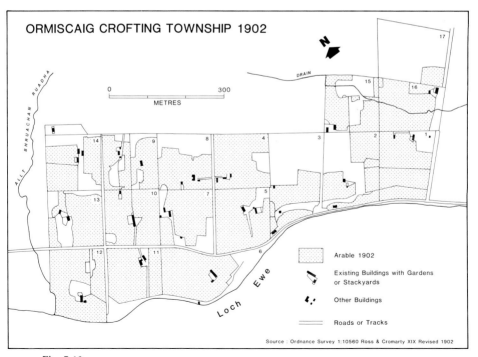

ORMISCAIG CROFTING TOWNSHIP 1902

17

DRAIN

| 15 | 16 |

| 14 | 9 | 8 | 4 | 3 | 2 | 1 |

| 13 | 10 | 7 | 5 |

| 12 | 11 | 6 |

Loch Ewe

| 0 | 300 |
METRES

Arable 1902

Existing Buildings with Gardens or Stackyards

Other Buildings

═══ Roads or Tracks

Source : Ordnance Survey 1:10560 Ross & Cromarty XIX Revised 1902

Fig. 7.10

153

Figs. 7.7-7.10 The evolution of Ormiscaig.

Two elements of the evolution of Ormiscaig are illustrated in these diagrams. Before 1845 [Fig. 7.7] the farms have five joint tenants sharing the arable land in periodic runrig, that is reallocating the rigs either annually, biennially or triennially. In 1845 [Fig. 7.8] this is transformed by the division of the farm into 14 square or rectangular crofts, giving each crofting tenant a discrete and permanent plot of land on which he had to build a new house.

The extent of the arable land before 1845 is identical in Figs. 7.7 and 7.8, but in Fig. 7.9 (Ormiscaig in 1875), much land has been reclaimed and two crofts, numbers 15 and 16, have been added to the township from the moorland common grazing. By 1902 [Fig. 7.10], further land has been reclaimed.

Comparison of Figs. 7.7 and 7.10 with Fig. 7.11 demonstrates that the cultivated land in 1981 is less than the land cultivated immediately before the creation of the crofts in 1845 and the arable area in 1902.

Figs. 7.7, 7.8 from the *Atlas of the Townships of Gairloch*, 1847; Fig. 7.9 from *O.S. 1:2500 Ross-shire XIX. 10*, 1875; Fig. 7.10 from *O.S. 1:10560 Ross & Cromarty XIX Revised*, 1902.

In a note of dissent to the 1893 Report, however, one of the commissioners, Sir Kenneth S. Mackenzie of Gairloch, had advanced the view that 'as speedily as proper considerations for the crofters will permit, encouragement should be given to the gradual replacement of the crofting system by one of small farms . . . and, with these, a few labourers' crofts of just sufficient size to provide the occupants with milk and potatoes' (Mackenzie [1892] 1893. Appendix 115-6).

Although certainly not exactly what Sir Kenneth desired to encourage, a type of small farm has, in fact, evolved in Gairloch (as in most other crofting communities), made up of effective units comprising scattered collections of crofts, tenanted and sublet from other tenants as depicted at Ormiscaig for 1981 [Fig. 7.11].

CONCLUSION

In retrospect, on an ancestral estate where relationships between the landowner and his people were different from those on most of the crofting estates with new Lowland or English proprietors, Sir Francis Mackenzie's recommendations for the improvement of the conditions of life of his small tenants and cottars seem so improbable as to be beyond achievement in the mid-19th century — even if most croft houses nowadays far exceed his recommendations. Dr. John Mackenzie's small allotments, replacing a very traditional pre-improvement agriculture by a system of spade cultivation and stall-fed cattle, also seem quite improbable. In 1856, Dr. Mackenzie resigned his Factorship and the crofters returned to their traditional agricultural ways, but much land had been and was to be reclaimed, the arable area increased and the standard of housing improved with rebuilding on the new crofts.

In the context of a rising population in Gairloch (a three and a half fold increase between 1801 and 1851), of heavy pressure on land which never produced the food supply required and an unwillingness on the part of the proprietors to promote emigration, what alternatives were available? The

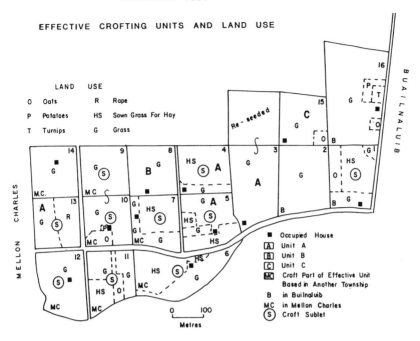

EFFECTIVE CROFTING UNITS AND LAND USE

Fig. 7.11 Ormiscaig, Gairloch Parish, 1981: Effective Units and Land Use.

This illustration shows both land units and land use in 1981. The 16 crofts were held by 15 tenants but only 6 crofts were worked by residents in the township of Ormiscaig — in one unit of four crofts and two units of one croft. The remainder of the crofts were tenanted by, or sublet to, residents of the neighbouring townships of Mellon Charles and Buailnaluib.

The land use could not be said to be intensive with 6 of the 16 crofts used only for grazing. There were four small patches of oats and six plots of hay, two potato plots and one patch of turnips on the other crofts, with the balance in grazing. Only one crofter had reclaimed and reseeded an area approximately the same size as the average croft in Ormiscaig. This was taken from the moorland common grazing adjacent to his croft, and in so doing enlarged his croft and his agricultural unit. (Data collected by J. B. Caird and Second Year Geography Students, 1981).

few sheep farms might have been converted to crofting townships, but estate income would have declined for the farms were more highly rented than the crofts: and after 1870, when sheep became much less profitable, clearance of crofters to expand the deer forests in order to increase estate income from shooting lets would have been unthinkable on an ancestral estate. The smallness of the crofts reflected Dr. Mackenzie's beliefs, and in any case there was insufficient reclaimable land on the estate to create more substantial units for the very large population in the 1840s. Even had there been resources available to employ at least three agricultural instructors, it is doubtful whether they would have succeeded in making the crofters operate the agricultural system prescribed by Dr. John Mackenzie, the Factor.

In the 1990s, most of the Gairloch coastal croftland might seem an early candidate for withdrawal from agriculture in an era of agricultural over-production in Western Europe, and the coast is not the most economic place for afforestation. Homes for indigenous residents, incomers and second home owners are already possible and established on crofts and on other estate land. But the trend seems established for multiple, if not consolidated agricultural units to form small scale, part-time units or larger full-time units, a few of small farm size, and for much croft land to remain as sheep grazing.

Sir Kenneth Mackenzie's vision of small farms and small part-time crofts with another salaried or wage earning occupation, rather than the intensive spade-cultivated units envisaged by his father and uncle, is, in the last analysis, the more likely future not only in Gairloch but throughout the crofting area in the Highlands and Islands of Scotland.

LAND USE IN NORTH GAIRLOCH, 1981

	Registered crofts	Tenancies	Effective Units	Average No. of Breeding cows per effective unit	Av. No. of sheep per effective unit	Effective units with cultivation	Units with cattle and sheep	Units with sheep only	Units not sublet with no activity	Full-time crofter	Crofter with regular employment	Crofter with occasional employment	Non-crofting	Crofter over 65
SECOND COAST	11	5	3	0	179	2	0	3	1	0	1	0	2	3
FIRST COAST	8	1	1	3	15	1	1	0	0	0	1	0	0	0
SAND	16	11	9	1.6	33	6	4	2	1	0	2	0	3	6
LAIDE	20	16	7	2.4	34	7	3	2	2	1	4	0	1	2
UDRIGIL	3	3	2	4.0	30	2	2	0	0	0	0	0	0	0
ACHGARVE	8	6	4	1.5	38	1	2	2	1	1	2	0	0	1
NORTH UDRIGLE	2	1	1	1.0	60	1	1	0	0	2	0	0	0	0
MELLON UDRIGLE	10	7	1	2.0	50	1	1	0	0	0	0	0	1	2
OPINAN	2	1	1	0	25	1	0	1	0	0	1	0	0	0
SLAGGAN	4	1	0	0	0	0	0	0	0	0	0	0	0	0
BADFEARN	5	4	2	0	33	1	0	2	0	0	0	0	1	1
AULTBEA	10	9	4	0.5	31	2	1	3	3	1	1	0	1	1
TIGHNAFILINE	11	11	2	3	25	2	2	0	8	1	0	0	3	1
CULCONICH	3	3	0	0	0	0	0	0	3	0	0	0	0	0
BUAILNALUIB	13	10	4	1.4	23	4	1	3	0	0	1	1	0	3
ORMISCAIG	16	15	3	2.5	77	2	2	1	1	2	2	1	0	0
MELLON CHARLES	55	44	9	1.5	36	2	3	6	36	0	9	0	28	7
TOTAL	197	148	53	1.7	44	35	23	25	56	8	24	2	40	27

	POPULATION												
	0-4		5-14		15-44		45-64		65+		Total		Total
	M	F	M	F	M	F	M	F	M	F	M	F	
SECOND COAST	0	0	0	0	0	0	1	1	2	1	3	2	5
FIRST COAST	0	0	0	0	2	1	1	0	0	0	3	1	4
SAND	1	0	0	0	1	3	4	4	8	6	14	13	27
LAIDE	0	0	3	2	4	7	2	5	3	2	12	16	28
UDRIGIL	0	0	0	0	0	0	0	0	0	0	0	0	0
ACHGARVE	1	2	1	0	2	3	2	3	2	1	8	9	17
NORTH UDRIGLE	0	0	0	0	1	1	0	2	0	0	1	3	4
MELLON UDRIGLE	0	0	0	0	0	0	1	1	1	2	2	3	5
OPINAN	1	0	1	0	1	1	1	1	1	2	5	4	9
SLAGGAN	0	0	0	0	0	0	0	0	0	0	0	0	0
BADFEARN	0	0	0	0	1	0	0	0	2	1	3	1	4
AULTBEA	0	0	1	1	1	1	3	3	2	1	7	6	13
TIGHNAFILINE	0	0	4	3	7	8	4	6	2	4	17	21	38
CULCONICH	0	0	0	0	0	0	0	0	0	0	0	0	0
BUAILNALUIB	1	0	0	0	1	2	0	2	3	1	5	5	10
ORMISCAIG	0	2	3	0	2	2	5	3	4	3	14	10	24
MELLON CHARLES	3	3	7	10	18	25	13	11	9	11	50	60	110
TOTAL	7	7	20	16	41	54	37	42	39	35	144	154	298

Fig. 7.12 Land Use statistics for North Gairloch. (Data collected by J. B. Caird and Second Year Geography Students, 1981).

Registered Crofts: Crofts are smallholdings entered in the Crofters Commission Register.

Tenancies: A tenant may have more than one croft.

Effective Units: May comprise one or several crofts tenanted by the same crofter, plus one or more crofts tenanted by the tenant's wife and one or more sublet crofts leased or informally granted by another tenant, which are worked together as one unit which has hay, potato or cereal crops and/or livestock. Units not sublet, but with no agricultural activity, are not effective units. All except one of the remaining crofts at Ormiscaig which are not parts of effective units based in Ormiscaig, are tenanted by or sublet to tenants in neighbouring crofting townships.

Acknowledgement

Grateful acknowledgement is made to the late Brigadier William Mackenzie of Gairloch and to Mr and Mrs John Mackenzie of Gairloch for their kindness in making the estate archive available for study; to Mrs Christina Byam Shaw for discussion of the contribution of Dr John Mackenzie prior to the publication of her excellent biography *Pigeon Holes of Memory: The Life and Times of Dr John Mackenzie (1803-1886)*, London, Constable, 1988; to Mr Donald Chisholm, Ormiscaig, Dr Malcolm Bangor-Jones, Mr D. R. Macdonald and Mr Roy Wentworth, Gairloch Museum. Grateful acknowledgement is also made to Mr James Ford for drawing the maps and to Mrs Pat Michie for producing the manuscript.

References

Byam Shaw, C. (ed.) *Pigeon Holes of Memory: The Life and Times of Dr. John Mackenzie, 1803-1886.* 1988.

Caird, J. B. The Making of the Crofting Landscape, in *Journal Scot. Ass. Geog. Teachers.* 1979. Vol 8.

Caird, J. B. The Creation of Crofts and New Settlement Patterns in the Highlands and Islands of Scotland, in *Scot. Geograph. Mag.* 1987. vol 103.

Cameron J. *Book of Reference to the Plan of the Parish of Gairloch* (Ordnance Survey of Scotland). 1876.

Campbell Smith, G. *Atlas of the Townships of Gairloch.* 1848. (Gairloch and Conon Archives).

Census: Census of Scotland: Ennumerator's Books, Gairloch Parish (Office of the Registrar General for Scotland, Edinburgh). 1841.

Cregeen, E. R. (ed.) *The Argyll Estate Instructions (Mull, Morvern and Tiree)* 1771-1805. Scottish History Society, 4th Series. 1964. vol. 1.

Dixon, J. H. *Gairloch and Guide to Loch Maree.* [1886] 1974.

[Drainage Act:] State of Sums Expended under the Drainage Act in Works of Drainage, Trenching etc upon the Estates of Gairloch and Conon, with the Interest payable thereon. M.S. list. 1850. (Gairloch and Conon Archives).

Inverness Courier Index: 30 October 1844; 19 September 1850.

McIntosh, D. Parish of Gairloch, in *OSA*, 1792. III.

Mackenzie, F. A. *Hints for the Use of Highland Tenants and Cottagers: by a Proprietor.* Inverness. 1838.

Mackenzie, J. *The Improvement of Highland Crofts.* 1842.

Mackenzie, K. S. *Statement for the Proprietor of Gairloch for the Crofters Commission.* 1885. (Gairloch and Conon Archives).

Mackenzie, K. S. Memorandum, in *Appendices to Report of the Royal Commission, Highlands and Islands of Scotland, 1892.* 1893.

Mackenzie, O. H. *A Hundred Years in the Highlands.* [1921] 1950.

Northern Chronicle: Fair Rents on Sir Kenneth Mackenzie's Property. 13 June 1888.

[Petition:] Petition Dame Mary Hanbury or Mackenzie etc. for Authority to Grant Leases, in Court of Session, Second Division, 25 June 1844. (CS/235/M/64/8).

[Rental 1843:] Rental of the Estate of Gairloch and Conon, for Crop and year Eighteen Hundred and Forth-Three, Testament Dative and Inventory, Sir Francis Alexander Mackenzie, inc. *Appendix 2,* registered 20 March 1844, Dingwall. Commissary Record. (*SRO* SC 25/44.4).

[Rental 1845-52:] Rental of the Estate of Gairloch, 15 November 1845 to 24 May 1853. (Gairloch and Conon Archive).

[Report:] Report to the Tutors by G. Campbell Smith, Land Surveyor, Banff, in *Appendix* to Court of Session, Second Division, 25 June 1844. (CS/235/M/64/8).

[Royal Comm.]: Evidence taken by Her Majesty's Commissioners of Enquiry into the Condition of Crofters and Cottars in the Highlands and Islands of Scotland. 1884. (C 3980-II).

[Royal Comm. Report:] Report of the Royal Commission, Highlands and Islands of Scotland, 1892. 1893.

Russell, J. Parish of Gairloch, in *NSA.* 1836.

Sutherland Papers: MacIver, Evander to Duke of Sutherland, 15 November 1850. (*NLS* Dep 313/1392).

BUILDING TRADITIONS
IN LOCHBROOM
AND GAIRLOCH PARISHES

Elizabeth Beaton

LANDSCAPE AND BUILDINGS

Similar to other west coast parishes, Lochbroom and Gairloch both embrace substantial geographical areas, sprawling the length of a serrated coastline indented with deep bays and over mountainous terrain carved by steep valleys and lochs. Townships developed and grew to fringe the coastline where there are pockets of fertile soil [Fig. 8.1]. 'Laird's houses', mostly built by various members of the Mackenzie family (see Bangor-Jones, this volume), occupy green tongues of land on favoured sites by the shore or in sheltered valleys, and there are a few 'improved' farms where there is land enough for spaciously enclosed fields. The other side of the agricultural coin is the crofting township squeezed between shore and the higher ground, the latter once entirely devoted to communal grazing. Besides its obvious value for subsistence and commercial fishing, the sea was the main artery of communication until this century, boats plying across the sea lochs or along the coast.

Traditionally the parish churches were near the coast, people travelling by boat to kirk for worship or to the burial ground with their dead.

Ullapool differs from other villages and townships in the area as it was a deliberately 'planned' town, though there was already a small settlement on the site chosen by the British Fisheries Society in 1788 for their fishing village (see J. Munro, this volume).

ECCLESIASTICAL BUILDINGS

Burial grounds frequently mark original medieval chapel sites. At Laide, on the south shore of Gruinard Bay, there is a simple roofless rubble chapel in the centre of the small graveyard [Fig. 8.2], whilst at Gairloch the earlier parish Church of Scotland was on the seaward side of its 18th century successor, fragments of the former church standing in the walled burial ground near the beach. In the two parishes, only Lochbroom parish church still occupies the original site, at Clachan at the head of Loch Broom. For in both parishes, these ecclesiastical centres proved inconveniently far from expanding settlements and both parishes have later 'Parliamentary' churches at Poolewe and Ullapool where independent *quoad sacra* parishes, each served by their own minister, were 'erected' in 1838 and 1833 respectively.

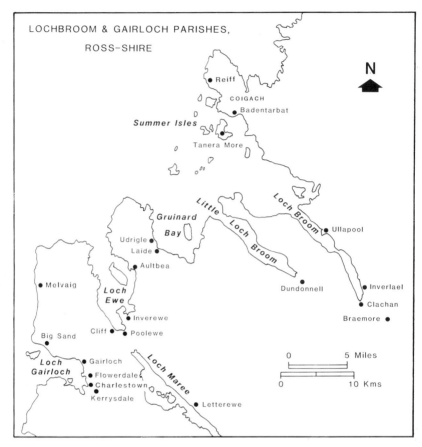

Fig. 8.1   Location map for buildings discussed. Most settlement in Gairloch and Lochbroom parishes is limited to relatively small patches of cultivable ground along the coast.

The subsequent Disruption of 1843 tore the established church apart, the newly founded Free Church of Scotland building independent places of worship locally as throughout Scotland.

Lochbroom parish church at Clachan is remarkable in that it is almost unaltered since it was build in 1817 (bellcote 1878). The austere, rectangular stone church is of two storeys, the clear sash windows revealing galleried construction. 'The purposeful simplicity of the interior is impressive' with pulpit against the end wall, a rectangular gallery and the central floor space occupied by two long parallel communion tables enclosed by a double box pew. 'Here is no preaching house, for the sacramental character of the building is unmistakable' (Hay 1957; see also R. W. Munro, this volume) [Figs. 8.3-8.5].

The little Gairloch parish church is earlier, built in 1792 but re-cast internally and given a large gable window in 1909, the alterations by A.

Fig. 8.2   The old medieval chapel at Laide, on the southern shore of Gruinard Bay. 1989.

Maitland and Sons of Tain effectively removing much of its original character [Fig. 8.6].

The large size and scattered populaton of both parishes made them candidates for the provision of 'Parliamentary churches' under the 1823 *Act for building additional Places of Worship in the Highlands and Islands of Scotland.* This made available the sum of £50,000 with which to construct church and manse at forty different sites, the buildings to cost no more than £1,500 together. Thomas Telford, with the assistance of James Smith and John Mitchell, drew up plans for church [Fig. 8.7] and manse, the latter of optional single and two storey designs.

The church in Argyll Street, Ullapool (1829, no longer in ecclesiastical use and now home to the Ullapool Museum), and that at Poolewe (1828), are both relatively unaltered examples of Parliamentary churches (and there were two others in Wester Ross — Plockton in Lochalsh and Shieldaig, Applecross — both 1827: see R. W. Munro, this volume) [Figs. 8.8-8.10]. These T-plan buildings have simple south elevations lit by two central shallow-arched windows with similarly shaped outer doorways closed by double-leaf doors, panelled at Poolewe. Both buildings have original lattice-pane glazing in the windows lighting the gables and rear wing besides the frontage, the cast-iron window frames brought from an Aberdeen foundry by sea: both have characteristic apex bellcotes decorated with stumpy pinnacles. No manse was provided at Ullapool, for the British Fisheries Society shouldered that responsibility (now Ornsay House in West Shore Street). The manse at Poolewe (The Old Manse) was of the single storey,

Fig. 8.3 Lochbroom Parish Church, Clachan, 1817. The church was renovated in 1835 and the bellcote added in 1878. Drawing by John Hume.

Fig. 8.4 The interior of Lochbroom Parish Church has simple galleries around three sides. Unusual and rare is the double row of parallel box pews and communion tables running down the centre from the demi-octagonal pulpit. Drawing by John Hume.

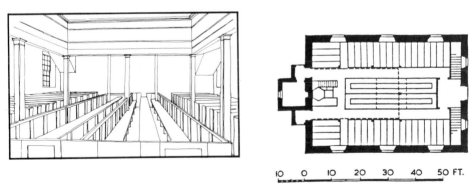

Fig. 8.5 Ground plan of Lochbroom Parish Church, showing the layout of box pews, communion tables, pulpit, precentor's desk and stairs to the galleries. From George Hay, *Architecture of Scottish Post-Reformation Churches, 1560-1843* (1957, 131-2). 'The purposeful simplicity of the interior is impressive . . . Here is no mere preaching house, for the sacramental character of the building is unmistakeable'.

162

Fig. 8.6 Gairloch Church of Scotland, built 1792, with alterations in 1909. 1989.

Fig. 8.7 Iona ca. 1830 — a typical Parliamentary Kirk. The same design was used for all, though some had a north aisle which produced the classic Scottish T-plan. On the ground plan, note the long communion table and (on the long wall, between the doors) the pulpit and precentor's desk flanked by the elders' pew and the manse pew. The elevation shows the distinctive bird-cage belfrey capped with a pyramidal finial. The windows had cast-iron mullions and transoms, and small lozenge-shaped panes. From Hay 1957. *ibid.*

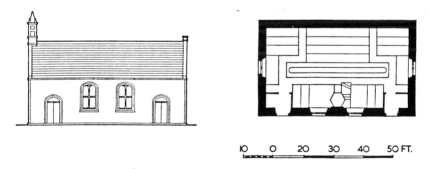

shallow U-plan model, but subsequent heightening to two storeys masks the original design [Fig. 8.11].

The congregations of all these 'Auld Kirk' churches were decimated by the break-away movement of the Disruption in 1843, the majority following the minister if he, too, 'came out' in support of the Free Church. Services were initially held in the open air — as illustrated by a fine collection of

Fig. 8.8 Telford 'Parliamentary Church', Poolewe, Gairloch Parish, 1828. 1989.

Fig. 8.9 Telford 'Parliamentary Church', Ullapool, Lochbroom Parish, 1829. 1992.

Fig. 8.10   Telford 'Parliamentary Church', Plockton, Lochalsh Parish, 1827. 1972.

Fig. 8.11   The Telford Manse, Poolewe, 1968. In May of that year the General Assembly of the Church of Scotland approved sale of this manse. The original roof-line is clearly visible across the main section of the house.

165

Fig. 8.12 Gairloch Free Church, 1878, overlooks Gairloch Bay. 1989.

Fig. 8.13 Aultbea Free Church, 1871-75. 1989.

Fig. 8.14   Church of Scotland, Mill Street, Ullapool, 1844. Formerly the Free Church of Scotland. 1992.

Fig. 8.15   The Free Church of Scotland Manse, Ullapool, ca. 1844, serves nowadays as the Church of Scotland Manse for both Ullapool and Clachan. 1992.

photographs in the Gairloch Museum — but when funds permitted, new places of worship were constructed. The pinnacled Gothic Free Church at Gairloch enjoys a fine open site by the shore overlooking Gairloch Bay (architects, Matthews & Laurie, 1878), while its somewhat stark Gothic counterpart at Aultbea (1871-5) has an equally dominant position [Figs. 8.12, 8.13]. The former Free Church and Free Church manse at Ullapool both now serve the Church of Scotland. The church in Mill Street was erected in 1844, probably to a design by William Henderson; it has a plain south elevation lit by five long round-headed windows and various later alterations. The manse is of about the same date, a wide gabled three-window fronted house with recessed centre entrance bay [Figs. 8.14, 8.15].

LAIRD'S HOUSES

Flowerdale by Gairloch (1738), and Udrigle near Laide (1745), are both important 'Laird's houses' in a Highland as well as a local context. Flowerdale stands in a sheltered valley, the site of a former moated house, the 'An Tigh Dige' of Osgood Mackenzie [Figs. 8.16-8.18]. The large two-storey crowstepped and M-gabled house is similar to the ruinous Eddercalda or Calda House on the shore of Loch Assynt, Sutherland (ca.1727) [Fig. 8.19] — the first symmetrical mansion of its kind in the North-West Highlands. Here the double pile, M-gabled house was probably influenced in design by the military barrack blocks at Bernera, Glenelg (1717-23) .

Flowerdale was built by Alexander Mackenzie of Gairloch and his wife Janet Mackenzie of Scatwell in 1738, the date incised on the east gable skewputts, and it still belongs to the same family. The principal entrance is in the raised ground floor, approached by a flight of steps. The keystoned doorway is dignified with moulded, lugged jambs and flanked by segmental-headed windows. A central crowstepped gablet, flanked by swept dormers, rises above the wallhead and the chimney stacks are enriched with string courses and moulded copes. In 1904 the mansion was doubled in size by extending it westwards to a reasonably sympathetic design by A. Maitland and Sons, Tain.

A slightly less prosperous Mackenzie of Gruinard, though equally fastidious regarding his home, built Udrigle House in 1745, on the shores of Gruinard Bay [Figs. 8.20, 8.21]. Externally the small gaunt crowstepped two-storey, three-window house appears unpretentious. The stark rubble frontage has off-set centre first floor windows to light the half-landings of the staircase while the main entrance is at the rear, sheltered by a gabled porch dated 1756. This unusual design is also found in the larger Applecross House, where the staircase is also set against the south wall, and is peculiar to this area of the west coast. At Udrigle the staircase is adorned with fine silhouette balusters: it leads to two panelled first floor rooms. The panelling in both rooms is raised and fielded with rare (in the Highlands) ogee detailing, the door frames are moulded and lugged, while the chimney-piece has a marriage stone inscribed '17 W MK I MK 45' together with a

Fig. 8.16 Flowerdale before 1904, from a painting by Finlay MacKinnon published in Osgood Mackenzie's *A Hundred Years in the Highlands*. 1921.

Fig. 8.17   Flowerdale, Gairloch. 1738 house at right, 1904 addition to left. 1989.

Fig. 8.18   Flowerdale, Gairloch. Crowstepped M-gable, 1738. 1989.

Fig. 8.19   Calda or Eddercalda House stands close to Ardvreck Castle (far left) at the upper
end of Loch Assynt. It was a MacKenzie house, superceding the MacLeod castle. Both are
long ruinous. 1992.

heart. The survival of these fine internal fittings is remarkable. The Mackenzies of Gruinard and Udrigle were a large and complex family in the
mid 18th century; the name William re-occurs and must account for the W
on the datestone.

Dundonnell House [Fig. 8.22] is another small Mackenzie mansion, the
Mackenzie of that name settling in the glen ca.1700. It was probably soon
after they arrived that the graceful small two-arched hump-back masonry
bridge spanning the Dundonnell River was constructed, while it may be
their old home that is incorporated at the rear of the present mansion. The
plain but dignified house, dated 1767, is approached through a tree-lined
lane; the regular five-window front was heightened, probably in 1816, to
accommodate dormers. Dundonnell stands in a wooded valley, whose
sylvan beauty and sheltered fields were largely the work of Kenneth
Mackenzie (1801-32). Mackenzie built and stocked the walled garden,
planted his policies with 'millions of firs and hard-wood trees' and
improved his land with great energy and taste during his short life, putting
so much into the estate that it was sold after his untimely death to clear his
debts.

Inverlael Farmhouse, near the head of Loch Broom, is also a plain two-
storey, five-window house [Fig. 8.23]. This was probably the former
spinning school and 'manufactory' established by the Trustees of the
Annexed Estates ca.1750 in an attempt to introduce skills, industry and
education to the Highlands (two other such schools were established, one in
Lochcarron and one at Invermoriston on Loch Ness). At Poolewe, Sròndubh

Fig. 8.20   Udrigle, 1745. South front: note off-set centre windows lighting half landings. 1955.

Fig. 8.21   Udrigle, rear elevation (north): gabled porch dated 1756 shelters main entrance. 1989.

Fig. 8.22 Dundonnell, 1767. Later attic storey. The house stands amidst trees planted in the early 19th century. 1962.

Fig. 8.23 Inverlael Farmhouse near the head of Loch Broom was probably the 'spinning school' and 'manufactory' established ca. 1750. 1989.

Fig. 8.24 Sròndubh House, Poolewe — mid 18th century. 1989.

Fig. 8.25 Kerrysdale, ca. 1800. House at left and cruck-framed barn set back at right. 1989.

dates from the mid 18th century in its present form but is said to incorporate an earlier dwelling [Fig. 8.24]. The long, low house has a regular frontage with single windows flanking the centre doorway but a five-window arrangement in the first floor.

SMALL HOUSES AND COTTAGES

The better farmhouse of ca. 1800 is merely a simpler version of the more prestigious symmetrical 'laird's house'. At Kerrysdale, near Gairloch (ca. 1800) [Fig. 8.25] and Cliff, Poolewe (ca. 1760), there are plain two-storey houses with regular three-window fronts. These are similar to some of the earlier dwellings in Ullapool, indeed throughout the Highlands as elsewhere in Scotland. The design is so simple that it can be expanded or contracted in size according to the resources of the owner. The early 19th century Old Bank House, Argyll Street, Ullapool, graced with a small wooden portico, is a good example [Fig. 8.26], though there are plainer versions elsewhere in the town, lining the streets laid out in grid pattern. Many of the simple original features of traditional 19th century Ullapool housing have largely been masked, particularly in Shore Street, by modern shop facias, widened windows and contemporary glazing [Fig. 8.27].

The later 19th century one and a half-storey house, with gabled dormers breaking the wallhead, appears throughout the area and has established its own tradition on the west coast as in other parts of Scotland. These are more substantial dwellings than cottages and, unlike the smaller cottage, provide accommodation satisfying late 20th century standards. Again, unsuitable replacement of the well-proportioned 2- and 4-pane sash and case windows detracts from their seemly appearance [Figs. 8.28, 8.29].

The plain single-storey cottage, with a door in the centre of the main front flanked by small windows, abounds in crofts and settlements throughout Wester Ross (and elsewhere), besides the streets of Ullapool. Most were thatched when first built though later examples may have been originally roofed with slate. Around Applecross, Gairloch and Loch Broom, thatching seems to have been mainly with rushes or straw. A little further south in Wester Ross, around Lochalsh, there appears to have been a greater use of heather [Figs. 8.30-8.33]. Some of these rubble cottages replaced earlier dwellings of cruder construction, of wicker frame clad with turf (creel houses) or walled with layered turf sometimes alternated with stones. There is continuous change in building materials and housing fashions, and the ubiquitous bungalow with concrete tiled roof has in turn replaced many a stone-built cottage. Alternatively, the cottage itself has been altered out of all recognition by such features as enlargement of windows, flat-roofed extensions and box dormers, generally to provide bathrooms, modern kitchens and (more) upstairs accommodation.

The small, unaltered thatched cottage at 27 Big Sand, on the north shore of Loch Gairloch, is therefore a rarity. Lived in until June 1981, it survives in its original form. The walls are of rubble with roughly-squared corner

Fig. 8.26 The Old Bank House, Ullapool, early 19th century. Its symmetrical frontage and slender columned portico emphasise its importance. Probably Ullapool's first bank. 1992.

Fig. 8.27 Shore Street, Ullapool, 1992. The original 19th century architecture has undergone considerable modification. Arcaded ground floor openings and enlarged shop windows were inserted mainly in the 1970s and 1980s.

Fig. 8.28 West end of West Shore Street, Ullapool, 1992. A mixture of one and a half-storey houses, mainly modernised, together with single storey houses, most with later added dormers and modern windows.

Fig. 8.29 Strathkanaird, Coigach; late 19th-century 1½ storey house with modern glazing. 1989.

Fig. 8.30 'A Highland Clachan' beside Loch Duich — a remarkable cluster of hipped heather-thatched houses and out-buildings. Beyond stands an improved house with gable-end chimneys. George Washington Wilson, late 19th century.

Fig. 8.31 Heather-thatched house near Dornie, Lochalsh. Internal chimney from the main room; the hipped end has been adapted to accommodate a modified gable chimney. 1962.

Fig. 8.32 Traditional thatched cottage with framework of thatched 'lum' (chimney) at left gable. 1989. This cottage, at 27 Big Sand, Gairloch, has now been re-thatched.

Fig. 8.33 Re-thatched cottage at 11 Melvaig, Gairloch, retaining chimney vents associated with former 'hinging lums'. 1990.

stones, and the off-centre door is flanked by a diminutive light at left and enlarged window at right. There is a masonry chimney stack at the east gable but the west still has its 'thatched lum', a small round vent through which the smoke seeped out, usually entrapped above the hearth by a canopy, or 'hinging lum', leading directly to the chimney and forming part of it. A small byre with corrugated-iron roof has been added continuously with the west gable. The dating of such a traditional dwelling presents difficulties but it is almost certainly of 19th century date, constructed when Big Sand was lotted as crofts or soon after. 27 Big Sand, together with a similar cottage at 11 Melvaig, further north, have both recently been re-thatched [Figs. 8.32, 8.33].

AGRICULTURAL CHANGES: BARNS & STEADINGS

Long, low rubble byres and barns, with corrugated-iron roofs replacing the original thatch, are still found throughout the crofting settlements — even where crofting has ceased these buildings form useful stores, so their life is prolonged. It is on the larger estates, however, that the 19th century agricultural changes have left the greatest mark, evident today in the landscape and buildings sited in the sheltered straths.

The improvements undertaken at Dundonnell in the 1820s and 1830s have already been mentioned. Besides his massive tree planting programme, Kenneth Mackenzie 'built a fine square of offices . . . [and] hundreds of yards of stone dykes'. Such improvements are also obvious in Strath More, the valley of the River Broom between Clachan and Braemore. Here the principal changes were effected by Sir John Fowler of Braemore (1817-88), a civil engineer. It was he who was responsible for the later 19th century improved farmhouses and steadings, together with many of the neat dry stone dykes that enclose the fields in this sheltered valley and much of the tree planting on the upper slopes. Sir John was Engineer-in-Chief to the Forth railway bridge; his memorial in Lochbroom Parish church at Clachan records that he had 'three light bridges' constructed over the River Broom. One of these is the fine pedestrian suspension bridge spanning the Corrie-shalloch Gorge and another the graceful and rare wrought-iron lenticular truss bridge with circular masonry piers near Auchindrean. The wooden deck was suspended from the convex truss by lattice girders and linked to the stone piers [Fig. 8.34].

Barns

The wet climate of Gairloch gave rise to a need for ventilated barns in which to store, and even to dry, hay and unthreshed corn. These 18th and 19th century barns are cruck-framed, the heavy timber cruck trusses or 'highland couples' forming a kind of 'A-frame' to carry the weight of the heavy heather-thatched roof as the louvred or wattle-panelled walls providing the ventilation are virtually non load-bearing. Heather thatch had

Fig. 8.34 Auchindrean Bridge, designed ca. 1870 by Sir John Fowler of Braemore: rare lenticular (fish eye) truss bridge with masonry end piers. 1989.

Fig. 8.35 Kerrysdale: interior of cruck-framed barn. Cruck blades have been sawn off above tie-beams to accommodate shallower pitch of replacement corrugated-iron roof. 1981.

Fig. 8.36   Heather-thatched barn at Mains Farm, Applecross. ca. 1976.

Fig. 8.37   Wattled ventilation panel in east wall of heather-thatched barn. Mains Farm, Applecross, ca. 1976.

a long life; even so the surviving barns of this type now have corrugated-iron or other roofing, the cruck blades usually truncated to accommodate a different pitch. Where available timber was not long enough to provide the height necessary for both the bulk of stored material and the up-stretched arm of the flailer, couples were jointed or 'scarfed' at the curved elbow at wallhead height, the two pieces of timber tenoned and fixed with wooden pegs or 'treenails'. In the parish of Gairloch, where there was a reasonable supply of local timber of quality and sufficient length, few examples of scarfing have been identified: the practice was usual, however, in other southward parishes where these barns are a feature of local vernacular building. The barns are always provided with opposing winnowing doors, usually placed in the centre of the building with the threshing floor between. There is a cruck-framed barn to the rear of Kerrysdale with five of the six pairs of cruck trusses surviving [Fig. 8.35]. At Letterewe, on the north shores of Loch Maree, two such barns are incorporated in the steading range, one now converted as a cottage.

The distribution pattern of ventilated cruck-framed barns spreads throughout Applecross, Lochcarron, Lochalsh, Kintail and Glenelg as well as Gairloch, which is on the northerly edge of the group. They are always associated with more prosperous holdings, the better farm or laird's estate, rather than at the subsistence level of crofting agriculture [Figs. 8.36, 8.37]. The corn and hay stored within was vital over-wintering feed for cattle intended for the southern fairs whence they were escorted in the summer by the drovers.

Just north of the church at Poolewe there is a 'bank-barn' built against the hillside, its two-storey elevation overlooking Loch Ewe. This mid 19th century rectangular building exploits the slope with access to byres accommodated in the ground floor of the east two-storey elevation while the upper barn is directly accessible from the west [Figs. 8.38, 8.39]. In front of and slightly to the left of the west doorway is a horse walk, a raised round platform formerly housing gearing to motivate thrashing machinery accommodated in the barn, the 'horse power' provided by horse or horses harnessed to sweeps and treading the circular track. This plain building of simple, composite design incorporates economy of space, for many agricultural functions are contained under one roof. This building is the only known example of its kind in the immediate area though a group of similar agricultural buildings has been identified further south in the Lochaber District, between Mallaig and Glencoe, and there are two or three known examples in Galloway.

Finally, possibly the earliest *dated* barn in the Highlands, perhaps in Scotland, is to be found at Flowerdale [Fig. 8.40]. It was erected by Alexander and Janet Mackenzie in 1730, the year of their marriage and eight years before they built their fine new house. The Mackenzies of Gairloch were also of Conon in Easter Ross and this barn is of east coast pattern, more suited to a dryer climate than the dampness of the west. It is possible that the slit vents in the ground floor, the usual provision in an east coast store, provided insufficient draught to ventilate the interior and that

183

Fig. 8.38 Bank barn, Poolewe — two storey front elevation. 1989.

Fig. 8.39 Bank barn, Poolewe — rear elevation, showing direct access from slope to upper floor and a horse-gang to the left of the (west) doorway. 1989.

Fig. 8.40   Flowerdale Barn, Gairloch, 1730. 1989.

Fig. 8.41   Flowerdale Barn:
Mackenzie coat-of-arms. 1989.

the large round-headed openings, probably originally slatted with wattling, were slapped at either end later. There is a central winnowing passage with a well-carved Mackenzie coat of arms commemorating Alexander and Janet Mackenzie of Gairloch, set in a panel above the door [Fig. 8.41]. Like Flowerdale house, this barn reflects the prosperity of a substantial Highland landowning family in the early 18th century, a period of both domestic and agricultural change and improvement possible in the more settled times immediately preceding the '45 rebellion.

BUILDINGS ASSOCIATED WITH THE FISHING INDUSTRY

While the ventilated barn features one aspect of the vernacular building in the parish of Gairloch, storehouses of a different type were required by the fishing industry. In Ullapool both the 'Captain's Cabin' and the building shared by Caledonian MacBrayne with the Tourist Information Centre, were stores both for fishing gear and for salt which was still subject to customs duty in 1788 when Ullapool was established [Figs. 8.42, 8.43]. Though early settlers in Ullapool were largely responsible for the construction of their own houses, buildings of a public nature such as these warehouses, church and pier, were the responsibility of the British Fisheries Society (see J. Munro, this volume). The warehouse, ca.1790, now known as 'The Captain's Cabin' is sited on the corner of Quay and Shore Streets, an imposing rectangular building of three-storey height, with regular fenestration and a forestair leading to a centre first floor entrance. The Caledonian-MacBrayne and Tourist Information Centre building is similar but was truncated ca. 1980 in the interests of road widening and ferry parking.

Fishing boats of many nations frequent Ullapool but few early buildings directly involved with the industry are evident today. Not so on Tanera Mor, the largest of the Summer Isles. Though roofless, the sizable two-storey rubble range fronted by a walled yard stands close by the shore [Fig. 8.44]. Besides storage and yard, the building incorporated a substantial house for the manager and other living accommodation. This herring fishing station was established in 1785 by a 'Mr. Roderick Morrison from Stornoway'. The crescent-shaped quay enclosing the little harbour was repaired in 1938 by Dr. (later Sir) Frank Fraser-Darling, the pioneer ecologist, when he farmed Tanera Mor, a project he recorded in his book *Island Farm*. Two hundred years after the development of Tanera Mor as a fishing station, salmon cages in the bay and modern bungalows for manager and staff reveal one aspect of on-going activity and change within the fishing industry.

The salmon fishing station at Badentarbat, near Achiltibuie on the Coigach peninsula is the centre for a seasonal commercial bag-net fishery for wild salmon. Illness prevented other than two men unsuccessfully working a sweep net in 1992 and 1993, but a new tenant re-set the bag-nets in 1994. Though most of the surviving buildings date from the 1850s onwards [Figs. 8.45-8.47], there may well have been a fishing station here from the early 1800s. The house was built ca. 1860-70, originally single storey with an

Fig. 8.42 Fishery storehouse, Ullapool, commissioned by the British Fisheries Society ca. 1790. Now known as 'The Captain's Cabin'. 1992.

Fig. 8.43 A similar fishery storehouse, now occupied by Caledonian-MacBrayne and the local Tourist Information Centre. 1992.

Fig. 8.44 Fishing Station 1785, Tanera Mór, Summer Isles. The old burial ground lies outside the dyke, above and a little left of the fish-farm manager's house. 1988.

attic pole store reached by an outside stair and a net store at one end. This building had a slated roof from the beginning. The present net store is said to incorporate an earlier icehouse, though the primary function was as a salt house, *tigh salainn*, earthed up on both sides. The salt was used for pickling the salmon (and herring). The present large vaulted icehouse (also converted for other uses) dates from the 1870s with its pitched roof added towards the end of the century. This semi-subterranean stone store was packed with ice collected from a man-made pond during cold weather, thrown in through a rear chute, and kept there until packed around the fish for transport to the urban markets, a pattern common to all late 18th/early 19th century salmon fishing stations. When the railway network was developed during the second half of the 19th century, the fish were taken by sea to Ullapool, onward by road to Garve and thence to Inverness and the south by rail. The ice pond at Badentarbat is identified by a shallow marshy lochan behind the fishing station, and by the remains of a sluice (W. Muir 1993).

Elsewhere, on the side of the road leading from Charleston to Flowerdale House, Gairloch, there is another small vaulted stone icehouse built into the slope for insulation against heat. This would have been associated with salmon fishing in Loch Gairloch.

CONCLUSION

The buildings discussed above are mainly of a traditional nature, their accommodation and design meeting the ecclesiastical, domestic, farming and fishing needs of the inhabitants of Lochbroom and Gairloch parishes over nearly three centuries.They were initiated, adapted or altered to accommodate changing work patterns, lifestyles and available construction materials throughout the period. Some of these building traditions are purely local, for example the M-gable, double-pile Flowerdale House and the cruck-framed barns. Other buildings, such as Lochbroom parish church at Clachan, have their counterparts elsewhere in the Highlands — austere edifices designed to accommodate presbyterian worship at the turn of the 1800s, at a time when many small ruinous churches were being superseded by larger buildings to accommodate larger congregations drawn from an expanding population. Where conscious ecclesiastical architecture is evident, this too is both regional and national; the regional style represented by the Telford 'Parliamentary' churches scattered in far distant Highland and Island settlements while the Gothic was common to much mid/later 19th century church design throughout Scotland.

The late 18th and 19th century fishing stations, both for herring and salmon, were built to exploit local stocks commercially. They were the centres where the industry became industrialised, the marine harvests packed, cured and exported to expanding urban markets at home, in Europe and salted herrings even to the West Indies sugar plantations! Herring stations similar to those on Loch Broom were developed in various coastal locations in the Highlands and Islands, either as private ventures or through

Fig. 8.45 Badentarbat Bay with salmon cobles, 1870s' ice house, Badentarbat Pier and Tanera Mór. 1972.

189

Fig. 8.46 The salmon-fisher's house, Badentarbat. In front is the bothy, and anchors for fixing the bag-nets in the sea. 1972.

Fig. 8.47 The net store formerly a salt store and ice house. To the left, nets are hoisted on the poles to dry. Further left is the marshy lochan once used as a source for ice. 1972.

the offices of the British Fisheries Society, though the fluctuations of the herring shoals dashed the high hopes of many of these undertakings. And commercial salmon stations similar to that at Badentarbat are common on the east coast of Scotland, particularly at the mouths of the rivers to which the fish return annually for spawning.

The greatest change, or series of changes, is in the cottages. Creel houses no longer exist, though the method of construction and use of materials survive in the cruck-framed barns. And abandoned, roofless, rubble cottages with a centre door flanked by very small windows are an-all-too-common sight. The associated small patches of land on which the former owners lived by subsistence farming have gone back to moorland or rushes, or have been incorporated into larger units. On the Coigach peninsula the last thatched cottage, at Reiff [Fig. 14.43], was abandoned in the early 1980s. It is thanks to grant-aid funding that two surviving examples have been restored near to Gairloch, and local traditional interior fittings and furnishings such as canopy chimneys and box beds can now be seen only in the Gairloch Museum.

The various national changes in ecclesiastical organisation and worship, the links with the many branches of the Mackenzie family both in Easter and Wester Ross, local settlement patterns and the development of both agriculture and fishing are reflected and still evident in the buildings of Lochbroom and Gairloch parishes.

Acknowledgement

This article is a reconstruction of an illustrated talk, rather than a formal paper, given at the Scottish Society for Northern Studies' Ullapool Conference, 1988. Notes prepared for that conference by Dr. Malcolm Bangor-Jones have provided a rich source of information and I am grateful to him for these and subsequent stimulating discussions about Highland buildings and their history. I am also grateful to Dr. E. Peters for drawing my attention to the bank-barn at Poolewe and to John Baldwin for information about Coigach.

I am grateful to the following for permission to reproduce illustrations: Royal Commission on the Ancient and Historical Monuments of Scotland (Figs. 8.9, 8.10, 8.14, 8.15, 8.20, 8.22, 8.26, 8.27, 8.28, 8.30, 8.31, 8.36, 8.42, 8.43); Scottish Ethnological Archive for photographs taken by John Baldwin (Figs. 8.45, 8.46, 8.47); Highland Regional Council (Fig. 8.33); Historic Scotland (Figs. 8.35, 8.44); R. W. Munro (Fig 8.11). All other photographs were taken by the author. Fig. 8.1 was drawn by James Ford; Figs. 8.3, 8.4 by John Hume; Figs. 8.5, 8.7 by Geoffrey Hay.

References

The buildings under discussion fall into mixed architectural, social, ecclesiastical and industrial contexts, and because of their varied nature a bibliography is of greater use than a profusion of detailed references. The following publications are relevant to these buildings and their background:

Allen, N. G. Walling materials in the Eighteenth Century Highlands, in *Vernacular Building.* 1979. vol. 5. 1-7.

Beaton, E. *Ross and Cromarty: An Illustrated Architectural Guide.* 1992.

Brunskill, R. W. *Traditional Farm Buildings of Britain.* 1982.

Close-Brooks, J. *Exploring Scotland's Heritage: The Highlands.* 1986.

Dixon, J. H. *Gairloch.* 1886.

Dunlop, J. *The British Fisheries Society 1786-1893*. 1978.

Ewing, W. *Annals of the Free Church*. 1914. vol. ii.

Fenton, A. & Walker, B. *The Rural Architecture of Scotland*. 1981.

Fraser-Darling, F. *Island Farm*. 1943.

Groome's *Ordnance Gazetteer of Scotland*. 1882-85.

Hackett, S. & Livingstone, N. Scottish Parliamentary Churches and their Manses, in D. Breeze (ed.) *Studies in Scottish Antiquity*. 1984. 302-36.

Hay, G. *The Architecture of Scottish Post-Reformation Churches. 1560-1843*. 1957.

Historic Buildings and Monuments (SDD). *Lists of of Buildings of Special Architectural or Historic Interest*. Ross and Cromarty District. 1983.

Hume, J. R. *The Industrial Archaeology of Scotland*. 1977.

Mackenzie, O. *A Hundred Years in the Highlands*. 1921.

Maclean, A. *Telford's Highland Churches*. 1989.

New Statistical Account. Gairloch Parish. 1836; Lochbroom Parish. 1835.

Old Statistical Account. Gairloch Parish. 1790; Lochbroom Parish. 1792-8.

Omand, D. (ed.) *The Ross and Cromarty Book*. 1984.

Scottish Vernacular Buildings Working Group. *Highland Vernacular Building*. 1989.

Smith, A. *Jacobite Estates of the Forty-Five*. 1982.

THE MACLEODS OF LEWIS . . .
AND OF ASSYNT,
COIGACH AND GAIRLOCH

Aubrey Halford-Macleod

In this paper I wish to examine in some detail the interdependence of the MacLeod families on both sides of the Great Minch [Fig. 9.1]. It is important to bear in mind that the sea, certainly during the centuries we shall be considering, was not a barrier, but an essential means of communication. The Outer Isles and the north-west mainland are linked geologically, geographically, archaeologically, socially and politically. They were part of the great Norse empire for some 500 years.

The MacLeods play only a part, albeit an important part, in the history of the region. I shall look first at the origins of the Lewis MacLeods and try to trace the course of their expansion until the extinction of the chiefly line in the early 17th century. Then I shall consider the subsequent fortunes of some of the cadet branches on the mainland. Finally I wish to offer some comment on Lewis MacLeods today.

MACLEODS OF LEWIS AND MACLEODS OF HARRIS

The first point concerns the relationship between the MacLeods of Lewis and the MacLeods of Harris and Dunvegan. The earliest genealogy we have was compiled by Sir George MacKenzie, first earl of Cromartie, in the second half of the 17th century. He was the grandson of Sir Roderick MacKenzie, the tutor of Kintail, who married Margaret, daughter of Torquil Cononach, reputed son of Old Ruari MacLeod, last legal baron of Lewis. This genealogy, preserved in Fraser's *Earls of Cromartie* (Fraser 1876. II. 510-11) is obviously defective. It asserts the seniority of the Siol Torcaill over the Siol Tormoid, a claim always made by the MacLeods of Raasay, descended from Malcolm IX Chief of Lewis, and by the Cromartie family itself. In his letter to Dr Johnson of 10 April 1775, John MacLeod of Raasay says that his ancestors 'disputed the pre-eminence for a long tract of time' (Johnson & Boswell 1924. 438-9). The Rev. John MacLeod, the Church of Scotland minister of the parish of Harris, writes (1791-92. XX. 69):

Among the first of the Danish invaders came that tribe, or clan, of which one branch has for several centuries held the property of Harris. The chief of this branch, who has variously been designed MacLeod of MacLeod, MacLeod of that ilk, and MacLeod of Harris, derives his pedigree from Magnus King of Norway, and latterly from the petty kings of Man. Two brothers Lodius, or Leod, and Turkill, or Torkill, the progenitors of two branches, who, to this

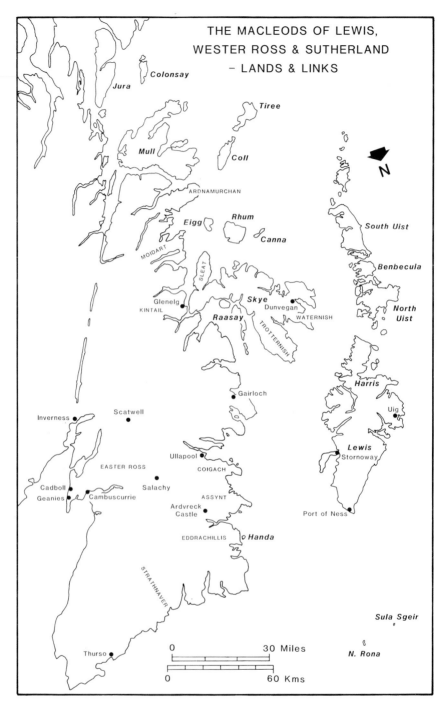

Fig. 9.1   The north-west seaboard and the Hebrides showing lands north from central Skye and Harris associated with the MacLeods. In a world where travel, trade and political power were dominated by the sea there was a natural interdependence between lands and families fringing the North Minch. The Lewis MacLeods took over this role for Assynt-Coigach/Lewis from the Nicolsons; and were later supplanted by the MacKenzies. The seaways between northern Skye and Harris were secured by the Skye/Harris MacLeods.

day, idly contend for the nominal honour of the chieftainship, seized upon the island of Lewis, or, as it was originally written, and as it should still be written according to the orthography of the Gaelic language, Leodhus, so denominated as the habitation of Leod.

The chiefly line of Lewis had died out nearly two centuries before he wrote; it is interesting that the question of seniority was still alive in his day. Some forty years later Gregory ([1881] 1975. 72) writes:

Although descended, according to tradition, from one common progenitor Leod (whence their collective appellation of ClanLeod), the Siol Torquil and Siol Tormod were, in fact, two powerful clans, perfectly distinct and independent of each other. We commence with the Siol Torquil, as having been connected with the Lords of the Isles for a greater length of time than the other branch of the ClanLeod.

For what it is worth, Gregory also points out that the armorial bearings of the two clans are different. Even today some people in Lewis would claim that the MacLeods never had anything to do with the Harris folk.

Harris tradition has always conferred a measure of exclusiveness on the clan names Leod, Tormod and Torquil. This is hardly justified. The Old Norse name *Ljótr* (ugly) appears in early Hebridean records and became Gaelicised as Leod. The famous Viking Sveinn Asleifsson in the spring of 1136 '. . . went first to Thurso in Caithness, and with him a man of rank called Ljótolfr' (Taylor 1938. 225). In 1151 Sveinn sent his brother, Gunni Olafsson, 'south to Lewis to his friend Ljótolfr, with whom Sveinn had been in days gone by' (ibid. 306). This Ljótolfr sounds like the Norse *vice-comes* in Lewis who appears in Hákon's saga. The Lewis antiquarian, Dr Donald MacDonald of Gisla, doubtless had this official in mind when he spoke of 'Ljotulfi, a chief of Lewis in the mid-twelfth century', as the progenitor of the Lewis MacLeods (1967. 7).

From Hákon's saga in the year 1230 (Mundt 1977. 166-167) we learn that:

Páll Bálki, Paul's young son, and Ottar Snaekollur then travelled south to Skye and there fought with Thorkel Thormodzson. He and his two sons fell there. But his son Thormod escaped from that meeting by jumping into a cask which was floating alongside the ship and it drifted to Scotland, to Gairloch. They travelled then north to Lewis. And Thormodur Thorkelsson was there before [them]. They pursued him from there and slew some men. They seized his wife and cattle.

Further examples could be quoted, but these suffice to show that the Norse names Thorkel/Torquil and Thormod/Tormod/Norman were in current use long before the MacLeods entered history. The Rev. William Matheson says that Tormod and Torquil were family names among the Nicolsons who owned Lewis and Assynt before the MacLeods arrived, and suggests that the persons mentioned in the above exploits were Nicolsons of Lewis (Matheson 1981. LI. 320-1).

According to Harris tradition, Leod, son of Olaf the Black of Man, was born ca. 1200 and died ca. 1280, leaving Harris, North Uist, Skye and Glenelg to his elder son Tormod, and Lewis to the younger, Torquil. Despite the adverse criticism of Lewis by Olaf the Black when as a young man he was *vice-comes* there (*Chronicle of Man*: Munch 1874; Young 1981. 112), the archaeological and geographic evidence suggests that Lewis was a more desirable portion than Harris, if not as good as Man. The official representatives of the Norse rulers, whether from Norway, Orkney or Man, had their residence there. The Lewis MacLeods argue, therefore, that it would be unnatural to leave such valuable holdings to a younger son.

A study of the charters and other acts of the Lords of the Isles (Munro & Munro 1986) reveals that both Harris and Lewis were often witnesses, sometimes to the same document. It ought to be possible to deduce from such evidence who had precedence, but there is no pattern. Sometimes the one, sometimes the other, makes his mark first in seemingly haphazard manner. It probably depended on who was thought to be more important at any given time.

In these circumstances, we should perhaps accept the tradition that all the MacLeods came originally from the same stock, whoever the eponymus — a tough, enterprising group which in the troubled political conditions of the mid 13th century saw the opportunity to seize land and power and took it boldly. As Matheson remarks, the name Leod is not common; only the MacLeods use it and they never again. It is unlikely that two independent clans emerging at about the same time in the same region should exhibit identical elitism. In short, a forceful young man from an increasingly successful family known as the MacLeods in the central Hebrides, appeared on the scene in Lewis in the latter part of the 13th century and there made his fortune.

THE MACLEODS OF LEWIS

Genealogies

Matheson has provided us with a new and realistic genealogy of the Lewis MacLeods (op. cit. 320-337). Using one of the tools of the genealogist — the recurrence of first or given names within a family group — he argues that the first use of the name Torquil and its regular re-appearance among the Lewis MacLeods, but never in the Harris family, indicate a marriage alliance with a family group other than the MacLeods. He therefore dismisses the accepted tradition of Leod's extensive land holdings, because at that time Lewis had been occupied, probably for several generations, by quite other Norse groups — the MacAulays around Uig; the Morrisons, the hereditary brieves, around Port of Ness; the Nicolsons on both sides of the Minch along the east side of Lewis, as well as Gairloch, Coigach and Assynt on the mainland opposite.

The three genealogies of Cromartie, Gordon and MacKenzie all agree that a Torquil MacLeod of Lewis was granted a charter in 1498 *(Register of the Great Seal.* 11. no 224), but before that the generations, starting with Leod, do not agree. Cromartie lists eight with a blank, Gordon five and MacKenzie seven. Confusion arises from the identification of a MacLeod of Lewis who witnessed a charter of lands in North Uist granted to Hugh MacDonald of Sleat, the date of which is variously given as 1409, 1449 and 1469. The Torquil of the 1498 charter married Catherine, daughter of Colin, first earl of Argyll — they are both mentioned in the charter and are celebrated in a poem in the *Book of the Dean of Lismore.* Matheson interprets this material as a list of three chiefs — Torquil son of Roderick son of Torquil — and dates them from 1498 back to 1432. Cromartie adds a great-grandfather, Roderick, and takes us back to 1405.

Further datings, by no means secure, are provided by the fight at Tuiteam Tarbhach close to Langwell in upper Strath Oykell, on the borders of Sutherland and Ross, which Matheson dates to 1406 (op. cit. 323). The Rev. J. Fraser (*Chronicles of the Frasers*: MacKay 1905. 87) says that the lady involved in the affair was called 'Shivag McKleud, Torkiloig of the Lewis his daughter' — Sidheag nighean Torcaill Oig — and Matheson reckons that the datings make her a sister of Roderick MacLeod who is on record in papal correspondence in 1405 and whose father was the chief known as Torcall Og.

Matheson recognises the difficulty of tracing the MacLeods further back than this, but cites a Gaelic genealogy in the archives of the Royal Irish Academy which sheds some light. It reads 'Ruaidhri McTurcaill McMurchada McTormoit McLeoid McOlbuir McRaoige McOlbuir snaige McAonghusa'. This can only be the Lewis line, and Ruaidhri can be identified as the Roderick MacLeod on record in 1405. The pedigree supports Matheson's argument that the founder of Siol Torcaill was not the younger brother of Tormod/Norman, son of Leod, but Leod's grandson, Murdo. He it was who married a Nicolson daughter and she named his son Torquil after her own father, thus bringing the name into the MacLeod family. Local oral traditions about this marriage vary in detail, but all suggest that the event was unexpected and radical in its consequences.

The following genealogy can now be constructed [Fig. 9.2]. Leod was succeeded by Tormod/Norman whose younger son Murdo married a Nicolson. He was succeeded by Torquil after whom the Siol Torcaill is named. Torquil was followed by his son Roderick *Ruaidhri Mor*, Roderick by his son Torquil, he by his son Roderick and he by his son *en secondes noces* Torquil. This Torquil was succeeded by his brother Malcolm. On the latter's death, Torquil's son John illegally took possession of the estate, but was succeeded by Malcolm's son Roderick — Old Ruari — whose four legitimate and five bastard sons ruined the estate between them. The family became extinct early in the 17th century.

Links with the Mainland

Putting dates to these generations is another matter. The first date in the history of the MacLeods is perhaps the most important of all. In the middle

THE MACLEODS OF LEWIS — SIOL TORCAILL

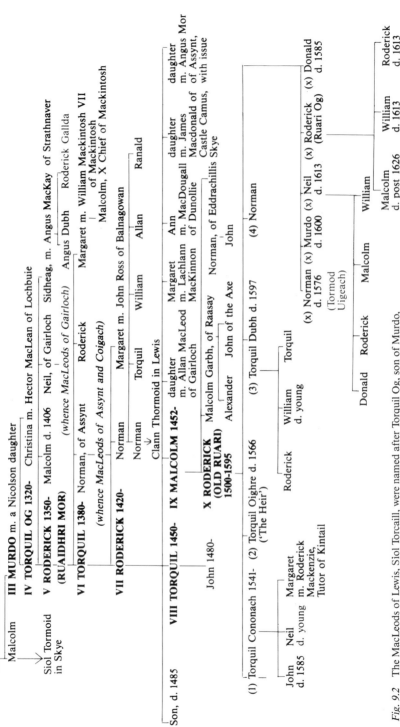

Fig. 9.2 The MacLeods of Lewis, Siol Torcaill, were named after Torquil Og, son of Murdo, son of Norman, son of Leod. The name Torquil would seem to be a Nicolson name brought into the MacLeods following Murdo's marriage to the daughter of a Lewis Nicolson. Earlier the MacLeods appear to have been based in Skye, which remained (together with Harris) the territory of the Siol Tormoid. (Genealogy based on Rev. W. Matheson 1979; dates of

1340s, between exile and the disaster of Neville's Cross, King David II turned his mind to the problems of the Highlands and Islands. About 1343 he granted two charters: the first to 'Malcolmo filio Turmode Maclode' of two thirds of the holdings (*tenementum*) of Glenelg; the second to a Torquil MacLeod of three davochs of land and the castle of Assynt in Sutherland. Malcolm and Tormod may be identified as the third and second chiefs of Harris respectively, although they are not so styled in the charter and would not call themselves 'of Harris and Dunvegan' for nearly two hundred years more (MacLeod 1938. I. 275).

The existence of the second charter is known only from Robertson's *Index to Missing Scottish Charters* (100). Torquil MacLeod was, however, lord of Lewis at the time and it may be assumed that the charter was granted to him. These were both crown charters and make no reference to other holdings — in Skye the MacLeods held from the earl of Ross, and in Lewis the MacLeods held from the Lords of the Isles.

The motivation for these grants becomes clear in the context of a passage in Dr Barbara Crawford's *Scandinavian Scotland* (1987. 25):

> The reason for King Magnus' journey across the Mull of Kintyre in 1097 was that the king of Scotland had agreed to 'let him have all the islands off the west coast which were separated by water navigable by a ship with rudder set'. The impracticalities of this arrangement which tried to distinguish the Scottish mainland from offshore islands must have been realized many times in a part of Scotland where it is sometimes difficult to tell whether land is mainland or island; the saga tale of King Magnus' attempt to include Kintyre in his lot no doubt reflects a realization that to separate Kintyre from islands to which it is linked by water made no sense in politico-geographical terms. This must have been the case in many other parts of the western seaboard which were linked by water with the offshore islands but separated from the interior of the country by difficult and sometimes impassable terrain. The agreement of 1098 was a political settlement made according to the growing principle of 'terrestrial empire' which attempted to cut the maritime links created by the Norse in the west since the ninth century. The immediate political results were negligible except for the boundary of the diocese of the Isles: the spheres of control established by the sons of Somerled in the next century were over island groups and the nearest section of mainland coast. One brief reference to a lost charter of resignation to the Scottish king tells us that Glenelg (opposite the Isle of Skye) had at one time belonged to the king of Man; probably much more of the western littoral belonged to other powerful Celto-Scandinavian chieftains of the Isles.

If you are a maritime people, the security of the sea lanes is probably more important to you than those on land. What had been true for the Norse in earlier times was no doubt equally true for Scottish rulers now. The Glenelg/ Skye/Harris and the Coigach/Lewis crossings have always been and still are vital for the safe navigation of the Minches. If he was to succeed in bringing law and order to the region as a whole, King David needed to have his own lieges in control on both sides of the water. Part of the duties of protecting the sea lanes was the maintenance of fire beacons at strategic points to assist shipping. Fraser (1876. vol 2. 510-11) says:

> Harold [ob. c.1250], sone of Godred Dound . . . was obliged to pey 100 merks
> yeirly for releive of the Scots King to the King of Norway, and at a certaine
> time of the yeir to keip tuo fired beacons, on in Lewis, ane other in the Ile of
> Skye, for directing the Norwegian shippes in their navigationes of the coasts.

The armorial bearings of the MacLeods of Lewis are 'a burning mountain proper' and the motto 'luceo non uro' — suitable for lighthouse keepers!

The importance of the Lewis/Coigach link is nowhere more sharply illustrated than in the struggle between Torquil Cononach MacLeod and his half-brothers during the last decades of the 16th century. On the death of Torquil the Heir by drowning in 1566, Torquil Cononach made a bid for the inheritance. He had the support of the MacKenzies, the Morrisons of Ness and his half-brothers Tormod Uigeach and Murdo. He seized Stornoway Castle and there imprisoned Old Ruari the Chief for the next two years (MacPhail 1916. vol 2. 262-288). In 1572 Old Ruari was conveyed to Edinburgh and resigned his lands to Torquil Cononach as his recognised heir, himself enjoying only the liferent. But on his return to Lewis, Old Ruari repudiated this resignation on 2 June 1572 on the grounds of coercion (MacLeod 1938. vol 1. 34-6). In 1576 the Regent Morton succeeded in reconciling Old Ruari and Torquil Cononach, and Torquil was again recognised as heir with immediate possession of the holdings on the mainland. These accommodations were, however, not to the liking of his bastard half-brothers. Moreover, Old Ruari now had two more legitimate offspring, Torquil Dubh and Norman. Tormod Uigeach, of the Morrison faction, was killed by his half-brother, Donald, who was in turn captured by Torquil Cononach (with Murdo's help) and carried off to Coigach, but soon escaped back to Lewis. Old Ruari then incited Donald to seize Murdo and hold him in Stornoway Castle. In reply, Torquil Cononach again invaded Lewis from Coigach, captured the Castle and shut up Old Ruari for the second time. At this date he took away all the MacLeod writs and charters and consigned them to the MacKenzies for safe keeping. He left his son John in charge in Lewis, but in 1585 the unfortunate young man was ambushed and murdered by his uncle Ruari Og who set Old Ruari free and restored to him his estate 'which . . . he did possess during the rest of his troublesome days' (Gregory op. cit. 220).

Torquil Dubh, Old Ruari's son by his third marriage, prosecuted the feud with Torquil Cononach with ruthless MacLeod intensity. In 1596 both of them declared their submission to the king, doubtless hoping thereby to profit at the other's expense. They were both withdrawn from the list of rebels who had been active while the king was occupied with the Catholic earls (*Balcarres Papers* VI. no 70). If anybody, the king favoured Torquil Cononach (*Register of the Privy Seal* LXVIII. 298), who nevertheless made little progress in his invasion of the Long Island. On the other hand, Torquil Dubh successfully took the war into Coigach itself (*Record of the Privy Council* 11 February 1596/7) and was consequently summoned to compear before the Council, of which Kintail was an influential member. Torquil Dubh was understandably reluctant to appear in such company, he was declared rebellious and soon afterwards was treacherously seized by the Morrison brieve and surrendered to MacKenzie. He was summarily beheaded in July 1597.

These events show how the internecine warfare of the chiefly family led to the disintegration of a significant social and economic unit. The collapse of the chiefly line gave rise to the depressing episode of the Fife Adventurers and, in the end, the MacKenzies' acquisition of Lewis. Some idea of the breakdown of society during this period may be gained from the journals of Bishop Robert Forbes who writes of the Rev. Farquhar M'Cra that he had served in Lewis in the 1610s:

> where he preached the gospel to the inhabitants, who were great strangers to it for many years before, as is evident from his having to baptize all under the age of forty years, which he did, and married a vast number who lived together as man and wife thereby to legitimize their children, and to abolish the barbarous custom that prevailed of putting away the wives on the least discord (Craven 1886. 110).

The Reformed Church of Scotland did not, of course, operate in the Islands until after the Synod of Glenelg was set up in 1724.

Standing and Status

The history of the chiefly line of the Lewis MacLeods has to be put together from the corpus of mediaeval material which has been at the disposal of historians for centuries — mainly public documents, since the family's muniments disappeared a long time ago. Such material can be interpreted in many ways. Some of the earlier chroniclers had few scruples about interpreting it to suit their own ends, even inventing new 'traditions' or rewriting defective passages. Through the permanent haze of speculation, however, we have a fairly consistent picture of the rise and heyday of a family which, if not of the highest rank and power, yet played a not insignificant part in the shaping of Highland history in the late Middle Ages.

The MacLeods were loyal supporters of the Lords of the Isles and their fortunes rose and fell with those of their overlords. In the Islands, the Lewis MacLeods were often at odds with their cousins of Harris and Dunvegan — thanks to the intractable dispute over lands and offices in Trotternish in Skye which the King of Scots artfully granted to both at the same time. On the mainland the Lewis MacLeods were usually at feud with their neighbours in Sutherland, the MacKays, but increasingly now with the rising clan of MacKenzie, a family whose influence spread throughout Easter and Wester Ross during the 16th century.

The MacLeods of both branches belong to that group of clans which began to come to notice in the 14th century — Campbells, MacLeans,

Camerons, MacNeills. Undoubtedly Norse in origin — *pace* Skene — they foreshadow a new society based on the clan, popularly a paternalistic society cocooned in legend and tartan (see Munro 1981. 117-129).

Morrison (1981. LI. 432-3) argues that the clan system in the Highlands differed in some subtle, unique way from the unjust feudal society which the kings of Scotland, latecomers to Norman ways, foisted on their reluctant subjects. The clan system, however it is defined, derives from a long and painful fusion of Old Norse democracy, Irish tribalism and Norman feudalism, the elements of which were inevitably modified by pre-existing social and racial structures.

That different layers of society existed in the 14th and 15th centuries is only to be expected. At the top, the *ancien régime* naturally discouraged innovation; at lower levels new ideas fermented and gained strength. The wry anecdote of Hugh MacDonald, the Sleat seannachie, aptly illustrates this uneasy relationship. John of the Isles (1449-1497), earl of Ross, once gave a great banquet at which he asked MacDonald of Moidart to be the master of ceremonies. MacDonald seated the leading guests in strict order of precedence and then sat down himself. Turning to the standing MacLeods, MacLeans and MacNeills, he exclaimed 'As for those fellows who have raised up their heads of late and are upstarts, whose pedigrees we know not, nor even they themselves, let them sit as they please' (Gregory op. cit. 54). The Scottish earldoms of Sutherland, Atholl, Crawford and Angus were created in the late 11th and the 12th centuries; Ross in 1226. Although the Lordship of the Isles is first used as a title only in 1336 (Munro & Munro 1986. XX. 3.), the MacDonalds trace their origins back much further, as the old style *Ri Innse Gall* implies.

The MacLeods certainly do not belong to this class of overlords. They never attracted the favour of the king of Scots. Royal recognition is conventionally based on usefulness or power, less on merit or gratitude. The history of the Lewis MacLeods shows only too clearly that they enjoyed none of these qualifications. Even their kinsmen in Skye — who survived when they failed — never came within touch of a peerage. Perhaps this lack of royal recognition lay behind the claim made by John MacLeod of Dunvegan in the early 1600s that his family was descended in the direct male line from the Norse kings of Man. He was probably influenced, as Matheson Šuggests (op. cit. Ll.71), by Camden's *Britannia* published in 1586, but it is also worth noting that the earldom of Seaforth was created in 1625. The MacLeods looked down on the MacKenzies as the MacDonalds had looked down on them; if the MacKenzies could be ennobled, perhaps the MacLeods had to be royal!

The MacLeods of Lewis were a luckless lot. Unlike their cousins in Skye, they were not clever at picking winners and even less clever at disentangling themselves from losers. Their unquestioning loyalty to the Lords of the Isles — splendid in Torquil's defiance in 1501 — degenerates into the hopeless succour which Malcolm, son of the illegitimate Ruari Og, brought to Sir James MacDonald during his rebellion in 1615.

In their family life the MacLeods were indeed ill-starred. Old Ruari was, by any standard, an erratic husband, but he was not lucky either. His first marriage was a disaster and it was perhaps not wholly his fault; arrest by an aggressive king was not to be foreseen. What might have happened if Torquil the Heir had not been drowned off Skye in 1566? Would Torquil Cononach, silent until that time, have still claimed the inheritance? Did someone deliberately send the young heir to sea in a leaky boat? Did Torquil Cononach's son John have to have a weakness for shooting swans?

'As far as writings could accomplish this object', says Gregory (op. cit. 270), Torquil Cononach put the future of his clan at risk by conveying the barony of Lewis into the hands of MacKenzie when he consigned all the writs and charters from the MacLeod chest to Roderick, the Tutor of Kintail. From then onwards the story of the MacLeods of Lewis is how the MacKenzies tell it.

As with Caesar's Celts and Germans, all we know about the Lewis MacLeods comes from outside, often unfriendly sources. The abundant muniments of the Harris MacLeods throw little light on their kinsmen across the Minch; recent research has in any case not been concerned with them. Our main sources of information are the histories of the first earl of Cromartie, Sir Robert Douglas and the clan historian, Alexander MacKenzie. It hardly needs remarking that all these gentlemen, honest historians according to their own lights, shared a certain attitude towards Clan Kenneth. The MacKenzies evidently wished to enjoy some of the royal Norse blood — however diluted — which the MacLeods claimed, but they were not always too scrupulous about individual MacLeods. They had access to public records, perhaps to some not now available to us. They also had access to the contents of the MacLeod charter chest, now lost or destroyed. In all fairness, but for the MacKenzies, we should know very little about the Lewis MacLeods at all. What one misses so sorely is the wealth of domestic detail which can be found for instance in the Dunvegan muniments.

Local tradition in Lewis unfortunately adds little to our knowledge. The Morrison MSS in the Stornoway Library were compiled by one Donald Morrison, a cooper by trade, who recorded his 'traditions' in the early decades of the 19th century. Two of the ten volumes are lost. There are a few references to the MacLeod chiefs — always respectfully called the 'proprietors' — but the bulk of the tales, mostly of the 18th century, are about the MacAulays, Morrisons, Mathesons, MacDonalds and, of course, the MacKenzies.

THE MAINLAND MACLEODS

On the mainland of Scotland, MacLeod families held lands in Gairloch, Coigach, Assynt, Eddrachillis and Handa. So long as the chiefly line survived in Lewis, these lands were held in vassalage to Stornoway and formed an important part of the heritage. Sometimes ownership returned direct to Lewis, as in the case of Torquil Cononach.

THE MACLEODS OF GAIRLOCH

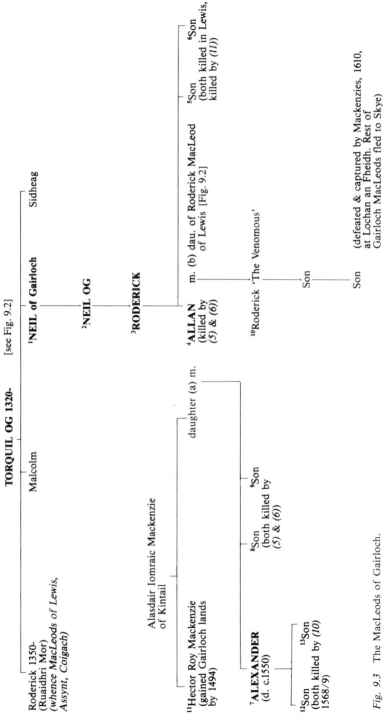

Fig. 9.3 The MacLeods of Gairloch.

MacLeods of Gairloch

The MacLeods of Gairloch are confused by the clan historian, Alexander MacKenzie, with the MacLeods of Raasay, probably because both these families used the same patronymic, MacGillechaluim. This hypothesis causes problems. It suggests that Neil, the ancestor of the Gairloch MacLeods, was the son of Malcolm, the younger brother of Ruaidhri Mor of Lewis, who was killed in 1406 at Tuiteam Tarbhach. According to Matheson's genealogy, however, Neil has to be Malcolm's younger brother This is probably right, but it leaves the business of the patronymic in the air.

Neil was the father of Neil Og who was the first to receive a royal grant of the Gairloch lands in 1430, although they had been in MacLeod hands for long before that date [Fig. 9.3]. Neil Og increased his holdings at the expense of the indigenous MacBeaths. Little is known of his son and successor, Roderick, who fathered Allan. Allan married a daughter of Alasdair Ionraic MacKenzie of Kintail, an alliance which, according to Sir Robert Gordon, was to bring disaster to the MacLeods:

> When the surnamed of Clankenzie began first to prosper and ryse, one of them did obtain the third part of Garlogh in mortgage or wedset from the clan — wic — Gillcholm. Thus the Clankenzie getting sitting therein, they shortlie and spedelie purchased a pretended right to the whole by some pretence of law, which the lawful inheritor did neglect.

By his MacKenzie wife, Allan had three sons, one of whom, Alexander, succeeded him. His second wife was a daughter of Roderick MacLeod of Lewis and bore him a son, Roderick, whose name, to quote Morrison (1968-76. section V) is synonymous with 'soaring ambition, crooked counsels and bloodthirsty deeds'. Allan's two brothers who lived in Lewis resented the MacKenzie alliance, came to Gairloch and murdered Allan and the two younger boys. Vengeance was exacted by Hector Roy MacKenzie, the boys' uncle, who in due course acquired the Gairloch lands by the sword and received a royal charter in confirmation in 1494.

The MacLeod family struggled to maintain its identity for 70 more years. Alexander succeeded Allan in the leadership and died ca.1550. His two sons were murdered, because of their MacKenzie blood, by Roderick the Venomous, their father's half-brother, at the infamous banquet on Eilean Isay in Loch Dunvegan in 1568 or 1569. This outrage provoked a new MacKenzie campaign of revenge. The final confrontation took place in 1610 at Lochan an Fheidh. The MacLeods were defeated; their leader, a grandson of Roderick the Venomous, was captured and the lucky ones escaped to Skye.

MacLeods of Coigach

The estate of Coigach was given by Norman MacLeod, first of Assynt, to his second son, John Riabhach, in the 1460s, thus founding the line of the Coigach MacLeods [Fig. 9.4]. John married a Nicolson lady and had four

THE MACLEODS OF COIGACH

[see Fig. 9.2]

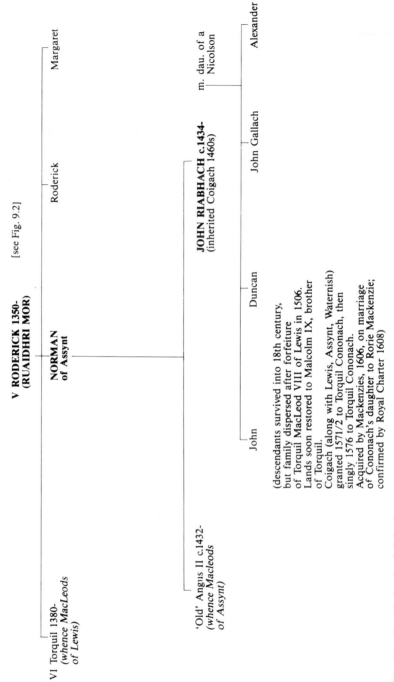

Fig. 9.4 The MacLeods of Coigach.

sons, John, Duncan, John Gallach and Alexander. The eldest son, John, was renowned for his martial prowess. He sired a line of descendants which survived into the 18th century.

The family was dispersed after the forfeiture of Torquil MacLeod of Lewis in 1506, when Coigach with Assynt was awarded in liferent to MacKay of Strathnaver. These holdings were, however, restored when Malcolm, Torquil's brother, was reinstated in 1511. By charter dated 14 February 1571/2 Torquil Cononach received Assynt with Lewis, Coigach and Waternish in Skye, as related above. Failing any legal heir of his, the estates were to go to Malcolm MacLeod of Raasay, failing whom, to the nearest legitimate male heirs of Torquil bearing the name and arms of MacLeod. Old Ruari repudiated this charter, but after their second reconcili-ation in 1576 Torquil Cononach received a direct grant of Coigach and used it as his base throughout the ensuing fratricidal struggle with the Lewis MacLeods (see above).

Coigach was still in his hands at the time of his death in 1620. The estate then fell to the MacKenzies.

MacLeods of Assynt

Assynt, as King David's charter of ca. 1343 shows, was one of the early MacLeod holdings. Roderick V of Lewis gave Assynt to his second son Norman (I) in the 1420s, retaining the superiority to himself [Fig. 9.5]. From the start the family had internal disputes about seniority and legitima-cy. Norman's son, Old Angus (2), married twice. This involved him with the MacKintoshes who in the end slew him. Angus III's succession (5) was disputed by his brother John (8), but confirmed by MacLeod of Lewis, Angus's father-in-law. The grievance festered, however, and Angus was murdered by his nephew, John Mor (17). Angus married twice, first to his chief's daughter and second to a daughter of MacLeod of Gesto. Three of the four sons of his first marriage were killed by their half-brothers or their sons or by Alexander, an illegitimate son of Angus. Of the first marriage only Donald Cam IV (9) survived, but he had no issue. The second marriage produced John Riabhach VII (12) who succeeded. It also produced Neill (13) who was to be the tutor of Angus Beag VIII (18) and also to murder his own younger brother Hucheon (14) and his son, Donald (29). The respec-tive progenies of these two carried the feud to the point of near extinction of both lines. John Riabhach VII (12) governed the barony for 15 years 'with great commendation' (*Geanies Papers*). He had married a daughter of MacKenzie of Fairburn and left a young family. His brother, Neill (13), became tutor to the minor Angus Beag VIII. Neill managed the estate with competence, but his crimes caught up with him and in the end Torquil Cononach seized him and had him executed in Edinburgh in 1581.

On attaining his majority, Angus Beag VIII (18) was not considered fit for the chiefship and after only one year was ousted by an unlikely alliance of the families of Neill the Tutor and his brother Hucheon, who divided the

THE MACLEODS OF ASSYNT — I

[1] **NORMAN I c.1400-**
m. Katherine Matheson
dau. of Lochalsh

[2] **"OLD" ANGUS II c.1432-**
killed by Young Lochalsh

   m. (1) dau. of Macdonald of Keppoch; no issue
   (2) Margaret MacKintosh, widow of Alexander
   Matheson of Lochalsh

[3] John Riabhach, c.1434-
I of Coigach
m. youngest dau. of MacNicol
(*whence MacLeods of Coigach*)

claimed elder through
Norman's "first" marriage
to Sinee neenn Clyann na Gayell

[4] Norman Ban c.1436-
went on pilgrimage
to Rome with
"Old Angus"

[5] **ANGUS MOR III.** c.1464-
killed by nephew.
John Mor (17)

[6] Roderick c.1466-

[7] Norman c.1468-

[8] John c.1470-

m. (1) dau. of Macleod of Lewis

[9] **DONALD CAM IV c.1496-**
m. Margaret, dau. of Alex.
Macdonald VII of Glengarry,
who later m. Torquil Cononach
of Coigach. No issue

[10] **NORMAN V c.1498-**
killed by his brother
Angus Beag (11)
No issue

[11] **ANGUS BEAG VI c.1500-1560**
m. Florence, dau. of Aodh
Ruadh MacKay of Farr.
No issue. Killed by
bastard brother, Alexander (15)

[12] **JOHN RIABHACH VII c.1520-1575**
m. dau. of MacKenzie
of Fairburn

[13] Neil the Tutor c.1522-1581
executed in
Edinburgh

[14] Houcheon c.1524-
killed by Neil
the Tutor (13)
issue [see II]

[15] (x) Alexander
killed by Aodh Ruadh
MacKay of Farr

[16] Neil, killed at Torran Dubh c.1500
m. (2) dau. of MacLeod of Gesto

[17] John Mor, c.1502
wounded at Torran Dubh,
killed Angus Mor III (5)

[18] **ANGUS BEAG VIII c.1560**

[19] John of Oldey

[20] Duncan

[21] Norman d. young

[22] Alexander d. young

[23] John d. in prison

[24] **DONALD BAN IX c.1560-c.1647**

m. (1) dau. of Pulrossie
m. (2) Margaret, dau. of Donald MacLeod of Lewis
[see II for continuation of
Neil the Tutor's family]

[34] Duncan c.1580-1609

[35] (x) Donald [36] (x) Duncan [37] (x) Neil [38] (x) Norman

[39] John [40] Angus

issue

m. (2) Christian Ross d. 1642

m. (1) Marion or Mor MacKay

[48] Neil c.1592-1633 fiar of Assynt

[49] Angus

[50] Rory

[51] James

[52] Margaret m. 1610 Sir Alex. Gordon of Navidale

[53] Katherine

[54] Annas

[55] daughter

[56] daughter

[57] **DONALD OG c.1610-c.1647** of Assynt and Annat (but MacKenzies effectively seized Assynt in 1646)

[58] **Hugh I c.1612** of Cambuscurry d. young

[59] John

[60] daughter

[61] daughter

[62] **NEIL X c.1628-1696**
m. Christian, dau. of Col.
John Munro of Lemlair

[63] John (*whence MacLeods of Geanies*)

[64] Alexander (*whence MacLeods of Flanders*)

[65] Alexander?

[66] dau. m. John Macleod? (last of Ardvreck)

THE MACLEODS OF ASSYNT — II

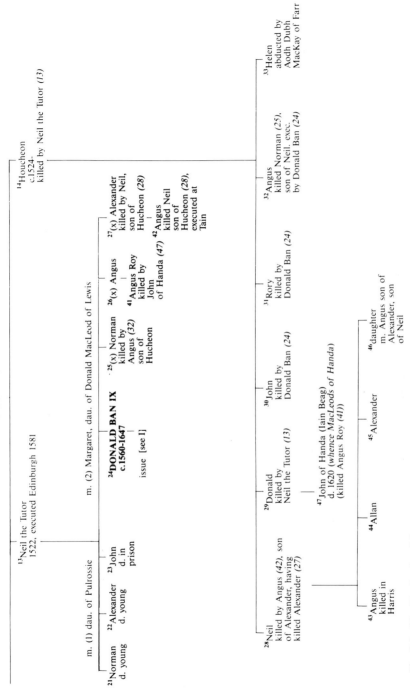

Fig. 9.5 The MacLeods of Assynt.

estate between themselves. A period of anarchy followed and ended only with the emergence as chief of Donald Ban IX (24), another son of Neill the Tutor by his second wife, Margaret, daughter of Donald MacLeod of Lewis. Donald Ban IX had to settle some of the old scores in the old-fashioned way, but he achieved much more through a policy of reconciliation between his fractious relatives.

On 8 November 1596 Donald Ban purchased a charter of Assynt from the first Lord Kintail and settled it on his posterity. In 1635 Colin, earl of Seaforth, granted Donald a new charter of Assynt, but Seaforth's successor, George, had other ideas. On winning a royal charter for Lewis on 13 November 1637, he decided to incorporate Assynt fully into the MacKenzie estate. As a result of much legal manipulation in which Seaforth's brother, MacKenzie of Pluscardine, and Kenneth MacKenzie of Scatwell played dubious roles, Seaforth now believed he could eject Donald Ban from his lands. A thousand MacKenzie troops invaded Assynt in 1640, but Donald Ban succeeded in getting a decree against Seaforth and was awarded compensation in the sum of £44,000 Scots. This was more than enough to discharge the estate's indebtedness and Donald's second wife, Christian Ross, who proved to be a good manageress, did what was required. In 1642 Donald Ban made over the estate to Donald Og (57), his son by Christian. The MacLeods now thought themselves secure, but the wadset due to Pluscardine, although paid off against receipts, continued to change hands amongst the MacKenzies and was still held legally valid as a debt on the estate as late as 1757. The MacKenzies raided Assynt in May 1646 and caused much material damage. They returned in 1672 and carried off the MacLeod charter chest, thereby extinguishing any hope of a MacLeod renaissance in Assynt. Donald Ban was still alive on 21 May 1646 when he left the estate of Annat to Donald Og.

By his first wife, Mor or Marion, daughter of Aodh MacKay of Farr, Donald Ban had four sons and three daughters; by his second wife, Christian, daughter of Nicholas Ross of Pitcalnie, three sons and two daughters. In succeeding decades, they and their children were to be dispersed throughout Scotland and Europe and to produce the cadet lines of MacLeods of Cambuscurrie (58), Cadboll, Sallachy, Geanies (63) and Flanders (64).

Donald Ban's eldest son, Neill (48), known as the 'fiar' or feuar of Assynt, married Florence, the fifth daughter of Torquil Cononach of Coigach. Neill predeceased his father in 1633. Donald Ban left Assynt and Annat to Donald Og (57) and the recently acquired estate of Cambuscurrie to Hugh (58), second son of Christian. Donald Ban and Donald Og both died about 1647. So far as the MacLeods knew, the estate of Assynt was quite unencumbered. Young Neill X (62), the eldest son of Neill the 'fiar', succeeded under the guardianship of his father's half-brother, Hugh of Cambuscurrie. While still a minor, Neill married Christian, daughter of Col. John Munro of Lemlair. He attained his majority on 24 November 1649, and his subsequent history is in the public domain. He died old, ill, embittered and impoverished in Edinburgh in 1702. He probably had issue by

Christian. When the sheriff of Sutherland was trying to eject the occupants of Ardvreck Castle [Fig. 1.11], mention was made of 'bairns and servants' (*Trial Indictment* no. 5). The defence of the castle was, it seems, in the hands of Neill's son-in-law, John MacLeod (66). The Rev Dr Donald MacKinnon asserted that Neill had a son named Alexander (65), but typically omitted to reveal the evidence. Officially the family died out. In 1954 a Mr. J.A.S. McLeod of Cooma, New South Wales, Australia, claimed descent from Neill, but this claim was judged to have no genealogical backing.

MacLeods of Eddrachillis and of Handa

The MacLeods of Eddrachillis trace their descent from Norman, a younger brother of Old Ruari, the last legal baron of Lewis. Their somewhat unedifying history may be deduced from the Geanies Papers. They lived mostly in Assynt. They were unluckily the neighbours of the MacKays of Strathnaver, by whom their rights in Eddrachillis were alienated. The direct line died out in the 18th century.

The small family of MacLeods of Handa sprang from Hucheon/Uisdean/Hugh (14) [Fig. 9.5], the youngest legitimate son of Angus Mor MacLeod of Assynt. The second chieftain, Iain Beag (47), distinguished himself by capturing Torquil Cononach whom he dutifully delivered to Stornoway for execution. To Iain Beg's fury, Tormod MacLeod, Torquil Cononach's half-brother, refused to commit fratricide and let him go free. Iain Beag shortly afterwards attacked, against odds, and killed the Morrison brieve of Lewis and some of his supporters. This is yet another example of the interplay between the mainland and Lewis.

Iain Beag spent most of his life feuding with Neill, the tutor of Assynt, who was his great-uncle and had murdered his father and grandfather. In later life he ran a profitable, independent piracy business out of Handa. Despite all this he died peacefully in his own bed in 1620 (MacPhail 1916. vol 2. 274). There is no certainty about his descendants. According to tradition they were decimated and scattered by the potato famine of 1845-46. A John MacLeod, crofter fisherman of Oldshoremore near Kinlochbervie, who was born in 1775, claimed descent from Iain Beag and there are some of his family still alive today.

MACLEODS IN THE 19th-20th CENTURIES

Despite massacres, murders, banishment and emigration over the centuries, families called MacLeod have survived in surprising numbers in Lewis, Ross and Sutherland, particularly in Lewis. The 1890-1 survey of schools in three parishes of Lewis reveals that the surname MacLeod headed the lists in all three parishes. Roughly 28% of the school population was called MacLeod (MacKenzie (1903) 1974. 64-5). The Annual Report of the

Nicolson Institute in Stornoway of 1925 shows that of the 31 duxes between 1895 and 1925, eleven were MacLeods — the MacKenzies were runners-up with 5! Of 255 children who took their leaving certificates between 1900 and 1924, 46 or 18% were called MacLeod. This does not necessarily mean that the MacLeods were more intelligent or hard-working; only that there were more of them than of other family names. In the current telephone directory of the Highlands and Islands Region there are 19 columns of MacLeod subscribers, making a total of about 2,500. Very roughly, 970 or 40% of these MacLeod subscribers live in Lewis. By contrast, in the MacLeod lands of Harris, North Uist, Skye and Glenelg, 244 MacLeods or only 10% of the subscribers are recorded. The other 50% of MacLeod subscribers are scattered all over the Highlands; most or many of them perhaps will have come from Lewis in the first place.

These random statistics merely show, however, that there are a lot of people called MacLeod! Despite lack of leadership and other misfortunes which have smitten the islands since the 17th century, a surprisingly large number of MacLeods have survived and multiplied in Lewis and the Highlands. Thousands of MacLeods exist also in the Old Commonwealth countries and the U.S.A., in France, the Low Countries and Scandinavia. Many of these will be descended from MacLeods from Lewis who emigrated after the beginning of the 18th century. Sadly, many of these descendants are ambivalent about their origins. The potent publicity which has come out of Dunvegan this century perhaps makes them all prefer to be cousins of the late Dame Flora MacLeod of MacLeod rather than descendants of humble and impoverished tenants of the MacKenzies!

By contrast, the MacLeods who still live in Lewis are notably impervious to the seductions of their Harris cousins. Attempts to enrol them in the world-wide Association of Clan MacLeod Societies have shown that they are not interested in the MacLeods of Harris and Dunvegan or indeed in their own chiefly line. The MacLeods of Lewis were Norse and brutish and feudal and Papist. They lived a long time ago and are best forgotten! The heroic figures of Lewis today are called Matheson or MacAulay or MacKenzie!

Acknowledgement

Grateful acknowledgement is made to James Ford for preparing Fig. 9.1.

References

Acts of the Parliament of Scotland.
Annual Report of the Nicolson Institute. Stornoway, 1925.
Balcarres Papers. Advocates' Library, Edinburgh.
Collectanea de Rebus Albanicis.
Craven, J.B (ed.) *Journals of the Episcopal Visitations of the Rt. Rev. Robert. Forbes, M.A. in Ross, Caithness and Argyll. 1762-1770.* 1886.

Crawford, B.E. *Scandinavian Scotland.* 1987.
Douglas of Glenbervie. *The Baronage of Scotland.* 1798.
Fraser, Sir W. *The Earls of Cromartie.* 1876.
Geanies Papers.
Gordon, Sir R. *Genealogical History of the Earldom of Sutherland*
Grant, I.F. *The MacLeods—the History of a Clan.* 1959.
Gregory, D. *History of the Western Highlands and Isles of Scotland* (2nd edition 1881)1975.
Johnson, Dr. S. & Boswell, J. *Journey to the Western Isles and Tour of the Hebrides.* 1924.
Macdonald, Dr. D. *Tales and Traditions of the Lews.* 1967.
McGurk, F. *Calendar of Papal Letters to Scotland of Benedict XIII of Avignon, 1394-1419.*
   Scottish History Society. 1976.
MacKay, W. (ed.) *Chronicles of the Frasers by James Fraser* [Wardlaw MS]. Scottish History
   Society. 1905.
MacKenzie, A. *History of the MacLeods.* 1889.
MacKenzie, W.C. *History of the Outer Hebrides.* (1903) 1974.
MacLeod, Rev. J. Parish of Harris, in Sir J. Sinclair, *The Statistical Account of Scotland 1791-
   1799.* 1983. vol XX.
MacLeod of MacLeod, Canon R.C. (ed.) *The Book of Dunvegan.* Spalding Society. 1938. 2
   vols.
MacPhail, J.R.N. (ed.) *Highland Papers.* Scottish History Society. 1916. vol 11.
Matheson, Rev. W. The MacLeods of Lewis and The Ancestry of the MacLeods, in
   Transactions of the Gaelic Society of Inverness. 1981. Ll.
Miscellanea Scotica. 1818. vol 2: *History of the Feuds and Conflicts among the Clans in the
   Northern Parts of Scotland and in the Western Isles from M.XXX.I unto M.D.C.XIX.*
Miscellanea Scotica. 1818. vol 2: *Extracts.*
Miscellanea Scotica. 1820. vol 3: *Supplement to the History of the Feuds and Conflicts among
   the Clans.*
Morrison, A. *The MacLeods—the Genealogy of a Clan.* Five Sections. Association of Clan
   MacLeod Societies. 1968-1976.
Morrison, A. The Feu of Berneray and the Sale of Harris, in *Transactions of the Gaelic Society
   of Inverness.* 1981. vol Ll.
Morrison MSS. Public Library, Stornoway. (Also published by the National Society of
   Daughters of Founders and Patriots of America. Stornoway 1975.)
Munch, P.A. (ed.) *The Chronicle of Man and the Sudreys.* 1874.
Mundt, M. (ed.) *Hákonar saga Hákonarsonar.* Norsk Historisk Kjeldeskrift-Institutt. 1977.
Munro, R.W. & Munro, J. *Acts of the Lords of the Isles. 1336-1493.* Scottish History Society.
   1986.
Munro, R.W. The Clan System—Fact or Fiction?, in *The Middle Ages in the Highlands.* 1981.
Record of the Privy Council. Haddington's Collection. Advocates' Library, Edinburgh.
Registers of the Great Seal and of the Privy Seal; Notes on the Register of the Privy Council.
   Haddington's Collection. Advocates' Library, Edinburgh.
Robertson's Index to Missing Scottish Charters.
Skene, W.F. *Celtic Scotland* (lst. ed. 1877) 2nd. ed. 1886. 2 vols.
Taylor, A.B. (ed.) *Orkneyinga Saga.* 1938.
Treasurer's Accounts.
Young, G.V.C. *History of the Isle of Man under the Norse.* 1981.

Fig. 10.1 Isle Martin, showing the Pier close to which John Woodhouse established a fishing station in 1775. *Clach Fear Eilean-Mhàirtean,* lies at the southern end of the little bay. The cross-slab stands within a small disused burial ground where a ruinous stone building was known as the chapel of St. Martin. O.S. 6 inch Sheet XIII, 1st edition, surveyed 1875.

214

TWO ECCLESIASTICAL SITES IN THE SUMMER ISLES, WESTER ROSS

Marilyn Brown

The Summer Isles are a group of about 20 islands and rocky skerries at the mouth of Loch Broom, most lying just off the Coigach peninsula, but with some reaching far out across to Greenstone Point [Fig. 10.4]. Several of the larger islands have been inhabited at one time or another, notably Isle Martin, Tanera More and Isle Ristol, whilst Priest Island also shows signs of some modest one-time habitation.

ISLE MARTIN

Isle Martin is the innermost of the Summer Isles, about 6km north of Ullapool and 1km off the coast of Coigach at Ardmair. It is a rocky island rising to a height of around 120m (393ft), roughly triangular in shape and measuring some 1.8km east-west by 1.4km north-south. There is an area of lower ground at its southern extremity close to the bay, where a fishing station was first established in 1775 and where the present houses on the island are situated [Fig. 10.1].

The burial ground, which lies near the south-east corner of the island, close to the shore and the landing place, is now defined on three sides by a stone wall and contains an upright stone cross slab and a roofless stone structure 4.2m square with an entrance on its west side. The latter is known as the chapel of St Martin; it appears to be of post-Reformation date and a number of roughly worked grave markers are visible around it. What may be the site of an earlier building running east-west lies to the south.

The cross slab, which is broken at the top and leans at a slight angle, stands about 1.3m high by 0.5m wide and 0.3m thick [Fig. 10.2]. Is has been suggested that it may have been re-set, upside down. The slab has been roughly dressed, with, on its east face, in low relief, an upright crossed by three horizontal bars creating a triple Latin cross. The shaft and the arms of the crosses are outlined by bead moulding and there is a raised moulding around the edge of the slab. A photograph of the cross slab as it appeared in the early part of the century accompanies J. D. Cairns' account of the island (Cairns 1912-13. 418-9).

The cross slab belongs to the Early Christian period. It is difficult to assign it to a precise date or to produce a very close parallel. Several stones from Iona bear more than one cross on the same face (RCAHMS 1982. 181, 183) [Fig. 10.3], but they are not linked together as at Isle Martin. Refer-

Fig. 10.2   Cross-slab, Isle Martin — an upright shaft with three horizontal shafts creating a triple Latin cross. 1988.

ence may also be made to the grave slabs on Isle Maree where, on one stone, the crosses are linked together [Fig. 6.4].

TANERA MORE

The island of Tanera More lies about 1 km off the Coigach peninsula, facing Badentarbat [Fig. 10.5]. It is irregular in shape measuring about 2.7km north-south, and 1-2km east-west, and consists of a number of rocky hills, the largest of which rises to a height of 124m (406ft). A large bay, nowadays known as the Anchorage (Gael. *an acarsaid*), lies on the east side of the island. It was an anchorage evidently well-known to the Scandinavians who named the island after it (ON *t-hafnar-ey,* Gael. *tannara,* harbour island). In the late 18th century this was the site of a fishing station, providing facilities for the herring catch, and from this period date the impressive

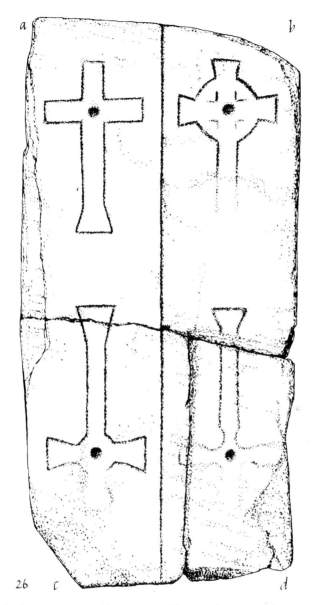

Fig. 10.3 Cross-slab, Iona Abbey Museum. The stone bears more than one cross on the same face, but they are not linked as on Isle Martin.

Fig. 10.4 The Summer Isles lie off Coigach in the mouth of Loch Broom. Tanera Mór (with Eilean Dubh behind), Tanera Beg (with An Chleirach behind) and Glas-Leac Mór. From Meall an Fheadain, 1972.

stone buildings near the pier, recorded in a view by Daniell [Fig. 12.3]. In 1939 this area was acquired by Frank Fraser Darling who described the island and its topography in his book *Island Farm* (1943).

The first mention of a burial ground on Tanera More, other than by the Ordnance Survey, seems to have been by Fraser Darling who describes it as a small triangular half-acre of ground, in use as a burial ground until late in the 19th century with graves marked by rough unlettered pieces of stone. The earliest inscribed stone yet found is dated 1790, and a number of other gravestones confirm that the cemetery was in use until the late 19th century. Fraser Darling tells how he found small crumbly fragments of human bone in the soil and judged the site to be one of great antiquity. He relates (1943. 42-3) that:

> in olden days people were brought from the mainland to be buried in Tanera More. There were several reasons for this, one being the freedom from wild beasts and dogs which tended to dig up graves. And another reason applied to the period when the resurrection men were busy stealing corpses from wherever they could for the anatomists.

There is no mention of any tradition of a church or chapel on the island. The centre of the medieval and later parish was at Clachan, at the head of Loch Broom, whilst earlier Christian presence centred on Annat (across Loch Broom on the north side of the Scoraig peninsula) and on Kildonan (Little Loch Broom).

On 31 March 1988, whilst finalizing arrangements for the Scottish Society for Northern Studies' Ullapool Conference, John Baldwin visited Tanera More and discovered in the burial ground part of a medieval gravestone. Sunlight coming from the south-west, over the low *bealach*, had picked out parts of the relief carving on the recumbent stone, and an initial sketch was made. When members of the conference visited the island the following week the stone was confirmed as the lower part of a cross-marked grave slab of unusual form, and the description which follows is based on a brief examination in the field at that time [Figs. 10.6, 10.7].

The fragment measures about 1.35m in length, 0.25m in width and 0.09m in thickness. It bears the shaft of what is presumed to be a cross standing on a stepped base. The cross shaft appears in low relief and the Calvary mount on which it stands is emphasised by two further rows of incised lines reflecting the design of the base. Below the stepped base is a much weathered scene. Immediately beneath the base is a horizontal figure wearing a short tunic. Under this is a centrally placed figure, again in a short tunic, grasping a large cross which has slightly splayed arms. To the left is an apparently seated figure holding some form of staff-like implement. Below this is a low shape which may represent an animal. The degree of weathering makes the identification of these figures difficult and consequently any interpretation is more than usually speculative. Below the figural scene the stone is roughly dressed. It is uncertain whether the stone was originally an upright slab set into the ground or a recumbent grave cover. The presence of a rough area at the base would suggest the former.

Fig. 10.5 Tanera Mór. The 18th-19th century fishing station was based at the pier. The cross-slab was discovered in the 'Burial Ground' in 1988. The same year a very large and substantial steatite bowl was uncovered by a mechanical digger on Rudh' Ard-na-goine. OS 6 inch Sheet IIIA, 1st edition, surveyed 1875.

220

Figs. 10.6; 10.7 The recumbent cross-marked grave-slab on Tanera Mór, probably 12th-14th century AD. At one time it may have been an upright cross-slab. The drawing [Fig. 10.6] is based on the photograph and field-notes. 1988.

The stepped base links it with the broad current of sepulchural monuments in Britain. The form is common from the 12th to the 14th century and is known in numerous examples throughout Scotland. The volume of material has perhaps precluded attempts to carry out a survey of these types of monuments on a countrywide basis this century, although Richard Gough's magnificent *Sepulchral Monuments of Great Britain* published in 1786 provided an inspiring example (Gough 1786: see also Steer & Bannerman 1977; Ryder 1987). References to medieval grave slabs with stepped bases occur in the pages of MacGibbon and Ross (1896) under the ecclesiastical monuments they are describing, and the *Proceedings of the Society of Antiquaries of Scotland* in the 19th and particularly the early 20th centuries contain papers dealing with this type of material as a part of studies of individual districts. The most relevant geographically to the example under discussion are those in Ross-shire, but none of these, as they survive, are a very close parallel to the slab on Tanera More, although they do provide evidence for comparable monuments in the area — for example at Urray, Convith, Killearnan, Contin and Kilmore (Rae MacDonald 1901-2. 688-732; MacLean 1914-15. 71-8; Grant 1908-9. 335-6).

Steer and Bannerman briefly mention a number of grave slabs in Argyll, which they date to the 13th and 14th centuries (one of which from Kilmartin has a stepped base) and derive these from English forerunners. They comment on a scarcity of such monuments in Argyll, and would use this as an argument in favour of the rapid replacement of the form by the products of the West Highland schools (Steer & Bannerman 1977. 14).

The fragment from Tanera More can be compared in size with, for example, a section of a cross shaft from Iona which measures up to 0.28m in width and 0.07m in thickness (RCAHMS 1982. 237). The stepped Calvary mount is the commonest form of cross base on cross slab grave covers, but the internal repetition of the stepped cross base is a rare feature recorded, for instance, from Kirby-in-Ashfield, Nottinghamshire (Gough 1786. 1. cviii). The presence of a scene below the cross base is also very unusual. Ryder discusses an *Agnus Dei* at the foot of a cross shaft at Sedgefield and draws parallels with examples from Great Milton in Oxfordshire and Wainsworth near Doncaster. He also cites a double-headed eagle and a robed figure inside the bases on a double grave slab at Barnard Castle, a possible heraldic dog from Bowes, and a Gainford example with small ornamental crosses below and to each side of the base. There is a 'beast', also, at the foot of a cross base from Bristol (Ryder 1987; Gough 1786. cix). However, Ryder records no figural scene comparable with that at Tanera.

The subject of the scene on the slab must, owing to its condition, be unclear. The figures in association with the cross recall the iconography of the True Cross as illustrated on the 12th century Kelloe Cross [Fig. 10.8]. The subject is extensively discussed by James Lang who refers to the mainly continental parallels (Lang 1977. 105-19). This free-standing cross was erected in the modest church of St Helen at Kelloe, County Durham. In the centre of its lowest panel is a large cross flanked by a crowned woman

222

Fig. 10.8 The Invention of the True Cross, St. Helens Church, Kelloe, Co. Durham.

holding a sword, and on the left a male figure holding a spade in his right hand and supporting a half-shrouded figure with his left. Two prostrate, shrouded corpses lie along the base of the panel. It is interpreted as showing ·

Fig. 10.9   Grave slab, Iona Abbey Museum. A priest in eucharistic vestments prays in front of an altar on which are a chalice and a ring-headed cross with a stepped base.

the Empress Helena threatening the Jew, Judas, who then digs to find the three crosses. The true one restores a corpse to life. The figure on the left of the Tanera More slab, holding an object which more resembles a sceptre than a sword, could be that of a woman. The central figure is depicted in a short tunic, indicating a male, probably lay, person. The recumbent figure at the top of the scene, but below the cross base, may represent a corpse. Another, quite different interpretation is suggested by a slab in the Abbey Museum at Iona (RCAHMS 1982. 222-3) [Fig. 10.9] which depicts a priest in eucharistic vestments, standing in an attitude of prayer before an altar on which are a chalice and ring-headed cross with a stepped base; the figure at Tanera More, however, seems to be holding the cross, but may be taking part in another liturgical scene. Poor preservation and the crudity of the carving prevent any certainty and leave the way open for other interpretations.

Elsewhere in the graveyard is a roughly-shaped stone of irregular form, about 1.65m in length, and there are slight indications of the former presence of a building, about 7m in length, aligned roughly east-west within the churchyard.

This discovery shows the need for more detailed survey in this area and points to the rewarding nature of future work. The Tanera and Isle Martin stones form an important part of the early ecclesiastical history of the north-west coast.

Acknowledgement

Figs. 10.2, 10.3, 10.6, 10.7, 10.9 are reproduced by permission of the Royal Commission on the Ancient and Historical Monuments of Scotland; Figs. 10.1, 10.5 by permission of the Trustees of the National Library of Scotland; Fig. 10.8 by courtesy of J. T. Lang, Durham University. Fig. 10.4 was taken by John Baldwin and is reproduced by courtesy of the Scottish Ethnological Archive, National Museums of Scotland.

References

Cairns, J. D. Note of an incised cross near the burying ground, Isle Martin, one of the Summer Isles, West Ross-shire, in *PSAS* 1912-13. vol. 47: 418-9.

Darling, F. F. *Island Farm*. 1943.

Gough, R. *Sepulchral Monuments of Creat Britain*. 1786.

Grant, A. Notes on a recumbent slab in Kilmore Churchyard . . ., in *PSAS*. 1908-9. vol. 43: 335-6.

Lang, J. T. The St. Helena Cross, Church Kelloe, Co. Durham, in *Archaeologia Aeliana*. 1977. vol. 5: 105-19.

MacDonald, W. Rae. The heraldry in the old churchyards between Tain and Inverness, in *PSAS*. 1901-2. vol. 36: 688-732.

MacGibbon, D. & Ross, T. *The Ecclesiastical Architecture of Scotland*. 1896.

MacLean, A. C. Notes on Contin Church, Ross-shire, in *PSAS*. 1914-5. vol. 49: 71-8.

RCAHMS. *Inventory of the Ancient and Historical Monuments in Argyll*. 1982. vol. 4.

Ryder, P. F. *The Medieval Cross Slab Grave Cover in County Durham*. 1987.

Steer, K. A. & Bannerman, J. M. W. *Late Medieval Monumental Sculpture in the West Highlands*. 1977.

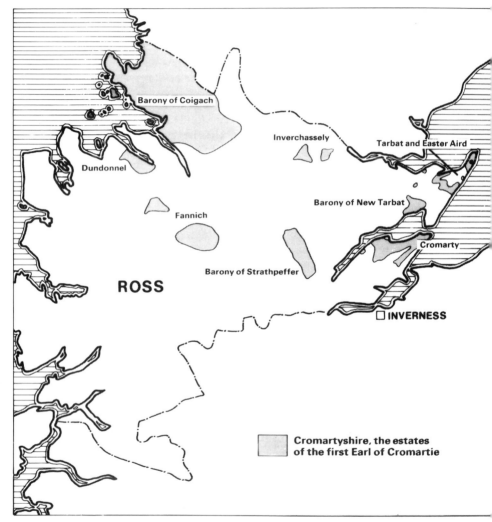

Fig. 11.1 Cromartyshire reflected the exact extent of the Regality of Cromartie in 1686. These were the territories acquired and held by George MacKenzie, 1st Earl of Cromartie and his sons. The major holdings were the Baronies of New Tarbat, Strathpeffer and Coigach. As well as being very remote, Coigach was Highland and essentially pastoral, compared to Lowland and agricultural Easter Ross.

226

EARLY FISHERY AND FORESTRY DEVELOPMENTS ON THE CROMARTIE ESTATE OF COIGACH: 1660-1746

Monica Clough

In the summer of 1756 Captain Forbes of New, Factor to the Annexed Estates of Cromartie, went over to the west to take a Judicial Rental of the Barony of Coigach, lying all along the northern side of Loch Broom [Fig. 11.1]. Both Forbes and the surveyor, Peter May, who mapped the Barony found it difficult to convey how remote they found it. The people, many of whom had recently fought in the Rising of the '45, were uniformly hostile to the government officers, and also strangely hostile to one another. 'I must beg leave here to take notice', wrote Forbes, 'that the Barony of Coigach is possessed by Macleods and Mackenzies mixt and that there seems to be a kind of Clan Quarrel in which I am as little interested — further than doing my duty as Factor — as I am in the disputes in Corsica' (*SRO* E 746. 74.4). It was almost exactly 150 years since this particular clan quarrel should have been ended by the marriage of the Macleod of Lewes heiress to Sir Rorie Mackenzie of Tarbat [Fig. 11.2]. The Barony of Coigach was part of the estates of the Mackenzies of Tarbat and Cromartie from that marriage in 1606 until their sale four hundred and fifty years later, bar the thirty-five years of annexation by the Crown after the Rising. A fairly comprehensive picture of their management can be found in the surviving estate papers, and much of the evidence has been presented and analysed in *Cromartie: Highland Life, 1650-1914* (Richards & Clough 1989).[1]

It was a pastoral community, with a population of about 900 adults in the Barony; a good recruiting ground for soldiers, part of one of the largest parishes in Scotland. Up to the end of the 17th century the presbytery was on the watch for pagan practices, especially bull-sacrifices and oblations of milk poured out in the name of St. Mourie (see R. W. Munro, this volume). With the exception of the Minister, a schoolmaster and a few of the tacksmen, no English was spoken or written; and because there was no castle or mansion house, no member of the landowning family lived in Coigach during this period. Rents were collected often at two or three yearly intervals, by the chamberlain of the other estates in Easter Ross, who made the hazardous journey by Garve and Fannich (another extensive forest wilderness, owned by the estate in Mid Ross). The chamberlain was always accompanied by a few men, a clerk and nominally at any rate, a piper. There was a resident ground officer unable (up to the mid 18th century at least) to sign his name. This lacuna put power into the hands of the principal tacksmen, self-appointed as the landlord's spokesmen. There was no civil

Fig. 11.2 Sir Rorie MacKenzie of Tarbat ca. 1579-1626, Tutor of Kintail, married the heiress to MacLeod of Lewis in 1606 and thereby gained Coigach.

law officer either, not even a baron-baillie-depute, though a visiting chamberlain sometimes held a court. From 1684 until 1891 the Barony was a part of the County and Sheriffdom of Cromartyshire.

Goods and news of the outside world tended to come from Stornoway by sea, rather than across the pathless hills. Once a year parties of men drove their black cattle on the hoof to sell at Beauly cattle market; they were sometimes pursued back by the chamberlain, who collected the rents while the tenants had the cash in their hands. It is worth noting that though all the Cromartie properties in Easter Ross paid rent in kind, and had assessments made in bolls of barley until the 1790s, the most distant barony of Coigach paid only silver mail (i.e. cash) from at least 1660 onwards.

The cattle trade, the only generator of income, was obviously established long before 1660. There were no services, and only a few minor rents: wedders, driven on the hoof to Castle Leod; butter and cheese; and pairs of white plaids, each twelve foot in length. These plaids were highly prized, only a pair was ever levied from each property, and they were probably of the fine quality of a modern Shetland shawl. Certainly George, the first earl [Fig. 11.3] was able to settle part of a large debt to a bookseller in London by trading in two years' rent of white plaids.

This paper, however, is not concerned with the cattle trade (see Baldwin 1986. 183-220), but with two efforts by the owners to develop the Barony of Coigach in other directions — fishing and forestry. Indeed, given the two hundredth anniversary of the founding of the British Fisheries' station in Ullapool in 1788, it is only fair to devote some time to the serious attempts of the first earl of Cromartie, ninety years earlier, to establish a fishing station there.

FISHING

Tarbat (he had not yet become the first earl of Cromartie) had a long pre-occupation with the possibilities of commercial fishing and he made two determined attempts to set up a fishery at Ullapool. Both failed, as the same problems which beset later developers were even more severe in Tarbat's day. These may be summarised as the difficulties of distance and transport — the lack of mainland roads, the lack then of government aid and of an assured market, the undependable vagaries of the herring shoals and (Tarbat's perennial problem) his lack of capital and support. In late Stuart times the Dutch continued to outfish the native Scots round all our coasts.

Tarbat's initial idea came in the form of a printed *Short Proposal for The Africa Company and Fishing,* undated but probably about 1697 and endorsed in his own hand 'Anent Fysery' (*SRO* GD 305. 163 (XVI) 218, 219). His proposal was that the funds raised for the Africa Company should first be invested in equipping a single seagoing Buss, to fish off Scotland on the model of the Dutch fishers' 'mother ship', processing its own catches and those of local small boats [Figs. 11.4, 11.5]. He estimated it would cost £500 Sterling to build and equip. One Buss would; he considered, land 30 lasts (360 barrels) and would make two loadings in a season. By simple and regrettably over-confident arithemtic he calculated that after four years the Company would have £72,000 sterling to re-invest, as well as much incidental profit to merchants and coopers. It would give 'supply to the poore and indigent', adding as a clincher 'and the whole stock to be pulled out of the sea'. The same proposal goes on to make the excellent point that the Africa Company (of which his brother was secretary) should first concentrate on investing up to £10,000 yearly in advancing current trade within Scotland — 'the Company would apply the greatest part of their Stock and Labour on Fishery and African trade [slaving] until they be sufficiently stocked for planting and sustaining a colony on probable and solid grounds'. In a scribbled draft for a speech in parliament at the same time he wrote with enthusiasm of the fisheries' potential — 'for mines of gold and silver in the earth do not renew their treasure verie slowly (if at all) whereas the

229

Fig. 11.3   George Mackenzie of Tarbat, 1st Earl of Cromartie, 1632-1714.

Fig. 11.4 A somewhat fanciful representation of hauling fish on shore, with fishing and trading boats offshore. From John Ainslie's *Map of Scotland,* 1789.

mines of the fish of the sea are yearly renewed'. There is also a draft Bill *Overtures for the Advantages of Fishing* dated 4th August 1698 and signed, modestly, Tarbat, J. P. requesting a bounty scheme to subsidise herring fishing (*SRO* GD 305. 163 (XVI) 211). Tarbat was out of office at this point, and it is tempting to think that it may have been enthusiasms of this sort which caused his contemporaries to dismiss his schemes as 'maggoty'. At any rate nothing but the full and disastrous attempt to establish a colony in Darien in Central America had any appeal to his fellow investors in the Africa Company.

Tarbat managed to convince at least one of his Edinburgh cronies, Sir William Binning of Bavelaw, of the profit to be made from private fishing. After some correspondence, upon terms now unknown, Binning and Tarbat agreed to set up a fishing station at Ullapool in 1698. The only evidence of its brief existence is a letter dated 9th November 1698 from H. Kynneir, servitor to Sir William Binning, writing from Ullapool (*SRO* GD 305. 153

(VII) 32). He enclosed two receipts for goods despatched by the two partners and left in Stornoway by John Manners — Master of the *Jennett of Leith* and known as a reliable skipper in the Cromarty grain trade (see Clough 1986. 88-97). The goods took three weeks to reach Ullapool from the Lewes, and are detailed twice by the careful Lowlander, Harvie Kynneir. The cargo included all necessaries for the setting up of a fishing station. Besides food, drink and tobacco, it included full coopering stores and tools, 24 fish-gutting knives, four rouping tubs, pickling pans, ladles and shovels, a measuring bar and a pair of scales, a ladder, a small quantity of Great Salt (14 bolls at £10.10 Scots per boll) and much more of small salt (72 bolls at £2 each). There was also one barrow, quite possibly the first wheel to appear on the roadless shores of Loch Broom, where there was not then a meal mill either. Nothing more is heard of this fishing station. An obvious weak point in the inventory of stores was the small proportion of good salt to the inferior sort. Binning, however, does not figure in later lists of Tarbat's creditors.

In 1712 Tarbat, now an earl and aged 80, was again out of office, this

Fig. 11.5 Fishing boats off Ross. A series of little vignettes from John Ainslie's *Map of Scotland*, 1789.

time for ever, and came north to his estates where he could perhaps dream of exerting more personal supervision over further fishery schemes. Even longer and more detailed *Proposals made by the Earl of Cromartie on the Fishing* are dated February/March 1712 (*SRO* GD 305. 163 (XVI) 216). The first page is missing, but it reads like a more business-like version of previous proposals, almost as a company prospectus. He implied that two Buss-type large vessels are already fishing on station, though this may be wishful and misleading. He claims that salt and casks must not only be provided for them but also for the 'country people engaged in coast fishing' — who were already fishing the Great Line of 800 to 1,000 hooks ('each which line should be very strong') and the Small Line of 300-500 hooks, together with hand-lines of several sizes for the 'great scaled fish' (cod and ling). A quantity of hemp-thread should be supplied for the making of nets and lines, especially for nets 'there being a great many nett-makers near these coasts'. Turning to the shore base he goes into great detail for the buildings. For example, a smoke house for smoking herring should be made of stone and built high 'since the same fire will smoak several stages'. And

233

roofing of canvas or thatch must be provided over the external drying-poles for cod and ling, for 'there is not one thing I fear more than the rain in time of drying cod and grey fish'. Evidently the intention was to employ all the methods subsequently adopted by the British Fisheries Society from 1788 on through the next hundred years — fishing by drift-net and by lines, to produce the standard three categories of fish; salt herrings in barrel, smoked herrings or haddock, and air-dried cod and ling. He ends on a characteristically optimistic note that 'Loch Kannorth' (Loch Kanaird) was 'swimming with herrings'.

A letter from the Estate Chamberlain, Norman Macleod, dated 15th August of the same year, 1712, confirms that the smoking-house had been built, but economically. Macleod had had experience of the old earl's schemes; he was cautious, 'whatever was done in either Lochs Broom or Gairloch was but an essay and therefore to lay out much expence was unfit'. The very bad news he gave was that no large ships had called to pick up the catch, or even to net it; and as an aside he remarks that the herrings are so plentiful that they are being used as manure by the country people.

The earl had apparently employed The Zetland Company of London as agents to supply the two boats, and to market the catch. The earl must have written urgently to his son-in-law, Major John Sinclair in London, who replied on 12th September, a bare month after the earl had heard the disturbing news of the non-arrival of the hired ships. Sinclair wrote a short letter, reporting that he had made 'with the utmost diligence inquiry about the Zetland Company but the more I inquire the worse I like them, they sham, they ly, they break appointments, they are "not at home" when thy ar, they will not shew their books to satisfy on how your money was applied for the Company's services, in short I am afraid they divided it amongst themselves'. Sinclair prudently enclosed a lawyer's endorsement of this verdict: Mr Hamilton wrote 'I am afraid it is a trick designed upon you from the beginning' and advised the only possible course would be to file a Bill of Chancery, 'a pretty tedious business' (*SRO* GD 305 Corrspondence: Major Sinclair to the Earl of Cromartie, 12 Sept. 1712). In 1721 there was a Bill of Roup of Fishing Stores lying at Cromarty and Coigach, set up for £292 1s. 3d. Sterling, last indication of the large scale of investment planned (*SRO* GD 305. 163 (XVI) 255). The total annual rent of the Barony of Coigach was about £50.60 Sterling at this date.

This appears to have been the end of Tarbat's second attempt to establish a fishery in Loch Broom. Forty-three years later, in 1755, the Factor for the Annexed Estates of Cromartie wrote hopefully of the great benefit the north side of Loch Broom derived from the herring fishing, and gave a well-argued case for a fisher town to be built at Ullapool 'as well situate for a village as perhaps any place on the western coast'. The Commissioners ignored this advice for another thirty years.

However, an international (and subsidised) market for salt herring had by then been established in Great Britain with growing demands from ships' victuallers, and from the plantations in the West Indes. Loch Broom and Gairloch were increasingly visited by freelance fishers. The estate benefit-

234

Fig. 11.6   Herring gutters, Ullapool. Early 20th century.

ted a little, by selling licences for the distilling of whisky; it was able also to increase several rentals, and to create new ones for Isle Martin and Tanera Mor, on the grounds of fishing profits. In 1756 the local Minister wrote to the Commissioners complaining of the behaviour of the fishers and the lack of any law-enforcement officer — behaviour which had encouraged back-sliding of his parishioners and at least one unfortunate girl to become a prostitute. By 1775 John Woodhouse of Liverpool had leased Isle Martin from the Commissioners and had claimed to have spent over £3,000 in the very first year in buildings, vessels sent, and casks. He already had his esta-blished market. In 1787 Directors of the newly formed British Fisheries Society visited the Western Highlands and, inspired by the success of Isle Martin and Isle Tanera in Loch Broom, decided upon a station at Ullapool. The purchase of land at Ullapool and Isle Ristol from the Cromatie heir Lord John Macleod, newly returned to his estates, was completed in September 1788, and the Society's investments and arrangements were more successful than the forgotten former attempts of the landlord (see Dunlop 1978; also J. Munro, this volume) [Fig. 11.6].

TIMBER

The attempt to develop an income from Coigach by selling the timber was the work of the second earl [Fig. 11.7]. His father died in 1714, an old man; John had had to wait a long time for his inheritance, and had spent the years in reckless living. By 1707 he was so much in debt that his father had drawn

235

Fig. 11.7   John MacKenzie, 2nd Earl of Cromartie, ca. 1665-1732.

up a complicated Will, leaving the properties in tailzie on his grandson, and
a life-interest only of the rents of the barony of Tarbat to his unreliable son
John. John was expressly charged not to sell any of the principle of the
estates, and the entire rental of Coigach was to go to the maintenance and
education of his two eldest sons. It was about £50 Sterling per annum, and
we have traced only one year when it actually went to the maintenance of
the little boys, George and Roderick at school in Inverness. George, Master
of Tarbat, had two other tutors as well as his father. Unfortunately, his
uncles Lord Royston and Lord Elibank were both rather distant and casual

236

about their obligations, whilst the second earl was unable to acknowledge that the estates he had waited so long to inherit were not his.

Earl John gives the clear impression of not caring for any inconvenient legal obligation. Almost as soon as he became earl his credititors began to put pressure on him, and by 1720 they foreclosed and were in the process of sequestering the rents of his remaining land at Tarbat. This should not have affected Coigach, legally the property of his son George, a minor. One outcome of his straits, however, was the second earl's quite illegal attempt to sell the standing timber of Coigach. The timber was presumably natural Scots Pine (*Pinus sylvestris*) growing up the south-facing slopes of Loch Broom, planted these days by the Forestry Commission; also what is now the bare 'forest' of Rhidorroch [Fig. 11.8].

There are indications that, originally, timber was cherished as an asset to the estate. A tack set in 1676, of the Oxgate of Ridorach and half-oxgate of Delvraid, has a special obligation written in — to 'look carefully to the woods of Ridorach' (*SRO* GD 305. 163 (XVI) 287). There is no standing timber now, though from evidence which we shall see, the average height of the boles was over 30 to 40 ft (9-12m). However, the old first earl had taken up as another 'maggoty scheme', the utilisation of the native timber of Scotland. There exists a draft, undated, of a speech to the Scots Parliament in support of a Petition to Queen Anne, begging that she would grant the same encouragement and premium for mastage and ship-planks from Scottish sources as was paid for the wood of colonial America — '. . . there are woods in our wildernesses . . .' (*SRO* GD 305. 158 (XII) 104). This seems to have led to an Admiralty Commission of Inspection which got lost in the woods of Strathspey, and never got to the real Highlands; it also may have given John the second earl the notion that that the woods of Coigach were a saleable asset, even though they did not belong to him. For in a contract dated 1719, the second earl assigned 'The Fir Woods of Coigach' to one John Innes, who died soon after, leaving his interest to William Innes, W.S., who was given the tack of Ullapool (*SRO* GD 305. 163 (XVI) 322). The second earl was already in debt to the Innes family.

Two long letters from William Innes give a good idea of the problems of extraction. The first is a quibble about the ownership of fallen timber — did such as had fallen between the signing of the contract and the start of operations belong to the Earl or Innes? The ground in question was 'the woods of Achall'. The second is longer, and Innes almost visibly tries to keep his temper with a difficult landowner. It is dated, from Ullapool, 1st June 1724 (*SRO* GD 305. Correspondence: J. Innes to John Earl of Cromartie). Firstly Innes answers objections clearly made by the earl, that an unidentified neighbour, 'the general', is getting far better prices for timber than Innes is giving. Innes replies, pointing out that the complaint would have been justified 'had your woods been kept as well and looked after as narrowly as theirs had been, but they have not, for they have been made havock of at pleasure, not only by all your own people in this country but also by the neighbourhood without much control'.

Innes goes on to complain that he made the bargain for 5,000 trees,

standing, fit to be manufactured into merchantable deals, 'and now since I came up here I have travelled the woods again and . . . after counting the trees we could not reckon on 3,000 trees to be yet standing'. Returning then to the grievance that the neighbour had cut much more profitable timber [Figs. 11.9-11.11], Innes explains that only:

> those trees which may br brought down whole in their full length and bigness to the sea, by which such as are fitt for masts or yards to ships have a praemium or bounteth of 20/- sterling payed by Government . . . But none in your lordship's woods, tho' they were more fit for Masts . . . can be brought down whole by reason of the Linn that is in the water through which they must pass, and therefore they must be cutt into Luggs of 12 or 14 foot lengths at most and even those of that length cannot be brought down without great pains and trouble, so that I am obliged to manufacture into Deals all the trees that are fit . . . whereas those of the Gentles' Wood are sent to the markets whole and get a far better pryce than the dealls doe, besides the praemium . . . the General obliges his tenants to work, paying what he states himself . . . so that the expense of every tree is but $10^{1}/_{2}$ pennies [Scots], but the price sought from he here is a merk the tree . . .

There follows intricate calculations of the cost of transporting a tree 'of the bigness to afford 3 luggs' to the mill, calculations which we fear were of no interest to the second earl. 'Every deal stands us a halfpenny to that mill, and a considerable expense more for carrying down the deals from the milns to the shoars'; the further expense that Innes had had 'to build the sawmills and provide all the materials necessary, the paying of £6 Sterling yearly to a Forrester for keeping the woods (which your lordship ought to pay) and many other expenses . . . If you had any thought before, that you were over-reached in the bargain, you will be now convinced of the contrary'. Innes ends by complaining of the harrassment he has had from the tenantry of Coigach, egged on, he fears, by Lord Cromartie's 'doers'. He demands that 'Your doers may undeceive the people and make them know that giving me any disturbance or discouragement in the work here is *not* agreeable to your lordship'. He will pay a reasonable rate for reasonable work, and 'thus the tenants will be able to pay their rents and perhaps make some profits to themselves'.

It is not clear how soon the teenage owner of the woods of Coigach found out that his father had sold them, but fortified by excellent legal advice he went into action in 1724, obtaining a judgement against his father who 'Most wrongeouslly and unjustly . . . has cutt a great deal and is going on to the destruction of the whole'. He also complained that the value put upon the woods was far too low — 'I might further represent that the woods were sold at an undervalue for £600 Sterling, when they were worth a vast deal more'. Young Tarbat becomes a little shrill at this point — 'This is a great loss to me to be deprived of such considerable woods by a sale at a very low price made by one who had no right to sell them . . .' The judge-

Fig. 11.8 Scots pine forest, Fochabers. Alasdair Alpin MacGregor Collection.

Fig 11.9   Felling timber with axes between Muirkirk and Sorn, Ayrshire. 1940.

Fig. 11.10   Taking out the felled timber, Glen Orchy. Alasdair Alpin MacGregor Collection.

Fig. 11.11 The long inland straths were well-suited to timber production. East over the watershed, at Contin, the upper part of the mill was built almost entirely of wood. Erskine Beveridge 1886.

ment was against the earl, who was required to repay to his son £400 Sterling. Meanwhile there was the contracting firm of Innes, two thirds through their extraction job, having had the heavy expenditure of putting up a saw mill. Eventually the aggrieved son settled with Innes to complete the job.

So, as part of his marriage and coming of age settlements in 1724, George Master of Tarbat assigned a new Tack to William Innes, in place of the one signed between Earl John and Innes on 2nd October 1719. Under the old tack Innes was to pay £600 in three instalments of which only the last remained unpaid: this was now to go to George. George, Master of Tarbat sells and dispones 'all and haill the remaining timber in the barronie of Coigach upward of 6" [15cm] diameter . . . particularly the fir woods in Achachall and Caulternath' . . . giving Innes authority:

> to cut down use and dispose of all and every of the said firr woods and to transport the same by land or water to the sawmilns already erected by him on

241

the water of Ullabull for manufacturing the said woods into dealls, and from thence to the shoar or harbour of Ullabull to be put on board such shippes or vessells as shall be employed by . . . William Innes . . . with full liberty to plane and flank the dealls so to be manufactured, and the loggs, joysts, sparroof or nails [stored] near the mills or shore until they are sold or carried off.

It seems Innes was into the prefabricated roofing business, not attempting the manufacture of ships' timbers. By the time of the Judicial Rental of 1755 the sawmills are mentioned as lying derelict, at Ullapool. Not only had Innes logged-out his contracted ground, but in the aftermath of the 1745 Rising a naval party was landed near Isle Martin and deliberately set the same woods on fire, part of the scorched-earth policy ordered against the homelands of the 'rebels'. The old MacLeod 'long house' of Langwell was also burnt, with the loss of all the old MacLeod of Lewis Charters (verbal comm: the late Earl of Cromartie).

The fishing and the forestry exploits in Coigach in the late 17th and early 18th centuries form a forerunner to the account of the 'formidable economic odds' in the chapter by Professor Eric Richards (this volume) in which he speaks of the increasing poverty and insecurity of the common people and the problems of capital investment in Coigach.

Note

[1]In Richards, E. & Clough, M. *Cromartie: Highland Life, 1650-1914.* (1989. 455, 459 and elsewhere), the present volume is referred to by its earlier, working title, 'Ullapool and Wester Ross'.

Acknowledgement

Permission to reproduce illustrations has been kindly granted by: the late Earl of Cromartie [Figs. 11.2, 11.3, 11.7]; Scottish Ethnological Archive, National Museums of Scotland [Figs. 11.4, 11.5, 11.6, 11.8, 11.9, 11.10]; Royal Commission on the Ancient and Historical Monuments of Scotland [Fig. 11.11].

References

Manuscript:

Scottish Record Office (SRO)

GD 305.153 (VII)
GD 305.158 (XII)
GD 305.163 (XVI)
GD 305 Correspondence: Major Sinclair to Earl of Cromartie, 12 Sept. 1712.
GD 305 Correspondence: J. Innes to John Earl of Cromartie, 1 June 1724.
E 746.74.4

Printed:

Baldwin, J. R. The Long Trek: Agricultural Change and the Great Northern Drove, in J. R. Baldwin (ed.) *Firthlands of Ross and Sutherland.* 1986.

Clough, M. The Cromartie Estate, 1660-1784: Aspects of Trade and Organisation, in J. R. Baldwin (ed.) *Firthlands of Ross and Sutherland.* 1986.

Dunlop, J. *The British Fisheries Society, 1786-1893.* 1978. (J. Munro).

Richards, E. & Clough, M. *Cromartie: Highland Life, 1650-1914.* 1989.

Fig. 12.1 Ullapool, Loch Broom. 1992.

ULLAPOOL AND
THE BRITISH
FISHERIES SOCIETY

Jean Munro

EARLY FISHERY SCHEMES FOR LOCH BROOM

The story of fishing developments on the north-west coast of Scotland is set mainly in the second half of the 18th century, but Loch Broom [Fig. 12.1] was notable some two hundred years earlier. In 1566 strangers applied to the Privy Council for a licence to fish there saying 'it has plesit God to oppin ane greit commoditie to the common weil of the realm throw the fisching of Loch Brume and utheris lochis of the north seyis' (*RPC*. i. 482: see also Clough, this volume, for details of late 17th-early 18th century initiatives by the Mackenzies of Tarbet and Cromartie).

Ullapool

It was not really until after 1745, however, that any detailed study was made of the western seaboard with a view to encouraging fishing — which was chiefly for herring. Reports to the Commissioners for Annexed Estates stressed the merits of the fishing in Loch Broom, though not in such glowing terms as Loch Hourn where the factor described how:

> In the year 1753 a shoal of herring was left by the tide in the inner loch . . . They were computed at half a mile square from three to five feet deep. All the way down to the Sound of Sky the herring were so thick that, a boat going on the loch, the oars made the herring fly out of the water like flying fish (E741/40).

Another great shoal was described in 1784. Even so, the factor listed among the advantages of Loch Hourn that it was 'but a short navigation' to Loch Broom which appeared to be visited by shoals more regularly than most nearby lochs. Captain John Forbes of New, the Coigach factor, went into some detail on the fishing in 1755 which he said 'frequently succeeds well' at Loch Broom:

> I am humbly of opinion that a village ought to be erected on this barony at a place called Ullapool, which lyes on the coast and north side of Lochbroom and as well situated for a village as perhaps any place on the western coast. There is a large field of corn land fit to be fewed out for houses and gardens, great plenty of improvable barren ground, and as the herring fishing succeeds so well here, it is mighty probable that numbers of sea-faring people would

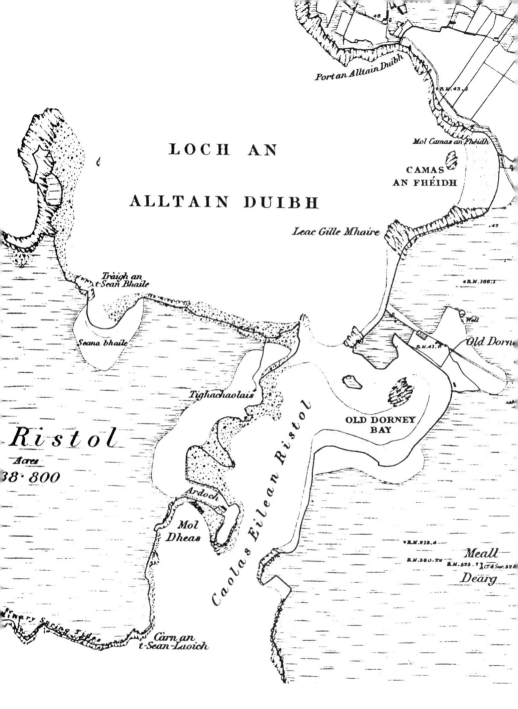

Fig. 12.2 Old Dornie is still the harbour for small local boats fishing for prawns, lobsters and crabs. At particularly low ebbs it is possible to walk across to Eilean Ristol. O.S. 6 inch Sheet IIIA, 1st edition, surveyed 1875.

246

resort to it and be fond of getting small feus for houses and gardens (E729/1/11).

One of the first buildings Forbes wanted to put up there was a prison — so perhaps his view of the human inhabitants was not so rosy.

But it was to be some thirty years before a village was founded at Ullapool. Various schemes of development were tried around Loch Broom in the meantime. A linen station was proposed at Inverlael near the head of the loch but, according to an observer, in 1787 the buildings were all 'a perfect ruin' and no manufacturing appeared to have taken place, so that 'a more flagrant instance of the abuse of public money, which appears to have been all jobbed away, can hardly be produced' (GD9/1/112). It was later found that the buildings, though paid for, had never in fact been completed. A settlement for marine officers at Loch Broom never even got to the practical planning stage but one for soldiers was more successful. After the end of the war in 1763, ex-soldiers were settled as crofters in various parts of Scotland with small bounties, rent-free houses and land. Of the eighty five who chose the Cromartie estate, twelve soldiers reached the farm of Ullapool. Their serjeant, John Mackenzie of Loudon's Regiment, was a diligent worker who remained in the district and later acquired some valuable property and prospered. The rest of the soldiers were employed by the factor in road-making, dyke building and other public work including a waulk mill, but seem to have cultivated their crofts as little as possible, failed to keep in repair the huts and tools provided for them, and soon left the district (E723).

Old Dornie

Among the papers of the Commissioners for Annexed Estates are two proposals from private people for establishing a fishing station in Coigach, both choosing a site at Old Dornie, on the mainland opposite Isle Ristol near the mouth of Loch Broom [Fig. 12.2]. In 1764 Ninian Jeffrey, then Coigach factor, sent in a scheme for building a storehouse for salt and casks and offering free houses to experienced fishermen who would teach the local population good fishing methods (E746/75). Apparently nothing came of this and six years later Colin Mackenzie, who described himself as a kelp merchant of Loch Broom, proposed to establish a fishery there on similar lines (E746/127). Again nothing further happened, but the area was evidently well regarded by possible entrepreneurs.

Isle Martin

It fell to private enterprise to open the way to success in Loch Broom. John Woodhouse of Liverpool had already set up a fishery on the Isle of Man and organised trade from there to the Mediterranean. In March 1775 he applied to the Commissioners for land for a similar undertaking in the Highlands and suggested Isle Martin as an appropriate place [see Fig. 10.1]. The Commissioners agreed to grant him a 41 years' lease with facilities for obtaining peat and limestone at Ullapool. By July, Woodhouse had chosen ten acres at the south-east of the island on which to build his station, which rose so quickly that in a year he claimed to have spent £3,500 on buildings, vessels, salt and casks (E746/103). But because of complicated salt laws, he soon found that it was impossible to trade from Isle Martin with no customs house nearer than Stornoway. He therefore applied to the Commissioners of Customs who agreed to form an 'incidental establishment' there. A collector and a surveyor were appointed who worked alone until 1789, when the staff was increased to five to extend its authority (GD9/3/209) .

The collector and surveyor were to be provided with land by the Commissioners for the Annexed Estates. After the soldiers had left, the farm of Ullapool was given to the factor 'with a good house, built with stone and lime three stories high and covered with slate'. In 1774 that factor resigned and his successor let the farm to his own brother who died in 1776. Serjeant John Mackenzie, meantime, had established himself on Isle Martin; and when he was ejected in favour of Woodhouse he was given two thirds of the farm of Ullapool. The other third, with the good house, originally built for an SSPCK schoolmaster, was leased to the customs officials, and this was occupied as the customs house, though official records called it Isle Martin until its removal in 1813.

After the advent of the customs officials Woodhouse increased his business very quickly. This was, of course, mainly directed at preserving the fish, for before the days of rail transport and refrigeration, the emphasis was on smoking or pickling. His chief aim was to cure red herrings on the Yarmouth method, for which he built a large shed where it was estimated that he could cure 1,000 barrels of herring at a time. The fish was salted for 30 hours, split through the mouth and hung on a wooden spit 4ft (1.2m) long over a fire for 14 to 21 days. The supplies of wood, generally oak, were sent as ballast from Liverpool, where it was bought cheap as shipyard refuse (Loch 1788. ii. 186). The fish was bought from local boatmen at the rate of 5s 6d per barrel. When cured the fish was shipped to London, Hull and Liverpool, as well as to the Mediterranean and all parts of Europe.

Tanera

Another market for fish appeared in 1784 when a curing station was set up at Tanera [see Fig. 10.5]. This was started by Roderick Morrison, who was described as a 'sober pushing Man' who had property in Stornoway and was said to be 'a man of extensive mercantile talents'. Morrison went into partnership with John Mackenzie, a cousin of Mackenzie of Torridon, who had business in Bishopsgate Street in London. In 1811 Daniell wrote that Tanera had been started by the British Fisheries Society, but this was not so. In 1787, according to Morrison, they erected warehouses for salt, casks, nets etc., five houses for smoking red herring and a pier where five vessels might unload at the same time. Morrison built himself a house and cultivated 16 to 18 acres of different crops on land which had appeared worthless (NLS MS2619. pl7) [Fig. 12.3].

Mackenzie described his trading methods. The firm owned six decked vessels and about thirty boats:

> Our great object was to purchase the herrings from the natives, having laid in annually a great stock of salt, casks, nets and meal, all of which, except the meal, were generally brought from Greenock and sometimes from Leith; the meal came from Caithness and the eastern coast of Ross-shire; the casks and nets from Greenock were generally sent in vessels going to the Baltic at 6d or 8d per barrel with nets in them; the salt chiefly from Liverpool and Lisbon and sometimes Leith was generally brought by our own vessels on return from the markets of Lisbon and Leith, but salt from Liverpool was brought on our own fishing vessels sent on purpose before the fishing season commenced. Our chief object was to supply the West India merchants in London with White herrings and the home market with Red herrings; we found that the fish caught in Great Britain was never equal to the demand for the West India market. (*Reports*. x.235).

Fig. 12.3 The Pier at Tanera Mór, Loch Broom. Print by William Daniell, 1814.

How to Extend the Fisheries?

Meanwhile Coigach, along with the other Forfeited and Annexed estates, was returned to its former owner — in this case his son, Lord Macleod, in 1784. This was a time of new beginnings in the Highlands and considerable interest in northern affairs. The Highland Society of London was founded in 1778 and one of its objects was to give practical encouragement to fisheries in the Highlands. As one member, George Dempster, rather gloomily put it:

> The seas abound with fish and the Highlands with industrious and good people. It will be the business of the legislature to bring these two to meet. But I fear it would in that country be an easier task for mountains to meet, at least they are much nearer together (Fergusson 1934.138).

There was much debate on how this should be done and a fashionable line of reasoning was that villages, of which there were virtually none in the Highlands, would promote employment and encourage the inhabitants in 'the love of Labour and Good Order'. As Professor Smout has written (1970.75) 'The eighteenth century village . . . was expected to provide a completely new framework for human life in the countryside'; and nowhere was this considered more necessary than on the shores of the west Highlands.

At the same time, in 1785, the old fishing regulations of 1750 became due for review and the House of Commons appointed a committee to inquire both into the state of the British fisheries and into the best means for their encouragement and extension. Many reports were made to this committee and, as a result, two acts were passed. The first, in 1785, among other provisions, abolished the old regulations which had naval training in view, which rewarded the sea-going busses rather than the catching of fish and which included the rendezvous required at Bressay and Campbeltown at the start of the summer and autumn season respectively. It also ended the apparently ineffective prohibition on buying fish from local boatmen. The act of 1786 dealt with the important subject of bounties: it introduced a system which combined the old tonnage bounty on larger vessels, now in a reduced form, with a barrel bounty; and it gave some help to local fishermen who used only small boats.

THE BUILDING OF ULLAPOOL

These new ideas and changes gave great impetus to the Highland Society of London, and in the summer of 1786 a new body was launched by them — called at first 'The British Society for Extending the Fisheries and Improving the Sea Coasts of the Kingdom'. It proved too ponderous a title even for the 18th century, and for years the members contracted it to suit themselves. Gradually it became known, though not officially until 1857, as the British Fisheries Society. I have told the story of the Society as a whole elsewhere (Dunlop 1978), and here will concentrate on Ullapool.

Selection of Sites

The first step was to select village sites, and in the summer of 1787 a number of Directors set out in two parties to visit possible locations. Before leaving London they decided to begin with only two villages on the west coast — one in the southern and one in the northern division (Skye was to be the site of a third village as soon as possible) (GD9/3/23). Tobermory was quickly chosen for the former and the Directors turned to consider the division between Skye and the Pentland Firth. This included lochs Torridon, Gairloch, Ewe, Broom, Inver, Laxford and Inchard. At Torridon and Gairloch the lairds already had schemes; Lochinver also had a station founded in 1775 by John Joseph Bacon from the Isle of Man and a local partner, although it was later said to have been founded by the British Fisheries Society. Laxford and Inchard were not then popular with either fish or boats. So they quickly eliminated all lochs but two — lochs Ewe and Broom.

It may have influenced them that they all saw Loch Broom first and fell under its spell. Loch Ewe had two great advantages: there was a road to the east coast while Loch Broom then had only a track, and the Stornoway packet boat left from Loch Ewe. The Directors were confident that they could change the packet's route (though it did not leave from Ullapool until the mid 20th century!) and they expected a road soon to be built which would be shorter than the one to Loch Ewe, so neither of these advantages weighed heavily. On the other hand, herring seem to have appeared less regularly than in Loch Broom. In any case none of the three harbours, one at Aultbea and two at the head of the loch, was available as the owners would not part with them. Had Aultbea been for sale in 1787 the Directors might have hesitated, but in the event they were agreed in recommending Loch Broom.

Here they inspected three sites. One at the head of the loch proved to have no good natural harbour and another on the southern shore (presumably Newton of Loggie) was thought to have too little flat land for a village. But all agreed with John Forbes that at Ullapool nearly all the conditions were favourable. The only objection raised — its distance from the open sea — was met by the purchase in 1787 of the island of Ristol at the mouth of the loch, which had a good natural harbour where the Directors planned to build curing and drying sheds. The stations at Tanera and Isle Martin did not offer any rivalry to the Society, but were welcomed as possible markets where the settlers might sell their fish (Beaufoy 1788.65).

At the Society's annual meeting in March 1788 members heard a lyrical description of Ullapool and endorsed the choice of the Directors. By the end of the month just over 1,000 acres of land, including 57 arable and 74 pasture, were sold by Lord Macleod to the Society [Fig. 12.4, 12.5].

The First Developers: Robert Melville and Roderick Morrison

During the same month of March the Society received an enquiry from a

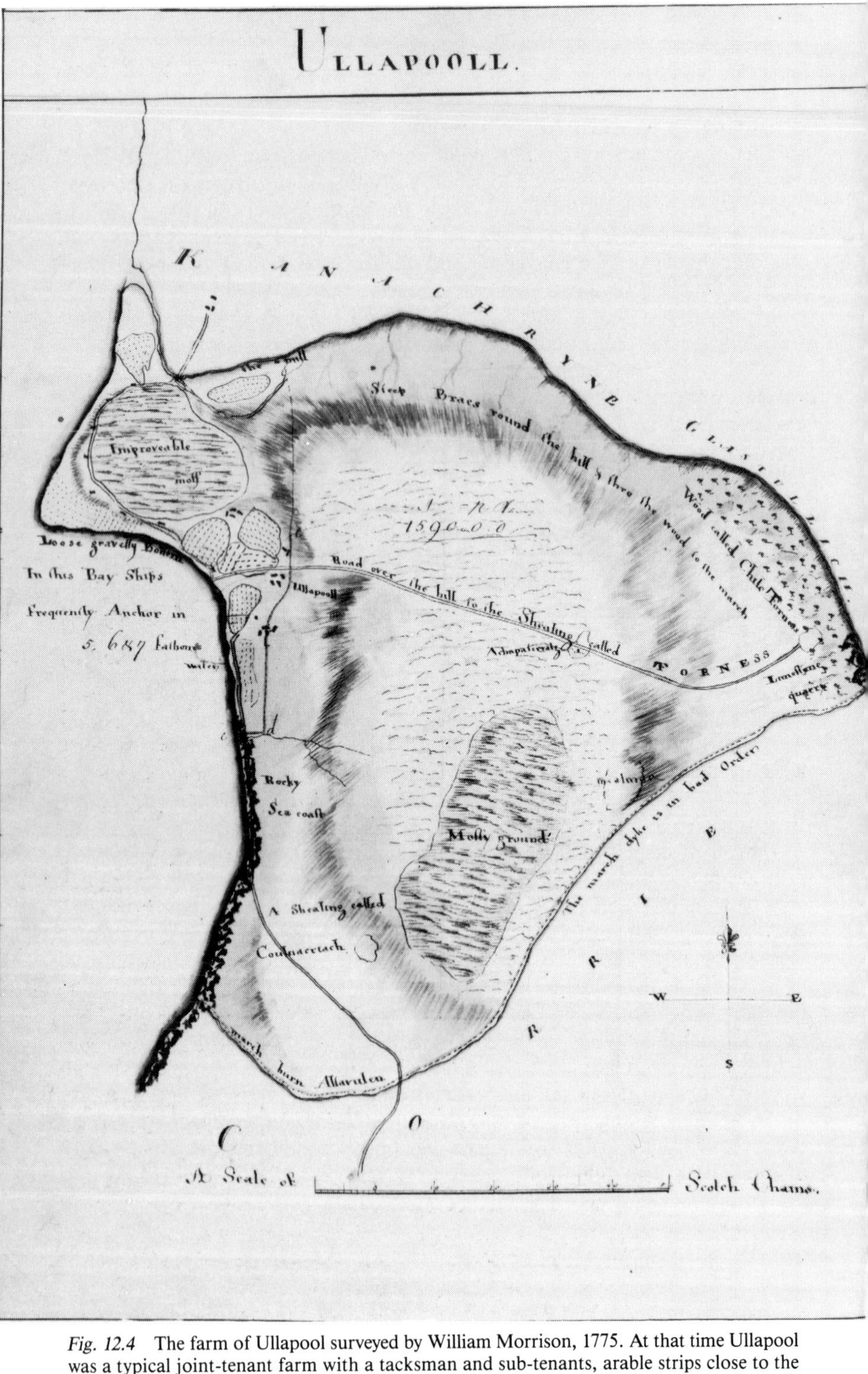

ULLAPOOLL.

Fig. 12.4 The farm of Ullapool surveyed by William Morrison, 1775. At that time Ullapool was a typical joint-tenant farm with a tacksman and sub-tenants, arable strips close to the clusters of buildings and shielings at a distance. There was also a mill on the Water of Achall.

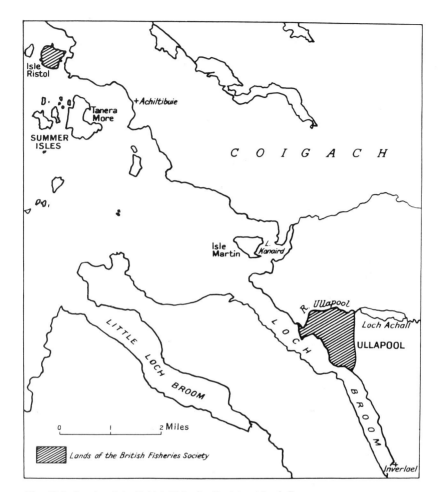

Fig. 12.5 Lands of the British Fisheries Society at Loch Broom.

would-be settler at Ullapool. Robert Melville was a nephew of Robert Fall, who owned a large fishery and commercial business in Dunbar. Melville had been a partner in the firm, but owing to losses in the corn trade Fall had recently gone bankrupt and Melville was looking for a job. He told Sir John Sinclair that he would be willing to make an offer to erect public buildings at Ullapool and to take charge of the trade and fishery. His uncle had been using his influence with George Dempster who thought Melville's intention 'a fortunate circumstance for the Society' and, after an interview, described Melville as 'a settler of great skill in the fisheries and one who will be supported with considerable capital by his friends' (Fergusson 1934.186).

As a basis for his scheme of development Melville wrote that he thought 'it most indespensable necessary to carry with me proper Artists so as by means of these I might, by apprenticeing the youth, instruct them properly in the various lines of business'. He enumerated boatbuilders, ropemakers, a net worker, blacksmith, coopers, fish curers and 'several of the most industrious and most experienced fishermen'. The building plan therefore included ten small houses for them. The Directors entered into a contract with Melville early in May 1788 by which he undertook to erect for the Society: *first* a house for himself to cost £100; *second* a shed for curing white herring for £80 (which was never built); *third* a smoking house for red herring for £290; *fourth* ten houses for his 'Artists' for a total sum of £200; *fifth* and *sixth* a shed for mending nets with tradesmen's shops behind for £80, and a storehouse for casks and nets at about £100 — making a total of £850. The Society was to lease these buildings to Melville at an annual rent of $7^1/_2$ % of their value on condition that he became a settler at Ullapool, that he kept the buildings in repair, and that he found adequate surety (GD9/4/31).

Meanwhile the Society had been considering plans for further building at Ullapool. Mackenzie and Morrison from Tanera had already suggested that their own experience in building would qualify them for a contract, adding 'We ask no favour, our claim to it will rest on the reasonableness of our proposals'. Morrison forwarded plans for a pier, warehouse and inn for a total cost of £1,063. The Directors found this 'not unreasonable' and wrote for further details, at the same time consulting with his partner John Mackenzie in London. But without waiting to study his second plan the Directors resolved 'that in the mean time Morrison do take measures for providing materials in such a manner as if a contract had actually been entered into on the terms he has offered' (GD9/3/33). The Society had much to learn in the matter of contracts for, after this arrangement had been made, Morrison's plans were given to Robert Mylne, who redesigned one wing of the inn and made considerable alterations to the plan of the warehouse. Morrison then had to persuade the Society to allow more money for him to carry out Mylne's more elaborate ideas.

Donald Macleod of Geanies: the Society's 'Superviser'

By this time work had already started in Ullapool. When Melville had gone away to make his preparations, the Directors turned to consider how a society of noblemen and gentlemen based in London could supervise building operations six hundred miles away. They knew that they needed an experienced person on the spot and, although several of the Directors had houses within reach of Ullapool, they spent too much time in London, especially during the early summer when building would be going on. It was therefore agreed to ask help from a member of the Society, Donald Macleod of Geanies, advocate and sheriff of Ross. He lived near Tain but rented the farm of Rhidorroch only eight miles from Ullapool, and agreed to visit the site and report on progress twice a year, in May and September, when his duties took him to Coigach. By the end of May 1788 Geanies had been supplied with ten pages of extracts on all the Society's proceedings on Ullapool, copies of Melville's contract, Morrison's proposals and a survey made by David Aitken in 1787. He was thus ready to begin his series of reports (GD9/4/74).

Already the two contractors had been busy. Morrison reported on 3rd June that he had collected enough material and workmen and was ready to begin. Melville had been equally expeditious, and two days later the sloop *Gilmerton*, loaded for Isle Martin, sailed out of Dunbar at 2 a.m. with a fair wind. The cargo included 8,000 bricks and tiles (another shipload of these was dispatched from Aberdeen); 1,967 pieces of timber; 20 cartloads of lime; six cartloads of household furniture and wearing apparel; two pairs of cartwheels, one cart and one plough. In addition the sloop carried 55 people — seven masons, two joiners, a slater, a blacksmith, a heckler, a netmaker, a fisherman, a cooper and a fish curer; the remaining 39 being wives and children. The party, which was increased by a number of masons from Dingwall, reached Ullapool on 13th June, while Melville and his partner James Miller, travelling by land, arrived on the same day. The farm was no longer left to Serjeant John Mackenzie and the customs officers (GD9/4/63).

On 30 June Geanies arrived on his first visit to Ullapool and found that Melville had proceeded much further than he could have expected. Aitken had appeared on 14th June and he and Melville had 'immediately proceeded to mark off the situations of the buildings to be erected this season, and set Masons to work on them, the lines for the streets of the town were traced out agreeable to the plan which Mr Aitken had formerly transmitted to the Society.' The first buildings were the cooper's and boatbuilder's shops and the net drying shed which, by the time Geanies saw it, had reached a height of five feet all round and in some places much higher. Geanies also sent for Morrison to consult with him about his work. The arrival of Morrison from Tanera produced the first clash in the history of Ullapool, for the two contractors failed to agree about the position of the pier. Morrison refused to build it in the place that Aitken had planned saying, correctly as it turned out, that the current would drive the shingle against it; Melville meantime said that Morrison's site, several hundred yards to the east, would be too far from the centre of the village. After reporting the arguments of both sides Geanies decided to leave the building of the pier until the following year, as Melville did not consider it necessary to his trade for that season (GD9/1/218).

The next report, early in August, told of Morrison's inn rising quickly under the hands of 15 masons — one wing being nearly finished. But when Mylne's plans arrived, Morrison found that 'the greatest part of all the mason work we had got done must be all pulled down before we could conform in any degree with his ideas'. On his next visit in October Geanies found that Melville's shed and workshops were all complete. He had commented in August that Melville's stonework was strong and substantial, but that:

he was sorry to observe that these buildings were meant to be covered with tiles, a kind of roof that will not suit that variable and tempestuous climate. The buildings both on Isle Martin and Tanera are covered with blue slate and will be found in the end cheaper than a tile roof though the immediate outlay is undoubtedly greater (GD9/3/151).

Melville would be accustomed to the pantiles of East Lothian and it was probably at his wish that the Society did not insist on slate roofs as they did at Tobermory. As late as April 1806 a cargo of tiles was sent to Ullapool, but in the course of the following year two loads of slates from Easdale and one from Ballachulish appear in the customs accounts (E507/19/1/511).

Further Developments: William Cowie and John Smeaton

Good progress had thus been made during the building season of 1788 and the Directors began to plan the work for 1789. In January a blow was dealt to the new settlement when Morrison asked to be released from his contract owing to ill-health. After some weeks of uncertainty he agreed to finish the inn, which he did before his death in 1790, while Geanies found a new contractor for the warehouse in William Cowie a builder and carpenter from Tain. Melville visited London in the spring and was given an additional contract to build 'a suitable schoolhouse to answer occasionally for a chapel' and a house for the schoolmaster who was to be appointed by the SSPCK (GD9/3/192). As far as the erection of buildings was concerned, the Directors had reason to be satisfied with the work of the first season and Dempster wrote 'If it does not rise to the sound of the lyre, it springs very fast to that of the bagpipe' (Fergusson 1934.194).

Work continued at a good pace in 1789 and the season saw the completion of Melville's contracts and of Cowie's warehouse. In addition there was the problem of the pier and breakwater postponed after the difference of opinion the previous summer. When Melville was in London he had told the Directors that 'the surf at present comes with such violence during a great part of the year upon the beach as to make it utterly unsafe and impracticable during a great part of the year for vessels of any kind to lie or land there' (GD9/3/183). The Directors consulted John Smeaton who advised them to build a pier and breakwater which he described in considerable detail. He said that he was too busy to design them himself but one of the Directors, John Call, who had been a military engineer in India, undertook to draw the plans. An advertisement for a contract was published, but as the matter was urgent Melville agreed to do some preliminary work, having himself sent in proposals for a contract. After some months, no other offer having been received, Melville was formally given the contract (GD9/8/119).

The pier was not a success, although it lasted until 1854. The designs were drawn without a preliminary survey of the bay at Ullapool, and Melville was not a professional engineer (there were very few of these at that time). The result was that the foundations of the pier, placed on too soft a surface, spread out causing the whole structure to come out much larger than planned. This in turn meant that the breakwater had to be placed in deeper water than was intended and even so allowed only a narrow passage for ships. From the start Melville had complained of the 'stones rising so very unshapely, it is next to impossible to lay them and they are of so cross and stubborn a quality as baffle all labour in dressing to any shape' (GD9/3/489). Geanies was asked to appoint a qualified surveyor to report on the work and one James Maclaren duly visited Ullapool and provided a report which the Directors found short and unsatisfactory. When the pier and breakwater were finished in 1790 the cubic content was much larger than intended and Smeaton, blaming Melville for bad workmanship, considered that he should bear the extra cost. Melville replied with truth that according to his contract a resident surveyor was to assist him, but the Society had never appointed one and the Agent, who was instructed to sign the certificates of progress, had no technical knowledge (GD9/32/3/86).

The Involvement of Thomas Telford

As a result of this controversy the Directors decided that they must have another survey which would include Melville's other work, which had been criticised, and all buildings at Ullapool (and at Tobermory also). Sir William Pulteney, a recently appointed Director, wrote to Thomas Telford, who agreed to undertake the whole survey for one guinea per day from the time of his setting out till his return — to cover both salary and expenses.

This was the beginning of the connection between Telford and the Society which lasted until the engineer's death in 1834. He began by charging fees, if very modest ones, but soon ceased to do so and his biographer records that shortly before his death the Society 'forced upon him a very handsome gift of plate, which, being inscribed with expressions of their thankfulness and gratitude towards him, he could not possibly refuse' (Rickman 1838.283). The Society minutes record that this was a silver inkstand and tea service.

On his first commission for the Society Telford reached Ullapool on 29th June 1790, his report being dated from Langholm six weeks later (GD9/3/583). In it he complained of the woodwork of all Melville's buildings and of several other features which the contractor tried to pass off as 'paltry differences'. Telford surveyed a red herring house, ten small houses, a shed for drying nets with boatbuilder's and cooper's shops behind it, and a storehouse for salt and casks; also the school/chapel and schoolmaster's house, the inn, and of course the pier and breakwater. Telford's verdict on the latter was that Melville was justified in enlarging the pier but not the breakwater, and therefore the Society was not liable for the total increase in cost. The report goes into considerable detail — the pews in the chapel were at least two inches too narrow; the floors in the storehouse were of flagstones and should be of brick; Melville's timberwork throughout was poor. His own house was inhabited though not quite finished — when it was put

Fig. 12.6 Fishery warehouse converted to a tourist gift shop and museum 1992.

Fig. 12.7 Fishery warehouse and harbour, ca. 1940.

up for sale in 1808 it was described as having three floors, with kitchen quarters separate and two acres of garden. Telford thought Morrison was an industrious, honest man but a professional builder could have produced the same results for less money. The inn came in for some criticism on detail — the windows had no pulleys or catches, the chimneys smoked, and there were no bells connecting the kitchen to the main house. He thought Cowie's warehouse too high and thin in its proportions but he commended the 'masterly and compleat manner in which every part of the building has been finished. The masonry of the walls is, I think, the best I ever saw of the sort, and the carpenters and joiners work is, if possible still better, in short I never saw better work in any building.' He suggested an outside crane or pulley on the gable at the harbour end [Figs. 12.6-12.9].

The report included a section on the general lay-out of Ullapool. The plan had the merit of being adaptable to any size and it is not clear how many streets were originally intended. The street fronting the harbour was reserved for store houses and public buildings but all the others were intended for dwelling houses [Fig. 12.10]. The east-west streets were placed wide enough apart to allow for gardens to north or south of the houses, while the communicating streets running north and south along the side of the gardens had no houses fronting them. The main features of this arrangement were planned by David Aitken in 1787, and laid out by him and Melville in July 1788. Aitken had intended that the whole street fronting the harbour should run parallel to the second street rather than follow the curve of the bay. But Melville had built his warehouses, shops and his own house along the shore line and Telford advised the Directors to continue the same plan. He suggested an elaborate market place in circular form within which there should be a row of houses with arcades or stalls in front and shops or parlours behind. The Directors approved the scheme provided it was shaped in a square, but it was never built. Thus Telford's part in the planning of Ullapool was confined to improvements and alterations on Aitken's general design and his original work for the Society was reserved for Pulteneytown (GD9/32/1/41).

ATTRACTING THE NEW SETTLERS

By 1790 most of the stone and lime was in position in the public buildings, and the Directors had to turn their attention to attracting settlers to make use of them.

Leases and Land Tenure

In the matter of land tenure the Directors were determined to give the longest possible leases, but this was not easy at first while they did not know how much of the land would be needed for houses. So the first leases were for five years only with much longer ones promised for later. The next problem was how much land should be granted to each settler. It was not a

Fig. 12.8 Surviving harbour buildings, Ullapool. 1992.

new one — on the one hand it was known that the herring was 'a shifting ambulatory fish' so that the settlers must have enough land to grow food to cover a bad season; but on the other hand the Highlander was thought to prefer a low standard of living to hard work, and if he was to fish at all he must not have enough land to live on entirely.

The resulting regulations were drawn up in 1789 and printed in 1790 (GD9/24). The land was classified into three types, at different values. The *first* was the town as planned by Aitken, divided into small lots just large enough for a house and kail yard, to be leased for 99 years — those nearest the harbour at £5 per acre and the rest at £2 2s per acre. *Secondly* every settler with one of these town lots was entitled to half an acre of arable land from what had been cultivated as the farm of Ullapool — this at first could only be leased for five years at ten shillings an acre. *Thirdly* each tenant might lease up to five acres of uncultivated land for ten years at one shilling an acre, with an undertaking by the Society to repay the cost of enclosures and improvements. *Fourthly*, there remained those parts of the farm incapable of raising crops and these too were available to the settlers — each was to have the right to dig peat, to pasture two cows in summer and to have stone, limestone and shelly sand freely for their own use.

Settlers' Houses

After settling the division of land the Directors began to consider building

Fig. 12.9   The old Custom House, Ullapool. 1992.

Fig. 12.10   Ullapool in 1875 (based on the Ordnance Survey).

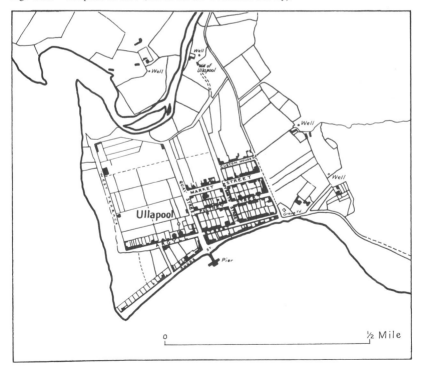

Fig. 12.11 Pulteney Street, Ullapool, crossed by Ladysmith Street, in the direction of Mill Street, ca. 1940.

Fig. 12.12 Pulteney Street/Ladysmith Street crossroads, 1992 — tarred road, kerb and pavement, grass verge given over to car parking, corner house raised, street lighting.

regulations for the settlers. Although six houses were built by Melville at the Society's expense for sale to incomers, it was decided that in the ordinary course the settlers should build their own to conform with the Society's regulations for simple white houses. They were to be built quickly. If a tenant had not begun to build within eighteen months of taking his lease the Society was free to let the ground to someone else. Each lot (a maximum of 60ft, 18.3m, along the street) was to have a dwelling house, shops or warehouse built along the whole line fronting the street, and on that line no stable, byre, outhouse or peatstack was to be erected. If the whole line was not built within 15 years the tenant must give up the part still empty. No detail survives of the building of houses, but in 1796 there were 39 houses, of which 28 were tiled or slated; there were also 40 thatched huts [Figs. 12.11-12.14].

Although the Society refused to build houses for settlers, a loan of money at legal interest could be obtained on the security of the house. This loan must not exceed 50% of the total value of the house and could not be given to the settler until the house was built and certified as habitable; and it must be repaid within ten years either at once or by instalments. A final rule prevented the Society from spending more than £500 on these loans. All this seems unfair to the settler, but the Society always worked under the shadow of former schemes where all the money was used for unfinished buildings.

The Directors were quick to realise their responsibility in regard to public health at the new settlement. Cleanliness was one of the main features of Telford's contribution to the town plan. There was to be a lane 18ft (5.49m) wide running at the back of the houses. When some of the settlers objected that this reduced the size of their gardens they were told:

The reason for making the lane . . . is that they may have a place behind for laying out the dirt and dung of their houses instead of putting it in the street in front; and the back lane ought to be so wide that carts may pass each other when necessary and this is of more importance to the neatness and cleanliness of the Town than the adding of a few feet more to their gardens (GD9/9/49).

In front of the houses the street was to be 49ft (15m) wide. Each settler was to dig a ditch at least 6ft (1.8m) from his door, the whole length of his lot with a level footway covered with shingle to a width of 3ft (0.9m) between his house and the ditch. The earth from the ditch was to be laid in the centre of the street which would then slope towards the ditch, and a strip of 7ft (2.1m) in the centre of the street was to be covered with shingle. The regulation on this ended 'It is not expected by the Society that this be done immediately but by degrees and according to the convenience of the settlers' (GD9/24). Telford included a system of drains and sewers in his town plan (sadly no early plan of the village survived and all we have are tantalising references to yellow and red lines on 'the enclosed plan') — the drains to be open and leading to the harbour or river. The water supply of Ullapool became a serious problem for a few years. Telford included twelve public fountains on his plan, and later it was suggested that a reservoir might be made from the burn or that springs might be piped. One Director even sug-

Fig. 12.13 Pulteney Street, Ullapool, between Quay Street and Ladysmith Street, 1992. The single-storey house was one of several house types erected. It had a direct parallel in the improved crofter's house and represented the simplest of those laid out on Aitken's 1789 plans.

Fig. 12.14 Numbers 2 and 4 Custom House Street, Ullapool. 1992.

gested refining rainwater, and it was the rain which solved the problem, for after several wet seasons the water from the old wells proved sufficient for the new village.

FISHING OPERATIONS

All this seems a long way from fishing, and in fact no detail survives of the operations at Ullapool because the Society was forbidden to take an active part in them, and Melville and his colleagues did not report to the Directors. But Mackenzie described his fishing at Tanera during the 1790s. He owned a number of decked vessels which he used as floating storehouses and the fishing was conducted entirely from boats, the property of local fishermen — Ullapool settlers probably among them. The herring were caught and brought to the vessels for packing, or taken straight to the curing sheds on Tanera [Figs. 12.15-12.17]. Boats varied in size from one to two tons and Mackenzie reported that they 'went to the extremity of Lochbroom, which is about fifteen miles long and were able to turn the headlands but not with safety when fully loaded; I believe that they have followed the fish from loch to loch but not to any great distance' (*Reports*. x.245). This description emphasises the uncertain nature of the boat fishery, for if the shoals did not appear as usual the boatmen were unable to go very far in search of them. The herring were always unreliable and even in 1788 the summer and autumn fishing failed in Loch Broom, but December brought so great a quantity that according to Melville enough could have been taken to supply the markets of all Europe and the West Indies.

In 1798 it was said that the population of Ullapool:

> consists of artizans, small dealers in various articles wanted for the use of the country, labourers and fishermen. But when the shoals of Herrings come to the neighbourhood the whole inhabitants of the village may be considered as Fishermen or Fish Curers; for they are then all more or less concerned in that business; some employing their personal labour and others their property in Fishing adventures. The natives in general may be considered as Fishermen on those occasions, for all of them who can be spared from necessary occupations at their farms, come down to partake of the profits of the Herring Fishery, according as their slender means and best endeavours enable them. Last season the Herrings visited the coast in great abundance, and the settlers and neighbourhood may therefore be considered at present as in a state of comparative opulence, of which the effect will probably appear in the rise of more houses at the station than have been erected for the last two or three years, which were years of scarcity of Herrings on that coast (*Reports*.x.246).

Alas, 1797 was to prove the exception rather than the rule, and by 1800 it was becoming clear that the east coast rather than the west was being favoured by the fish. It was also evident (ibid.) that:

> when the Herrings are in plenty in the Neighbourhood, every thing else wanted by the inhabitants is so also. The vessels follow the shoals bringing along with them a supply of all necessary articles; but when there are no shoals, the Directors have sometimes found it necessary to lend from £50 to

£100 to some person of credit at the settlement, for the purpose of importing a cargo of meal to be sold by retail to the settlers at short credit.

And this was to become the predominant pattern.

THE DECLINE OF ULLAPOOL

By 1798 there were, in addition to about 30 boats belonging to settlers, three vessels of between 20 and 70 tons which belonged to Ullapool (one having been built there), and several more visited the station for import and export. But gradually, with poor seasons of fishing, the village ceased to be in a state of readiness, so that when shoals did suddenly come to Loch Broom necessary supplies and equipment were not to be had there — salt could not be obtained quickly so the curers could not operate, boats were no longer seaworthy when herring came, and nets and barrels were not available.

There were many reasons for the decline of west coast fishing as well as the non-appearance of shoals. The markets were disappearing. In the West Indies most of the fish had gone to feed the slaves and as the number of slaves declined, those paid wages preferred to spend their money on better food sent from America. For the standard of British red herring was so low, especially when barrels had been delayed in their wartime passage of the Atlantic, that only slaves would eat them.

The war and the blockade of Europe not only interfered with markets, but enemy ships and the fear of press-gangs cut down the enthusiasm of boat fishermen; in addition, emigration had begun to affect the Highlands. Also at this time the general influence of the Society was lessening — partly because the original Directors began to die off and were replaced by men with excellent qualities but with little connection with the north. For example when Sir William Pulteney (who was a Scot and began life as a Johnstone of Westerhall before marrying the heiress of the earl of Bath) died in 1805, his successor as governor was Sir William Smith, a member of Parliament, financier and supporter of Wilberforce (and incidentally grandfather of Florence Nightingale). His only apparent previous connection with the Highlands was that his father Samuel Smith had sent presents of tea and other luxuries to Flora Macdonald when she was in the Tower of London. Smith did valuable work for the Society, but he seems to have regarded it as one among his many rather impersonal charitable designs. The Society also had much of its influence transferred to the new Fishery Board set up in 1808, which took over all regulation of the industry and passed to official inspectors most of the intervention with the government. This was a triumph for the original aims of the Society, but curtailed its later activities.

Ullapool gradually sank from its hopeful beginnings, and in the first half of the 19th century there was little work and much hardship there. The Society finally withdrew from its western settlements. Tobermory was sold in 1844 and Ullapool went in 1847 to Sir James Mathieson of Achany for

Fig. 12.15 Gutting the fish. Rags were bound around the fingers to try to protect cuts and raw skin. Ullapool, 1940s/50s.

Fig. 12.16 Preparing herring for curing. The vat on the left contains salt. Ullapool, 1940s/50s.

Fig. 12.17 Packing the herring in barrels for export. Ullapool, 1940s/50s.

Fig. 12.18 The pier at Ullapool filled with boxes of herring. 1940s/50s.

Fig. 12.19 Motor lorries would take the herring to the curing yards. Ullapool, 1940s/50s.

£5,000 — the money being devoted to the Society's successful venture at Pulteneytown. Ullapool had to wait another hundred years before the fishing once again came its way and many of the Society's buildings could be used as they had been planned [Figs. 12.18, 12.19].

Acknowledgement

I am most grateful for permission to reproduce photographs to the following: R. Scott Morton RIBA [Figs. 12.7, 12.11]; Royal Commission on the Ancient and Historical Monuments of Scotland [Figs. 12.1, 12.6, 12.8, 12.9, 12.12-12.14]; Scottish Record Office [Fig. 12.4]; Trustees of the National Library of Scotland [Fig. 12.2]; National Museums of Scotland [Figs. 12.15-12.19]. The print for Fig. 12.3 has been very kindly provided by Monica Clough.

References

Manuscript:

Scottish Record Office:

GD9   Papers of the British Fisheries Society
E   Exchequer Papers of the Commissioners for Forfeited and Annexed Estates
           723 Reports to King and Treasury
           729 Factors reports
           741 Barrisdale estate
           746 Cromartie estate

National Library of Scotland:

MS 2619   Extracts of Answers to the British Fisheries Society

Printed:

Beaufoy, H. *Speech to the British Fisheries Society.* 1788.
Dunlop J. *The British Fisheries Society: 1786-1893.* 1978.
Fergusson, J. *Letters of George Dempster to Sir Adam Fergusson.* 1934.
Loch, D. *Essays on Trade.* 1778.
Reports. Reports of the Committees of the House of Commons.
Rickman, J. *Life of Thomas Telford.* 1838.
RPC. Register of the Privy Council. 1877.
Smout, T.C. The Landowner and the Planned Village in Scotland, in N. T. Philipson &
    R. Mitchison (eds), *Scotland in the Age of Improvement.* 1970.

ULAPUL DÀ CHEUD BLIADHNA

1788-1988

ULLAPOOL BI-CENTENARY

<u>*EMIGRATION.*</u>

Free Grants of Land in Canada.

160 ACRES IN MANITOBA.
100 TO 200 IN OTHER PROVINCES.

OPENINGS FOR THE INVESTMENT
OF CAPITAL IN MANUFACTURES, &c.

IMPROVED FARMS at REASONABLE PRICES
in Nova Scotia, New Brunswick, Prince Edward Island,
Quebec, Ontario, Manitoba, & British Columbia.

ASSISTED PASSAGES
For Farm and General Labourers
and their Families.
SPECIAL FACILITIES OFFERED TO DOMESTIC
SERVANTS.

Pamphlets containing full information respecting the
investment of capital, land regulations, demand for labour,
rates of wages, cost of living, assisted passages, &c., can be
had on application to the Office of the High Commissioner
for Canada (Mr J. G. COLMER, Secretary ; Mr C. CAMP-
BELL CHIPMAN, Assistant-Secretary and Accountant),
9 Victoria Chambers, London, S.W. ; or to the following
Agents of the Canadian Goverment :—JOHN DYKE,
15 Water Street, Liverpool; THOMAS GRAHAME,
40 St Enoch Square, Glasgow ; CHARLES FOY, 29
Victoria Place, Belfast ; THOMAS CONNOLLY, North-
umberland House, Dublin.

Fig. 13.1 Opportunities for emigrants occurred throughout much of the 19th century. From
Historical Sketch of the Agricultural Progress of Scotland, Highland & Agricultural Society
of Scotland, Centennial Show, 1884.

POVERTY AND SURVIVAL
IN
NINETEENTH CENTURY COIGACH

Eric Richards

A PEASANTRY IN ADVERSITY

The survival of the heavily-populated communities of Coigach through the 19th century was achieved against formidable economic odds. Until the 1860s Coigach was one of the most remote and inaccessible districts in the mainland of the British Isles. It was also one of the poorest and most vulnerable to crop failure. Its isolation indeed had helped to preserve one of the best surviving examples of a peasant community within the industrialising nation. The people of Coigach existed in resolutely pre-industrial living conditions at a time when most of Britain moved rapidly towards complete industrialisation.

It was remarkable, therefore, that in such an age this peasant society should not only survive and persist, but also demonstrate signs of expansion. For instance, despite great poverty and periodic food crises, the population of Coigach and Lochbroom (the very large parish in which it fell) continued to grow rapidly and did not reach its maximum until the 1860s. Moreover, towards the end of the 19th century, the common people of Coigach were able to grasp a much firmer hold on their relatively small resources of land. In the teeth of the far greater economic strength of the landlord, the sheepfarmers and the great sporting tenants, the will of the people prevailed in the political campaigns of the 1880s. The peasantry, that is the crofters and the cottars, were by the terms of the Crofters' Act re-affirmed in their occupation of their lands. It was the victory of the small-holder against the forces of economic rationalisation; it was a demonstration of survival against the odds.

The tenacity and the triumph of the crofting communities in Coigach (and, of course, elsewhere in the West Highlands) was all the more extraordinary in terms of the adversity which they had faced. For, while the population rose at very high rates, continuously from about 1780 to 1860, some of the fundamental sources of income of the district lapsed into periodic or permanent decline. The great hopes raised by investments in the local herring fishery in the 1790s had been dashed by 1820: as Lord Teignmouth said, Ullapool, once the great hope of the district, had fallen 'victim of herring-caprice' (Teignmouth 1836. 68). The income derived from kelp manufacture had also collapsed by 1830. Recurrent efforts to introduce industry, in flax and wool processing, failed; and so did much of the old domestic manufacture of goods for local consumption (*NSA*. XIV. 89). The introduction of large sheep graziers to the district by the 1810s, producing wool for distant markets, placed greater pressure on the resources of the region. In agriculture the arrival of the potato in the late 18th century was a mixed blessing. A remarkable, almost miraculous, addition to food sources, the potato was extremely susceptible to disease, however. Its ease of cultivation and high productivity encouraged monoculture. Indeed throughout the 19th century Coigach remained in a precarious balance with its food supply. For most of the time the people of Coigach were unable to feed themselves from their own crops and depended on imported meal supplies (*OSA*. X. 562). A substantial proportion of the community lived near the margin of subsistence, near the edge of life. And beyond all this was the heightened competition for the land itself, the endless pressure from sheepfarmers and graziers for the lands of the west. Survival in such circumstances was itself a triumph.

There can be no doubt that the people of Coigach lived in poverty and insecurity throughout the 19th century. The conditions in which they lived were essentially pre-industrial. The economic foundations of life were narrow and still depended largely on the weather and the seasons; there was a continuous but unpredictable alternation of good times and bad. There was little industry or differentiation of employment. But the most telling indicator of pre-industrial circumstances in Coigach was the persistence of famine.

The primary purpose of this paper is to explore the meaning, extent and incidence of famine in 19th century Coigach, and the manner in which these emergencies were faced by the people and by the public agencies of the time. A broader question lurks behind this agenda. It concerns the means by which a growing population was able to sustain itself on the basis of ostensibly declining resources, the expedients which were required for this feat of survival. In part it involves the changes in the relationship between Coigach and the outside world, but this is not the main point of attention in this paper.

Access to the inner history of the crofter community is obstructed by formidable problems of evidence. It is characteristic of most peasant societies that they generate little written record of their own workings. This is true of Coigach. Apart from the brief appearances before the Napier Commission in the summer of 1883, it is extremely difficult to find any evidence deriving directly from the people of Coigach. We are necessarily thrown back on the observations of outsiders — on the reports of estate factors, of tourists, of government officials, of newspaper reporters, of police officers and visiting agriculturalists. We see Coigach through a filter, through alien eyes. Consequently we know most about Coigach when the Barony was subjected to extreme circumstances: during times of privation, of riot (Richards 1973) or of governmental intervention (Smith 1982). The dangers of these types of evidence are palpable: they tend towards a selective and unbalanced perception of the realities of common existence.

The best and most recommended type of evidence to counterbalance such distortions in the written record is that contained in oral testimony, by folk tradition, song or recent oral history. The only example I know in Coigach is the fascinating material collected by James M. Fraser in 1982 from Morag Shaw Mackenzie (see also Baldwin, this volume). This indeed adds several dimensions to our understanding of the inner world of Coigach. What is extraordinary is that these vivid recollections, which stretch across two centuries and more, make virtually no reference to famine or hunger in Coigach (Fraser 1982). In this, the oral testimony is in accord with other such evidence recorded in the West Highlands (Cregeen 1974). It is as though the phenomenon of famine and hunger has been systematically suppressed in the collective memory of the people. In reality famine was a central danger in the lives of the people, and it is possible to put this in a long perspective.

REMOTENESS AND DEMOGRAPHY

In 1793 the people of the Aird of Coigach gave themselves rare expression. In a petition to the Scottish Society for Propagating Christian Knowledge they pleaded for the services of a missioner. In doing so they drew attention to their circumstances and exposed several themes which were to recur throughout the following century. They were, they complained, 'Living at the extreme distance of Thirty Miles from our Parish church and Twenty Miles from the nearest place of worship, to which we have only access over roads almost impracticable to active and vigorous youth, and totally so to the *Old, Frail and Infirm!*' Mostly they travelled by sea which itself, they claimed, was hazardous. Their own description of Coigach was a passionate plaint against isolation. Coigach was, they said:

> an extensive tract of Country about sixty miles in circumference, inhabited by about One Hundred and Ten families, supposed to number at least five hundred and fifty souls, who have not the advantage of hearing publick worship more than twice in Twelve months, and during the rest of the year the poor Ignorant and Illiterate Inhabitants, only know the Lord's Day from the other days of the week, by resting from Bodily labour, which the Brutes of the Field enjoy in common with them! How then can this poor and dark corner be said to enjoy man's greatest boast, the Comforts of Religion!

The petitioners, to emphasise their case, claimed that their isolation was affecting adversely even their demographic behaviour. 'To the poor Inhabitants of this much and long neglected, dark and unenlightened corner, it is particularly distressing, when baptism and marriage' required the prompt services of a minister. They explained thus:

> This is thought to be no small check in our poor population, as weak children by cold and fatigue frequently loose their lives tho' it happens for most part that they are several months Old, before they are baptised; and Our Youth are deterred from the Honourable Bonds of Matrimony, from the apprehensions of the extreme trouble, to which the circumstances as above related expose them.

In so many words the people of Coigach were saying that their remoteness from church was seriously inhibiting both marriage and reproduction in the community (Petition to S.S.P.C.K. from the Inhabitants of the Aird of Coigach, Parish of Lochbroom, 1793, Cromartie Papers, Vol.19).[1]

There was obvious exaggeration in the 1793 petition, the proof of which was to be found in the extraordinary growth of population which had already occurred in the district. Precise estimates of Coigach's population are difficult to achieve because it was located within the great parish of Lochbroom which also incorporated Ullapool. The development and subsequent decline of the fishing village at Ullapool complicates the local demography and so also did seasonal migration. Nevertheless it is clear from Dr Webster's estimate of Lochbroom's population in 1755, and those of the Old and New Statistical Accounts which were reinforced by those of the Censuses, that population growth was accelerating in the late 18th century. The population of Lochbroom more than doubled between 1755 and 1831; the population of Coigach may have trebled between 1791 and 1834 (*OSA*. X. 564-5; *NSA*. XIV. 89). Moreover, population growth continued further until 1861, though at a diminishing rate after 1841.

Isolation, therefore, had not insulated Coigach from the demographic revolution; it may indeed have exacerbated the accumulation of dense settlements on the west coast. And the problem of isolation itself was not solved until new roads began to breach the mountains in the middle decades of the 19th century. These roads were constructed partly in response to the continuing recurrence of famine in Coigach.

FAMINES IN COIGACH: 1780-1840

One of the consequences of extreme isolation was that little reportage of famine can be found before the middle of the 19th century. Recent studies in the population history of Scotland have demonstrated that famine was a recurrent fact of life in many parts of the country well into the 18th century. These food crises, however, had been diminishing in both ferocity and scale for some time. Famines were becoming increasingly localised in their incidence and were, eventually, entirely exorcised from southern Scotland (Flinn 1977. 376). In the Highlands famine continued to wreak its penalties even into the 19th century.

Famine is a word notoriously difficult to define and is here used to denote severe shortfalls in the harvest which posed a threat to life and to future seed crops: a subsistence emergency which produced the imminent danger of a leap in mortality rates. In the 19th century Highlands such a crisis was commonly called a 'destitution'. By then, of course, the population of the entire region was much larger than before, and more people were at risk. Concurrently, however, communications with the outside world (and the sources of food) were improving, and various agencies emerged which were far better placed to counteract food emergencies. Nevertheless it would be a mistake to understate the severity of the 19th century famines in the Highlands. For, although there was no catastrophe to compare with that of Ireland in 1846-49, there were times when terrible danger hung over tens of thousands of people along the western littoral. Coigach was in the centre of the region still at risk throughout the 19th century.

Until the 1830s the subsistence emergencies in Coigach did not enter directly into the historical record. It is the contention of this paper, however, that the harvest crises of the 19th century were the last acts in the age-old saga of famine in the region, and certainly not the beginnings of communal hunger (see Donaldson 1938. passim). For instance, it is practically certain that Coigach suffered in the general Highland food crises of 1772, 1782, 1796, 1807, 1812-13 and 1817-18. It is hard to believe that Coigach escaped the hungry fate of so much of the Highlands in these years. The historical record, unfortunately, is virtually silent though we do know that the fishing merchant Ross gave people of Lochbroom meal on trust during the dreadful crisis of 1782. Ross's good feeling was fully reciprocated according to a recollection of the time: 'All paid him that could. When any died in debt, their directions were invariably to sell their effects to pay their meat, meaning meal. On their deaths their whole effects were sold by auction to pay this sacred debt — these might produce an average from 6s to 6s 6d' (*The Bee*, 30 May 1972). This brief glimpse of the famine indicates the significance of credit and external meal supplies in the crisis, and the high priority given to communal responsibility in facing adversity.

The first time that Coigach enters directly into the account was in the severe crop shortage of 1836-37. At last there was some public disclosure of conditions of life in the Barony although, of course, under the extreme circumstances of famine. Even so, partly because contemporary newspapers made relatively little reference to the famine, and partly because few estate records survive from the 1830s, our knowledge of the emergency in Coigach is derived primarily from a retrospective account given before the Parliamentary Inquiry into Scottish Emigration in 1841. It was contained within the evidence of Andrew Scott, the factor of John Hay-Mackenzie, proprietor of the Cromartie Estates of which Coigach comprised the westernmost extremity. Scott was a Roxburghshire man who had been employed in this role since 1831, a modern manager much frustrated by the immense difficulty of improving either the land or the people of Coigach. In addition, however, Scott's testimony revealed the extent and intensity of the 1836-37 crisis..

Scott provided some basic economic and demographic data about the people of Coigach. He had made his own count of the population in 1838 and provided the remarkable figure of 1,512 of whom more than one-third were less than 12 years of age; they lived in families of an average size of 6^1/$_2$ people and subsisted on eight great 'lot farms' to which were attached communal grazings; their arable land was a mere 450 acres, presumably almost exclusively devoted to the cultivation of potatoes. The cultivable land, indeed, was absolutely limited; there was virtually no possibility of any expansion of cropping area. Even more significant was the parallel existence in Coigach of an unofficial population, another 500 squatters, the marginal people who had no claim on the land whatsoever except as illegal subtenants.

The Highland subsistence crisis had made its first approach as early as 1835 when the *Inverness Courier* had reported a poor crop. The harvest of 1836 was much worse and great distress was reported in general terms (Barron 1907. II. 196). Public meetings were held in Edinburgh in February 1837 to mobilise relief on behalf of the West Highlands and Islands. A communication from Skye indicated the impending danger: 'We know not that the history of the British people ever presented such pictures of severe unmitigated want and misery as are exemplified at this moment in the case of our poor Highlanders' (Barron 1907. II. 197). A Glasgow Committee was also at work raising funds from various parts of the British Isles (Macleod 1898. 125) .

The famine crisis in Coigach, apart from Scott's testimony, passed virtually unrecorded except as subsumed into the general emergency in the West Highlands. The main element in the crisis was an almost total failure of the potato crop, but the corn crop (mostly oats) had also been damaged by frosts before it had been able to ripen. The herring fishing too had been very poor during the bad harvest years. Scott testified that the general health of the people of Coigach was good, yet every year some families suffered privation: 'living almost altogether on shellfish from the shore, with a little water gruel at night, and not a bit of bread or potato in their house'. Such people lived on the outer limits of subsistence and suffered want in the hard season of each year. As Scott said, 'There is positive distress every year'. But it is clear that in 1836-37 the deprivation gathered in a much larger proportion of the population.

Relief measures in Coigach were strictly limited by the financial capacity of the proprietor, Hay-Mackenzie. Certainly he recognised the responsibility to prevent death and disease on his estate, for these were regarded as the ultimate shame of the landlord (*PP*. 1841. Q.1817). But Hay-Mackenzie's finances were already strained and he was not equipped to deal with a mass emergency. In 1835 he had imported 200 bolls of meal from Aberdeen to be distributed in credit to the people and he allowed arrears of rent to accumulate (*PP*. 1841. Q.1676). Only one half of the small tenantry's rent was paid in 1835 and in the following years much rent was entirely lost. This relaxation of rent demands was the orthodox means by which a landlord could cushion the impact of famine, thereby allowing the people to use their cash reserves to buy imported meal for present consumption and as seed for future years. But in 1836 and 1837 the crisis outstripped Hay-Mackenzie's capacity to care for the Coigach community — as Scott put it candidly, 'if relief [from outside] had not come, I do not know what would have been the consequence, the distress was so severe.' The work of the Glasgow Committee was decisive in co-ordinating charitable subscriptions and its intervention was probably the most important element in the avoidance of fatalities during the famine. Hay-Mackenzie had contributed to the fund but his Coigach estate received far more than his contribution for its famine relief. The intervention from the south was an echo of the government assistance provided to the east coast in the famine of 1782-83 (Flinn 1977. 235). In a vital sense the isolation of Coigach had been effectively breached; southern agencies were now able to counteract the dire effects of subsistence crises. Scott was able to say, 'I never heard of any one dying from starvation' (*PP*. Q.1815).

It is too easy to assume that the crofting community, labouring under elemental difficulties, simply awaited its fate or, better, its relief at the hands of external agencies. It is clear, from hints in Scott's own evidence, that there was a measure of reciprocal, mutual, support in times of crisis. As Scott pointed out, there was minimal regular public support for the poor and the hungry: each harvest shortfall was treated as an emergency and resources within the community used as best as they could be. At such times the people were 'all poor together' and the poor looked after the poor. As Scott put it, simply but eloquently, 'they are very remarkable for that; a poor man would divide his potatoes with his destitute neighbours'. Charitable funds from the church were derisory, and the landlord gave only a few pounds each year by way of supplementation. There was no other mode of supporting the poor who were, necessarily, thrown back on the community itself. There was no compulsory poor relief and the landlord was certainly against its introduction. So also, claimed Scott, were the people themselves because it would diminish their sense of independence: 'that independent feeling which the poor in that country generally cherish'. He said 'They have a decided objection to be on the poor roll' (*PP*. 1841. Q.1803).

Thus, as far as can be detected, the community created its own minimum standards of security even in a context of perennial poverty and rapidly rising numbers. Despite annual hardships and periodic harvest shortfalls no one starved in 1836-37 and the poor were looked after in the bosom of the community. It was a precarious balance of welfare which required the co-operation of the landlord in two ways. He was expected to step into the breach when *extremis* threatened (as in a famine). In the last resort the factor (or the minister) would intervene and no one was allowed to starve — 'it would reach the ears of the proprietor or his factor'. Second the landlord forbore to extract the economic rent for the land occupied by the numerous small tenantry. As Scott implied, the people were simply not economic: the landlord would have been better off without them. Considerations of humanity (and perhaps also the fear of physical resistance) stood between the proprietor and the maximisation of his income (*PP*. 1841. Q.1798)

Two central facts emerged from Scott's account of the 1836-37 famine. One was the fundamental vulnerability of the people. Coigach commonly produced less than half of the subsistence requirements and, consequently, imported substantial quantities of oatmeal every year and more, of course, during local harvest shortfalls. This explains the central role of meal dealers in these communities, not simply as organisers of food imports but also as sources of credit. The second salient matter was the role of cash income.

Each lotter kept between one and three beasts, and cattle sales effectively paid the rent. The rest of the buying power of the community, its margin between hunger and comfort, was generated externally from seasonal employment in the Caithness fishing and harvest work in the south and east, supplemented by the increasing availability of construction work on the railways. As Scott said, 'The people . . . are all poor together as they must necessarily be; they go away to Caithness, to the herring fishing, and look out for such kind of work as they can undertake' (PP. 1841. Q.1810). The fishing at Wick could not have continued without 'the ample supply of hired men' from districts such as Coigach (John O'Groat Journal, 5 August 1853). The payment of rent at Coigach fluctuated directly with the success of the northern fishing. In effect, and increasingly so, the Coigach economy was propped up by this external income: it enabled the community to survive through its great growth of population. The people were poor but were able to make ends meet by the quite un-peasant method of selling their labour outside their own district.

The peripatetic character of the Coigach labour force gave the census takers decennial headaches. Local people were highly sceptical of the official figures. In the 1831 census it was known that 'some hundreds of the parishioners of Lochbroom, away at sea, at Caithness and deep sea fishing, and at south country labouring of various kinds, must have been omitted in their own, and returned from other parishes' (NSA. XIV. 83-4). But local observers were agreed that the population growth in Coigach continued unabated through the 1830s and 1840s; one claimed that it had grown by 10% between 1836 and 1847 (CP. Scott to Hay-Mackenzie, 4 April 1847). The community was able to absorb the increase only by uncontrolled subdivision of the crofts and further growth of its 'unofficial population'. The people continued, for the most part, to reject the option of permanent migration — partly because of the support of their external earnings, partly because they were prepared to tolerate a level of poverty unacceptable in other parts of Britain. The dangers were palpable. Further famine was openly predicted. As the Rev. Norman Macleod said in March 1841: 'I am afraid a very fearful crisis is approaching' (PP. 1841. Q.842).

THE FAMINE OF 1847-1848

The great disaster which produced the Irish catastrophe of 1847-48 also created extreme danger in the Highlands and Islands of Scotland. As in Ireland there was a large and growing population heavily dependent on potatoes. By December 1846 the destruction of the potato crop was reported widely, and the best known and best-documented of the 'destitutions' which descended upon the west coast had begun. In March 1847 the minister at Ullapool reported the imminence of disaster in his parish (Macleod 1847):

> The destitution of the people here from want of meal is truly alarming, and unless some immediately arrive, death will be the consequence. Great

numbers of people have nothing to eat but herrings [and] as there is no store of meal . . . starvation is surrounding its victims.

The Ullapool minister, three months before, had already signalled the onset of hunger. There was 'a considerable number of families in absolute want of food, raiment and money, subsisting wholly on the charity of their poor neighbours — a great many of whom will become equally destitute in a few weeks, unless a kind Providence send some relief from some unseen source'. Reports early in 1847, to the General Committee of Edinburgh for the Relief of Destitution in the Highlands and Islands, confirmed the severity of the emergency. In Lochbroom there was a dense, hungry and vulnerable population; two thirds of the potato crop had been lost; the seed potatoes were now also in jeopardy. Potatoes constituted three-quarters of normal food consumption. The general view was that it was already the worst crisis in living memory. In February the minister reported that no food had yet been imported to Lochbroom. So far only one hundred and fifty families were destitute but it was certain that many more would fall to this level unless food and employment were provided. 'At present they are mutually assisting each other and bearing their hard lot without murmur or complaint'. Some of the people were already scouring the countryside for employment, being 'desperate for work', and already local spokesmen were suggesting that subsidised road construction would be the best solution to the emergency.

The 1847 crisis soon generated an extraordinary panoply of relief, both public and private. Unprecedented efforts were made to prevent starvation. At Coigach the landlord was disadvantaged by his own financial difficulties, and eventually he accepted considerable philanthropic aid from external sources, as did many other West Highland lairds. By mid 1847 Hay-Mackenzie had already advanced to the people of Coigach, in meal and seed-oats, the equivalent of one year's rent, 'a great part of which he will not be able to recover', as his factor realistically predicted. Hay-Mackenzie also responded promptly and enthusiastically to the policy of the Board of Supervision for the creation of an employment scheme to construct roads in Coigach. It was designed as a form of relief for the able-bodied among the destitute. According to Andrew Scott, the road (later known as the 'famine road') would be a great boon to 'so remote and neglected a country'. It would educate the people into regular habits of work, and provide 'a taste of comforts that hitherto they have not discovered the want of'. The scheme combined development work with relief. It applied a work-test to the issue of food and other assistance in the name of an economic philosophy which was convinced that unrestrained charity was a moral danger to both recipient and donor.

The actual execution of relief works was a major challenge to the organisational capacities of the local estate factor and the relief officials. Anomalies and disputes were rife and the construction of roads presented great technical problems. The utilisation of untrained local labour was difficult and sometimes unpopular. Meanwhile the landlord was required to secure supplies of meal at a time when the general trade in cereals was in considerable disarray (Richards 1982. passim). Hay-Mackenzie eventually made arrangements for clippers to bring meal from Banff and Aberdeen to Ullapool, and potatoes were preserved for distribution in the following season. Yet proprietorial interference in the meal trade was itself regarded as a dubious practice since it would deter the operations of the regular private suppliers. So some of the people of Coigach received relief employment and food in clear contravention of the rules for distribution set down by the organising committees. The entire district was clearly in a turmoil of poverty and activity: in late 1847 there was an astonishing report that 1,671 people on Hay-Mackenzie's property were in receipt of some form of assistance. The total population was probably about 2,000. Such numbers were, of course, a measure of the emergency along the west coast.

The relief schemes were occasionally undermined by the seasonal migratory habits of the Coigach people. For instance, in the summer of 1850, the road construction work, especially that involving rock cutting, was seriously disrupted by the departure of many of the people to the Wick fishing. It was explained that ' at this season many of the people usually go to Caithness to the Herring fishing where they can gain better wages than in road-making'. Consequently the relief managers found themselves employing extra labour in order to proceed with the road (*CP*. Andrew Scott to Lord Stafford, August 1850).

Several features of the famine need emphasis. First, there can be no doubt about the scale and intensity of the crisis, nor its persistence. Crops through the years 1847, 1848 and 1849 were severely ravaged by the blight. The emergency, therefore, was much prolonged — again, in 1850, the potatoes were reported as rotting in their pits, road construction was continued, and special food supplies were still being brought in from the east coast. As late as March 1851 the potatoes were failing but now an excellent catch of herrings in Lochbroom rescued the people. As Andrew Scott explained 'Although their potatoes have mostly failed by this time, yet there is nothing like want among the small tenantry' (*CP*. Scott to Mrs Hay Mackenzie, 5 March 1851). Later that year the new potato crop was reported as abundant and sound. The famine was over.

Second, the famine had roused an unprecedented and widely co-ordinated system of relief which effectively combined local and external assistance. Suffering and real destitution undoubtedly occurred but the clear priority was that no death should occur. In effect the relief systems brought employment and income to the district supplementing the income usually brought into the district by external seasonal labour. As one official said, 'but for the interference of relief, the gravest consequences would have been in fatal operation'. This contemporary verdict accords well with the findings of modern demographic historians. It has been suggested that the relief measures were not only effective in preventing starvation during the famine: it is now argued that the levels of mortality *declined* during the famine years in the West Highlands and Islands (Flinn 1977. 433-4). Here, therefore, the contrast with the tragedy in Ireland (and indeed with famines in pre-1750 Scotland) is astonishing. For, though population had increased dramatically and had become dependent on a highly unreliable monoculture of potatoes, the mobilisation of relief was able to comprehensively counteract the consequences. The impact of famine had been radically curtailed: indeed it had been defeated. And so the events of 1847-50 in the Highlands leave a definitional conundrum. In what sense can they be designated as 'famine' when mortality rates are observed to decline?

FAMINES IN COIGACH: 1850-1900

The famine of the late 1840s is generally regarded as the last such event in British history. Living standards rose, food supplies were placed on a permanently secure footing, and Britain left its pre-industrial past forever. Famine was banished from the face of the country. In the Highlands the great famine was followed by relative prosperity. In 1852 there were serious fears of labour shortage in the Highland economy (*Ross-shire Journal*, 19 June 1852). Living standards for the small tenantry in particular improved: cattle prices and wages rose for several decades while most small rents remained static or rose much more slowly. In Coigach the relative trends were especially clear. Better standards of consumption were observed in those years and, even in the 1850s, it was increasingly difficult to persuade West Highlanders to accept free passages to Australia. It is apparent that in Coigach and other districts in the West Highlands, migration was slow to siphon away the recent increments of population growth [Figs. 13.1, 13.2]. The contrast with Ireland is again worth emphasising: in many parts the population was actually higher in 1851 than in 1841 and rose marginally for another decade. In Ireland, of course, the population fell dramatically during the famine years and after.

Yet this broadly optimistic version of West Highland conditions should be modified to take into account the continuing recurrence of famine conditions *after* 1850. Coigach provides clear evidence of these crises: its significance is to emphasise the persistent poverty and vulnerability of the communities of small tenants and cottars along Scotland's north-west coastline.

Measuring the intensity of famine is always difficult but it is unlikely that the severity of the years 1847-50 was ever again repeated. Nevertheless in each succeeding decade there were subsistence crises which demanded the mobilisation of relief measures on behalf of the Coigach crofters. These episodes are now mainly forgotten, yet at the time they caused great alarm even though they were less publicised than the previous emergencies. For example, in Coigach in the early 1860s a succession of poor crops eventually threatened the return of destitution. Petitions for help were received in May 1861. By January 1862 the people were reportedly worse off then they had been for many years. Potato supplies were exhausted and the small tenants were buying up reserves of oatmeal. Then the herring season failed and the subsequent potato harvest was also meagre. By the end of 1862 the position had demonstrably deteriorated into a full scale

STATE LINE.

STATE OF NEBRASKA.	STATE OF INDIANA.
STATE OF NEVADA.	STATE OF ALABAMA.
STATE OF GEORGIA.	STATE OF PENNSYLVANIA.

The Steam-Ships of this Line are appointed to sail from

GLASGOW TO NEW YORK,

EVERY FRIDAY, CALLING AT LARNE HARBOUR (BELFAST) THE FOLLOWING DAY.

All the vessels of the Company are of the most approved construction in hull and machinery, and built of a strength and quality of material surpassing the highest description of first-class ships. They have been proved to be superior boats of good average speed, and admirably adapted to contend with the heaviest gales which have been known to occur on the Atlantic Ocean. They have also been fitted up specially for the conveyance of passengers, and the accommodations for all classes are of the best description.

RATES OF PASSAGE.

Saloon, £10, 10s. to £15, 15s. per adult ; Second Cabin, £7, 7s. per adult.
Return Tickets available for 12 months at reduced rates.

STEERAGE AT LOWEST RATES.

Passengers booked to Boston, Philadelphia, and Baltimore at same rates as to New York, and at special low rates to all parts of the United States and Canada.

A liberal amount of luggage allowed to each passenger free. Experienced Surgeons and Stewardesses carried.

For freight or passage apply to AUSTIN BALDWIN & CO., 53 Broadway, New York ; GEORGE C. PIM & CO., 20 Corporation Street, Belfast ; JOHN POLLEN, 19 Eden Quay, Dublin ; ROSS SKOLFIELD & CO., 2 Old Churchyard, Liverpool ; THOMAS COOK & SON, Ludgate Circus, Fleet Street, London ; or to

THE STATE STEAMSHIP COMPANY, LIMITED,

JOHN BRUCE MURRAY, Manager.

65 GREAT CLYDE STREET, GLASGOW.

Fig. 13.2 Emigrants were welcomed by most of the old 'Commonwealth'. countries — Australia, New Zealand, Canada — and by the United States. From *Historical Sketch of the Agricultural Progress of Scotland,* Highland & Agricultural Society of Scotland, Centennial Show, 1884.

emergency. The Cromartie Estate, now partly subsumed under the administration of the Duke of Sutherland's estates, mustered its resources for the needs of the moment. Famine relief in Coigach in 1863 was a replication of the events of 1847-50 with one exception. This time there was no external intervention by charitable or government agencies; instead the estate administration organised its own methods of relief. By January 1863 road construction and cottage building had been set going by the estate factors; relief was made available, under the strict rules of a work test for the able-bodied. This time however there was no landlord interference in the import of foodstuffs which was deliberately left in the hands of the customary meal-dealers. Nor was there any subsidisation of meal prices. As the Sutherland estate commissioner insisted, 'our duty is confined to averting absolute want and starvation', and this required great stringency in the provision of relief and charity. Self-help and the freedom of trade must not be subverted. Relief employment on wages and the unfettered operation of the market were the two pillars of the system created to combat the famine. But the community was promised that 'not a single person [would] suffer from absolute starvation'. Local factors were given unambiguous directives: 'You must let no one starve' (CP. George Loch to Andrew Scott, 1 February 1863, 21 February 1863, 22 February 1863, 27 February 1863). In part the relief system was designed to provide employment and income until the Caithness fishing season began, and until the new harvest was got in. Indeed by late 1863 the crisis was over and a good harvest celebrated. One consequence of the famine was that it revealed once more the mass of poverty that existed below the surface of estate life even in normal times. Once again, too, famine had further accelerated road construction in Coigach and thereby diminished again its isolation.

For as long as so many people lived in conditions of virtually pre-industrial seasonal dependence, any shortfall in the harvest was bound to bring hardship, certainly to the most marginal elements in the population. Localised famine recurred. In the middle of 1870, for instance, it was reported from Coigach that the people had been without potatoes since the early part of the winter and, though food was still relatively cheap, they had already exhausted their money and their credit. Once more the local economy had no internal means of generating employment and income. Rent arrears mounted again. As one estate factor remarked: 'There will always be a heavy list of defaulters on the West Coast among the small tenants'. The Duke of Sutherland was persuaded to finance further road construction in Coigach, partly for development purposes and the encouragement of the sporting tenantry, but more particularly to offer relief to the people by means of employment. One of the more outspoken factors remarked, 'I rejoice to hear that the Coigach road is at length to be made — it will not only afford much valuable employment for your people and afterwards tend to improve and civilise them — but it will teach many of them to work with pick and spade which is a valuable species of education for them through life'. The food crisis was little reported at the time even though the potatoes continued to fail: in October 1872 half the crop was yet again destroyed by disease (*CP*. Gunn to Loch, 19 October 1872).

There were, naturally, good times between the crop failures. The local arable economy may also have diversified, though our knowledge of this is meagre. When the herring fishing was successful the people of Coigach lived in greater ease, for instance in 1879, and the landlord received better rents. Two years later conditions worsened dramatically and created another serious subsistence crisis. This new emergency in the western crofter communities provided the essential economic context to the great crofter agitation which was played out during the following years. The renewed food crisis had several causes. One was the accumulated effect of three exceptionally bad seasons within five years. In February 1881 all categories of tenants were in grave difficulty, suffering from very poor prices for their saleable stock at a time when their potatoes had been destroyed by frost. The Cromartie factor exclaimed, 'It has been a most trying winter for poor people out of employment, and for the sake of all concerned I do trust an improvement will come soon' (*SP*. Gunn to Kemball, 7 February 1881). Another cause was the severe weather and storms of December 1881 which damaged many of the fishing boats of the Coigach district. This was then followed by a very poor fishing season, and many of the people came back penniless from Caithness in late 1882. The markets for sheep and cattle were also much depressed. In October 1882 it was evident that the potato crop was again failing and that the oats had been ruined in the fields by gales.

By late winter, in March 1883, signs of hunger began to re-appear in Lochbroom where already fifty families were reported to be in danger of destitution having exhausted their own food supplies and pleading with the landlord for relief. William Gunn, factor on the Cromartie estate, described the terrible food shortages and the ensuing destitution: 'there has been nothing like it for the last forty years or more', he claimed. It was especially severe for widows in the community, women with large young families and no able-bodied workers. They faced many months of hunger before the new season. But there was also a shortage of seed and another emerging problem at the centre of the distress was the decline of local meal merchants. There had been a long term decline in country meal-mills in the region and grain was now sent to Aberdeen for processing. More critically, distant traders would not extend credit to the people, and credit had been the traditional means by which famine was mitigated and its economic effect spread across a longer period of time.

The local Parochial Boards were clearly unequal to the task of widespread relief in Coigach. It also became clear that the problem in Coigach was merely a part of a wider West Highland crisis. Rapidly and efficiently external charitable assistance was assembled by the Mansion House Committee in London, attended by much publicity on behalf of the crofters. The Cromartie Estate once again activated itself to prevent starvation. Road works were instituted together with other small relief works — notably a series of ' branch and peat moss roads [which] will be most useful to the people when completed'. Once again, however, the estate expressly refrained from interfering with the food supply trade. Moreover the dangers of charity were stressed. As the factor put it:

I am fully alive to the necessity for the greatest care and discrimination in dealing with these people at such a time. In every possible instance the labour test should be applied and *charity* should only be given in cases of real and proved necessity.

Relief employment was confined to one man per family.

It was during this crisis that the Cromartie estate found itself in the position of relieving people who were publicly resisting the authority of the estate and withholding their rents in a concerted political campaign of protest for land rights. Nevertheless the estate policy was unambiguous: 'The utmost watchfulness will . . . be needed . . . to anticipate any risks of loss of life from starvation'. In March 1883 forty-five families were in immediate need of relief in the form of food; 135 families also needed seed for oats and potato sowings, and many of these families had no breadwinner whatsoever. By April 1883 a ton of meal was on its way by steamer from Glasgow, arranged by charitable organisations. For, though the Sutherland administration was loathe to admit the need to involve external assistance, the crisis had awakened the conscience of the British people. There was no question that relief would be forthcoming or that people would die of hunger. Death was averted (*CP*. Finlayson to Gunn, 7 May 1883; Kemball to Gunn, 12 April 1883; Gunn to Mackenzie, 8 May 1883; *Scotsman*, 21 March 1883, 23 April 1883).

The crisis of 1883 had followed the pattern set in 1837: famine conditions were effectively nullified by prompt and sufficient measures of relief. Without them death rates must have worsened. By the mid 19th century internal and, more vitally, external resources were far greater and far better co-ordinated than in previous centuries. As the experience of Coigach demonstrated, starvation was avoided, not because the basic food deficiency was less severe but because the modes of relief had become so much more successful. Nor should it ever be thought that agricultural improvement had now put the region beyond the cold reach of destitution. In 1885 the potato crop was yet again diseased and storms destroyed the crops: the season was regarded as the worst in eighteen years; rent was remitted by 50% and the people were able to subsist mainly on the strength of a good herring fishing (*CP*. Gunn to Duchess of Sutherland, 30 April 1885). Two years later the potato crop was attacked again by disease and it was reported that the seasonal migrants from Caithness 'male and female are returning home from the east with little money, partly from the low prices of herring'. Continuing road construction work helped once more to cushion the effects (*CP*. MacIver to Gunn, 12 September 1887). Finally there were fears of destitution in January 1891 again (*Ross-shire Journal*, 2 January 1891), and a further recurrence of potato disease in September 1896 — in both cases, however, the extent seems to have been relatively confined.

In a strict sense none of the subsistence crises in these years could be classed as 'famine', since short-term mortality rates appear not to have increased. In a broader sense however it is clear that in at least four of the episodes here described the failure of the harvest would have occasioned actual starvation had it not been for the intervention of external assistance. These episodes were the clearest sign of persistent poverty and the recurrent danger under which the western crofter communities laboured. The reliance on the weather, on the seasons, and on the direct production of an ungenerous land had changed little over the past century.

A SELF-SUSTAINING COMMUNITY

The economic and social history of Coigach in the 19th century, therefore, was one of survival against adversity. To concentrate on times of famine and emergency is, of course, to produce a biassed and pessimistic account of life in the Barony. There were also times of feasting and relative comfort. Nevertheless the continuing recurrence of severe food shortages exposed not only the vulnerability of the population at large but also its general poverty. The subsistence crises caused great distress among the people and embarrassment to the landlord. The Duke of Sutherland (husband of the Countess of Cromartie) was one of the richest men in the kingdom and he effectively presided over one of the country's poorest populations. Mostly the people of Coigach looked after their own needs but, during subsistence emergencies, it was necessary and expected that the landowner would intercede with direct assistance. Relief required the constant vigilance of the landlord since famine was regarded as a great humiliation to both the people and the proprietor. The record of famine relief in the 19th century sometimes appeared doctrinaire and harsh in its regulations but, in the last analysis, must be considered successful since no one starved to death.

In 1883 Alexander Mackenzie described the people of Coigach as 'the most comfortable crofters in the north of Scotland' (Richards 1973. 164). Neither this, nor the clear improvements in welfare since 1850, should obscure the persistence of shocking levels of poverty even at the end of the century. The records of the Cromartie estate bear eloquent testimony to the harshness of existence, of dozens of families living in conditions of helpless poverty, submerged in debt and facing rent arrears completely beyond their means of recovery. The Cromartie rent books are catalogues of primary want, of endless biographic accounts of large families with virtually no means of employment and income, of old people living on the margins of subsistence, of infirmity, desertion, ill-health and, increasingly, of reports of children 'gone away'.

The question that looms over this study is not so much the sheer existence of poverty but the means by which the community sustained itself and coped with its adversity. It was a great feat of survival. Perhaps the most important point was that the local economy was underpinned by income from outside. The willingness of the people to sail or tramp out of Coigach in search of employment was remarkable and consistent. Working in the Caithness fishing, in the harvests of the Lothians, in the kitchens of

Edinburgh, all produced income for the landlord's rents, for food imports, for old and young relatives. In effect, ordinary life in Coigach was subsidised since the district simply could not yield sufficient income to sustain the people from its own resources. It was a remarkable balancing act maintained for more than a century. It was so successful that twice as many people lived in Coigach in 1860 as in 1760. Yet this of course was itself a great paradox: of demographic growth in an age of recurrent crisis.

Another element in the context was the behaviour of the landlord. Either out of considerations of humanity, or out of simple political expediency (or both), the Cromartie lairds were compliant in a *modus vivendi* which allowed the land to be rented at less than its next alternative use. The crofters did not pay an economic rent and their real rents fell during most of the 19th century. The small tenantry had persisted and expanded their numbers despite the fact that they could not compete against alternative uses of the land they occupied. This itself was part of their triumph against the stark forces of economic rationality. It was also an index of the tenacity of the people to resist such rationalisation — best and most sensationally demonstrated in the Coigach riots of 1852-53 (Richards 1973. passim; Richards & Clough 1989. 236-45; Baldwin/MacLeod & Payne, this volume). It was a status which was ultimately institutionalised under the legislative consequences which flowed from the Napier Commission of 1883.

Survival, however, was also related to one of my original themes, that is the remoteness of Coigach. Isolation, despite the mobility of the people, had tended to preserve the community from certain types of change. Coigach (and other districts in the West Highlands) had sustained the last of the peasantries on mainland Britain. Many of its agrarian arrangements were survivals from the pre-industrial age. As late as the 1860s some of the remnants of the old tacksman system remained and sub-tenancies persisted. Labour services were slow to die, and even in 1896 some of the land was still worked in the ancient runrig methods. Large families were valued for the insurance that growing children gave to ageing parents. The direct reliance on agriculture and fishing remained central to all existence, and they continued to impose their age-old disciplines of time and season on the community (Richards & Clough 1989. passim; Baldwin, this volume).

These, however, were the outward forms: within the society survival was assisted by methods of mutual support in times of difficulty which both surprised, and were admired by, outside observers. As far as it is possible to penetrate the detailed life of the community it appears always to have rallied to its own emergencies, though this was not always enough to preserve life. Land itself, ironically, was regarded as the greatest security against adversity, and land was clung on to with extraordinary perseverance even though, in reality, it provided very meagre security let alone comfort. It was a society which, in some important sense, exhibited a tolerance of poverty and occasional deprivation. Here, however, the evidence is ambiguous: there were indeed times when emigration was popular and people sought to leave Coigach altogether; sometimes it seemed even their own poverty hindered their departure. Yet, when free emigration became available, especially in the 1850s, the outflow was relatively small (Hildebrandt 1980. 261) [Figs. 13.1, 13.2]. For the most part the community seems to have preferred to use seasonal migration in order to preserve their life in Coigach. Seasonal migration was an alternative to emigration, a means of putting off expatriation.

The chronology of Coigach's population changes is significant. The local population appears to have grown continuously until 1861. In the next decade net migration for the first time exceeded the natural increase of population. After that the decline was rapid, falling by one third between 1861 and 1901: it was like a sudden release of people, a swift reduction of the long-standing demographic pressure.[2] The interesting aspect of this exodus is that it began to occur in times of rising living standards. The people of Coigach began to migrate permanently only when their living standards began to improve. Rising expectations undoubtedly played their part. So too did the erosion of Coigach's isolation which was conquered primarily by the physical effort of the people of Coigach themselves during times when the failure of their own resources had reduced them to mendicancy and destitution. Eventually the people were confronted with the choice between the croft and the outside world. The remarkable thing was that they delayed the choice much later than most agrarian communities in the British Isles.[3]

Notes

[1] On the fate of this petition, see *OSA*. X. 564-5.
[2] These remarks are based on the successive censuses, mainly extrapolated from Lochbroom figures. The 1881 census provided detailed statistics for Coigach including evidence that the number of males exceeded females. This is either a mistake or the consequence of a freakish boom in male births five to ten years before.
[3] All references are to the Cromartie Papers unless otherwise indicated.

References

Manuscript:

Cromartie Papers [*CP*], in Scottish Record Office.
James M. Fraser, Manuscript of Interviews with Morag Shaw Mackenzie, 1982 — with particular thanks to the author.
Highland Destitution Papers. 1847. Vol. B.10, B.11, in Scottish Record Office.
Sutherland Papers [*SP*], in Stafford County Record Office.

Printed:

Barron, J. *The Northern Highlands in the 19th Century.* 3 vols. 1907-1913.
Correspondence from July 1846 to February 1847 relating to measures adopted for the Relief of Distress in Scotland. 1847.
Cregeen, E. Oral Tradition and Agrarian History in the West Highlands, in *Oral History.* vol. 2. 1974.
Donaldson, J. E. *Caithness in the Eighteenth Century.* 1938.

Flinn, M. W. Malthus, Emigration and Potatoes in the Scottish North-west, 1770-1870, in L. M. Cullen & T. C. Smout (eds), *Comparative Aspects of Scottish and Irish Economic and Social History 1600-1900.* n.d.

Flinn, M. W. (ed.) *Scottish Population History.* 1977.

Highland Destitution, in *Blackwood's Magazine.* vol. 62. November 1847.

Hildebrandt, R. W. *Migration and Economic Change in the Northern Highlands.* Unpublished Ph.D. thesis, University of Edinburgh, 1980.

Letters on the Present Condition of the Highlands and Islands of Scotland. Reprinted from the Scotsman newspaper. 1847.

Macgregor, A. On the Causes of the Destitution of Food in the Highlands and Islands of Scotland in the Years 1836 and 1837, in *Quarterly Journal of Agriculture.* vol IX. 1838-9.

Macleod, J. N. *Memorials of Rev. Norman Macleod.* 1898.

Macleod, N. *Destitution in the Highlands and Islands of Scotland. Speech of the Very Rev. Norman Macleod D.D.* Pamphlet. Glasgow, March 1847.

[*NSA:*] *New Statistical Account of Scotland.* 15 vols. 1835-45.

[*OSA:*] *Statistical Account of Scotland.* 21 vols. 1791-99.

[*PP:*] *Parliamentary Papers: First Report from the Select Committee on Emigration, Scotland.* 1841.

Political Economy of a Famine, in *North British Review.* May 1847.

Richards, E. Problems on the Cromartie Estate 1851-3, in *Scottish Historical Review.* 1973.

Richards, E. The Last Scottish Food Riots, in *Past and Present Society Suppement No. 6.* 1982.

Richards, E. & Clough, M. *Cromartie: Highland Life, 1650-1914.* 1989.

Smith, A. M. *Jacobite Estates of the Forty Five.* 1982.

Smout, T. C. Famine and Famine Relief in Scotland, in L. M. Cullen & T. C. Smout (eds), *Comparative Aspects of Scottish and Irish Economic and Social History 1600-1900.* n.d.

(Lord) Teignmouth, *Sketches of the Coasts and Islands of Scotland and the Isle of Man.* 2 vols. 1836.

Newspapers:

Inverness Courier
John O'Groat Journal
Ross-shire Journal
Scotsman
The Bee

AT THE BACK OF THE GREAT ROCK: CROFTING AND SETTLEMENT IN COIGACH, LOCHBROOM

John R. Baldwin

INTRODUCTION

General Background

Assynt and Coigach were once in the possession of the Clan Nicol, a family traditionally said to have held lands in Lewis since the 10th century. The remains of their modest mainland stronghold are commemorated in the name 'Castle Street', in Ullapool. In the mid 14th century, however, Torquil MacLeod of Lewis was granted a charter for the lands of Assynt by David II, and although Coigach was not specifically mentioned he continued to hold both districts — which had been seized by his father from the MacNicols. The 'transfer' had been regularised by his father Murdo's marriage to Margaret, the MacNicol heiress. MacKay of Strathnaver subsequently held what was effectively a liferent for some years and the Earls of Ross appear to have claimed a superiority, but essentially Coigach remained in the hands of the MacLeods of Lewis until the early 17th century.

By the early 1600s, however, the MacKenzies had come by Coigach — albeit not straightforwardly. Kenneth MacKenzie of Kintail was active in subduing Lewis and 'acquired' the lands of the MacLeods of Lewis. In 1608 he granted Coigach to Rorie MacKenzie of 'Cultaloid' (Castle Leod), who had married Margaret MacLeod in 1605. Like the earlier Margaret, she was also an heiress — in this instance to Torquil 'Cononach' MacLeod of Lewis. In a manner of speaking, therefore, the lands of Coigach were once again brought as a dowry, even if technically they were no longer Margaret's to bring. The Royal Charter for Coigach of 1609 was effectively royal confirmation of Kintail's grant of 1608 to Rorie. In his own right, Rorie MacKenzie ('Rory Mor', the Tutor of Kintail) had earlier inherited the lands of Castle Leod in Strath Peffer, Easter Ross, which gave the expanding Estate its eastern base. It was an Estate that his descendants were to own for over 400 years (Cromartie 1979. 29, 71, 93, 293; R&C 1989. 7; M. Bangor-Jones 1992. pers. comm.) [Fig. 11.1].

The lands of Coigach were wild, inaccessible and remote; more like an island than a part of the mainland until the coming of roads. The first, but inadequate 'road' to Ullapool from the east was built between 1792 and 1797; it proved impassable within twelve years and there was to be no satisfactory road west of Garve until after 1847. Efforts to build roads in

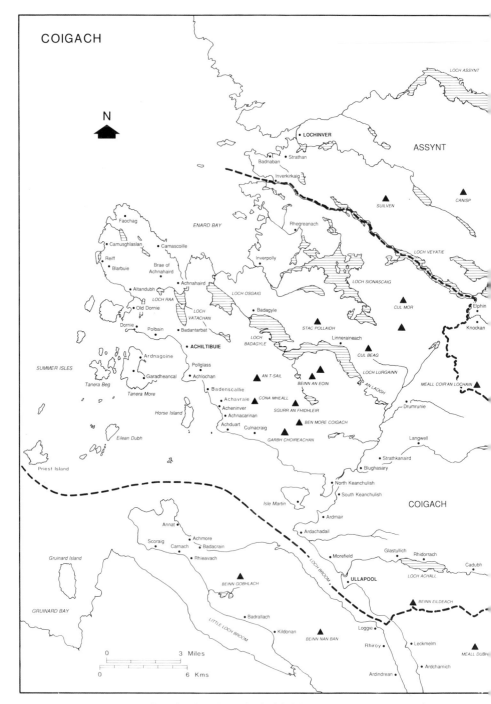

Fig. 14.1 Settlement in Coigach at the peak of mid 19th century population growth. Field survey reveals a small number of additional, tiny coastal settlements broken out by fishermen, cottars or squatters.

Coigach and Wester Ross in subsequent years, eg the 1850s and 1870s, were linked primarily to famine relief. Indeed, cattle and sheep were still being taken out of Coigach 'on the hoof' into the early 1930s (Cromartie 1979. 267-8; Baldwin 1986. 207 et seq; R&C 1989. 209-12, 286-7). Until relatively recent times, therefore, travel was either on foot or — much more easily and rapidly — by boat.

Coigach divides into two distinct areas, split by the mountains of Ben More Coigach, Cùl Beag and Cùl Mór [Figs. 14.1, 14.2]. Southern/eastern Coigach encompasses Ullapool, Glen Achall and Rhidorroch, Strath Kanaird and Langwell; northern/western Coigach includes Inverpolly and Sionascaig in addition to Achnahaird, Achiltibuie and the coastal lands out beyond Ben More Coigach on outer Loch Broom. Northern Coigach also includes most of the Summer Isles, and either in part or in whole was once referred to as 'the Aird of Coigach'. The one-time 'davoch of the Aird' appears to have stretched from Badenscallie to Rubha Coigach, and from there to the Kirkaig river (Bangor-Jones 1986. 157; 1992. pers. comm.).

Present-Day Coigach

This paper focuses primarily on those parts of Coigach that lie north and west of A'Bheinne Mhór, the big mountain (Ben More Coigach). It seeks to reflect aspects of everyday life and work in the late 19th-late 20th century as recalled and experienced by local families — notably the last MacLeods in the tiny township of Culnacraig. The MacLeod pedigree can be traced to early 19th century clearances for sheep of lands around Inverpolly and Loch Sionascaig, marching with Assynt some five to ten miles (8-16 kms) due north. In the mid 18th century, Culnacraig was uninhabited — it appears merely as a grazing on the Badenscallie farm [see Figs. 14.64-14.66] so in seeking to set that culture within the framework of evolving settlement patterns more widely in Coigach, there is a certain focus on the earlier farm of Badenscallie. Nonetheless, given that the Culnacraig MacLeod traditions and recollections are generally representative of those of the wider indigenous population of Coigach, this paper reflects more fully the rise and fall of crofting in Coigach.

Today, Culnacraig and the neighbouring townships of Achduart and Achnacarinan have reverted to sheep grazings — generally in association with outward migration, sub-leases and croft amalgamations. By contrast, privately-planted coniferous plantation covers much of the Achavraie infield (much of the rest being private lawns and gardens); whilst recently-planted mixed woodland is transforming Acheninver — a private conservation project by the leaseholder. All these townships are early 19th century pendicles of the 18th century (and much earlier) Badenscallie farm. At Achduart, Achnacarinan and Acheninver, a little traditional crofting continued into the mid 1960s; it survived into the early 1970s in Culnacraig, with a few drills of potatoes laid down for a number of years thereafter. Badenscallie, too, is now used mainly for grazing (cattle still, as well as sheep); but Badenscallie

Fig. 14.2 Cùl Mór, Stac Pollaidh, Cùl Beag, Beinn an Eoin and Ben More Coigach rise starkly beyond the crofts of Brae of Achnahaird. 1972.

alone retains an indigenous and active, albeit small crofting population [Fig. 14.3; see also Fig. 14.56].

In other words, the outermost townships mark the furthest expansion of settlement and cultivation at the time of the clearances, land hunger and peak population. At the other end of the peninsula the abandoned settlements of Faochag, Camascoille, Camusghlaslan tell the same story. So does Achlochan, and so do the townships on Tanera Mór [Fig. 14.1]. As pressures reduced, the smallest, poorest and least accessible townships on the outer limits of cultivation have emptied soonest and most completely. Certainly there is some contemporary diversification with local cooperatives developing small fresh-water fish farms at Culnacraig and Acheninver (as well as on other small burns in Coigach), but most of the former croft houses on these erstwhile Badenscallie pendicles have become holiday homes or retirement cottages. The new timber-frame house at Achduart serves a similar function, whilst the two large newish houses at Achavraie and Acheninver are owned respectively by the family of a former (post-Cromartie, mid 20th century) proprietor of the Ben More Estate, and by a titled land-owning dynasty from central Scotland which also owns the fruitful waters of Loch Osgaig. Ironically, the Cromartie family itself, constrained managerially and financially after (and indeed before) the Crofters

Fig. 14.3   The outermost crofts at Badenscallie have long ago gone empty and fallen into ruins as the core area of croftland and settlement has contracted. 1992.

Act of 1886, retains just one small unimproved cottage, also at Achavraie. It, too, is now scheduled for renovation and extension.

These trends, taken along with the immigration into Coigach of proportionately large numbers of elderly retired (mainly from England or non-Highland Scotland), and of younger individuals and families in large part opting out of urban unemployment and soul-less housing schemes in the English Midlands, have had a major impact on a cultural tradition, now much decayed but essentially little changed until the mid 20th century for perhaps 1,000 years.

This culture is presently undergoing a period of rapid transformation, such as probably it has not experienced since the arrival of the Norsemen and the Gaelic-speaking Scots. Because outward migration and the breakdown of the old economy have been so regular and substantial over the past 50 and more years, and because immigration has equally been so sustained and rapid over the past 30 or so years, not only does precious little now survive of the Gaelic language and culture but what does remain has largely 'gone underground', replaced by a remarkable interface of what would be termed elsewhere as mainly middle and working class lowland Scottish and English cultures. Recollection and understanding of the old ways, where this survives, is now largely fragmentary, and it has been submerged by new cultural waves with quite different cultural roots and aspirations. Whilst many newcomers may have an interest in what went before, by and large they cannot have a detailed, inherited or first-hand experience of Coigach's distinctive past (see MacLeod & Payne, this volume).

Whilst to some degree perhaps a lament, this is not a criticism. For whatever reasons, cultural change has taken place and is irreversible. Perhaps Gaelic will hold on in the area, taught as it is in the local school? — but this would seem unlikely given that Gaelic *learning* is minimal. And perhaps there are lessons to be learnt with regard to the nature and sustainability of economic change and the long-term intrinsic value of human cultures and natural environments that will help avoid a repetition of past errors and injustices? Meantime all cultural and ethnic strands within the present population of the 'Aird of Coigach' look to securing a future where community size and geographical location make cooperation and collaboration a necessary virtue.

THE TRADITION OF DONALD MACLEOD, CULNACRAIG

Family History

Donald MacLeod (1898-1979) [Fig. 14.4] possessed a good memory and eye for detail. From his own recollections it is possible to sketch an outline history of the family. His grandfather Donald (1816-1898), who died the year his grandson was born, was one of three brothers (Roderick, 1815-1857; Murdo, 1816-1897) all of whom were born 'in the Lodge area of Inverpolly'; his great-grandfather, Murdo Bain (1776-1863) was born 'somewhere between Inverpolly and Lochinver' [Figs 14.5-14.7]. All four were victims of the Clearances and formed a nucleus of the first recorded (although not the first) settlers in what came to be known as *A'Chulachreige* (Culnacraig: at the back of the rocky buttress, *A'Chreige Mhór*, on the steep western end of the ridge of *A'Bheinne Mhór*, Ben More Coigach).

Donald was well able to outline his genealogy (confirmed in good part by the stones in Badenscallie burial ground); he was also able to put at least a little flesh on the bones. His grandfather Donald used the shielings below the precipitous east/south face of Ben More; his grandfather's brother Murdo put in the well below the track below his house, built a wall around it and covered it; his grandfather's other brother Roderick emigrated with his family to New Zealand, where he died of 'galloping consumption' (tuberculosis). As for his father's generation, one sister (Hannah, 1858-1927 or Etta, 1864-1939) moved to Tain; the other two (including Annabella, 1870-1935) stayed in Culnacraig. Of his father's brothers, his uncles, Alex, the youngest (1876-1878) died in infancy; Duncan, the eldest (1855-1939) emigrated to Queensland, Australia, as a plumber; John (1862-1927) spent a few years as a shepherd at Raddery Mains, Tongue, before returning home; Roderick (the second eldest, 1855-1951) stayed at home as a salmon/herring fisherman and was 18 years bedridden with rheumatism from the fishing. In other words, four of the eight stayed at home. It is unlikely that the croft and

Fig. 14.4   The late Donald MacLeod, Culnacraig, cutting bracken to use as a base layer to his corn stacks. 1972.

Fig. 14.5   The farms of Inverpolly and Dalpolly, Coigach, based on a survey by William Roy, ca. 1747-52.

297

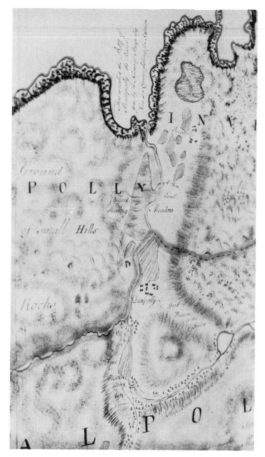

Fig. 14.6 ⁴Inverpolly and 'Dealpolly' Farms, as surveyed by Peter May, 1756.

the fishing could have supported more — even assuming it adequately supported four.

Donald's father, Murdo, was born in 1866 (died 1922), the sixth of eight children and the youngest of the four surviving brothers. According to Donald, he left for Glasgow to look for work; he married and settled down at '58 Miller Street, Motherwell'. His wife, Elizabeth Marshall, died one month after giving birth to Donald; Murdo was unable to look after his infant son; so Donald was sent north to Culnacraig to live with his 71 year old grandmother and uncles and aunts, mainly in their 30s and 40s. He was brought up, therefore, in a small remote township by kinsfolk who (with the exception of his grandparents) remained unmarried, and whose direct personal experiences went back to the 1820s-1850s/60s. Perhaps more than many, therefore, Donald MacLeod fell privy to the experiences, attitudes

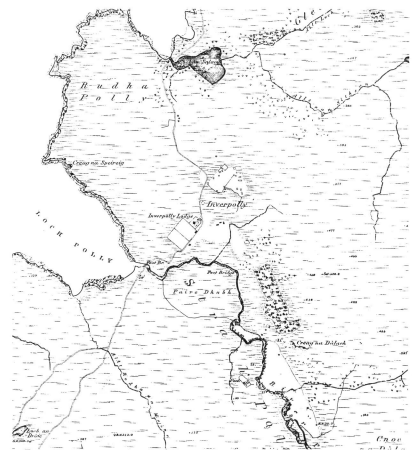

Fig. 14.7 Inverpolly, surveyed by the Ordnance Survey in 1875. Dalpolly has disappeared entirely by this time, though May's secondary cluster on the west bank of the river survives as a sheep fank. By contrast, the layout of the Inverpolly township remains not far from the subsequent Inverpolly Lodge.

and memories less of his parents' but of his grandparents' generation.

Development of the Township

From them, no doubt, he heard that prior to the clearances no-one lived in Culnacraig [Figs. 14.8-14.10; see also Figs. 14.65, 14.66]. He recounted that four families lived in the old Culnacraig; that when they first arrived their land was all down by the sea, and that it was they who created the patch-work of now long-abandoned turf dykes (*gàradh fàil*) and lazy-beds (*fean-nagan or màgan tumaidh*) that feature so clearly still in the landscape [Fig.

299

Fig. 14.8 Culnacraig, Coigach, 1972. The large flat field was known as Am Blàr; the smaller dyked fields below the nearest house were created in the late 19th century after security of tenure had been guaranteed by the Crofters' Act of 1886.

14.11]. They lived, he recounted, off herring and tatties; and their first houses were clustered around the site of his own house (171) and out-buildings [Fig. 14.13].

The question then is more 'why there?', rather than simply 'where?' According to Donald MacLeod, the original Culnacraig was below present-day Culnacraig, running down to the sea. He suggested that the people were

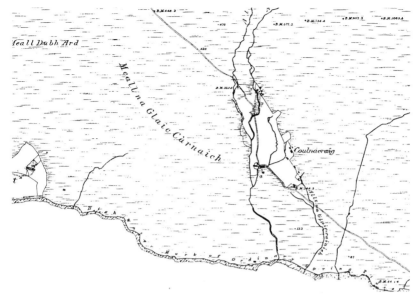

Fig. 14.9 Culnacraig, surveyed by the Ordnance Survey in 1875. Dwellings had become scattered, though the keeper's house at the upper end of the valley was not yet built. Nor was much of the infield yet enclosed other than by the hill-dyke. By contrast, none of the earlier lazy-beds are marked, lying below the present-day fields and running down to the sea between the two burns — evidence that they had long since been abandoned.

Fig. 14.10 Culnacraig by the time of the 2nd. edition of the Ordnance Survey 6 inch Map, 1906. This is close to the optimum period of settlement — the infield is at its greatest; the new houses have all been built; new tracks have been constructed, including the cart track down to the fishermen's bothy and the track leading to the school in Achduart. The main access track over the moorland has been realigned better to follow the contours.

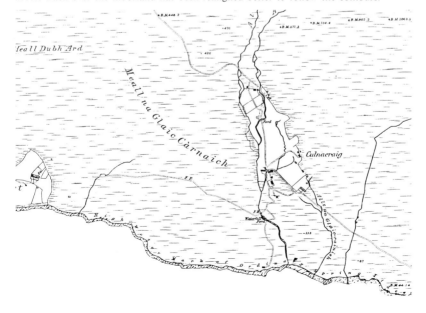

Fig. 14.11   Long-abandoned cultivation rigs below Culnacraig. 1992.

put there because, being more dependant on the sea, they preferred to be near it; but also because the flat and fertile Culnacraig croftland of today was then a marsh.

Some 14 ins or so (36 cm) under the big field (*Am Blàr*) is pure sand, and he heard it said that in former times it was a loch whose waters burst out and flooded down the hillside creating both the deep steep-sided gorge behind his own barn and the small gorge, *A'Chlais dubh*, below his neighbour's house (173). A marsh, it was said, remained; when the new settlers arrived, the steeper seaward rigs were broken out and cultivated whilst the marsh was being drained. Subsequently the people abandoned the early rigs, *A'Bhuaile Mhór* and moved to the better land.

Donald MacLeod's traditions apart, the first documentary record for Culnacraig appears to be in the proposals to improve the Coigach farms accompanying Morrison's plans of 1775 (E 746/189):

| To 38 [Roods] Stone to inclose Culchreg at 4/6 | £8 11 0 ⎫ |
| To 74   do.   feal on the same line at 2/- | £7 12 0 ⎭ |

It is not until 1815, however, that we become aware of any settlers, when Alexander MacLeod and Roderick MacLeod are cited as defendants in a process for payment of debts. They are listed as living at *Culcraggie of Badscallie* (SC 25/22/54).

Thereafter, the evidence is primarily that of the Rentals and various other Processes (Rentals from 1855 sampled on a five-yearly basis):

1820 (Rental):	Alexander MacLeod	£4
	Rory MacLeod Senior	£4
	Rory MacLeod Junior	£4
	Murdo MacLeod Senior	£4
	Murdo MacLeod Junior	£4
	(GD 305/2/2050/18)	

1826 (Processes):	Murdo MacLeod senior
	Roderick MacLeod senior
	Roderick MacLeod junior
	Murdo MacLeod senior
	Murdo MacLeod junior
	(SC 25/22/102)

1830 (Processes):	Murdo MacLeod alias Baillie
	Roderick MacLeod senior
	Roderick MacLeod junior
	Murdo MacLeod senior
	Murdo MacLeod junior
	(SC 25/22/119, 120)

1835 (Rental):	Rod. MacLeod Jn	£5 3
	Rod. MacLeod Sn	£4 16
	Murdo MacLeod Sn	£5 6
	Murdo MacLeod Jn	£5 3
	Murdo MacLeod	£4 12

In this rental Achininver, Achavrae, Achnagarron, Achduart and Culmacraig [*sic*] are all described as 'Pen.' — Pendicles of Badenscallie. (GD 305/2/85)

1853-1865 (Rentals):	Neil MacLeod	£5 1
	Murdo McLeod (Bain)	£5 8
	Robt. McLeod & Mother	£10 8
	Murdo McLeod (Black/Dhu)	£5 8
	(GD 305/2/119, 120, 121, 122, 132)	

1865 (Rental):	Niel McLeod [*sic*]	(168)	£5 1
	Murdo McLeod (Bain)	(169)	£5 8
	Robt. McLeod	(170)	£10 8
	Murdo McLeod (Dhu)	(171)	£5 8
	(GD 305/2/136)		

1870 (Rental):	Neil MacLeod	(170)	£5 1
	Murdo MacLeod	(171)	£5 8
	Robt. MacLeod	(172)	£10 8
	Murdo MacLeod	(173)	£5 8

By 1870, the Lot numbers allocated by 1865 had been amended and appear to equate with present-day house/croft numbers.
(GD 305/2/139)

1875 (Rental): As 1870, except that Robt. MacLeod's Lot is divided between himself, I. Grant, J. Grant and S. Grant.
(GD 305/2/142)

1880 (Rental):

Neil MacLeod	(170)	£6 8
Murdo MacLeod	(171)	£7 1 6
Robert MacLeod	(172)	£6 13
Murdo MacLeod	(173)	£6 11 6
Alexr. Grant	(174)	£6 6
(GD 305/2/147)		

1885 (Rental):

Neil MacLeod	(170)	£7 16
Murdo MacLeod Bain	(171)	£9 1 6
Do. Kate Int 12/-		
Robert MacLeod	(172)	£6 13
Murdo MacLeod Dhu	(173)	£7 19 6

On the statement of Rent Arrears for 11/11/1886, Neil MacLeod has been replaced by Wm. MacLeod.

The 'double' croft that Robt. MacLeod held 1850s-1870s, and then shared with Grants, has now reverted to a single tenancy. The 'second' croft has apparently been divided amongst all the tenants except Robert.
(GD 305/2/150)

1890-1892 (Rentals):

William MacLeod	(170)	£6
Murdo MacLeod Bain	(171)	£7
Robert MacLeod	(172)	£5 2
Wid. Anne & Don^d MacLeod	(173)	£6 2
(GD 305/2/156,157)		

On occasion the Rentals have been annotated. Thus on 4 January 1887 William MacLeod, Culnacraig, bought a Drumvaich tup off the Estate for 12/-; and on 16 April 1887, Murdo MacLeod Dhu paid £8 cash towards rent arrears.

Without further research into, say, the Census returns or oral family histories, it is not easy to identify more detailed inter-relationships between the various MacLeod families, or indeed the various Murdos or Rodericks. Donald MacLeod's recollections tell only that the original settlers included twin brothers, a grandfather and the grandfather's uncle; and that Murdos in his family were referred to as Bain — as opposed to Dhu. He was, however, able to point to Ruaridh Og MacLeod as being the great-grandfather of his former neighbour Christie MacLeod (173). 'Young' Roderick, also 'born at

Inverpolly' according to Donald, would presumably be one of the Rories of the 1820 Rental. In which case perhaps he could be the Roderick Og who, as told by Morag Shaw Mackenzie in 1982, 'took his father on his back out of the burning village of Sionnenscaig when the people were evicted'[1] (R&C 1989. 443)?

With five tenants and their no doubt increasingly extended families to feed it must be asked whether all the lazy beds down towards the sea would have been abandoned at once (as Donald suggested), or whether — and when — gradual contraction took place? For they would surely have needed as much land as possible? Perhaps it coincided with the allocation of individual crofts, apparently in 1829? By way of comparison, the high point of cultivation in the crofting areas of neighbouring Assynt appears to have been reached during the 1830s — given that efforts by the estate to encourage the improvement of crops led subsequently to better cultivation of a smaller, contracted area (M. Bangor-Jones 1992. pers. comm.).

Another enigma relates to the names *Tigh a'Bhaillie* and *Lios a'Bhallie* (the house and garden of the 'baillie', close by the Culnacraig sheep fank), and to 'Murdo MacLeod alias Baillie' in 1830. Oral tradition says that the fank was built out of the old house, and there are certainly enough ruins close by to have provided outbuildings and a dyked 'garden'. Perhaps the said Murdo MacLeod came to live in a house formerly occupied by 'the Baillie'? There is no known (Baron) Baillie ever resident in Coigach, however, and more realistically Murdo MacLeod simply acquired his alias as a result of a personal standing, status or reputation locally — triggered perhaps by his involvement in the legal 'processes', maybe standing up for his rights? A 19th century date for the name is undoubtedly the most likely — in which case it suggests that not all the older houses were necessarily clustered.

Donald MacLeod could identify only three stone houses for his four settler families — one in what was latterly his hen house, one in his garage, and a third a little below his garden wall, close to the well. Their very first houses may have been rapidly-built turf houses close to the shore; indeed tradition has it that one evicted family lived for over a year in a cave, *An Uamhag*, along the rocky shore towards the Geodh Mor [Figs. 14.12, 14.13]. The old stone houses, clustered between the 'old' and the 'new' infields, remained as outhouses once more substantial stone houses were built in the late 19th century — a beneficial effect, no doubt, of the 1886 Crofters' Act. Instead of being clustered, the new houses were scattered about the township. The family from below the track built their new house on the hillside (170); another built the outermost house in the present settlement (173) — thatched until 1905 when the house roof was raised and covered with corrugated iron (the steading was corrugated later with a Board of Agriculture Grant in 1922) [Fig. 14.14]. Donald's own uncles and grandfather built the present house (171) in 1879 — the roof timbers were sledged across from the Osgaig woods and it was roofed with Ballachulish slate. (Dormers and rear outshot were added in the mid 1980s by the new owner).

The fourth habitable house, by contrast, at the road-end, was seemingly

Fig. 14.12 According to local tradition, the cave behind the rowan tree was inhabited for over a year by an evicted family. 1992.

first put up by one of several Grants (who appear to have acquired a share of croftland in Culnacraig shortly before 1875). By 1885, if not before, they had moved off; the Estate put a new roof on it and allocated it to a keeper. The keeper found it too far to walk regularly into Achiltibuie and was relocated at Greenhill, just west of the present Community Hall (ex Drill Hall). It seems that Robert MacLeod came to rent it off the Estate and used it as his croft house; John Alec Campbell bought it in 1947 when he married Peggy MacLeod, Robert's granddaughter, and took on the croft she inherited at Culnacraig. This house has recently been improved by John Alec's son Ian, in 1990-91 (J. A. Campbell 1991).

Tales and Stories

Donald MacLeod was also heir to a modest store of stories and sayings which, in the 1960s/1970s, he recalled hearing from his grandmother in the 1900s/1910s — 'a long, long time ago', when he was very young. A slight, slender, sprightly figure in his 70s/early 80s, with expressive bony hands, he would sit back in a chair in his old baggy trousers, black boots, old brown tweed jacket and open-necked shirt, a smile on his thin, high cheek-boned, weather-reddened face and an innocent — perhaps mischievous — twinkle in his sharp blue eyes. Over many an evening he would recount how things had been; and he would tell, for instance, of how the fire-blackened stumps of trees in the peat had come to be burnt:

Fig. 14.13 Part of the cluster of buildings at the lower end of Culnacraig. Barn, byre, hen-house, cart-shed and garage in more recent times, they once formed a nucleus for the post-Clearance settlement. 1992.

Fig. 14.14 The outermost house in Culnacraig was formerly occupied by the descendants of Ruaridh Og MacLeod. 1992.

... Hundreds of years ago, long before the evictions a Norwegian lady called *Dubh a'Ghiuthais* [black fir] came and burnt all the fir trees so that only the black stalks were left ... the stumps of burnt trees in the peat banks. She had been sent to destroy ...

The trees had been set on fire by a witch who came from Norway ... She had wings and flew ...

The *Dubh a'Ghiuthais* could turn into a hare ... They tried to shoot the hare with a shotgun, but couldn't get a spark. They were told to put a 6d into the barrel of the gun, and they fired ...

The hare disappeared into a hole — that was a witch. Hares could 'disappear into all appearances'.

(Further Wester Ross versions of this story have been recorded and analysed by Donald Archie MacDonald: MacDonald 1984. 269 et seq.).

And in 1976, on seeing the smoke-blackened candlesticks, victims of a blocked chimney in his neighbour's holiday house, he remarked with a chuckle: 'The candlesticks are as black as the trees in Glaic na Phris that were burnt by the Norwegians'. 'The hollow of the thicket' is down towards the shore, a little west of the old fishing bothy; it was his own, live cultural tradition on which he continued to draw.

He would also tell of the fairies:

The fairies lived up the hill above Loggie, on the moor. They had lots of festivities at Christmas time ... in their mounds, filled with electric light ... At Christmas they danced the Highland Fling ...

One man was mesmerised and went to dance ... and danced and danced ... there was a very bright light. When he came out his feet were worn away to the knees ... He was in the mound for 100 years but thought it was only a day.

Loggie was his wife's place of birth; maybe the hill or mound referred to was the prehistoric fort of Dun an Ruigh Ruadh or Dun Lagaidh? (see MacKie, this volume).

On yet other occasions, Donald MacLeod would tell of:

The Druid stones ... down towards the sea *Aite (?)Ùrnuigh* ['Urie': place of prayer?] where people used to worship in a circle ...

There was another stone, further west, nearer the shore ... past the bothy ... near to where peats were once cut ... one stone only, about four feet high ...

This single stone appears to be a standing stone; the 'Druid stones' (which also include what may be considered a standing stone) appear to be the remains of a hut circle adjacent to the old cart track running down to the *port* where boats were hauled up on the shore. Both are evidence of prehistoric settlement — the former perhaps 3,500 or so years ago; the latter some 1,600-2,500 years ago.

At Achnacarinan, a couple of miles or so north round the coast, stands another standing stone, *Clach na Biodaig*, the Dirk Stone, linked to another circle of stones [Fig. 14.15]. Angus MacLeod, Achnacarinan (1992) tells how this was called a Druid's stone by one Major de Hamill, an ex-Army

Fig. 14.15 Clach na Biodaig, the Dirk Stone, Achnacarinan. 1992.

padre who had the old Achduart Schoolhouse from the mid 1940s to the mid 1950s. De Hamill seemingly found an antiquarian reference to the Dirk Stone. In this instance, therefore, it seems as if Donald MacLeod's reference to 'Druid stones' and 'a place of prayer' at Culnacraig *may* have a specific and recent provenance (or overlay) — and exemplify the power of oral tradition, however originated. For Donald's wife was once housekeeper to de Hamill.

Both Donald and his wife, Dolina, were native Gaelic speakers, but it was only after his marriage that Donald was taught to read in Gaelic, by his wife, from the Gaelic *Bìobull*. Both were staunch Free Presbyterians and good church people, worshipping at the simple corrugated iron church in

Achiltibuie — latterly a craft workshop, 'Picture Shack' and hay store. They were strong observers of the Sabbath and, as others, Donald would always shave on Saturday night, for instance; nor would they cook meals on a Sunday.

At the same time, earlier concepts and stories could co-exist easily enough for Donald alongside his religion, without the incongruity apparent perhaps to outsiders. For Dolina, there was rather more tension maybe, for she could become quite agitated when her husband talked about the 'Druid circle' (*An Deilbh*) at Badenscallie, and about the 'Giant's tombstone' below the cemetery. Dolly poked the fire in great agitation when this came up and said 'There were giants here in those days' (J. & D. Armstrong 1973. pers. comm.).

These tales and recollections give a flavour of the world in which Donald MacLeod (and Dolina MacLennan) grew up — a world whose roots lay in a blend of Celtic and fragmentary Norse attitudes and beliefs, overlain by an almost overwhelming acceptance of Free Presbyterianism which did not remove totally, nonetheless, the much earlier cultural substratum. Along with its economy, it is a world far removed from present-day Culnacraig and Coigach.

For some, Donald MacLeod, *An Slaiseadh (An Slasag)* was maybe eccentric, perhaps naive. He had a simple, childlike sense of wonder and humour, a trusting nature and an impishness that must have got him into many a scrape when young. His nickname, indeed, is said to refer to the many little slaps around the legs that his uncles felt obliged to give him. Iain Slaiseadh, his uncle John, is said to have told him frequently to 'come here and I'll give you a little slap' (A. MacLeod 1991).

Yet it would be this open and unsophisticated gently mischievous nature, linked to his curiosity, his clarity of mind and eye for detail, that made Donald a natural repository for such stories of times past — accepted, in so far as one could tell, at face value (which is not to say that they were necessarily or totally believed).

And his recollections on other, more mundane matters — crofting, fishing and everyday life — are equally clear and detailed. Even though he was often more interested in talking about cars, watches and how he would have liked perhaps to have been a doctor had things been different, he would happily talk of the past, and could still turn his mind to a gentle Gaelic tongue-twister:

Naodh ba breac dàmhsa air an leac
Nine speckled cows dancing on the floor [flagstone].

At the same time he was just as taken with such prosaic purple prose as 'Happiness is a perfume you cannot pour over others without first getting a few drops yourself' (1970) — first uncovered perhaps in an old Reader's Digest or People's Friend!

Donald died alone, of hypothermia, one cold November night about a month after our last discussions. He had gone out in his normal working clothes, probably in the evening, and seemingly to tidy up some rubbish in the little burn below the simple stone bridge, not far from the house. For some time now he had become increasingly frail and shaky on his feet, and had difficulty getting up again if he fell. And he would often not tie up his bootlaces, for he could hardly bend far enough to reach them. He apparently slipped and fell on the rocky slabs; and with loose boots and freezing fingers he tried in vain to get back on his feet and back up to the old cart track. He became progressively weaker and exhausted as he struggled; he lapsed into a coma; and the following morning was found dead beside the burn. It took three men to lift him, a slight light figure, and to carry him indoors (Miss M. F. Watt 1992. pers. comm.).

A far better end for Donald, however, than the old folks' home. He had rejected all talk of a move; he wanted to remain in his own house, on his own croft, with his cats and his hens; on the land his ancestors had worked. An old folks' home would have seared his soul.

Dolina had died of a weak heart in 1974 after many months in hospital in Inverness; Donald MacLeod was the last of his line. His family had lived at Culnacraig for around 160-170 years, a period that encompassed the rise and fall of crofting in the township.

CULTIVATION AND HARVESTING

Before they went away to the fishing, by the first week in May, the men would have prepared the land and sowed the seed. Traditionally spring work began on 12 March, and on 24 March (old calendar) the cattle were put out to the hill; dykes, fences and gates that had been open all winter were repaired and closed, and sowing began (D. Fraser 1972).

In practice, times would vary — not least according to the weather, the nature and extent of the land and availability of labour. For a five acre croft in Coigach it might take two weeks to gather enough seaweed, and a further three weeks to dig over the land (A. MacLeod 1972). With a plough, manure and a bit less land on the other hand, it might take a week or ten days (D. MacLeod 1972). Either way, if sown in April oats could normally be harvested around the beginning of September; if in May, by late September/early October — weather permitting! Meantime an enclosed 'park' or yard like that below Donald MacLeod's garden would be dug in February, from the bottom up, and planted with oats and potatoes, part being left in grass. It would give a threefold return (D. MacLeod 1976).

Turning over the Earth

Latterly, Donald MacLeod's neighbours would tractor-plough the land he was to cultivate. In 1972, the year of his last harvest, this was done on 5 May, when the Campbells also prepared their own drills for potatoes and turnips. Ministry tractors were first used in Culnacraig in 1942 (1941 in Achiltibuie); previously the land was turned over by horses or with the *cas-chrom*.

The *cas-chrom* was once well-known in Coigach. A man could dig more in one hour than in two or three hours with the spade — though the spade was better because it went deeper. It was widely used on Tanera Mór (as also on the steep lands of eg Letters on Inner Loch Broom and Diabaig, Loch Torridon); and it was no doubt equally widely used on the once-cultivated, long-abandoned rigs that cluster around eg Dornie, Alltandhu, Badentarbat, Achnahaird and Inverpolly, and on the rough wet hillsides below present-day Culnacraig. Even on the gently-sloping heartlands of what were once the old 18th century farms, the *cas-chrom* was used for odd corners, rig ends or bits of land too steep, too rough, or too small to be ploughed with horses.

The *cas-chrom* was made locally from birch or other hardwood, carefully chosen so as to give a wide angle between the shaft (commonly 6 ft; 1.8 m long) and the sole (about 2.5 ft; 0.8 m long) [Figs. 14.16, 14.17]. It had a foot-peg inserted in the reinforced 'ankle' and one made by Donnie Fraser's grandfather also had a horn fixed to the upper end of the handle. The length of the shaft was made to suit the man; the iron blade was inserted into the earth at approximately 25° to the ground; and every man liked his back straight, not bent, when using it.

On a small rig or lazy-bed, particularly on rough ground, you had first to notch a line with a spade; for a *cas-chrom* can only cut one way, slicing in and forward. Then you started at the top, working backwards a single width

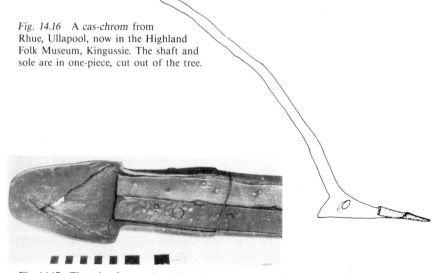

Fig. 14.16 A *cas-chrom* from Rhue, Ullapool, now in the Highland Folk Museum, Kingussie. The shaft and sole are in one-piece, cut out of the tree.

Fig. 14.17 The sole of a *cas-chrom* from Coigach, collected by Iain Crawford and now in the National Museums of Scotland (PA 34). As well as an iron blade, the base of the sole is shod with iron to protect it against wear.

down the rig, returning repeatedly to the top [Figs. 14.18-14.21]). A *feannag* was a narrow rig; *gead*, a somewhat wider lazy-bed or portion of arable land; *màg*, a very broad rig; *raon*, a field. If there were two or three men in the house they would work the rig together, in parallel, following each other down (D. & D. MacLeod 1972, A. MacLeod 1972, D. MacLean 1972, D. Fraser 1972).

The iron blade or *caibe* (*ceapa*) for the *cas-chrom*, as for other implements, was made by the Achiltibuie smith, William MacLeod in Polglass (A. MacLeod 1972) — but not everywhere did *caibe* refer simply to the blade. In the compound *cas-chaibe* it was a common enough mainland term for the Hebridean *cas-dhìreach* or straight delving spade (Dwelly). And around Gairloch, Kinlochewe, Torridon and Applecross the term *cas-chaibe* was also used instead of *cas-chrom* for a crooked spade (*cas-chrom* apparently re-appearing around Kyle of Lochalsh). When she first heard *cas-chrom*, Alex MacDonald's sister in Fearnamore, Applecross, did not realise that it applied to what she knew as the *cas-chaibe* (A. MacDonald 1972, R. & M. Beaton 1972).

Ploughing with Horses

In Culnacraig, however, as on other suitable land, horses were commonly used in the decades prior to the first tractors [Fig. 14.22]. For the bulk of modern Culnacraig is flat, stone-free land — some 14 ins (36 cm) of good black soil overlying an inch or two (2-5 cm) of coarse sand, and below that 'as good pure building sand as you could wish for' (D. MacLeod 1970, J. A. Campbell 1991).

In those times, each house had one horse, paired up to work each other's land in turn — three horses, that is, since the land attached to the keeper's house at the top of the settlement was insufficient to feed a horse. And on Tanera, where land was equally scarce, a pair of horses were temporarily shipped in each year to work the land (A. MacLeod 1972).

Donald MacLeod had had two horses (consecutively) since his marriage to Dolina in 1936. One, *Prince*, was 'a bit too big', presumably for easy yoking. *Jeannie*, brown with steel-grey hairs and a black stripe, was more than (?)30 years old when she died ca. 1940 — bought at Scoraig ca. (?)1913 and brought over the hills to Letters and thence to Coigach by the bridge at the head of Loch Broom. *Jeannie* was used in partnership with *Bessie*, a jet black mare 'bigger than a Shetland', bought from Strathan (Lochinver) around 1915 and kept by Christie MacLeod's family in the seaward-most house in Culnacraig (173). Bessie died in 1941 and was buried in *A'Chlais dubh,* the big rock-girt ravine below Christie's house.

When not working, horses were put out to graze on the moorland between Culnacraig and Achduart, though at one time in Coigach horses were grazed in several places in the hills. *Glaic nan Each* is a hollow high above Culnacraig, across the Allt nan Coisiche and under the buttress of A'Chreige Mhór, the great rock of Coigach; there were further horse grazings under the north-west slopes of Beinn an Eoin and at the Osgaig shiel-

Fig. 14.18

Fig. 14.19

314

Figs. 14.18 - 14.20 Stages in using the *cas-chrom* demonstrated for the writer by the late Alex. MacDonald, Fearnamore, Applecross, 1972, and now part of the Scottish Country Life collections in the National Museums of Scotland. Inserting the blade (14.18); cutting deeper and beginning to twist (14.19); turning the furrow (14.20).

ings; and *Eilean nan Eich* (Island of the Horses) was regularly used for the wintering of horses (Fraser 1957. A.l. 22, 55) — reminders perhaps of the days long past when droves of horses, not just cattle, were sold out of Coigach.

According to Donald MacLeod, in earlier times ('about 200 years ago', but more likely perhaps in the later part of the 19th century), there was a meeting of all those with horses on the hill to agree grazing restrictions — horses being included in the souming. Just one man from Culnacraig attended that particular meeting — William Macleod, who took over his tenancy in 1890 and whose house (170), occupied by MacLeans from Achduart after ca. 1907-10, still stands on the steep hill-slope above the fank. It is said that discussion focused at one point on the horse kept by those at the Achavraie shop. Some referred to it as a water-horse *(each uisge)* — no doubt as a joke or an insult! 'What about the *each uisge* then, that was up at Achavraie?' 'Oh well we never heard of a water-horse that ate grass', so its grazing was not restricted!

Donald MacLeod's long rectangular strips of land lay across the level field at Culnacraig, rising steeply up the eastern slope. The steeper land has not been much cultivated since 1942, with the advent of tractor-ploughing. On the flat ground his strips were about 120yds (110m), long from the

Fig. 14.21   Using the *cas-chrom* and planting potatoes in Lochcarron parish. The women frequently did the sowing, whilst the men dug. (?) Early 20th century.

township track to the bottom of the brae. It would take a pair of horses an hour to plough a 7 yard (6.5m) wide strip — seven yards being the most convenient unit allowing for the horse to be turned at either end.

Manuring the Ground

The detailed sequence of cultivation depended on the fertiliser to be used. If cow manure, accumulated during the winter in the byre, this was spread evenly across the ground with a graip before ploughing; if seaweed, the

Fig. 14.22 Ploughing at Achiltibuie, 1930s. From an album in the National Monuments Record of Scotland.

ground was sometimes ploughed first and the seaweed put into each furrow/drill afterwards so as not to get tangled around the plough (or *caschrom*) [Fig. 14.23].

Though it might take Coigach people about two weeks to gather enough seaweed for their land, and it might take perhaps a further three weeks for it to rot adequately, it would take only a few hours to spread — four or five tons being the equivalent to one bag of today's fertiliser!

Last century, weed was taken from every bit of shore [Figs. 14.24, 14.25]. Anyone could take *feamainn chura*, the ripe weed washed up on the shore by the tides — it belonged to the first man who got to it and piled it up with a graip. Otherwise the shore rights were allocated to townships and sub-divided amongst the crofts. Shore divisions were determined by marks

Fig. 14.23 A team at work on a Skye croft. The men dig with the *cas-chrom*; one woman is carrying a creel filled with seaweed; the other woman teases out the seaweed onto the freshly-turned earth. George Washington Wilson, late 19th century.

Fig. 14.24 Cutting seaweed on Skye, from a Valentine's postcard. The women have sickles; one man rests on the boat; the other man stands beside a creel. 1880.

Fig. 14.25 Archie MacEachern, Kinsadel, Arisaig, carrying seaweed for fertiliser, ca. 1910. M. E. M. Donaldson Collection.

off the land; the Summer Isles too were allocated; and the resident factor kept the peace in the event of a quarrel.[2] Once cut (perhaps 4-5 tons per day), seaweed was gathered in creels and loaded either into a cart or a boat. On Tanera, for instance, boats homeward-bound from other islands would be moored below the crofts at high tide and unloaded at low tide. The seaweed was then taken right up to the croftland in creels as there were no carts on Tanera (A. MacLeod 1972, M. MacLeod 1972, D. MacLean 1972, D. Fraser 1972). At Badenscallie too, it was unloaded from the boats at *Creag a'Chléibh*, the rock of the creels (Fraser 1957. A.I.32), and a pair of creels could be hung on a *srathair*, pack saddle, either side of a pony's back.

Apart from *feamainn chura*, Coigach people would collect *feamainn dubh*, the bubbly black/dark green bladder wracks used extensively for corn and (sometimes) potatoes. Some, however, preferred not to use seaweed on potatoes, and certainly not tangles, for they were too rich and made the potatoes watery or 'cheesy' — they preferred 'smiling' potatoes! Tangle leaves (*barr-stamh*) might be used on turnips, however, and some sought out the long, wide-bladed phosphorous-rich *liaragach* for their potato ground — weeds that grow far out, accessible only at the very low spring tides (M. MacLeod 1972, D. Fraser 1972).

More particularly at Culnacraig, black weed (*feamainn dubh*) and reddish/brown weed (*feamainn dearg*) were put on the corn land — byre manure being used mainly on potatoes. Cutting took place at low tide, particularly during the big March tides. Sometimes all the people in Culnacraig would cut weed together, bring it back and share it out; other days each would cut his own. It was cut on the boulder-strewn shore below the old rigs, taken in a creel (*cliabh*) to the mouth of the big burn (*Sruth mór/Allt a'Chulacreige/Allt a'Choire Reidh*), and then carted up the zigzagging *Ceum nan Cuirn*, the track of the carts, to the crofts. Donald MacLeod was in school at Achduart when cutting seaweed stopped — probably just a little before 1910 — though the system of shore rights had fallen into disuse long before.

The seaweed was cut with reaping hook or sickle (*corran*) [Fig. 14.26]. Although smooth-edged sickles seem to have been used around Applecross (Alex MacDonald of Fearnamore had never seen a *corran fiachach*), toothed sickles were certainly preferred in Coigach. They would be bought, toothed, from the local store (originally from Glasgow), but Donald MacLeod filed the teeth coarser so as easier to cut the seaweed. Moreover, a well-worn sickle, narrow in the blade, was also preferred — it slipped more easily between the rocks on the shore.

In addition to seaweeds and manures, the land needed lime. Shell sand from Tanera Beg was a local source, though apparently little used (Fraser Darling 1943. 146). When John Alec Campbell first went to Culnacraig in 1947 he found that yields were poor. After discussions with Ministry officials, and soil testing in Aberdeen, he put three tons of lime per acre on to the croft, bought at £2 per ton from the quarry at Ullapool. This brought him greatly improved crops of potatoes, oats, swedes and turnips, and magnificent hay; and it allowed him to winter half his sheep flock on the infield. But now the land is exhausted once more. 'If I were younger, I'd start it all over again — drain, lime and use the land' (J. A. Campbell 1992).

Planting and Harvesting Potatoes

Around the end of April/beginning of May potatoes were planted by hand by the whole family, about 18ins (45cm) from each other in ploughed drills about 2ft (60cm) apart, which were then closed up. Alternatively, they could be dropped into holes made with a *pleadhag* (dibble) — *putag* in Gairloch (Ian A. Fraser 1992. pers. comm.). If planted too early, when cold and wet, weeds would grow with the potatoes.

At Culnacraig, a *croman* or mattock (though latterly just a hoe) was used either side of the drill for weeding and earthing up; and elsewhere around

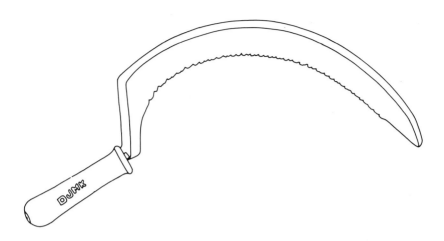

Fig. 14.26 Toothed sickle, from (?) South Uist, now in the Scottish Country Life collections, National Museums of Scotland. This has a considerably wider blade than was generally preferred in Coigach.

Loch Broom it was used occasionally to harvest potatoes at the ends of rigs or for digging out just a few for immediate use [Fig. 14.27]. More usually a *gràp* (graip, fork) was used — and in the early 1970s it would take the Campbells three days or so to lift their crop. Or as at Loggie, Inner Loch Broom, a horse plough opened up the drills and, after an initial gathering, a harrow was used to bring up the remainder. This was in the days before the spinner digger!

In the 1970s Kerr's Pink were preferred for human use [Fig. 14.28], and Pentland Dell for animal fodder. Earlier it was Champion and Golden Wonder — and 'Cows Horns', an old variety so-called because they were curly. Golden Wonder were often preferred, but as they were a late crop they had to be planted earlier. Seemingly they first came into Coigach in 1922 when Christie MacLeod's brother, a salmon fisherman in Prince Rupert Island (British Columbia, Canada), brought back a hundredweight (approx. 50 kgs). Shared around the district, they produced a sevenfold return.

Once lifted, potatoes were taken in creels and stored in a *toll buntàta* (potato pit) — a special place, well-drained and dry, and used year after year. At Culnacraig the MacLeods' *toll buntàta* was just below the *Ceum nan Each,* the track of the horses, just on the township side of the footbridge going towards Achduart. This pit, overhung by deep heather, still survives. In the old days, the heap of potatoes was simply covered with turf. Donald MacLeod's last potato pit was made in 1971, but close to his house. About 4ft (1.2m) square he first dug out a few inches of soil and then put in the potatoes — which were left to dry off during the day. The heap was covered with about 14ins (36cm) of earth, with a few extra inches added to the north

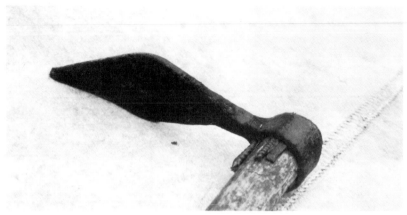

Fig. 14.27   Croman owned by the late Alex. MacLeod, Polbain, Coigach. 1972.

side to give added protection against the weather. Covered with divots cut from behind the house (dry bracken when the supply of turf was exhausted), the whole mound was chapped down with a spade.

At Loggie meantime, in the 1960s/70s, potatoes were alternated with layers of hay and 3/4ins (9cm) of earth to an overall height of about 8ft (2.5m). Bracken could be used instead — a good air space avoids sweating; whilst the earth was best taken from around the pit so as to make an 'island' and encourage good drainage (D. MacLeod 1972, D. MacLean 1972, A. MacLeod 1972, D. Fraser 1972).

Sowing and Harvesting Corn and Hay

Potatoes (introduced around 1750) are a relatively modern crop, though considerably earlier than turnips in the area.[3] In the 18th century, bere (an early form of barley) and oats were the two main crops, the former having the far longer history (Mrs A. Muir 1972; M. Bangor-Jones 1992. pers. comm.). However, Donald MacLeod remembered only two or three men ever growing barley — one at Achduart, John Alec Campbell's father at Polglass and one at 'Achiltibuie or Alltandhu.' Even then it was grown essentially as a fodder crop rather than as human food. *Clach an Eòrna*, nonetheless, the 'barley stone' down on the shore below Culnacraig and east of the Allt nan Coisiche, indicates a place where barley was once shelled and pounded into meal with a wooden mallet or *plocan*. There were seemingly several such places along the Coigach shore where barley was thus ground in natural holes in the rocks — even though it had to be carried there and back from the croft (Mrs A. Muir 1972).

However, at least within living memory, croft work revolved primarily around oats, hay, potatoes and livestock. On a five acre croft with three cows and three followers for instance, four stacks of corn and two of hay would be needed to see the beasts through the winter — and on Tanera this would be

SEED POTATOES--A SPECIALITY.

New and Improved Varieties.

WILLIAM KERR,

Seed and Potato Grower,

The Royal Scotch Potato Establishment

DARGAVEL, DUMFRIES.

MR KERR having the Largest and Best COLLECTION OF POTATOES in SCOTLAND specially grown for Seed, he is enabled to supply all the best Varieties, **Warranted True to Name,** and at the lowest price consistent with truthfulness of Kind. **Several Special New Varieties,** recently introduced by Mr KERR, are strongly recommended for extensive Cultivation.

Descriptive List of these and over 100 *other Leading Varieties,*
Free on Application.

100,000 one-year Unnamed Seedling Potatoes from Kerr's Hybridised Seed. Price 100 tubers, 25s.; 50 tubers, 15s.; 25 tubers, 8s.

Free by Post or Rail.

Fig. 14.28 Advertisement for William Kerr's seed potatoes, from *Historical Sketch of the Agricultural Progress of Scotland*, Highland & Agricultural Society of Scotland, Centennial Show, 1884.

Fig. 14.29   The late Donald MacLeod's coles of oats on his croft at Culnacraig. 1972.

supplemented by a special kind of seaweed found along the top of the shore, boiled and with potatoes added (A. MacLeod 1972). According to Dwelly, this *feamainn chìreag* is but a few inches in length, short and crisp, and grows only on rocks that are seldom under water at neap tides. His Skye and Uist source, Rev. J. MacRury (Snizort) adds that it had a strong laxative property when fed to cattle suffering from 'dryness'.

Be that as it may, by the early 1970s Donald MacLeod had need of but two stacks of oats for his black cow and calf — enough to last them from November through till May. Traditionally, after ploughing and manuring, the earth was broken up with a *ràcan* (rake) prior to sowing. Oat seed might be carried in a pail held in one hand and sown broadcast with the other, generally around mid-April. After harrowing with a wooden, later iron harrow (*cliath*) with iron teeth (*fiaclan*), there was nothing more to do until harvest — other than make sure livestock did not stray on to the crop.

Toothed sickles seem to have been widespread in Coigach and much preferred to the smooth-edged reaping hook. The scythe arrived in the early 20th century, just before the 1914-18 war, but the hook continued in use to take off what the scythe could not manage (A. MacLeod 1972).

With his Y-snedded scythe (the 'Scots' type was much better, he felt, than the S-snedded or 'English' version he once tried), Donald MacLeod would cut the oats, then tie them into sheaves with straw bands made from a handful of the crop, and put them up into *tùdan* (stooks). He put 12 sheaves to a stook, and after about a week raised some 20 stooks into a *sgrùthan* (cole), twisted slightly around a centre base and built around and up, heads inwards. *Sgrùthan* would be about 4-5ft (1.2-1.5m) diameter by 6ft (1.8m) high. Sacking over the top, secured by a bit of netting and binder twine, would protect the ears from the rain and the sheaves from the wind [Fig. 14.29]. By contrast, John Alec Campbell's *sgrùthan* were often thinner, more pointed and not covered by sacking; in Polbain 12 sheaves (*sguab choirce*) made a *sgrùthan* rather than a *tùdan* and would then be transported direct to the stackyard (A. MacLeod 1972); whilst a little further south, at Kinlochewe, a *dais* would be raised on the field, in addition to a *sgrùthan* (Mrs A. MacLean 1972). These basic techniques, common to all such communities, were highly susceptible to localised differences in practice, influences and terminology — so that by Loch Laxford, some way further north along the coast, a stook would be a *stùcan* and a cole a *tùdan* — a term which applied equally to the stack built and left all winter in the stackyard (A. MacAskill 1974).

Stacking the Corn/Hay

When sufficiently dry, and on a good dry day, the coles would be taken down and the sheaves taken to the stackyard.

Fig. 14.30 Having cut the bracken with a Y-snedded scythe [Fig. 14.4], Donald MacLeod carried it to his stackyard in a doubled rope. 1972.

Preparing the Foundations

First, however, Donald MacLeod had to prepare the foundations for the stack. Bracken cut from a strip about 15ft (4.6m) long by one scythe-swing wide was pitchforked onto a double rope and taken the 50-80yds (46-73m) to the rough circles of field stone foundations at the back of the barn [Figs. 14.4, 14.30]. Spread and patted down with the pitchfork, it was finally trodden down to a height of 1-1½ft (30-45cm) — which reduces considerably further under the weight of the corn. At Polbain the foundations were of stone and then heather; the purpose was the same — to keep rising damp away from the stack.

Building the Corn Stack

Taken out of the *sgrùthan*, the sheaves were placed across a double rope (*ròp uallach*) laid on the field, heads of the sheaves alternately to one side, then the other. Some 20 sheaves made a burden (*uallach*); the ends of the rope were taken over the sheaves and threaded through the loop at the end; the rope was tightened and the whole load hoisted on to the back over one shoulder. It was a heavy enough burden for a 74 year old man (or, for that matter, for one less than half his age!) [Figs. 14.31-14.33].

At the stackyard the sheaves were unloaded and spread around the perimeter of the foundations, to be close to hand [Figs. 14.34-14.38]. The first sheaves were set up in the centre (as for building a *sgrùthan*), one twisted slightly round the next one to aid balance. Sheaves were then built up around the core, always working sunwise, clockwise, for as Donald said 'you should not go against the sun'. When the stack was one sheaf high across the full diameter, binder twine was used around this first tier to prevent it sliding outward when he climbed on top.

From then on it was building tiers all the way up. The second tier was also secured with twine, and trodden down at the centre to flatten it at a point just below the ears. Then the third and fourth tiers were added, now all but horizontally rather than vertically. The tiers were regularly trodden down, and some 12 sheaves added to the centre to maintain an outward slope — important for shedding any rain that might penetrate. A fifth tier was added, and then a half row to even up on the side where the foundations were not quite level — to prevent slippage and spillage.

At this point, Donald MacLeod took a spade and with the end of the blade (not the back) firmed the outer sheaves into position to make a neat, straight vertical line all around the circumference.

The process of adding tiers, treading down, tying and trimming continued until the stack was about 4ft (1.2m) high. From then on, narrowing of the stack began. And every two or three tiers, the stack was firmed and shaped — now with a pitchfork rather than the spade, and with the straw always sloping downwards to the outside.

Eventually the stack had narrowed almost to a point. Access had first required a short ladder; now a longer one. To position the last few sheaves, ears ever upwards, he had to turn continually around the point, and when

Fig. 14.31 Taking down the coles and laying the sheaves across the loop end of the doubled rope. 1972.

Fig. 14.32 Securing the burden by passing the loose ends of the rope through the loop and pulling it tight. 1972.

327

Fig. 14.33   Carrying a burden of some 20 sheaves back to the stackyard. 1972.

Fig. 14.34   The sheaves have been laid out around the stone stack foundation, already covered in a bed of freshly-cut bracken. The first sheaves are set up in the centre, in a slight twist. 1972.

Fig. 14.35 Once the stack is one sheaf high, it is secured with binder twine to prevent sideways slippage. 1972.

Fig. 14.36 Two tiers high, and the stack is trodden down to flatten it. Trampling continues as further tiers are added. 1972.

Fig. 14.37 After five or six tiers, the bottom edge of the spade is used to firm in the outer sheaves and to give the stack a neat, vertical face. 1972.

Fig. 14.38 The stack is narrowed, then firmed and shaped with a pitch-fork. The sheaves should always slope a little downwards so as to shed water. 1972.

the top was reached it was covered with sacking — four bags, opened out, and then covered with old salmon-fishing net. Later, when the stack had settled, the net and sacks would be removed and the conical top thatched with rushes and re-netted — or maybe he would put rushes over the sacking. Before the days of old fishing net or bought rope, rope (*sìoman*) was made at home, twisted by hand from rushes (*luachair*) — as were chair seats. The three/four ropes always passed up and over the stack (never around it), so that six/eight ends hung down, sometimes weighted with heavy stones (A. MacLeod 1972) [Figs. 14.39, 14.40].

The stacks were not built 'all in one go'. Rather was stack-building alternated with the more strenuous work of carrying in the sheaves from the field. For in one day Donald stacked 4¹/₂-5 coles — the equivalent of nearly 100 stooks or 1,200 sheaves. This is probably an average day's work for, although helped by the writer on this occasion, had she not been unwell Dolina would normally have worked alongside her husband. In all he had 9 coles (180 stooks, 2,160 sheaves) from a field 14yds (12.8m) wide by 100-120yds (92-110m) long — where the width reflected two plough strips, each 7yds (6.4m) wide. These 9 coles made one complete and one all-but-full-size stack, 10ft high by 7ft diameter (3.1 m x 2.1m) — sufficient to keep cow and calf from November through until May.

But October 1972 saw their last harvest. By then Donald was 74 years of age and his wife Dolina 78. She was taken into hospital within months and died in 1974. Right up until her illness, however, she had taken the view that 'We have the land and should therefore use it and have a cow'. With no wife to help, the beasts had to go; and without the beasts there was no call for the oats. True crofting had effectively died in Culnacraig.

Building the Hay-Stack

The Coigach term for such circular corn stacks is *cruach choirce. Cruach fhèoir* is a haystack, circular or rectangular, constructed from *tùdan fhèoir*, little stooks set up in the fields after the grass had been let lie loose to dry for two or three days. Normally, and particularly in wet weather, stands or tripods of three/four pieces of wood were set up, around which the *tùdan* were built — so as to let the air circulate better. In Coigach, hay was left in the *tùdan* as long as was required [Fig. 14.41]. Around Kinlochewe, by contrast, after the initial spreading of the wet cut grass, very small coles were built (*coileag bheag*), later amalgamated into larger coles 3-4ft high (3.5m) — *coileag mhór*, occasionally referred to as *tùdan* (Mrs A. MacLean 1972). And beside Loch Laxford, north of Scourie, a cole would be called a *gorag*. There, a stack (*cruach*) built on foundations of stone would be rectangular; otherwise circular (A. MacAskill 1974).

Preparing the Corn

Threshing and Riddling

The harvest was of critical importance in crofting life. When grown more

Fig. 14.39   Once the stack is complete, it is covered with a few opened-out sacks and secured with old fishing net. After a few days the stack will be lightly thatched with rushes. 1972.

Fig. 14.40   Alistair MacLeod's thatched stacks, Brae of Achnahaird, 1972. The tops are tightly secured and covered in net.

Fig. 14.41 Hay continued to be made in Polbain for a few years after Donald MacLeod's last corn harvest. 1972.

widely, oats were threshed straight from the sheaf with a flail (*sùist*) or with a stick. In later years Donald MacLeod no longer used a flail; he continued however to use a threshing stick, *siòlpan*, occasionally a somewhat thicker *buailtean* (by Loch Laxford a *plocan*). It was about 3ft (92cm) long, with a slight bend in the head (5-6ins, 13-14cm) and resembled a *camag* — his word for a shinty stick, *caman*. He would lay two sheaves at a time on a flat stone in the barn, just to one side of the door, and beat them for five minutes. Brushed up and bagged, this would feed his nine hens for two days.

In his younger days, two men would thresh with the flail — there were in fact two flagstones on the floor. Threshing normally took place at night in winter, the two men striking alternately. It took perhaps an hour fully to thresh four/five sheaves.

After threshing, seed corn was sieved in a calf-skin *criathar*, the skin perforated with a red-hot rod and laced to its circular pliable wooden frame with leather thongs. The MacLeods' sieves were made by one of Donald MacLeod's uncles. In use, the seed (*coirce*) fell through on to an old canvas sail laid out below — the hens pecking at it as it dropped, whilst the chaff (*mogul*) went away with the wind, helped by a split door with a small window in the opposite wall (Mrs A. Muir 1972, D. MacLeod 1972).

Drying and Grinding

The corn was not dried artificially prior to threshing — leastways not in so far as was recalled. Nonetheless, placename evidence certainly indicates that drying kilns were once used on the larger (pre-crofting) farms — *Lios na h'Athainn* at Badenscallie, for instance; *Cnoc na h'Athainn* at Polglass (formerly part of Achiltibuie farm); and *Larach na h'Athainn* at Achnahaird (Fraser 1957. A.I.7, 31; A.II.27).

The Cromartie Estates built the meal mill, *Am muillean (allt an Ruisteal)* at Achiltibuie ca. 1880. [Fig. 14.42]. The late Mrs Abie Muir's father, a Fraser (whose people had come from 'behind Ullapool'), was miller — renting the mill from the estate. But during his tenure bagged meal began to come in from the North of Scotland Milling Company of Inverurie, brought by rail to Kyle, thence by steamer to Badentarbat. The mill fell into disuse at the beginning of the 20th century; Mr Fraser continued to keep an oatmeal store and sold the imported meal; and the old mill was rented as a store to the shop-owner (Mrs A. Muir 1972, A. MacLeod 1972, D. Fraser 1972). It was subsequently sold and renovated as a holiday house.

Before the Estate mill was established (seemingly between 1876 and 1884, during that period from 1849 to 1888 when the Cromartie Estates were amalgamated with and run by the Sutherland Estates), corn was either ground in a hand quern (*brà*) at the croft, or taken to one of a series of small horizontal water-mills (*tòn ri làr*: backside to the ground!). Hand querns were still used in Mrs Muir's early days — the turn of the century; the *tòn ri làr* survives in the placename record and ruinously on the ground. According to Donnie Fraser (1972), surviving placenames suggest about eight such mills locally — at Achnahaird, Reiff (by the sea below Loch na Totaig), Alltandhu (down by the shore), Achiltibuie, Acheninver (2), Achnacarinan, (?)Culnacraig. One on Tanera Mór is credited by the Ordnance Survey to the wrong loch; there are also mill ruins and a name at Badenscallie.

At Achiltibuie *Tigh Alaidh Ghairneilear* (the house of Alexander the gardener), now a ruin close to the shore below the Achiltibuie Stores (*Bùth an arcaich*: the shop of the Orkneyman), is said to have been built on the site of a former meal mill and grain-drying kiln, water being diverted from Allt an Ruisteal. At Achnahaird also, both functions are reflected in *Làrach a'Mhuillean* and *Làrach na h'Athainn* — the site of the mill/kiln on the burn flowing out of Ruadh Loch (called *Lochnamoullen* in Peter May's 1756 Survey [Fig. 14.70]). Fraser suggests that the mill was situated at the lower boundary of the later crofting settlement of Brae of Achnahaird, whilst May indicates structures close to the outlet of the loch. Meantime, at Badenscallie, *Muileann na Goile Duibhe* survives fragmentarily on the *Allt Bad a'Sgalaidh/Allt Mór*, the mill of the black throat — perhaps an abusive reference to a former inhabitant, or more likely a reflection of the dark, twisting ravine through which the burn passes at this point. And at nearby Acheninver, the names *Muileann Iomhair* and *Muileann Iain Ghrannd* refer respectively to Ivor and to Ian Grant — the last to work each mill (Fraser 1957. A.I.27-8, 32-3; A. II.53-4).

Fig. 14.42   The Estate mill, built ca. 1880. It was obsolete by the beginning of the 20th century, largely on account of the expansion of the railways. Part of the lade survives in the foreground. It led to an overshot wheel. 1992.

The age of these mills, like the kilns, is uncertain. In Assynt, although there are some very old mill sites, most date from the 1770s-1830s and a few kept going until the 1860s (M. Bangor-Jones 1992. pers. comm.). In Coigach, such as at Acheninver and Loch Totaig, Achnacarinan and (?)Culnacraig, seem most likely to date from the 1810s-1830s, following the post-clearance settlement of outlying parts of earlier tenant farms. The mills close to the earlier farms however — at Achnahaird, Achiltibuie, Baden-scallie, Alltandhu — were presumably older, presumably horizontal and presumably the model for the later township mills. For only the Estate mill is known to have had a vertical wheel.

Otherwise, the only reference to an older mill in the district concerns a possible tide-mill at the entrance to *Loch na Ribhe*. According to William Muir (1991), William Matheson, late of the Department of Celtic, Edinburgh University, had identified an early 16th century documentary reference. Given that the loch of Reiff, in spite of the reef, is said once to have been one of the three key harbours in this part of Coigach (the others being Old Dornie and Tanera), and that its entrance was subsequently altered, the location of a tide-mill here remains a possibility [Fig. 14.43].

335

Fig. 14.43 The loch of Reiff enters the sea through a channel straightened by man. The former postman's house (George Frame's), now modernised, was the last inhabited thatched house in Coigach. 1972.

LIVESTOCK HUSBANDRY

However critical the annual harvest, livestock formed the core of the Highland economy and numbers were strictly regulated. Prior to the '45 it appears that the Earls of Cromartie would grant to certain of the aged and poor free grazing for a cow and follower and a few goats. Tacksmen continued this privilege, and because of labour shortages were obliged to extend it. Inevitably abuses arose, and in 1768 the Cromartie factor, Ninian Jeffrey, initiated a survey of 'the Persons who has catle [*sic*] and pays no rent' (E 746/72/4; Mitford n.d. 19-21). It is little wonder perhaps that other tenants and subtenants had complained — free grazing was enjoyed by some 23 horses, 84 cattle and 272 sheep and goats! In consequence, a new Souming was also compiled (E 746/72/5). Whether or not this Souming was ever implemented is unclear. Jeffrey certainly considered it 'very hard upon the present manners of management of cattle in Coygach for these Tenants to pay the higher rent' [Fig. 14.44].

Today, the scattered townships from Achnahaird by Reiff to Achiltibuie and Culnacraig have substantial common grazings — areas that have ebbed and flowed over the past 250 or so years in line with clearances for sheep farming and deer forests, and subsequent declines in these monocultural activities. There are still a small number of cattle grazed on the lower moorland beyond the old township dykes, notably around Achiltibuie, Badenscallie and Polbain, as well as at Inverpolly Farm. Until very recent times, however, the hill ground has been intensively stocked with the crofters' sheep and roamed by red deer. Deer there still are, culled annually by a free-lance stalker contracted by the Benmore Estate. Sheep there still are, but in

REVISED SOUMING: COIGACH, 1768

E 746/72/4-5	Cows	Horses	Sheep	Goats	Soum Total	Value of each Soum
Achnahaird (with Eisbrecky added instead of Ouscraig) [sic]	80	20	10	10	120	3/4
Reeve	40	6	5	5	56	3/-
Altandow	20	4	3	3	30	2/6
Runabreck	30	4	2	2	38	3/-
Leorebircaig	35	4	3	2	44	3/-
Sheanascaig	25	3	2	2	32	3/-
Inverpollie	65	6	6	5	82	3/-
Dalpollie	50	8	5	4	67	3/-
Dornie (£2 grass added)	70	13	5	5	93	3/4
Badentarbat (£1 grass added)	35	6	3	3	47	3/-
Island Taurara	—	—	24	—	24	3/-
Achiltybowie (do. when Ouscaig added)	40 80	10 20	5 10	5 10	60 120	3/4 —
Badenscallie	60	10	5	5	80	3/-
Forest					300	1/-

Fig. 14.44 Proposed new Souming for Coigach, 1768, prepared by Ninian Jeffrey (Factor), Alexander MaCra (Achyouran) and Alexr. MaCra (Invershin). E 746/72/4-5.

The switch in grazings may be linked to the removal to Dalpolly of Mrs MacKenzie, widow of Roderick MacKenzie, tacksman in Achiltibuie, so as to accommodate Lieut. Daniel MacKenzie in Achiltibuie [see also Fig. 16.67]. In 1777, Achnahaird also acquired Runabreck as grazing.

considerably lesser numbers than in the 1960s-1980s. Sheep are territorial and keep to given areas once hefted. Gradually those hefted to the high hills — the one time Forest of Coigach — have been sold off as the last generation of traditional crofters grew older, so that most now stick to the lower ground and are regularly grazed on the former infields.

In Donnie Fraser's father's day, 'crofters had a house, cow, wife and children, potatoes and hens'. On a two and a half acre croft you were allowed half-a-horse, six cows and six followers and 30 sheep; and with only half a croft his father had to go to the herring and salmon fisheries (D. Fraser 1972). Individual crofts were not economically viable, in other words, without such supplementary activities as fishing, shepherding, gillieing, working on the roads, delivering the mail, and seasonal migration.

Sheep

At Culnacraig, with a wife, four children and elderly relatives, John Alec Campbell had taken on and worked his wife's croft there, along with his own at Polglass. He was a gillie; he was also a shepherd and maintained over 300 sheep on the Benmore grazings. By contrast, Donald MacLeod and his wife, childless and with no close relatives remaining in the area, continued as simple, traditional crofters, keeping 30-40 sheep, a few cows and followers, hens, cats, a dog . . . the norm for most crofter-fishermen. Within memory, the sheep have always been Cheviots, with an admixture of black fleeces — perhaps a throwback to pre-clearance stock, or influenced by the *caora Sealtanach* introduced experimentally to Tanera in the early 1940s by Fraser Darling. The dominance of Cheviots appears strange, however, given that this extremely bleak land looks far better suited to Blackfaces (better still to the pre-improvement breeds). According to Fraser Darling, the reason is to be found in earlier mismanagement and the lack of planned husbandry. Cheviots are kept and do well in the limestone country a little further north, beyond Elphin, and on through the hills into mid-Sutherland. Years ago, however, the poorest lambs, L Sc s*hotts*, were consistently sold to the coastal crofters for a few shillings apiece. In this way, the poorest Cheviot stock came to be kept on some of the poorest hill ground that would not have well-suited even the best Cheviot stock. Thus it was that the Coigach crofters could not keep up an adequate ewe stock without regularly buying in more of the same class of poor sheep (Fraser Darling 1938.32). It was a vicious circle that well-suited the commercial sheep-farmers to perpetuate.

The crofters would go to the hill four times a year — for lambing, lug-marking and dipping at the end of April, for clipping in June and July, for dipping and taking off lambs in September. Tupping was carefully controlled so that the lambs would be born when there was enough new grass to put milk on the mother; it took place around New Year, and both these Culnacraig crofters would hire Board of Agriculture rams for a month at the end of November rather than feeding their own year-round.

338

In the old days it was usual to fix a patch of cloth to the tail of the gimmers (two year old females) to prevent them from breeding. This was made illegal however, for when the gimmers were on heat the tup was in danger of destroying his penis. Instead, the gimmers were kept in and only the sheep and the tups sent to the hill. Two to four men would go to the hill daily during tupping, to round up the animals and check both sheep and tups. More recently, however, with very few gimmers and with reduced manpower, the tups and sheep were kept inbye, with the gimmers sent to hill (D. Fraser 1972).

Until regulations required regular immersions, the main dipping took place in the autumn. In earlier days still, however, sheep were smeared. Each sheep in turn was laid on a *stòl-smeuradh*, smearing stool; one man stood at the end of the stool and 'split' the wool every two inches (5cm), smearing the split with a mixture of tar and linseed — as waterproofing and to control vermin. The tar and oil came in barrels; you mixed it yourself, using more tar than oil. The speed of smearing a sheep (like shearing) was the index of a good or poor smearer. The tar made the fleece heavier, and therefore more profitable — in theory at least. But it remained in the fleece after shearing; it was difficult to remove; and it was seen increasingly by buyers as a disadvantage. (When the men were away at the fishing, the women and older men/children looked after the shearing, the women shearing with scissors rather than the strongly-sprung shears) [Figs. 14.45, 14.46].

Fig. 14.45 A stool once used for smearing and/or shearing sheep — trapped beneath the collapsing roof of an abandoned croft house. Polglass. 1972.

CRAWFORD, CREE, & CO.,
Wool Brokers,
14 INGRAM ST., GLASGOW.

WOOL STORES—

COLLEGE GOODS STATION (Glasgow & South Western Railway),

HIGH STREET.

Terms of Business—2½ per cent. Commission.

6d. per Bag or 1s. per Sheet per annum for Fire Insurance.
6d. per Bag or 1s. per Sheet per annum for Porterage, receiving, weighing, and delivering the Wool.

SHEETS OR BAGS SUPPLIED. NO CHARGE FOR USE.

☞ *No Storage is charged except on Wool consigned with a price limit. In such cases storage is free for one year, after which period 1d. per bag or 2d. per sheet per week will be charged.*

All kinds of DIP, and DIPPING and SMEARING MATERIALS, of the Best Quality, supplied. Also FEEDING STUFFS for Sheep and Cattle.

AGENTS IN SCOTLAND FOR

THE GLYCERINE DIP FOR SHEEP.

PUBLIC SALES OF WOOL are held periodically, and SALES by PRIVATE BARGAIN are always energetically pushed.

CONSIGNMENTS are requested, which will meet with careful attention.

Fig. 14.46 The wool crop would be sold away to help raise cash to pay the rents. From *Historical Sketch of the Agricultural Progress of Scotland*, Highland & Agricultural Society of Scotland, Centennial Show, 1884.

340

Smearing went out of fashion before the 1914-18 war, when the men learnt new ways, working on sheep farms further south. Donnie Fraser's father built the first dipper, in wood, down by the Achiltibuie mill (the fank is still used, although gradually being eroded away by the sea). It was used by crofters from both ends of the road; the ingredients came from Glasgow. Solid cakes of McDougall's Dip were melted down and boiled together with whale oil, also bought from McDougall's. And on occasion soft soap might be added to the large black pot [Fig. 14.47]. Gradually, however, dippers were built at fanks in townships across Coigach — sometimes an old bath was used; and a new concrete dipper was added at Culnacraig in 1950 (D. Fraser 1972, M. MacLeod 1972). At Badenscallie a brand-new fank and dip have recently been completed (1993) — evidence of a determination to continue aspects of crofting on the part of a handful of younger crofters.

Marking

The other key task was to mark the sheep. Keel was never used as a mark of ownership, only to recognise sheep on the hill. Keel marks could be applied, for instance, to the side of the sheep, top of the tail, head, shoulders, hindquarters — and in the olden days maybe right over the back, from one side to the other. There were also back-end keel marks used during tupping — red for breeding sheep, blue for gimmers. (Today it is the spray-can of paint!).

Ownership marks, by contrast, were either lug-marks or nose brands (horn brands on the occasional stray Blackface) [Figs. 14.48, 14.49]. Some believed nose-brands to be best — eg a bar, spot or band straight up and down. And nose-brands would certainly be preferable for those sheep whose ears went black, shrivelled and eventually dropped off (Yellows disease) — for otherwise they could only be keeled.

Nose-branding, like keeling, was generally introduced into the Highlands during and following the 18th/19th century development of commercial sheep-farming; lug-marking, on the other hand, has a much older pedigree. Certainly the southern flock-masters brought north southern shepherds' lug-marks and terminology, not to mention custom-made pliers for eg the nip, fork, hole and cut; and undoubtedly Coigach shepherds would return home with new ideas, whether from the south or Montana! But small subtenants and crofters continued to keep their handful of sheep alongside the large commercial flocks. And whilst gradually they, too, acquired the new marks and breeds (Cheviots in Coigach), nonetheless they retained some of the older Highland marks and names (D. Fraser 1972, A. MacLeod 1972) [Fig. 14.50].

Over-Wintering

North-west coast winters are harsh, particularly away from the coastal fringe; in more recent times the generally scarce arable land allowed only a modest crop of turnips; and traditionally other fodder crops were always in short supply.

LOOK AT THE SAYING!

Users of MIXED DIPS

Save 50 per cent. by buying **ROBERTSON'S**

HIGHLAND SHEEP DIP,

which combines the strength and ingredients of a bath made with Non-Poisonous Carbolic Dip (Paste or Fluid) and Poisonous Powder Dip. Waterproofs the Fleece, Destroys Vermin, and Cures Scab. Price 6s. 6d. for each 16 lb. (1½ gallons), makes 80 gallons bath.

Users of Non-Poisonous DIPS

Save 1s. on every gallon (10 lbs.) by purchasing

NON-POISONOUS HIGHLAND DIP

(Waterproofing Paste), which is superior to most Compositions of this class, and is not excelled by any.

Soluble Fluid Non-Poisonous Dip

costs 4s. 6d. per gallon; 20s. for 5 gallons. Each gallon makes 100 gallons bath to dip 120 sheep, and is identical in composition with Fluids sold at 7s. 6d. per gallon. Try it.

Users of POWDER DIP

May have on application a copy of the analysis of the

SCOTCH POWDER DIP

by the City Analyst of Glasgow, showing that this Powder (which is the ONLY POWDER DIP MANUFACTURED IN SCOTLAND), contains more than double the amount of Soluble Sulphide found in the best known English Powders. Price 1s. per packet, to dip 25 sheep.

Users of PITCH OIL

Are supplied with **PITCH OIL** so concentrated that 1 gallon makes 100 gallons of the strongest Sheep Dip without any addition of Soap or Soda, needs no preparation, mixes instantly with cold water, and never Stains the Wool. Recommended by Wool Brokers. In 40 gallon casks, 2s. per gallon, costs 1s. 6d. to dip 100 sheep.

Write for Particulars and Testimonials to the

SOLE MANUFACTURER,

ALEX. ROBERTSON,

Argyle Chemical Works, OBAN.

Proprietor of Terebene Balsam for Lamb Cutting.

Fig. 14.47 Advertisement for Robertson's sheep dips, from *List of Sheep Marks for the Counties of Aberdeen . . . and Inverness.* 1897.

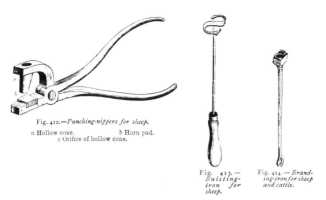

Fig. 412.—*Punching-nippers for sheep.*
a Hollow cone. *b* Horn pad.
c Orifice of hollow cone.

Fig. 413. —
*Buisting-
iron for
sheep.*

Fig. 414.—*Brand-
ing-iron for sheep
and cattle.*

Fig. 14.48 Commercially-produced tools for marking sheep. The punching-nippers cut lug marks; the buisting-iron tar marked the fleece of a sheep; the branding-iron was used on the horn or the face. From H. Stephens *Book of the Farm*, 4th edition, 1891.

Fig. 14.49 Brand marks for selected sheep farms in Skye and Western Inverness-shire, from *List of Sheep Marks for the Counties of Aberdeen . . . and Inverness*, 1897.

Tracing of Brand Iron.

William and Hugh Cameron, Ben-more, Portree.

Iron, runner on left side of nose. Tar—Ewes and Lambs, ⊕ left side on ribs. Ear mark—Ewes and Lambs, fork and fore bit right ear ; fork left ear. Paint—Ewes and Lambs, two Red marks, one across shoulders and one across hips.

Bernisdale Club Farm, Bernisdale, Snizort, Portree.

Iron, [⬚] on cheek. Tar—One, Two, and Three-year-olds, B right ribs ; Ewes and Lambs, B left ribs. Ear mark —One, Two, and Three-year-olds, fork and back bit out of right ear ; Ewes and Lambs, fork out of right ear and back bit out of left ear. Paint, Red right side

Allan Cameron, Dundreggan, Urquhart, Glenmoriston.

Iron, ⊢, stroke down bridge of nose and from centre to left. Tar, O on rump. Ear mark, fork out and hole in right ear ; back bit out of left ear.

The Macleod of Macleod, Uiginish, Duirinish, Dunvegan.

Iron, runner above nose. Tar, U left ribs. Ear mark—One-year-olds, back bit right ear ; Two year-olds, fore bit right ear ; Three-year-olds, fork right ear ; Ewes and Lambs, two fore bits right ear. Paint, Red keil back of neck.

343

(i) Lamb Houses:

Whilst most crofters' relatively small numbers of sheep could be left safely enough on the hill and allowed to graze the croftland during the winter, special arrangements were needed for some. The ruins of small lamb houses are found in the hills above Polglass (J. A. Campbell 1990); whilst at Culna-craig, each of the houses had a *bothan uan* a short distance outside the hill-dyke on the lower slopes of the hill. One bears the name *Tigh na Creig* (Fraser 1957. A.I.51); the ruins of all are still to be seen. Small, rectangular, drystone buildings with a narrow entrance and formerly thatched, they were used in winter to house the hoggs day and night, to protect them from the snow and the frost. A dozen or so such lambs were kept loose inside, fed on

SOME COIGACH LUG MARKS: 1972

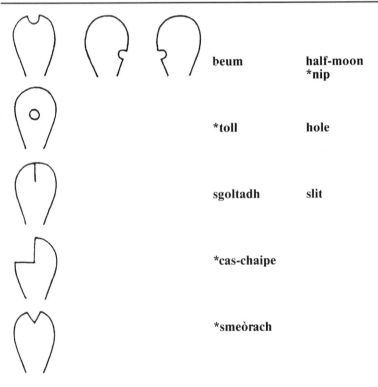

beum	half-moon *nip
*toll	hole
sgoltadh	slit
*cas-chaipe	
*smeòrach	

**Those marked * from Donald MacLeod, Culnacraig
Remaining marks from Alex MacLeod, Polbain**

Fig. 14.50   Some Coigach lug-marks, collected in 1972.

344

oats and turnips (cut into halves or quarters with a spade and left on the floor), with hay left lying in little slatted wooden racks.

Quite separately, down by the shore, tucked into former beds of the Allt nan Coisiche, a number of small dry-stone structures survive to a height of one to three courses. Like similar structures a little above the settlement, above the road bridge beside the Allt a'Chualacreige (Allt a'Choire Reidh), these provided shelter for lambs (J. A. Campbell 1990) [Fig. 14.51]. At the same time, they suggest a re-use of earlier buildings, perhaps associated with one-time shielings (see below).

(ii) Winter Transhumance:

Lambs were frequently weaned in the first week of August so that they would put on plenty of fat before winter. In many parts of Coigach, female lambs in their first winter (L Sc *hoggs*) were herded by the children in autumn, given good food and conditions and then, October to February/ March, over-wintered on the Summer Isles [Fig. 14.52] — an alternative to lamb houses and of much greater antiquity. Traditionally they could not generally be left on the islands much after the end of February without heavy loss from pining and braxy; so after their return they would be kept around the crofts during the hard months of March and April and given extra feed before being moved to higher ground and new grass in May.

The grazing on the islands, it was said, strengthened the uterus, making them better for breeding in their third year (as two year old gimmers they were not to be tupped). Put another way, low islands almost always provide better pasture than the adjacent mainland, and the soil on the north-west seaboard is unusually deficient in the mineral salts that are necessary for growing sheep. On the islands, however, not only is the climate milder and the pasture lower, the rainfall is much lighter, the drainage is better and the land generally less waterlogged. But in addition, high sea-bird populations on the islands help manure the ground — the knolls occupied by the lesser black-backed gulls, for instance, grow short sweet grass that is eagerly eaten by sheep. And there can be seaweeds to graze (Fraser Darling 1938. 31-2).

Wedders also (the castrated males), if kept for several years could be overwintered on the islands; whilst Willie Muir's father would overwinter Highland cattle on An Cleirich (Eilean a'Chleirich, Priest Island).

Virtually all the islands with grazing might be used, even including such as Glas-leac and Sgeir nam Mult, where the spray and the surf would shoot right over in winter storms. It was accepted that some animals might be lost in these conditions (Fraser Darling 1944. 129-131; D. Fraser 1972, W. Muir 1991; see also Baldwin 1986. 187-190).

This practice of winter transhumance still continues — in 1991 the sheep were brought back to the mainland on 26 March; 8 March when Fraser Darling observed the operation in 1938. A boatload of men go out, round up the sheep and manhandle them into the boat from often slippery rocks in a frequently heaving swell (W. Muir 1991, A. 'West' MacLeod 1990,1991).

By contrast, winter transhumance of a different kind took place amongst the larger flocks. In earlier centuries the farmers and tacksmen with stock in

Fig. 14.51   Sub-square dry-stone enclosures in the old stream beds of the Allt nan Coisiche, just above the shore south of Culnacraig. Used as shelters for lambs, they may mark the site of earlier shielings. 1992.

Coigach would sell off or transfer a proportion of their droves of horses and cattle to dealers or to low-country farmers in Easter Ross who had the arable to overwinter substantial numbers. The later flock-masters and crofters with sizeable sheep flocks acted likewise — taking the sheep out on the hoof along the old drove routes, or later in motorised floats (D. Fraser 1972; see also Baldwin 1986. 194 et seq.). In this way, there would be enough fodder and winter grazing available to maintain locally a smaller flock through until the following spring. But it was costly if they were simply out-wintered and later returned — 10 shillings a head ca. 1938. For the ordinary crofter, therefore, out-wintering on the islands was much more economic (Fraser Darling 1938.31).

Goats

At one time goats were quite widely 'kept' in Coigach — though not normally at the croft, for their grazing habits are destructive. Recent attempts at goat-keeping by incomers have stripped the bark and killed 40/50 year old alders regenerating in the MacLeods' former potato 'park' or yard at Culnacraig; on the other hand Donald MacLeod would relate with relish the particular agility with which goats would climb onto thatched roofs early in the century, and eat the grass growing out of the thatch!

Culnacraig goats were kept out past the Garbh Allt, along the low route to Ullapool; and on occasion they were kept in a 'park' at Geodha na

Cailliche, opposite Eilean Martain — the infield of a tiny, long-ruinous cottar settlement where, it is said, the old woman (*cailleach*) regularly climbed the very steep short valley with a creel of either shellfish or seaweed, all the whiles spinning on her distaff (Fraser 1957. A.I.61-2).

Fairly wild, most were quite white; a few 'with sprechans on them', were black 'sprecheld'. Christie MacLeod's family (173) and Donald MacLeod (171) each kept five or six goats; others, including Angus MacLeod, Achnacarinan, also had some — a total of about 25. The herd had been there at least since their parents' time (? mid 19th century), and part of their value was in grazing the very steep rocky slopes either side of the Garbh Allt. Nimble on their feet, in so doing they rendered the area less attractive to sheep which would slip and fall more easily or get stuck on narrow rocky ledges. The writer rescued one such animal from a ledge a little south of the Garbh Allt in the early 1960s; it is widely believed however, that once a sheep has found a way onto such a ledge, if rescued it will return again subsequently (see Baldwin 1986. 188-9). In hard weather the goats would shelter in *An Uamhag nan Gabhar* — a cave below the steep shore track to Ullapool, *Cadha nan Tòn*, just a little before the Garbh Allt, where you would frequently fall on your backside! (Fraser 1957. A.I.43).

This apart, some families (but not Donald MacLeod's) milked the *boirionn* (female) — it was stronger than cows' milk. And latterly they would take the kid (*cid*) from the mother in the autumn to prevent the latter becoming too thin. Each summer, moreover, they would drive the herd back to Culnacraig with dogs, just like sheep. They would select one to kill and salt down for the winter, then release the rest and let them work their way back along the hillside to their customary grazing. Subsequently, these goats were shot at periodically by Ullapool people in boats, and eventually died out (D. MacLeod 1972).

At one time, however, goats were not restricted to these far-off cliffs. *Meall nan Gabhar*, Goat Hill, a little island lying just north of Eilean nan Eich, was no doubt once used to graze goats (and Horse Island, horses); *Clach nan Gabhar*, the stone of the goats, stands just west of the Allt nan Coisiche, below the Eas Dubh; whilst *Lòn nan Gabhar* lies just past the top of Culnacraig in a flat shallow valley, a little to the east of Meall Dubh Ard. Here in the wet meadow of the goats (used later for peat cutting) is *Làrach an Tigh Dhuibh*, the site of a one-time bothy where Ruaridh Og, Christie MacLeod's great-grandfather would distil whisky and cast out the dregs on to what became a greener spot! A copper pot is said to be buried there still, hidden from two maurading excisemen.

Cattle

Donald MacLeod (1972) tells of two families locally once keeping a pig — one in Achduart and one in Badenscallie. And he recounted how he used to push pins into the Achduart pig on his way to school there! But in times past, it was not pigs or goats or sheep, but cattle that were the most valuable

Fig. 14.52   The Summer Isles from above Altandhu, across Old Dornie harbour. Isle Ristol (right), with Tanera Beg beyond. 1992.

animals on the farm or croft.

Over-Wintering

Just as certain sheep were put to the Summer Isles during the winter, so also were non-milking cattle and horses. Horses were put to *Eilean nan Eich*; and back in the mid 18th century *Eilean Martain*, then uninhabited, was considered 'a good place' for winter grazing. As for *Achlochan*, between Badenscallie and Achiltibuie (almost as good as an island!): 'This Isthmus has cover and good Pasture for Wintering to black cattle' (May 1756).

In more recent times, in the early 20th century, Donnie Fraser's father would buy stock in Dingwall for £5-£7 per head — he 'couldn't pay more than £7 10/- if he was to make any profit at all'. The beasts were sold the following season after over-wintering on the islands — the converse of the more usual practice of selling stock east out of Coigach for over-wintering! Willie Muir's father (married to Donnie Fraser's sister) once kept Highland cattle on An Cleirich; it is probable that his father-in-law grazed his in-bought stock there also, for the tenancy of the island had been transferred to the Frasers after others had been discovered distilling whisky there — 'the sheep had scab, they said, which required many visits to treat them!' (D. Fraser 1972, W. Muir 1991).

Otherwise, cattle were over-wintered in the byre [Fig. 14.53]. In those days there were no turnips and no bought-in hay. The cattle lived on oat straw, and earlier this century every scrap of grass was cut from the roadside and elsewhere to provide winter fodder.

The cows became leaner as winter progressed; and had become so weak by the spring that, when they were let out, the old men had to follow them all day in case they fell into a bog and could not haul themselves out. The men followed until the cattle were strong enough; and they occupied themselves by twisting rope from heather freshly-pulled from the moor — for it had to be new, green heather (D. Fraser 1972). A not dissimilar sight was noted at Easter 1960. The surviving croft at Achduart, hard by the road-end, was still occupied by an elderly couple — MacLeans, originally from Skye. Their three or four cows were grazing on the topside of the Achduart hill-dyke, one in particular staggering and stumbling as she went (Baldwin 1986. 189-90). Shortage of winter fodder was always a problem on the marginal lands.

Summer Transhumance: The Shielings

The secret of successful cattle husbandry was to ensure that they got as much good grass as was possible, for as long a period as possible. Once cultivation began, however, all stock was banished from the infield until the following autumn.

Commonly, of course, hens were kept around the house and steading, and individual larger animals might be tethered on odd bits of uncultivated infield ground. Otherwise a well-developed system of transhumance existed in Coigach, as elsewhere in the Highlands — making use of a carefully structured sequence of seasonal grazings and shielings.

Given the extent of the Cromartie Estates, it comes as only a partial surprise to learn that, in the 18th century, the Forest of Fannich — a part of the first earl of Cromartie's Regality of Cromartie in 1686 [see Fig. 11.1] — was used in conjunction with the Coigach grazings. Because of its distant and disjoined location, not only was a forester employed there in 1755 to prevent illicit fuel gathering, but a 'Yeald Bowman' was responsible for the cattle, particularly the barren cattle and heifers before their first calving. For the stock was driven from Coigach to Fannich for the summer grazing — a practice that was evidently profitable given the presence of two Bowmen there by 1783 (R & C 1989.32; M. Bangor-Jones 1992. pers. comm.).

(i) The Culnacraig Shielings:

The use of many, if not most, shielings and pastures was discontinued in the later 18th/early 19th centuries, when the lands were taken away from the small (sub-) tenant farmers and leased out to sheep farmers. But not all became obsolete, and such was the need of the dispossessed on their new coastal marginal holdings that, where they could, they looked out new areas

Fig. 14.53 The MacLeods still kept a cow and follower until the winter of 1972/73. Their oat crop provided winter fodder — though the hens would get a share! 1972.

for summer grazing. Thus *Na Bothan Airigh*, immediately below *Na Baic* on the face of *A'Bheinne Mhór* (Ben More Coigach), were discontinued only in the time of Donald MacLeod's grandfather, perhaps around the mid 19th century.

The ruins of up to six small, rectangular, once-thatched stone bothies can still be seen stretched out on relatively flat but broken land a little above and west of *Na Luban Ruadha* (a maze of knobbly little humps and winding little valleys) in the vicinity of *Na h-Ach'ean Beaga*, the small meadows. They lie to the west of *Cnoc an t'Suidhe*, the hill of the sitting — a suitable place for the herds to rest perhaps when following the cattle onto the steeper ground.

At the beginning of the season the cows were taken up to the shieling across the steep screes and rocky slopes below *A'Chreige Mhór*, the big rock. ('Cross the scree that looks like an elephant', said Donald MacLeod). Then they followed *An Ceum Meadhon*, the middle path, before branching off along *An Ceum Ard*, the high path. Subsequently, the herds would climb up from Culnacraig in the morning and stay overnight in the bothies, eating food they had taken with them. The following day they would return to the settlement with the milk, to be made into butter, cheese and crowdie at home; and they would climb back up to the *bothan* the same day, with a further night's provisions. They would milk night and morning at the shieling, therefore, and spend every night there.

How long *Na Bothan Airigh* were in active use is unclear. For they do not feature on the 1756 Survey Map, and given that Culnacraig was uninhabited at that time, they may have been built by the incoming MacLeods in the 1810s/20s. In which case they may have had a life of perhaps 30-60 years — a lingering remnant of the pre-clearance, pre-crofting economy, in a post-clearance setting. That John Alec Campbell (1991) considers it 'a very queer place for cattle . . . very difficult to get the cattle up to', would tend to confirm its late development — under pressure of land shortage for grazing. The grazing is quite attractive, but it is also high at between 750 and 1,000ft (230-300m), with an inevitably restricted growing season. Significantly perhaps, the land there had not previously formed a part of any recognised Coigach farm; rather was it a part of the Forest of Coigach, unallocated in 1756.[4]

In other words, we do not know if there were shielings high up at the back of Ben Mor in earlier times, though this seems unlikely. What we do have, however, is circumstantial evidence of likely shielings much lower down and closer to Culnacraig that would correlate with Culnacraig's 18th century role as a grazing for the Badenscallie Farm, as suggested by the 1756 Survey Map.

Structures used at a later date as winter shelters for lambs have already been mentioned, but with an earlier function suggested. Down by the shore, in the boulder-strewn, bracken-infested former stream beds close to the mouth of Allt nan Coisiche, there are the ruinous remains of at least three sub-square stone-built huts, each about 7ft (2.1m) internal diameter [Fig. 14.51]. Each appears to have a secondary, adjoining structure closely paralleling 'double' shieling huts elsewhere; and each is partly built into the east side of the low bank separating one former rocky stream-bed from the next, thereby protecting the huts from the prevailing weather coming up and across Loch Broom from the south-west. Likewise the doorways face east, away from the weather, as they do in two nearby prehistoric hut circles.

This would indeed be a classic shieling site. Westward is the land later taken in as cultivation rigs; eastward *Allt an Achan Fheàrna*, the burn of the little meadow of the alders, runs into the sea at nearby *Am Port Driseach,* the 'port' of the thorns/brambles. This meadow is a tussocky, gently albeit unevenly sloping piece of wet moorland, showing possible signs of drainage, that runs back and up to the Allt nan Coisiche; and it is surely no coincidence that at its western, slightly higher end lies one of Culnacraig's hut circles. By its location close to the shore and to good fresh water, and by its general disposition for grazing, cultivation and fishing, it lends itself to human use. The surprise is, rather, that it seems not to have been taken into cultivation following the early 19th century settlement of Culnacraig. Perhaps it was just too wet to be drained satisfactorily? Perhaps it was just beyond the 'pressure zone' of the new, post-Clearance township? Or perhaps it was considered even more valuable as grazing? Indeed, perhaps the Estate forbade its cultivation?

That said, the documentary sources do not confirm unambiguously that there was ever a shieling at Culnacraig. The Mitford ms. (n.d. ? mid 20th century[5]); indicates 'a ³/₄ shealing' at Achduart; May, 1756, gives the name *Grackenarie*, across the point of Achduart, glossed by Fraser (1957. A.I.47) as *Creag an àraidh*, 'rock of the ladder', rather than *Cnoc an airidh*, 'hill of the shieling'; and Morrison (1775) refers to a shieling called *Achduard* located at what later became Culnacraig (not close down by the shore, but at what maybe emerged as early post-clearance cultivation rigs)! Mitford's designation, whatever '³/₄' may mean, is quite unconfirmed; the May Map is a copy, redrawn not without errors by Jon Scott — he dates it 'Surveyed . . . 1758', and gives 'A Tabee [*sic*] of the Contents' full of mathematical inconsistencies; whilst more generally in Coigach Morrison did not record all the shielings (or arable for that matter) mapped by May, nor did May map everything recorded by Morrison!

(ii) Shielings across Northern/Western Coigach:

Whatever the specific arrangements at Culnacraig and Achduart, there is evidence of substantial exploitation of northern and western Coigach for shielings and summer grazings. Donnie Fraser's collection of placenames, made in 1957, taken along with other surviving oral tradition and the Ordnance Survey 6 Inch map (1906), identifies some 14 shieling sites — as reflected in the elements *airigh/airidh, ruigh, bothan*. Peter May's Survey (1756) suggests at least 27 sites mostly identifiable as shielings either by their name (incorporating *arie*) or by the designation *Shealing*, but including sites (eg. Culnacraig) referred to as *Grass* or *Grassing* [Fig. 14.54].

There seems little logic behind this differentiation unless 'grassings' were to be distinguished from 'real' shielings. Might it be then that *Grass* or *Grassing* indicates an unattended grazing for eg young or dry animals, as opposed to milking stock? In which case it might be confirmation that Culnacraig's role as a one-time milking shieling, suggested by the ruinous huts by the shore and by Morrison, had indeed ended by the mid 18th century. In which case it might indicate an effect of the '45 and/or reflect the growing importance to the Cromartie Estates of cash-crop production of cattle for the droving trade — in evidence at least from the mid 17th century (Baldwin 1986.196). By the 1750s, therefore, Badenscallie farm could have had a milking shieling at Achduart, and an unattended grazing for non-milking cattle at Culnacraig — unless, that is, the shieling called 'Achduard' really was at Culnacraig!

Discrepancies apart, it is clear that shielings were variously located close to the sea, beside freshwater lochs, beside burns on the higher moorland — but not at this period, right in amongst the high mountains. And the Survey Maps make it very clear that by the mid/late 18th century, population pressure had caused a number of shielings and grazings to be cultivated — and perhaps (or about to be) occupied on more than a seasonal basis. Faochag,

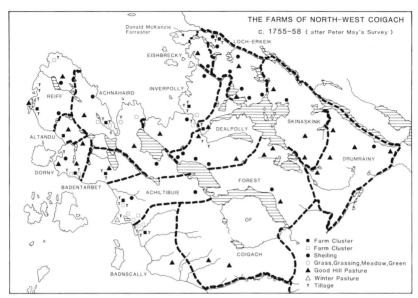

Fig. 14.54   The farms of north-west Coigach based on the survey by Peter May, 1756. Names are as written on the survey map; shielings marked do not include names incorporating Gael. *airidh* given by May, only those formally designated as 'shealing'. Building clusters shown by a solid black square appear to be the principal tacksmen's buildings, as opposed to sub-tenants'/cottars' buildings (open squares) — though not all farms show such differentiation. No settlement is indicated for Drumrunie; no cultivation is indicated on Eishbreaky or Sionascaig (though elsewhere Sionascaig is noted as under corn).

on the point of Coigach out past Reiff, is a good example.

Of particular significance in the longer evolution of settlement might be sites at Sionascaig, Osgaig and Calascaig — the latter at the foot of Loch Achall, inland from Ullapool and going with Corrie Farm in the mid 18th century. Sionascaig was apparently inhabited at the time of May's Survey; the other two were shielings — all of them in prime inland locations, with good land, beside substantial and fish-rich rivers/freshwater lochs. It is no coincidence, perhaps, that of all the shieling sites, these three alone are re-presented by Gaelicised forms of Norse names — ON *sjónar-skiki* (observation/lookout strip), *óss-skiki* (strip beside the mouth/outlet of a river/loch), *Kali-skiki* (Kali's strip). They appear to reflect a continuing ebb and flow of permanent settlement of considerable antiquity on narrow attractive strips of land between loch and hill (Watson 1904. lxxxii).

Indeed, the attractions of Osgaig live on in oral tradition. For it was evidently a well-loved shieling, in use in Donnie Fraser's grand-mother's time, well after the 1800s. Willie Muir remembers his mother (a sister to Donnie Fraser) talking of the 'happy thoughts' people related regarding life at the shieling, whilst Angus MacLeod, Achnacarinan, tells of the women staying at *Airigh Osgaig* from June until late August, sleeping on heather beds on the floor of the shieling huts. The men would walk over on Saturdays with food and clean clothes, and carry back the butter and cheese. *Pigean* (earthenware 'pigs' or jars) were put two or three at a time into the corn stacks, so that the salted butter and cheese would not all have been eaten before, say, March. It was a way of ensuring you had food left late in the season (D. Fraser 1972, W. Muir 1991, A. MacLeod 1991).

Tradition has it that the last dairy maids there were disturbed by a huge monster, an *each uisge* or water horse. They drove the shape or form into Loch Oscaig with sticks and stones (another version has them at a shieling at *Bun a'bhig*, driving the beast into nearby Loch Bad a'Ghaill) — but what frightened them most was that their missiles seemed to go right through the creature, and the dairy maids never returned (Fraser 1957. A.II.85 et seq.; J. A. Campbell 1991). A similar creature was said to live in *Loch na Beiste*, where the boundaries of Achnahaird, Alltandhu, Dornie and (almost) Badentarbat farms met (Cromartie 1979. 330).

Bun a'bhig was a shieling on the southern side of Loch Bad a'Ghaill, marked on Peter May's Survey (1756) and recorded by Fraser as *Airigh na Banachaig*, the shieling of the dairy maid. The name *Airigh Osgaig* refers to both sides of the burn running into the southern corner of Loch Osgaig, as does *Na h'Achaidhean*, the meadows — where the ruins of the shieling huts and calf pens can yet be seen. *Achadh Innis Bhràighe* is a pasture in the upper part of the shieling area, whilst *Grunnd Oscaig* is the bottom land of Osgaig. The whole area sits between the loch and *Meall Doire an t-Sithein*, the hill of the wood of the fairy mound — though the exact location of both fairy mound and wood is uncertain. There are many fragments of mixed, mainly birch woodland surviving in what would once have been a much more densely wooded area, and it is from these woods, for instance, that the birch roof timbers for Donald MacLeod's house were cut in the 1880s/90s, and sledged across the moorland, back to Culnacraig (A. MacLeod 1991). Indeed the peat either side of the Allt Druim Fuarmailt (Druim Mhór Osgaig on the OS 6 inch Map), was renowned for its long straight sticks of bog fir, much sought after for rafters (Fraser 1957. A.II.81).

At the head of the burn in *Coire Osgaig*, above the main shieling area, lies *Glaic nan Each*, horse hollow — presumably a horse grazing or place where horses were kept; whilst the whole area is bounded by ancient dykes. An unnamed dyke links Lochan Sgeireach to Loch Osgaig, whilst between Lochan Sgeireach and Loch Bad a'Ghaill lies *Garadh Glaic na Cullaidh*, the dyke of the hollow of the boar.

The *Abhainn Osgaig* completes the link between Loch Osgaig and Loch Bad a'Ghaill, fordable in at least two recognised places, *An Àth* and *An Damhàth*, the ox or stag ford. This last name refers to the fine pool below, rather than to the ford itself — a pool poached at night for salmon, with a torch (Fraser 1957. A.II.80-81, 84-87).

Two old tracks once made for the fords from Achiltibuie, passing by the western end of Lochan Sgeireach. Several small cairns, said to be funeral resting cairns, lie just south of the burn (en route for Badenscallie or for the ancient burial ground on Tanera Mór? — see Brown, this volume), whilst the bog to the south of the lochan bore the name *Blàr na Fala*, moss of the blood/bleeding — perhaps the site of a clan battle or a place where cattle were bled for food? Just south of the west end of this lochan stands *Clach na Comhalaich*, the stone of the meeting — probably a natural spot when travelling to rest or wait for others.[6] For past this tiny lochan and across the Abhainn Osgaig ran a key route to the Easter Ross fishings, harvests and religious festivals — by way of Gleann Laoigh, Elphin and the Oykell. (Other routes to the east/north-east led via Culnacraig through Strath Kanaird and Glen Achall).

The Osgaig shielings, therefore, were close to a major trackway; they were also close to the meeting of several major farms (Inverpolly, Dalpolly, Achnahaird, Badentarbat and Achiltibuie). It was less a remote shieling; rather a focal point near a key river-crossing on a lengthy system of large freshwater lochs and wide fast-flowing rivers stretching from Enard Bay to the River Runie and to Strath Kanaird: a system that effectively made the southern part of northern Coigach an island.

It would be little wonder perhaps, were this kindly shieling, located in a well-watered and wooded valley, once to have held a certain strategic importance. It is probably no accident that Osgaig has a Norse name, nor that it outlasted all other Coigach shielings; for it is a sheltered and fertile area, critically central to northern Coigach, and close to a good look-out point north, west and south to Enard Bay, Loch Broom and the Minch.[7]

SETTLEMENT PATTERNS

These accounts of generally early-mid 20th century land-use and crofting practice are based mainly on the evidence of oral history. Further accounts of eg fisheries, domestic and social activities, placenames and field-names must await another occasion.

This final section seeks to give an overview of the evolution of settlement in northern Coigach — from traditional tacksmen's farms and clusters of sub-tenants, to the modern crofting townships that have now outlived their original role as subsistence smallholdings for the remaining descendants of that local population once moved at will by landowners [Fig. 14.55].

Given the wealth of oral evidence relating to crofting specifically at Culnacraig, much of the material has been selected to focus on change and continuity within the area covered by the one-time Badenscallie farm [Fig. 14.56; see also Figs. 14.62-14.66].

Coigach in the mid 18th Century

Coigach as a whole (extending from the River Kirkaig to the Summer Isles and south to Strathkanaird and Glen Achall) once comprised four davochs of land (Gael. *dabhach*, a vat, measure of land: see Bangor-Jones 1986. 153 et seq.). The exact extent and sub-division of the four davochs of Coigach is not entirely clear, but they appear to break down as follows (M. Bangor-Jones 1991. pers. comm.):

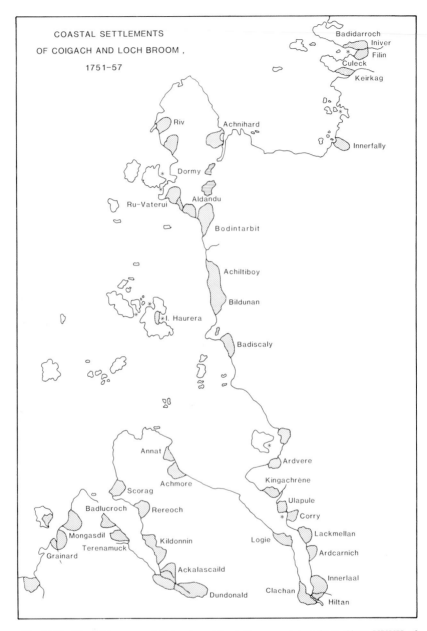

COASTAL SETTLEMENTS
OF COIGACH AND LOCH BROOM,
1751–57

Badidarroch
Iniver
Filin
Culeck
Keirkag

Riv
Achnihard
Innerfally

Dormy

Ru-Vaterui
Aldandu

Bodintarbit

Achiltiboy

Bildunan

I. Haurera

Badiscaly

Annat
Ardvere

Kingachrène

Achmore
Scorag
Ulapule

Badlucroch
Rereoch
Corry

Mongasdil
Lackmellan

Terenamuck
Kildonnin
Logie
Ardcarnich

Grainard

Ackalascaild
Innerlaal

Dundonald
Clachan
Hiltan

Fig. 14.55 Townships around Coigach and Loch Broom redrawn from Chart XXVII of Murdoch Mackenzie's *North West Coast of Scotland*, 1776. Because this is primarily a sea-chart it does not record such inland settlements as Dalpolly, Sionascaig and the numerous farms in Strathkanaird and Glen Achall. It does give a good general impression, however, of the extent of 18th century coastal settlements. An * indicates 'anchorage'. (NB: The names for Aldandu and Dormy are incorrectly placed on the original chart.)

356

2 davochs:	Strathkanaird (including Langwell)	
1 davoch:	Ullapool and Glen Achall	

1 davoch:	¹/₈ Badenscallie ⎫	
	¹/₈ Achiltibuie ⎬ ²/₄	
	¹/₈ Badentarbat ⎪	
	¹/₈ Dornie ⎭	

	Achnahaird ⎫	
	Reiff ⎬ ¹/₄	
	Altandubh ⎭	

	¹/₈ Inverpolly ⎫	
	¹/₈ Dalpolly ⎬ ¹/₄	

Whilst this helps correlate land divisions with the layout and listing of farms given by Peter May in 1756, it does not account for the northernmost part of Coigach: neither *Skinnaskink* (noted by May as under corn, with buildings), nor those areas he describes as grazings in the *Kierrograve*, the rough quarter — *Eisbrecky, Kennabreg* and *Knockbreck* [*sic*]. One must assume, however, that the 'davoch of the Aird' encompassed all the lands as far north as the Kirkaig river (M. Bangor-Jones 1992. pers. comm.). For in earlier Rentals, 1725 and 1740, the rough Kerrowgarve is certainly tenanted (GD 305/1/64, 126, 129), and a complementary list of farms for 1775 (E 746/189) indicates corn land at *Runabreck & Eishbrechy*, as well as at *Sheanascaig* [*sic*]. It may be, indeed, that Kerrowgarve signifies the fourth part of a davoch or possibly of a half-davoch — Gael. *ceathramh* (cf. Watson 1904. lxxxi; 1926. 236) [Figs. 14.54, 14.57-14.61].

What should not be assumed, however, is that all the farms were fully let or in good heart in the mid 18th century. For following the Jacobite Rising and the Battle of Culloden, the Earl of Cromartie's estates were forfeited and annexed to the Crown.

On the one hand, contemporary references by Munro of Teanninch and the annexed estate's new factor, Captain John Forbes of New, confirm the physical 'wasting' of Coigach referred to nearly a century later in the *New Statistical Account*. In 1746, Hanoverian ships under Ferguson appeared in Loch Broom. They stayed for eight days, during which time parties of Marines ransacked the Mackenzie house at Langwell, burnt a trunkful of estate papers (including, it is said, MacKenzie's title deeds to a wadset right and possibly any surviving charters of the MacLeods of Lewis), and drove off some 50 head of black cattle. Elsewhere, they fired the Forest of Coigach, seized cattle, sheep and goods wherever they could, and generally laid waste to the area (Ross 1834. 82-3; Cromartie 1979. 199, 245-6; R&C 1989. 72-79; M. Bangor-Jones 1992. pers. comm.).

On the other hand, given that virtually all the Coigach tenants were said to have been in rebellion supporting the Jacobite cause, large numbers of the young men would have been taken prisoner and transported to America — a factor which must also have led to a great part of the Barony lying waste (unoccupied) for several years. Indeed, according to the 1755 *Judicial Rental*,

Fig. 14.56   South-east towards Ben More Coigach (left), Beinn Dearg and the Fannichs. Achiltibuie, Polglass and Badenscallie (left to centre); Achlochan, Acheninver and Achnacarinan (right), with Isle Martin beyond. 1988.

Achnahaird, Reefvater of Garve (=Reiff, Water of Garve) and *Kerrowgarve* 'was [formerly] unrentalled and lying waste', as well as the *Forest of Coigach* (E 746/70/77 et seq.).

Although the Cromartie estates, including Coigach, were forfeited after the '45, Cromartie's own factor John MacKenzie of Meddat continued to collect rents for the family as late as February 1747. In 1748 the Barons of Exchequer Court in Scotland appointed an Edinburgh lawyer, John Baillie, as Estate factor, and he proceeded to lease the whole of Coigach for three years to Alexander MacKenzie of Fairburn at a yearly rental established in 1748. In October 1749 Fairburn sub-let Coigach to Murdoch MacKenzie of Achilty, and following Fairburn's resignation in 1751 Achilty continued to act as sub-factor for the new factor, Forbes of New (Bangor-Jones ms. 1988. 1-2).

To combat the evident depopulation occasioned by the Rebellion, Achilty brought in new sub-tenants 'from the island of Lewes and the neighbouring countys', including his own son-in-law Donald McAulay who settled in Inverpolly and is listed as having possession of the town, lands and fishing from 1753. Elsewhere, Angus McAulay was $^2/_3$ tenant of Badentarbat and the Summer Isles, with Hector MacKenzie $^1/_3$ tenant; whilst one Aulay McAulay appears to have held Auchindrein since at least ca. 1725 — holding a wadset to those lands (*Judicial Rental* 1755) [Fig. 14.61].

Factors, Tacksmen and Tenants in the later 18th Century

By 1755 the barony was let out to 64 tenants — out of a total population of 896. Given an average family size of say 5 people, perhaps some 115 or so families (nearly ⅔ of the population) were sub-tenants, labourers/cottars or otherwise dependent upon the principal tenants.

This was a period of considerable unrest and instability, with increasingly poor relations between tacksmen and their sub-tenants, who were generally allocated the worst parts of the farms at exhorbitant rents.

In a letter of 1755 John Forbes comments on 'Various grievances of the Coigach subtenants against principale Tacksmen'. He continues:

> It is the custom in the Highlands and in the greatest part of the North that when a tenant takes a large farm he subsells the skirly and worst parts of it to poor people at as high a rate as he can, and makes them obliged to perform many services, and the rent and services paid by them is generally much higher in proportion than what is paid by the aforesaid Tacksman. Some times he subsells so much of it in this way that he enjoys the best part of it to himself for nothing at all, and that this is at present the case in Coygach and several other parts of the Annexed Estates, I believe to be very true, and cant at all doubt but these poor creatures the subtenants are frequently oppressed by these tacksmen their Masters (E/746/74/1).

COIGACH FARMS: 1756

Names of Farms or Divisions of the Plan	Arable			Meadow			Improvable Land		
	A	R	F	A	R	F	A	R	F
Achnahaird	54	2	30	—	—	—	4	2	—
Reiff	37	3	20	—	—	—	5	1	—
Altandu	26	3	—	—	—	—	—	—	—
A Grassing on Kierrograve called Eisbrecky	—	—	—	—	—	—	—	—	—
A Grassing on ditto called Kennabreg & Knockbreck	—	—	—	—	—	—	—	—	—
Locherkeick	7	2	—	—	—	—	—	—	—
Shinaskink	5	3	20	10	—	—	4	3	30
Inverpolly	10	—	10	8	2	20	—	—	—
Delpolly	11	—	10	—	—	—	—	—	—
Dorny	21	—	—	—	—	—	—	—	—
Badentarbet	11	2	30	4	3	20	—	—	—
Achiltibuie	78	—	20	3	—	—	—	—	—
Badenscallie	30	—	20	5	2	10	6	3	30
The Forrest of Coygach	—	—	—	—	—	—	—	—	—
Drumrainy	—	—	—	—	—	—	3	2	10

Fig. 14.57 Extent of farms in north-west Coigach, from Jon Scott's 1758 copy of Peter May's Survey Map of Coigach, 1756. (RHP 85395).
'Meadow', 'Improveable Land' and 'Marshy Ground', if taken together correspond to 'Grass & Good Pasture' on Morrison's 1775 Survey. Similarly, 'Moss' and 'Barren Ground' correspond to 'Hill & Moss' [see Fig. 14.58].

MacKenzie of Achility, MacKenzie of Corrie and Aulay McAulay seem to have been a particularly rapacious lot, even if George MacKenzie of Achnahaird seems to have been the only tacksman still demanding services from his sub-tenants. Around 1755 the same George MacKenzie paid rent of £233.6.8 (Scots) for his farm and received £220 (Scots) per annum back, taken from his 17 sub-tenants — who 'being poor . . . make not punctual payments' however! [Fig. 14.61]. There was widespread land hunger and widespread conflict. Dykes were broken down, sub-tenants' cattle were illegally pastured and tacksmen's sheep harried. At the same time, tacksmen evicted sub-tenants and others at will (R&C 1989. 82-84).

The finer details of the affairs of Coigach and the inter-relationships of factors, tenants, sub-tenants and cottars can be gleaned from *Cromartie:*

COIGACH FARMS: 1756

Continued

Marshy Ground			Moss			Wood			Barren Ground			Whole Contents		
A	R	F	A	R	F	A	R	F	A	R	F	A	R	F
9	3	30	140	—	—	7	3	20	3157	—	—	3374	—	—
7	—	—	50	—	—	—	—	—	1828	3	20	1929	—	—
—	—	—	7	3	—	—	—	—	405	2	—	440	—	—
—	—	—	—	—	—	20	3	30	442	—	10	463	—	—
—	—	—	—	—	—	10	—	—	226	—	—	236	—	—
5	3	20	9	3	30	7	2	10	1627	—	20	1628	—	—
14	—	—	8	—	—	10	—	—	3817	—	30	3860	—	—
7	3	30	50	1	10	5	—	—	1743	—	10	1825	—	—
3	—	—	18	2	20	12	3	—	3004	2	10	3050	—	—
—	—	—	15	3	30	—	—	—	703	—	10	820	—	—
—	—	—	30	2	—	—	—	—	1044	3	30	1092	—	—
20	2	—	80	3	30	16	3	—	2305	2	10	2505	—	—
60	2	20	40	2	10	—	—	—	1902	—	30	2046	—	—
90	3	—	250	—	—	20	2	30	10924	2	10	11286	—	—
18	2	20	30	—	30	15	1	20	5086	—	30	5154	—	—

Fig. 14.57

Highland Life 1650-1914. Richards & Clough have ably quarried the Cromartie Papers to give a tantalising picture of a Highland Estate seeking to integrate the development of Highland (Wester Ross) and Lowland (Easter Ross) properties within a philosophical and cultural framework far removed from that of the people who actually lived and worked in Coigach, Strathpeffer and New Tarbat. It is hardly surprising perhaps, that the tension and discontent so clearly visible at the time of the Estate's annexation, should have continued in one form or another right through until the Crofting Acts of the 1880s gave a real security to the indigenous population.

As elsewhere in the Highlands, sheep farming was seen as the Estate's economic saviour. A Borderer, Ninian Jeffrey, was appointed local factor in Coigach 1764-81, and it was he who sought to introduce sheep-farming. In

COIGACH FARMS: 1775

	Corn Land			Grass & Good Pasture			Hill & Moss			Wood			Total		
	A	R	F	A	R	F	A	R	F	A	R	F	A	R	F
Achnahaird	54	2	30	14	1	30	3297	0	00	7	3	20	3374	0	00
Reeve	37	3	20	12	1	00	1878	3	20	0	0	00	1929	0	00
Altandow	26	3	00	00	0	00	113	1	00	0	0	00	140	0	00
Runabreck & Eisbrechy	2	0	00	0	0	00	224	0	00	10	0	00	236	0	00
Leorchircaig	7	2	00	5	3	20	1637	0	10	7	2	10	1650	0	00
Sheanascaig	5	3	20	28	3	30	3825	0	30	10	0	00	3870	0	00
Inverpollie	10	0	10	16	2	10	1793	1	20	5	0	00	1825	0	00
Dalpollie	11	0	10	3	0	00	3023	0	30	12	3	00	3050	0	00
Dornie	21	0	00	00	0	00	799	0	00	0	0	00	820	0	00
Badatarbat	11	2	30	4	3	20	1075	1	30	0	0	00	1092	0	00
Achiltibuie	78	0	20	23	2	00	2386	2	00	16	3	00	2505	0	00
Badenscallie	30	0	20	73	0	20	1912	3	00	0	0	00	2046	0	00

Fig. 14.58 Extent of farms in north-west Coigach accompanying Morrison's *Plans of Coygach*, 1775 (E 746/189).

1765 he suggested that Coigach men go south to learn about grazing methods; he proposed that the Forest of Coigach be let experimentally, rent free, to a southern sheep farmer to show the potential of the area; and he offered personally to transform Tanera into a sheep farm. However, the first sheep-farming tenant failed, despite a long lease and low rent; and in general the Board of the Annexed Estates did not appear to favour sheep-farming (or any other enterprise) that could have triggered large-scale evictions (Smith 1982. 86-87).

It was important to differentiate between the main tenant (whether old-style tacksman or new-style farmer), smaller tenants (also holding directly of the landlord), and the sub-tenants. In the regular famines of the 1760s/70s (eg in 1763, 1768, 1771-72, 1773) it was primarily, though not exclusively, the smaller tenants, sub-tenants and cottars who suffered. Crop failure, increased rents, social division, land hunger and American attempts to entice new settlers that continued until (and indeed after) the American Revolution in 1776, led to substantial emigration. In 1772, for instance, 26 persons left Coigach; in 1773, 11 more families had renounced their leases and sailed off in the 'Hector' to Pictou, Nova Scotia. Also in 1773 Lieut. Alexander MacLeod, tacksman in Inverpolly, gave up his lease; and in 1776 tenants in Runabreck, Badentarbat and Tanera wished to be relieved of their leases and to leave (R&C 1989. 90-92; Mitford ms. p29).

By contrast, the Estate was successful in setting farms to new and progressive tenants — which unsettled yet further many of the lower orders. In 1767, for instance, eight sub-tenants in Achiltibuie [Figs. 14.62-14.64] were removed to furthest *Rubha na breige* to make room for Lieut. Daniel Mackenzie, then living in Lewis. In 1777 the five who remained at Runabreck (the others had seemingly left in 1776) were again removed so that the Achnahaird tacksman could have Runabreck as a grazing. Four of these five settled on Tanera, and were evicted yet again in 1784 when the fishing station was established. Small wonder that on occasion the people refused to remove and that the factor found them 'so stubborn and unruly' (Bangor-Jones ms. 1988. 8).

In another instance, it would appear that Easter Ross-based Donald MacLeod of Geanies, a descendant of the MacLeods of Assynt, was keen to lease Cromartie land. Perhaps by the mid/late 1780s, 'At Coigach, on the west coast, Mr MacLeod possessed a large farm, which maintains about 300 horned cattle and 60 horses during the summer months . . .'; around 1790 he was thinking of replacing the cattle with sheep; in 1791 he was paying rent on Badenscallie [Figs. 14.62-14.66]; and in 1795 he is recorded as holding the leases of Badenscallie, Rhidorroch and half of the Forest [of Coigach] (GD 305/1/135, 163, 200, 203; Mackenzie 1810. 130; Baldwin 1986. 194-97; M. Bangor-Jones 1991. pers. comm.). The contrast is clear: MacLeod of Inverpolly was struggling and failing under the old system; MacLeod of Geanies had the political vision, muscle and capital to see where economic success would lie.

Nonetheless, he did not find it easy and was evidently in conflict with the sub-tenants. For three years later, in 1798, a *Petition of Donald MacLeod of*

COIGACH RENTAL: 1725

GD 305/1/126(129)	'Land Duty, bicardys, ffishing and ffow Duties'		
	marks	sh	p
1. Auchnahaird and Roiff	180	00	00
(Auchnahaird) 'of bicaradys' [*sic*]	015	00	00
2. Kerowgarw (Keriwgariew)	200(290)	00	00
do.	015(025)	00	00
3. Inborpolly (Inborpollie)	090	00	00
do.	007	06	08
4. Dabinhionphollunds (Dallphollig) Dalsichionphollunds	090	00	00
do.	007	06	08
The ffishing (The watter of Pollie)	020	00	00
5. The Ivion of Dornie (Dornie)	110	00	00
do.	007(007)	00(06)	00(08)
6. Baidinterrbutt (Baidintarbatt)	110(110)	00(06)	00(08)
do.	007	06	08
[mainland] ['Somar jllds']			
7. Aicbilibuy (Auchilibiy)	120	00	00
do.	007	06	08
8. Baidsbullie (Baidsballie)	110	00	00
do.	007	06	08

Fig. 14.59 Part of the Coigach Rental, 1725. (GD 305/1/126, 129). Entries in brackets are taken from the second copy (129).

COIGACH RENTAL: 1725

'Customs as usually peyd' Stones Wedders Plaids Butter			'Entries' ('Grassum') marks		Principal Tenant
8	6	1			
			1,000	(2,000)	(Ardloch)
8	6	1			
4	3	½	400		
				(650)	(James mbonye)
4	3	½	250		
—	—	—			
4	3	½	300		(Sallachy)
4	3	½		(500)	(?—)
			300 200		
4	3	½	400		(Allon. mLeod)
4	3	½	400		(Donald mLeod)

365

COIGACH RENTAL: 1740				
GD 305/1/64	Merks	Sh.	D.	Principal Tenant(s)
1. Achnahard 2. Kerowgarve Water of Garve	1,065	00	00	Corrie
3. Inverpollie 4. Delpollie	459	00	00	Alexander Mackenzie younger of Keppoch
5. Dornie	304	10	00	Alexander McKenzie of Achilty
6. Baditarbat [mainland]	237	2	4	Hector Mackenzie John Mackenzie John MacRa
Summer Island	99	8	00	Donald McLeod
7. Achlbuy	324	10	00	Alex^r McLeod
8. Badishally	324	10	00	Donald McLeod

Fig. 14.60   Part of the Coigach Rental, 1740 (GD 305/1/64). In an accompanying *Account of the Arrears of Coygach Rent 1737*, the following tenants are listed:

Dorny	Kenneth Mackenzie
Ackilbuie	Allasidr MacLeod
Badiskallie	Donald MacLeod
Badintarbat	Tennants

JUDICIAL RENTAL OF BARONY OF COIGACH: 1755

E 746/70/77 et seq.	Annual Rent (Scots) £ sh. d.	Entry Money /Grassum	Tenant(s)
Auchnahaird Reiff Water of Garve	233 6 8 (= money rent + customs)	14-15 guineas in whole to Auchilty	*George Mackenzie, entered Whit 1750 without Tack *+17 subtenants who pay him 'yearly £220 Scots or thereby but being poor they make not punctual payments'
Eisebrecky in Kerrowgarve	44 3 4 (= money rent + customs)		*Roderick McKenzie of Achillibuy, entered 1751
Kergarve Ruenabreage } part of Knockbreck	44 3 4	None	*Donald McKenzie of Achale, entered 1750
Shianscaig Lochangavich	26 13 4 26 13 4	}	*Angus McLeod, entered 1745 * Let to him by deceased Alex. McKenzie of Corry at 40 merks Scots each. Heard that old rent of Lochangavich was 20 merks Scots. Has paid that yearly since 1750 to Murdoch McKenzie of Achilty
Inverpolly + Fishing	78 5 8 4 stone butter 2 wedders 1 plaid	None	*Donald McAulay, entered 1753 without Tack *+ 3 sub-tenants
Dallpollie	32 10 0 (+ wedders etc)	Since 1750 to Murdoch McKenzie of Achilty. £17.16.8 Scots for 1st. three years £12.12 for 4th year	*½ lands — Roderick McLeod, entered Whit 1744 *½ lands — Murdoch McLeod, entered 1754 *Alike in everything: i.e. both pay the same

Fig. 14.61

● Continued on next page

JUDICIAL RENTAL OF BARONY OF COIGACH: 1755
CONTINUED

E 746/70/77 et seq.	Annual Rent (Scots) £ sh. d.			Entry Money /Grassum	Tenant(s)
Dornie	78	6	8 + customs 4 stone butter 3 wedders ½ white plaid	None	*Wm. McKenzie, entered 1754 * + 4 subtenants
Badentarbat Summer Isles	78	6	8 4 stone butter 3 wedders ½ white plaid	240 merks (⅔) 100 merks (⅓) since 1750 to Auchilty	*⅔ Angus McAulay *⅓ Hector McKenzie * + 5 subtenants
Achillibuy	78	6	8 4 stone butter 3 wedders ½ white plaid	£82.10 Scots yearly for 3 years past to Murdoch McKenzie of Auchilty	*Roderick McKenzie, entered 1745 * + 10 subtenants who 'pay him 200 merks Scots yearly but being poor do not make exact payments'
Badiscallig				£16.18.4 Scots yearly, each, for 2 years past to Achilty [sic]	⎧ John McLeod (son) ⎪ Roderick McLeod ⎨ (son) ⎩ Mrs McLeod (mother) *Entered 1751 without Tack
Forest of Coigeach	Formerly £30/£31 sterl.				*Alexander McKenzie of Corrie, deceased Laid waste in 1745

Fig. 14.61   Farms in north-west Coigach as detailed in the *Judicial Rental of the Barony of Coigach, 1755* (E 746/70/77 et seq.).

Geannies and others (GD 128/36/8) to the Estate sought protection for their sheep-farms from 'depredations' on their flocks. One of the signatories is given as 'Alexander MacCulloch of Badscallie', probably the tacksman and/or Geanies' local manager of the grazing lands in Coigach, the rent of which had risen sharply over the previous few years (GD 305/1/146, 147, 200, 203; R&C 1989; M. Bangor-Jones 1991. pers. comm.) [Figs. 14.67, 14.68].

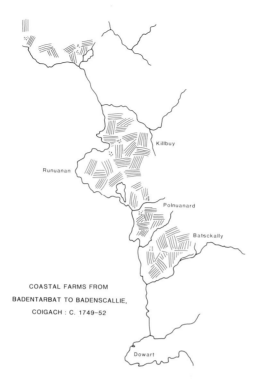

Fig. 14.62 The farms of Badenscallie, Achiltibuie and Badentarbat, based on the survey by William Roy, ca. 1749-52. The later plans [Figs. 14.63, 14.64] suggest this to have been a much stylised and inaccurate survey.

Into the 19th Century: Sheep Farms and Lot Farms

The turn of the century was a critical time both for Badenscallie and for other farms in northern/western Coigach. In spite of all the talk about sheep farms, an enquiry into Highland emigration reported in 1803 that there were only two in Coigach — one large and one small (*NLS* ms. 9646 p.43); though it did point out that the estate would be out of lease within ten years and that movements were beginning to be detectable.

In 1807 a 'good tenant' offered John Macrae, Edward Hay-MacKenzie's western factor, a bid of £150 for 'Badscally Farm', as opposed to its current rental of £30 (*CP* Bundle xxix, Macrae to Edward Hay-MacKenzie 18 April 1807). Then in 1808-09, 15,000 acres at Badenscallie (in addition to 2,400 acres at 'Altandow' and nearly 80,000 acres in eastern Coigach) were put up for letting (*Inverness Journal* 1808, 1809). The proposal was to have 14 sheep farms when the existing leases ran out in 1810. The market was all; as additional bait, sporting and commercial fisheries were highlighted along

369

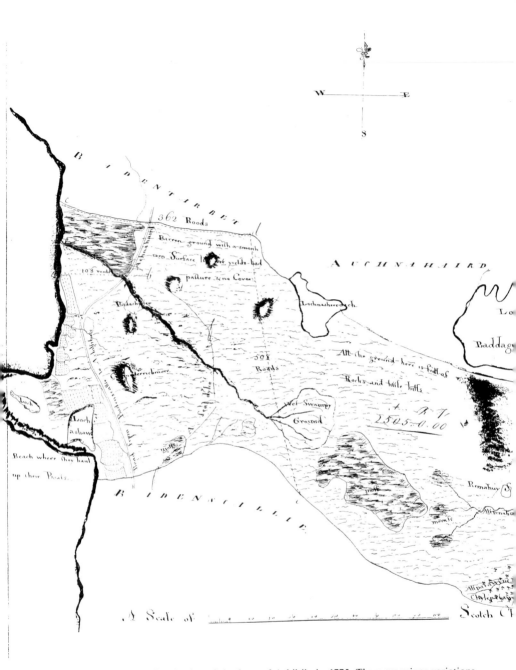

Fig. 14.63 Morrison's plan of the farm of Achiltibuie, 1775. There are minor variations
in the layout of parcels of infield land, and he does not appear to pay as much attention
to buildings as does May [Fig. 14.64]. On the other hand he names a shieling near to Loch
Badagyle as 'Remahuy' and that behind Achiltibuie as 'Badachylleo', nowadays *Bad
a'c(h)oitear* — the place of the cottar (though *Bad a'coitcheann*, place held in common,
has also been suggested: Fraser 1957. A.II.83) (E 746/189).

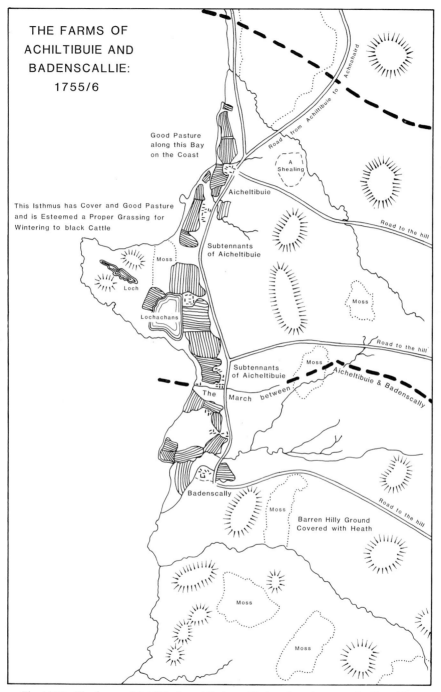

THE FARMS OF
ACHILTIBUIE AND
BADENSCALLIE:
1755/6

Good Pasture
along this Bay
on the Coast

Road from Achiltibuie to Achnahaird

A
Shealing

Aicheltibuie

This Isthmus has Cover and Good Pasture
and is Esteemed a Proper Grassing for
Wintering to black Cattle

Road to the hill

Subtennants
of Aicheltibuie

Moss

Loch

Moss

Lochachans

Road to the hill

Subtennants
of Aicheltibuie

Moss

Aicheltibuie & Badenscally

The   March   between

Badenscally

Moss

Barren Hilly Ground
Covered with Heath

Road to the hill

Moss

Moss

Moss

Fig. 14.64 The farms of Achiltibuie and Badenscallie based on the survey by Peter May, 1756. At Achiltibuie the tacksman's farm was in the vicinity of what is now known as Raon Mór, the big field; at Badenscallie the tacksman's farm was on the south side of the burn. For Achiltibuie there is a clear distinction between a buildings cluster for tenants (on the best land) and those for sub-tenants. (RHP 85395).

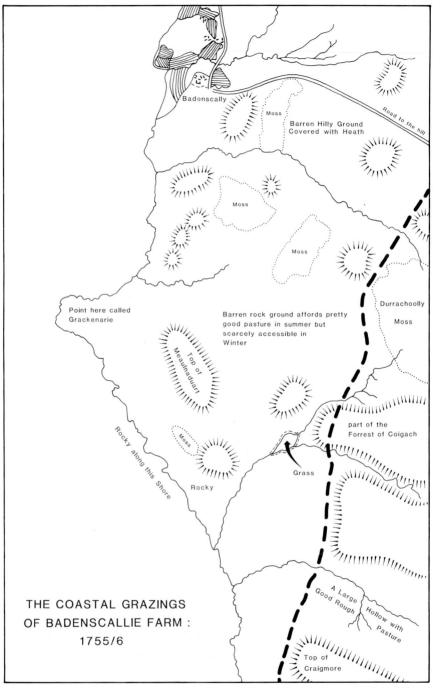

Badenscally

Moss

Barren Hilly Ground
Covered with Heath

Road to the hill

Moss

Moss

Point here called
Grackenarie

Barren rock ground affords pretty
good pasture in summer but
scarcely accessible in
Winter

Durrachoolly

Moss

Top of
Meadhnaduart

Moss

part of the
Forrest of Coigach

Rocky along this Shore

Grass

Rocky

A Large
Good Rough

Hollow with
Pasture

THE COASTAL GRAZINGS
OF BADENSCALLIE FARM :
1755/6

Top of
Craigmore

Fig. 14.65   Re-drawn from May's survey of the grazing lands of Badenscallie farm, 1756.
What was later to become Culnacraig is designated simply as 'Grass'; 'Grackenarie' perhaps
indicates the site of a former shieling, though Morrison [Fig. 14.66] places a shieling called
'Achduard' at Culnacraig.

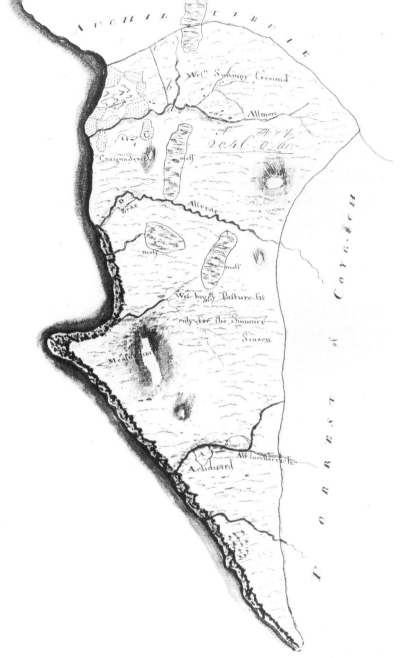

Fig. 14.66 Badenscallie farm, surveyed by Morrison, 1775. By this date there appears to be a cultivated area at 'Brae' (=Achavraie/Acheninver); and according to the facing page, 'Brae' was to be enclosed with a stone dyke. The shieling 'A', given as 'Achduard', was to be enclosed with a turf dyke; whilst 'Culchreg', a little upstream, was to be enclosed partly with a stone, partly with a turf dyke. If the latter area corresponds to the big field at present-day Culnacraig (though it is curiously placed with regard to the burns) then the shieling, in spite of its name, corresponds perhaps to part of the old cultivation rigs still visible below Culnacraig. In which case surviving turf foundations across the main burn, by the waterfall, may be the ruins of a shieling hut, not simply a 19th century old man's bothy (see also note 1).

COIGACH RENTAL: 1785

GD 305/1/146-147	Rental £	sh.	d.	Principal Tenant(s)
Achnahaird	13	6	8	George Mackenzie
Rive	8	8	0	10 tenants
Altandow	3	15	0	5 tenants
Rhunabreck	5	14	0	{ Malcolm MacLeod (Tack) + 4
Leorchirkaig	6	12	0	{ Hector MacLeod Donald MacLeod
Shiniskaig	4	16	0	{ John MacLeod Roderick MacLeod
Inverpolly	13	11	0	{ Lt. Donald Mackenzie + 6
Dalpolly Fishing }	10	1	0	Widow Mackenzie + son
Dornie	13	6	8	7 tenants
Baddintarbat	7	1	0	{ Angus MacAulay Donald MacLeod Murdoch MacLeod
Island Tanera	2	13	4	Rod. Morison (Feu + Tack)
Priest Island + Fishing }	17	4	5	Capt. Mackenzie, Avoch
Auchillibuie	20	0	0	{ Heirs of Lt. Daniel Mackenzie (Tack)
Badinscally	12	0	0	{ Roderick McLeod John McLeod Hugh McLeod (Tack) Murdoch Stewart
Forest	7	1	1 4/12	{ John MacKenzie Hector McLean
Island Martin	4	4	0	John Woodhouse

Fig. 14.67 Part of the *Coigach Rental of the Cromartie Estates, 1785.* Lieut. Daniel MacKenzie had by this time succeeded in acquiring the tack of Achiltibuie — indeed it is now credited to his heirs. The widow of Roderick MacKenzie and her son, after an acrimonious and long-drawn out struggle, had finally been removed to Dalpolly (GD 305/1/146-7) [See caption to Fig. 14.44].

COIGACH RENTALS: 1795 & 1799

GD 305/1/200, 203	Rental £	sh.	d.	Principal Tenant(s)
Achnahaird	18	15	8	Roderick Mackenzie
Rive	22	0	0	{ John MacLeod + others
Aultandow	5	18	1	{ Kenneth MacLean + others
[Runabreck]	—			—
Leorchirkaig	10	0	0	{ John MacAulay Don. MacLeod
Shiniskaig	6	10	0	{ Roderick MacLeod John MacLean
N. Half of Inverpolly	15	0	0	{ Murdo MacLeod + others
Delpolly	12	9	4	Mrs Mackenzie
Dornies	28	12	0	Heirs of Mr. Roderick Morison
Badintarbat	20	0	0	{ John MacAulay Angus MacAulay
Isle Tanera	3	12	0	Don^d MacDonald (Feu)
Isle Ristol [+ Ullapool]	50	9	1	British Fishery Society (Feu)
Achiltybuie	20	16	8	Mrs Mackenzie of Hilltown
Badinscally	30	0	0	Geanies
½ of the Forest (+ Rhidorach)	20	13	7$_{4/12}$	Geanies
Isle Martin	2	4	0	John Woodhouse (Feu)
Salmon Fishing	14	0	0	{ Ken Mackenzie Rod^k Morison
Kelp Shores of Coigach	25	0	0	Donald Shaw

Fig. 14.68 Part of the *Coigach Rental of the Cromartie Estates, 1795 & 1799.* By this time Isle Tanera, Isle Ristol and Isle Martin had been feued to herring fishery interests, and Donald MacLeod of Geanies had a lease on Badenscallie (GD 305 1/200, 203).

with ease of communication to Liverpool and elsewhere; no mention was made of the occupying tenants. In 1813, 'the whole district of Coigach is about to be let'; and by 1814 considerable areas of inland Coigach had been cleared, including Inverpolly, Langwell and what may well have been Badentarbat. Inverpolly had been taken over by Roderick MacKenzie of Achnahaird as early as 1810, when Sionascaig was cleared; further parts of Badenscallie and Achiltibuie farms were advertised for sheep in 1815; and more sheep farms were created over the period up until 1840 (M. Bangor-Jones per W. Muir 1991).

In 1814, Hay-MacKenzie's agent in Coigach, James Laing, was also 'supervising the rearrangement of Coigach lands' — the resettlement of people, the creation of lots for crofters, 'removals' and a rapid increase in rents (MacKenzie 1813. 256; R&C 1989. 144-150):

> I shall settle the small Tenants as far as in my power at present and should the Badenscallie Tenants not give £250 Badenscallie will bring more Rent and be better improved by letting it out the same as Achiltibuie — indeed were the present Tenants or any native to have the whole, they would just subsist and enslave the poor creatures as formerly, which I know is against your wish.

Richards & Clough highlight several key points in Laing's document:

* individual lots were being created for 'crofters' in Coigach (and had already been fixed in Achiltibuie)

* efforts were being made to eliminate the old system whereby tacksmen rented the whole land and sublet it in a quasi-communal fashion

* this was justified not simply because it would bring higher rents, but because it would reduce oppression by the tacksmen

* tacksmen were to be given the chance to bid at the new rentals, but outsiders were preferred for the main part of the land

* the majority of the people were to be placed on small lots, with most of the land to be let to a single tenant at a large rent

* a rapidly increasing local population would be granted reduced access to grazings, thereby turning them into 'crofters' whose continuing, albeit limited grazing concealed a substantial loss of land rights.

Clearly the existing (sub-)tenants were under heavy pressures, and by 1814 many had already agreed to the higher rents and to lotting — Rive (=Reiff) £60, Altandhu £70, Achiltibuie £300, Badenscallie £250. The Achiltibuie tenants agreed to add four more tenants to their number; those at Badenscallie a further six (R&C 1989. 146-149). Laing intended that in future the landlord should have a much greater degree of control, with a consequent reduction in the power of the tacksman. He had already ensured that rent payments were up-to-date in 'the Boreraig of Coigach' (= ?), and he looked to a more direct and regular system than hitherto. The elimination of the tacksman as middle man, however, was not to be completed until the 1860s.

Although the tenants of some at least of the farms had accepted the new rents and conditions in 1814, in most cases the allocation of individual crofts (as opposed to run-rig holdings) seems not to have taken place for another 11, 15 or even 34 years. Records are but sketchy for the 1820s and 1830s; and the surviving lists, which are evidently incomplete and show a number of minor discrepancies, were compiled some 40-60 years later:

1884 Crofters Statistics (*CP*: to Kemball & Green; R&C 1989. 346)			**1886 Crofters Statistics** (*CP*: November 1886; R&C 1989. 170)	
1825	Keanachrine		1825	Keanchrine
1828	Achindrean	(ca.)	1828	Achindrean ·
1829	Culnacraig		1829	Altnacraig [=Culnacraig]
	Polglass			Polglass
				Achlachan
				Achanduart
				Achnahaird
				Strathan
				Rhive
1831	Reiff		1831	Isle Martin
	Isle Martin			Altandhu (15 lotters)
	Altandhu			Canniscoil
	Camuscoil			
1846	Isle Tanera		1846	Isle Tanera
1848	Polbain		1848	Polbain (19 lotters)

It is difficult, moreover, to square these lists with Laing's letter to Edward Hay-MacKenzie of 26 September 1814: '. . . the new settlers on Keanchrine have got most of their houses up. I have got it all divided into lots . . . there are fine crops all along the coast they were never so good . . .' (R&C 1989. 149-50). Perhaps it is the difference between lots marked out on a plan and lots fully marked out on the ground — the latter taking a considerably longer time? In which case, plans for the lotting of other townships may have been prepared long before their implementation in the 1820s-1840s, new tenants being accommodated first of all within a run-rig system that required a considerable extension of rigs on to the surrounding moorland.

In other words, most of the new lots/small-holdings were only formalised between 1828 and 1831; the rest by 1848. Altandhu had 15 lotters initially; Polbain 19 lotters. The overall amount of infield land available to the community was not necessarily any less than previously. Moreover, the new holdings were each much of the same size — which, in adversity, must have given the 'crofters' a sense of (more or less obligatory) social cohesion, reducing rivalry and encouraging cooperation. At the same time, virtually all the new lots (as opposed to re-lotted farms) were created coastally on rough marginal land — often small patches of grazing between and beyond the old farm infields.

In 1831, one Andrew Scott from Roxburghshire became John Hay-Mackenzie's factor. He was to remain factor until 1869 and had a local sub-agent on the west coast, Kenneth MacKenzie. Scott's factorship saw further remarkable events and changes in Coigach.

In 1841, when anything from 40,000-80,000 people were destitute in the Highlands, the Government set up a Select Committee on Emigration (Scotland). Most of the Cromartie evidence was given by Scott, who testified that the tenants were located on 'eight lot farms' or 'townships' (R&C 1989. 482) [Figs. 14.69, 14.70]:

Achiltybuie:	52 tenants	Tanera:	7 tenants
Badenscallie:	34 tenants	Ardmair:	26 tenants
Altandow:	20 tenants	Keanchrine:	46 tenants
Reiff:	21 tenants	Auchindrean:	25 tenants

— which helps confirm, if the surviving records are sufficiently complete, that Dornie and Badentarbat were not lot farms at that date,[8] and neither was Achnahaird (even though it had apparently been lotted in 1829 — Brae of Achnahaird?). Until 1848, moreover, Polbain was let to a single tenant with the power to sub-let (*CP* Crofters Statistics. November 1886).

At that time the Coigach estate (including eg Langwell, Rhidorroch, Glen Achall) covered 145,000 acres — roughly a third of Lochbroom parish. Of this the lotters of the entire estate (not just the western part) had access to but 450 acres of arable for oats and potatoes, with no significant scope for expansion or reclamation. Additionally each township was allocated 1,000-5,000 acres of hill grazing, depending on the amount of arable. Tenants grazed 1-3 cows and 2-20 sheep which raised cash to pay their rents — augmented by fishing and seasonal employment in Wick and the Lothians.

In 1838, meantime, Coigach's total population was 1,512 and rising — a third of them under the age of 12. This represented 231 tenants, averaging $6\frac{1}{2}$ to a family and paying an average annual rent of 65-70 shillings per tenant. But in addition there were 500 others — squatters who were not officially there and who officially did not even exist. To discourage early marriage and thereby to slow down population growth, sub-letting and sub-division of lots was prohibited. So also was the building of additional houses on lots, other than as direct replacements, room for room, for old houses, which had to be converted into barns or byres. On the limited grazings, shielings too were forbidden lest they became permanent dwellings — though ostensibly to prevent some tenants gaining greater hill grazing advantages than others (*CP* Scott to Alex Ross n.d.; to James Mitchell 3 December 1842; R&C 1989. 201-205). Perhaps inevitably, however, squatting was uncontrollable.

The situation was exacerbated, according to Scott, by the tenants' continued reliance on and preference for a traditional, semi-communal peasant life-style based on what remained of the old ways and the old economy. For the 'lot farms' were an inadequate response for those removed from extensive

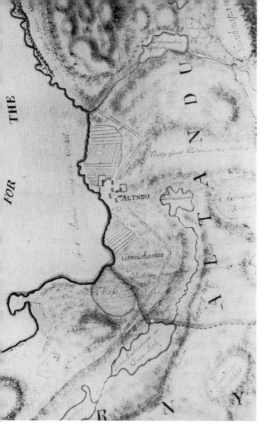

Fig. 14.69 'Altndu' with 'Camishanea' as surveyed by Peter May, 1756. A shieling lies on the north side of 'Locknarickielaphetre'. On the adjoining farm of 'Dorny', a further shieling lies just a little inland from the farmland of Old Dornie beside the harbour. Altandhu appears to have been broken up into 15 lots in 1831; and by 1841 there were 20 tenants. The 1835 Rental, however, gives 17 tenants, with a further 4 in the dependent pendicle of 'Camiscoil', nearly 3 mls (4.8 km) away on the northern coast of Rubha Coigach — a pattern reinforced in subsequent rentals.

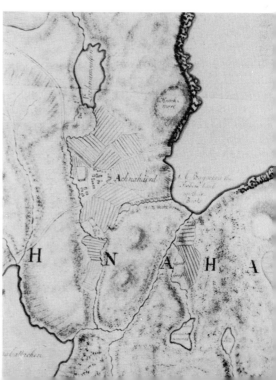

Fig. 14.70 Achnahaird as surveyed by Peter May, 1756. Unlike Altandhu, which became a 'lot' farm, Achnahaird remained largely as a single unit. Tacksmen/tenants included Roderick MacKenzie (±1820), George and Roderick MacKenzie (1833-48), George MacKenzie (1848-55: died 1851), George MacLeod (1851-66), heirs of George MacLeod (1864-5 . . .). By 1868-70 Alex. Munro was tenant — when there were also 9 smaller tenants (? Brae of Achnahaird), who appear to have co-existed alongside the principal tenant (Rentals).

Morrison (1775) marks May's 'Good Grass' east of the river as a 'shealing', but omits the two buildings, presumably mill and kiln, at the outlet of 'Lochnamoullen'.

old-style farms: the expropriation of the vast proportion of these lands turned the tenants into all-but landless labourers, and the factorial conviction that fishing would support the people was as ill-researched as it was cruelly optimistic (though it held up times enough when the potato crops were blighted).

Resultant poverty and the injustice of the surviving system of tacksman and sub-tenant are well illustrated by the case of a Badenscallie sub-tenant Mrs A. MacKenzie, who travelled across to Tarbat (Easter Ross) in 1841, to petition Hay-MacKenzie to save her from eviction by the over-tenant. She had to look after her aged and bed-ridden mother on her 'lot' and sought help to pay £2 per annum rent for her arable; she also asked for old grazing land to be added to an adjacent croft (she had neither cattle and sheep). It appears that her petition was granted, provided that no new houses were built and no strangers allowed on to (work) the land. (*CP* Letter Book 1841-48. Scott to Mrs A. MacKenzie, 20 February 1841).

Yet if Laing's stated intention in 1814 had come to pass, this incident might have been avoided — namely that the landlord should exercise greater control by cutting out the tacksman and leasing directly to the tenants.

Eventually townships were held directly from the landlord:

1848:	Polbain	1853:	Achiltibuie
	Dorney		Badenscallie
	Altandhu		Achavraie
	Reiff		Acheninver
			Achnacarinan
			Achduart
			Culvercraig [=Culnacraig]
1866:	Achnahaird		

(*CP* General Statement relating to the Crofter Holdings on the Cromartie Estate in the parish of Lochbroom, 1890; R&C 1989. 379).

However, this had been a long-drawn-out affair, largely it would seem of the Estate's own choosing — for the Estate found it much less troublesome to leave it to the tacksmen to collect rents from an impoverished tenantry.

When a later factor, William Gunn, set about making a survey of tenants' rentals in 1869, he noted of the small tenants:

It is right to mention that having traced the Rentals back for a period of 40 years I find that there has been practically no increase of Rent during that period. At that time the Crofters of Achiltybuie and other smaller townships as far as the Big Rock [ie as far as Culnacraig] were all sub-tenants of Messrs MacKenzie, Merchants, Ullapool, and so continued until 1853 when much to their satisfaction they became the tenants of the Propr direct at the old rents. (*CP* William Gunn's 'Remarks on the recent valuations of Crofter Holdings on the Cromartie Estate', October 1878; R&C 1989. 292-5).

In 1841, certainly, both William and Alexander MacKenzie, tacksmen respectively of Badenscallie and Achiltibuie, were still shown as collecting the rents. In 1850 they unsuccessfully petitioned the Estate to be allowed to relinquish their tacks on account of their difficulties in collecting the rent;

and only when their leases expired in 1853 were the small tenants made direct tenants of the Estate. There were over 82 such tenants, paying £320 to the MacKenzies; and after the landlord had tried unsuccessfully to re-settle them in Badentarbat, the tenants subsequently paid £370 per year (*CP* Gunn to Kemball, 22 February 1884; R&C 1989. 348).

New Attempts at Clearance: 1850s

This reference to resettlement highlights perhaps the most important event in mid 19th century Coigach. Back in 1841, Scott's personal conclusion was that emigration was the only answer to poverty and overpopulation:

> I think it would be a decided benefit to the people themselves, as well as to the landlord, to get rid of the burden of the support of these people . . . [after which Hay-MacKenzie] . . . would make the farms into sheep-grazings. (*PP* Select Committee on Emigration (Scotland) 1841-2 Report, Q.1636-1828; R&C 1989. 204).

In other words, the predicted famine of 1846-7 was simply one of a string of such disasters (1850 was another), which encouraged the Estate to think again about clearances and emigration — partly to reduce an impoverished and dependent population, and partly to increase income by extending sheep farms and the increasingly popular sporting tenancies. Scott's letter to Smythe, Secretary of the Board of Supervision in Edinburgh, 22 June 1848, says it all:

> a large proportion of the Parish is in farms let on lease and a considerable extent is in townships or allotments of land to which are attached extensive hill grazings occupied in common by the tenants of the townships respectively.

As Richards & Clough remark (1989. 213), this was the traditional, un-cleared pattern of settlement — substantial grazing areas in Coigach still in the hands of tacksmen and small tenants had remained untouched and uncleared since the first round of changes in the first quarter of the century.

Albeit on a modest scale, piecemeal, and thinking of local relocation of communities rather than massed emigration, in 1848 Scott was planning evictions at Dornie and on Tanera. But the people were not for removing (*CP* Scott to J. Hay-MacKenzie, 2 June 1848; to G. MacKenzie, 1 August 1848; to K. MacKenzie, 3 March 1849; R&C 1989. 213-5).

Even so, there was an emigration in 1853, when 15 Coigach families from Dornie, Reiff, Tanera, Isle Martin (and also Morefield/Kenachrine, Ardmair and Auchindrain) left at a total cost of £1,425 for Van Dieman's Land (Tasmania). The local factor, Kenneth MacKenzie, accompanied them by sea as far as Glasgow; for various reasons however they were unhappy, awkward and abusive towards him. This echoed the passive resistance to removal shown by the Dornie and Tanera crofters five years earlier; it served also as a forerunner of what was about to unfold in Coigach (R&C 1989. 233-5, 484 note 42).

The Coigach Riots: 1852-53

The 'Rebellion at Coigach' is described in considerable detail in *Cromartie: Highland Life 1650-1914* (see also MacLeod & Payne, this volume). Following the abortive attempts to clear Dornie and Tanera, the Estate did not want to risk difficulties at Achnahaird. Thus, although in 1851 Scott received an offer from a Border sheepfarmer, Purves, at a rent well above that of the current 11 sub-tenants, this would have required the removal of the sub-tenants. It was rejected, therefore, in favour of one from George MacLeod in Assynt who would pay only a little more than his predecessor, but agreed to retain the small tenants provided they paid their rents and behaved peaceably (CP Scott to Purves, 4 March 1851; to MacKenzie, 12 April 1852; to MacLeod, 21 January 1852).

However, the following year, 1852, in addition to the MacKenzies seeking yet again to get out of their leases of Badenscallie and Achiltibuie, Mundell of Badentarbat (created a sheep farm by 1848, but possibly some 10, 20 or even 30 or so years earlier[8]) decided not to renew his lease 'on account of the trouble and loss he has had to suffer since he became the tenant at the hands of the Lot tenants on every side'.

The Estate's solution was to shift the Badenscallie tenants to Badentarbat and to make a sheep farm out of Badenscallie — which marched with no other farm but Achiltibuie. The Badenscallie tenants included, of course, those of Achavraie, Acheninver, Achnacarinan, Achduart and Culnacraig, not simply Badenscallie.

Scott's problem was transparent. The tenants would be unlikely to remove voluntarily, so he set about making his proposal as attractive as possible whilst recognising — albeit with serious misgivings — that he would almost certainly be obliged to take legal action.

He first sought to persuade the 93 tenants[9] to sign letters agreeing to move. Although there would be a reduction in the hillgrazing and a greater encouragement to fisheries, they would only have to move about two miles (3.5 kms), and they would be given time to harvest their crops and to build new houses. In the event, 75 tenants signed the letter; only 18 refused. The 18 were to lose their crofts and all their hill-grazing (ie total eviction), but their refusal blocked the entire scheme — at least initially.

In March 1852, the sheriff's officer sought to serve eviction notices on the 18. Men and women waited all night, and when the group arrived from Ullapool they were attacked and the summonses burnt. A second attempt produced a similar result — summonses were again burnt and the boat dragged some 300 yards (275 m) over the shingle. The resettlement plans were postponed for a year.

By mid 1852, however, a new and financially much more attractive tenant from the south wanted a long 15-19 year shooting lease. Lord Dupplin demanded the removal of both people and sheep so that he could stock the western Coigach hills with deer; Lady Stafford rejected a petition from the tenants and gave her full support to Scott. She had reacted badly to the treatment meted out to her factor the previous March and wrote to Scott: 'I think the sooner and the more decidedly the Badenscallie people are taught their lesson the better, and it will also be a warning to the other small tenants' (*CP* Scott to Johnston, 24 February 1853; Lady Stafford to Petitioners of Achnahaird, 3 June 1852).

It was the next confrontation, in February 1853, that has left its mark in the oral as well as the documentary record. According to the latter, nightly watches were kept, with 'spies' or 'Scouts' in Ullapool. Eventually the sheriff's party left by boat for Culnacraig; they were violently assaulted by a large number of (mainly) women; yet again the summonses were seized and burnt; and the sheriff's officer 'was put on board the Boat in which he went to Coigach in a state of almost absolute nudity'. Women were said to be the leaders, but Scott was in no doubt that all the men were also present, as the previous year (*CP* Scott to G. MacKenzie, 10 February 1853; to Melville, 11 February 1853; to Loch, 18 February 1853; R&C 1989. 236-45).

Mary Shaw MacKenzie's recollections (J. N. Fraser 1982, in R&C 1989. 443) recall the early warning system in Ullapool and tell of the women, and men disguised as women, gathering in a barn at Culnacraig — 'this suggests that the evictors were coming by foot rather than boat', although it is an extremely rough route that leads out from Keanchulish to Culnacraig, underneath A'Chreige Mhór. Mrs MacKenzie suggests that 'The purpose of the disguise was the notion that if the worst came to the worst women would be treated more leniently than men'. Indeed, in her version one of the officers 'swore that no Coigach women would stop him. He received a blow from one of the women which did him permanent damage. He averred that the blow was so hard that it could only have come from a man'.

Donnie Fraser adds that the boat arrived at Ra Chamas; that it was met by young women and by some men dressed as women who stripped the whole party; that the warrants were found nailed below the step of the mast and subsequently burnt in 'a merry little bonfire made on the beach'. He also adds that a woman was put in the stern of the boat with her hand on the rudder, 'a lady skipper'; and that the boat was then carried shoulder high $^1/_4$ - $^1/_2$ ml (400-800 m) inland and dumped on the top of a potato pit. According to Donnie Fraser, *An Gàradh Ùr*, the new dyke, was built to form the new eastern boundary of Achiltibuie but was never finished (Fraser 1957. A. I.2; 1972). That would have required removals from all lands east of the present-day school and community centre, and would have included, therefore, Polglass and Achlochan.[9]

Mrs MacKenzie refers in particular to three women — Mary MacLeod, Anna Bhàn (the 'hefty woman') and Katie MacLeod Campbell. 'Katie Campbell took the shoes of the leader to ensure that no papers were secreted there. The officer was subsequently thrown into the sea'. Mrs MacKenzie continues by saying that Katie Campbell was later identified and the officers demanded of the factor that she never live on the estate again. When she was married, therefore, 'she was forced to build a house below the high-water mark'.

Further corroboration comes from John Alec Campbell of Polglass and Culnacraig. His version is similar, whilst offering additional detail with regard to the ringleader Katie Campbell — Cait Bheag, small Katie. She is said not to have had a croft, and to have lived in what is now a ruin immediately south of the burial ground at Badenscallie, just above the low coastal cliff. It was she was hit the sheriff's officer with a stick and knocked him out. Afterwards the Estate refused her a house and she eventually emigrated to New Zealand (J. A. Campbell 1990).

These, then, were the Coigach Riots of 1852-53 — an event of more than local significance as tenants more widely were taking the initiative regarding their traditional lands. In the event, the Estate had backed down; it dropped its attempts at removing the Badenscallie tenants; and in 1857, not getting any satisfaction regarding the adjoining Lot tenants, Walter Mundell refused (again) to renew his lease of Badentarbat. Scott had found it impossible to re-let Badentarbat, and wrote with great exasperation of the triumphant attitudes of the 'natives' or 'wretches' who so taunted the shepherd — 'We were here before you and will see you out and so on tormenting the poor fellow'. By 1857, the tenants were effectively beyond his control (*CP* Scott to J. Scott, Hawick, 18 February 1857; to MacKenzie, 13 April 1858; R&C 1989. 245).[8]

The 'victory', however, did not put an end to the problems of poverty, overpopulation and famine. In the spring of 1861, a letter from Badenscallie showed two tenants unable to pay their rent and offering to relinquish a third of their croft by way of compensation to the landlord. Indeed, over 1861-62 crops failed again, leading to a further petition from Badenscallie, signed with many crosses. It said that the small tenants could pay no more than one-third of their normal rent. Kenneth MacKenzie, the local ground officer acting for Scott, opted to take cattle in lieu of rent with which he could stock the large Rhidorroch farm; but prices could not be agreed and the rents remained unpaid (*CP* Angus and Hugh MacLeod to Scott, 14 March 1861; MacKenzie to Scott, I January 1862; R&C 1989. 259, 349).

And so it continued. By the 1880s Coigach was, if anything, even more unmanageable — even though a new factor, William Gunn, had replaced the ageing Scott. It was partly the continuing failures of crops and fisheries; partly the growing campaigns by crofters throughout Scotland for a 'new deal'. Thus it was, in 1882-83, that a situation emerged reminiscent of the Riots 30 years previously — except that this time the sheriff officer was collecting School Board Arrears. When he arrived in the traditional way, by boat to Badenscallie, he was opposed, assaulted and sent away. He was told that cattle and sheep were virtually unsaleable; that the potatoes (in October) were deteriorating rapidly; and that the fishermen had returned penniless (*CP* Gunn to Kemball, 13 April 1883; R&C 1989. 301).

Eventually the Napier Commission was established (1883); in 1886 the Crofters' Act gave crofters security of tenure at a fair rent; and gradually, through their own efforts, the crofters developed a more secure albeit still overpopulated and fragile economy. It was only in December 1992, with entry in February 1993, that the nearby crofters of the 'North Lochinver' estate, mobilised as the Assynt Crofters Trust, finally succeeded in buying out their lands — a date that may prove to be as significant for the indigenous population as the Coigach crofters' successful resistance to removal

140 years earlier.

POSTSCRIPT

In Culnacraig, Donald MacLeod's grandfather, born 1816, was in his prime at the time of the 'Coigach Riots'. He would have been fully aware of what was happening. His eight children were born in the 35 years following, beginning in 1855 — a period that would still have been filled with fear and insecurity, whether of eviction or starvation. For only when Donald's grandfather reached the age of 70, and his father 20, did the Crofters' Act become law; and whilst this offered security and fair rents, it could not guarantee a freedom from famine. Indeed his father, the youngest of the four surviving brothers, left for Motherwell at some point during the 12 years after 1886.

This is the background to the culture and oral history of Donald MacLeod and others of his generation still alive in the last quarter of the 20th century. Their tradition spans four generations, more or less — generations which saw a remarkable transformation from the role of oppressed sub-tenant on an old tacksman's farm, to dispossessed settler on the coastal fringe, to secure crofter with a title to his own land and house. In the event the land allocation proved insufficient and the standard-of-living too low — even on the most fertile parts of Achiltibuie or Achnahaird. And given opportunities to move away, large numbers of crofters in Coigach have seized them. By contrast, those few and younger crofting tenants who remain have become a new elite. They have gathered around them a multitude of assigned or sublet crofts, often across several townships, which provide them with ample infield grazings, considerable agricultural potential and substantial influence over what takes place both on the common grazings and on the enclosed land. For it has been the empty houses that have gone to outsiders and incomers, not the crofting leases by and large.

The future of the Highlands, however, cannot continue to depend upon monocultural exploitation — whether of sheep, deer, trees, fish, potatoes, tourism or nature conservation. It is to be hoped that both proprietors and politicians recognise this. It is also to be hoped that the descendants of the indigenous population, whether or not they have retained their Gaelic language, will feel encouraged to work along with others for a long-term, interdependent and sustainable use of the land — where natural resources and human cultures are recognised as of substantially greater importance and value than short-term economic gain, the maximisation of profits or political expediency. For now that the population is much reduced and subsistence activity and deep poverty are largely things of the past, the opportunities are there to work for a carefully-balanced, collaborative and attractive long-term future for the community. As Dolina MacLeod said in 1972, at the age of 78: 'We have the land and should therefore use it'. Twenty years later, aged 87, John Alec Campbell concurred: 'If I were younger, I'd start it all again — drain, lime and use the land'.

Notes

[1] The theme of carrying people, whether in flight or old age, is a recurring one. At Culnacraig, the grandfather of an occcupant of Christie MacLeod's house (173) lived in a bothy a little down from the old wooden footbridge on the Achduart side of the Allt a'Chulacreige (see Fig. 14.66, caption). The outline of the turf bothy, overrun with bracken, yet remains. When he fell ill he was carried up to the higher house on the man's back (Mr & Mrs D MacLeod 1972). Could this even have been the same Roderick Og who was carried out of Sionascaig?

There are versions also of an old Fingalian tale associated with Loch Lurgainn. In one story, Fionn escapes with his mother after coming to blows with an Irish giant in the direction of Garve. He carried her on his back all the way to Loch Lurgainn. When he found only her shanks or shins remained, he threw them into the loch — hence the loch of the shanks (Fraser 1957 A. II.91; see also MacDonald 1984. 265 et seq.; Watson 1904. 257). In another version the writer has heard it applied to the Norsemen. Escaping from Norsemen raiding on the east coast of Ross, a man ran all the way, without stopping, across to the west, with his father on his back. He ran through the woods and forests — 'for at that time the land was well-afforested' — but by the time he reached Loch Lurgainn he discovered that all of his father, except for his legs, had been torn off by the trees and branches as he ran.

[2] During the 18th century there were periodic attempts to develop a kelp industry in Coigach: before the Rebellion, by the Earl of Cromartie; afterwards by a succession of 'entrepreneurs'. In 1764 Ninian Jeffrey, the factor, argued that kelp manufacture would make the people 'shake off the lazy idle habits they have hitherto been accustomed to'; and by being prevented from using seaweed as manure they would be obliged to use the shell sand much favoured by agricultural improvers. It was left to James Robertson, the minister of Lochbroom, to stress to the Board of Commissioners for the Annexed Estates in 1766 the importance of seaweed as a manure, as well as reminding the Board of the inaccessibility of the banks of shell sand (eg Tanera Beg at low spring tides: Fraser Darling 1944. 146).

The conflict with tenants' rights appears frequently; in general, coastal farms continued to be allowed the right to use seaweed from their shores for manure. Kelp was certainly made from time to time (eg Tanera 1774/5, Auchtascailt 1781), and Donald Shaw rented the 'Kelp shores of Coigach' for £25 in 1795/99 (GD 305/1/200, 203). But there was never the same concentration or economic dependence on kelp as in the outer isles or parts of Orkney (Bangor-Jones ms 1988. 9-11). Whether the £211. 5. 9. rental for 'Sea Ware', charged of the 'Coigach tenants' in 1835, referred to manure or kelp manufacture is unclear (GD 305/2/85).

[3] In 1768 it was noted that 'Rory MacLeod & Son has built a drye stone House & Barn near the march wt Altendow and has taken in some moss or muir wt potatoes which will save about 8 or 9 pecks of bear, this where his grass is set apart from ye rest' (E 746/72/4). They would appear to have been subtenants/cottars in Reiff.

[4] The rough and rocky Forest had certainly been let for grazing prior to 1745, but had been laid waste in the Rebellion. The *Sworn Judicial Rental of the Barony of Coigach of 1755* (E 746/70/77 et seq.) gives two perspectives on its immediately preceding tenants and rental. In his own deposition Aula(y) McAula(y) — principal tenant in Auchindrein, between Keanchulish and Drumrunie — considered that its former rent of £31 sterling was far too high, 'being occasioned by two gentlemen in the Country, their bidding on one another out of humour'. He adds that 'those who took it at that rent were obliged to give it up'; also that he was one of those appointed to value the Forest at the time of the first survey, when it was valued at 100 merks Scots. Even then he thought it was 'not worth even that, excepting to the tenants within the Country in order that they may be free of a Forester'.

By contrast, Alexander MacKenzie — in Ardmair since 1745 — related that about 20 years previously (ca. 1725) the late Earl of Cromartie was in Coigach setting tacks and offered to set the Forest at about £100 Scots yearly:

2 gentlemen of the Country, the dec. Alex McKenzie of Corrie and Aulay McAulay of Auchindrein in odium of each other did raise the same by roup to £31 sterling yearly which was continued to be paid until the year 1745 by Alex McKenzie who was the highest offerer.

Shades of pique, resentment and animosity on the part of Aulay McAulay?

Although exploitation of the Forest intensified during the latter part of the 18th century, at the time of May's Survey in 1756 there was no tenant. In the vicinity of the later shielings May simply notes:

This end of the hill is called Beian-more and is like the other, very Steep and Rocky. These two hills are among the largest in Coigach, they abound in a Number of Fine Springs and have Sundry patches of Grass in the hollows and towards the Bottom it is Generally pretty Good Pasture.

[5] The 'Mitford manuscript' is a typed document acquired by William Muir (Achilitibuie) from Kenny John MacLeod, Achduart Schoolhouse, ca. 1960.

According to Mr Muir and Angus MacLeod, Achnacarinan, it was based on papers held by the late Mrs Mitford (née Fowler, of Braemore Estate), giving the names of Coigach crofters in the (?) 1770s. The papers are said to have been found in the fishery warehouse in Ullapool when it was cleared out prior to conversion as 'The Captain's Cabin'. Enquiries of the Troughtons of Leckmelm in 1991 failed to identify these papers.

Examination shows the manuscript to include material extracted from Morrison's Survey of Coigach (1775), as well as from other Forfeited Estate Papers and from the Cromartie Papers. In spite of discrepancies, the manuscript seems to be based exclusively on material now available through the Scottish Record Office, and it appears to have been prepared for serialised publication in a newspaper or magazine.

[6] In local tradition, *Clach na Comhalaich,* the trysting stone, is said to have been the meeting place of three brothers who were the first to have settled in Coigach. *Sgàl* gave his name to Badenscallie; *an Gille Buidhe,* the yellow boy, settled at Achilitibuie — the field of the yellow boy; and Watson (1904. 258) failed to learn the name of the third!

[7] In 1596 for instance, Torquil Dow MacLeod of Lewis, with 700/800 followers, fought with Torquil Cononach MacLeod of Coigach close to the mouth of *An Garbhaidh,* that exceedingly short length of river between Loch Osgaig and the sea. This attempt to seize Coigach was almost the last in a series of family feuds, spread over some 30 years, which ended in the early 1600s when the MacKenzies took over the MacLeod territories in Lewis and the adjoining mainland (Cromartie 1979. 174-75; see also Halford-MacLeod, this volume).

It is a battle still remembered in oral tradition as the battle with the Lewismen; that the Lewismen fled; and that after the battle, swords were thrown into a small loch still known as the loch of the swords — *Loch nan Claidheichean.* Stones nearby are said to mark graves; and when draining the land it is said that a local man once came upon the body of a Highland soldier. The drain was diverted so as to avoid the body (W Muir 1987).

A slightly different version suggests that 'peace was made without bloodshed and swords or possibly one from each side cast into the loch as a token of good faith' (Fraser 1957. A. II. 31). It is also said that 'one of the Torquils' was taken and hanged on the gallows hill, *Cnoc na Croiche* — the second highest point on the peninsula behind Achlochan (W Muir 1993).

[8] William McKenzie was removed from Badentarbat at Whitsunday 1842 when his ten year lease expired. Walter Mundell, who had the lease of Horse Island, Rhidorroch, Dalcanloch and part of Corry in 1835, took a four year lease of Badentarbat and the Isles in 1848 (1850 Rental). Given the difficulties that both Mundell and the Estate had with the local population around this time, Mundell gave up his lease in 1852. Badentarbat and the Isles appear to have been virtually unlettable at this point, and Lady Stafford herself is credited with the tenancy from Whitsunday 1852 (1851 Rental).

In 1857 Lady Stafford is 'removed' from the tenancy and Duncan Urquhart set on a 19 year lease until 1876 (GD 305/2/85, 113-116, 119-122, 132).

[9] Acccording to the 1853 Rental (GD 305/2/119-120), Badenscallie and its pendicles had

387

33 tenants; Achiltibuie (including Polglass and Achlochan) 60 tenants — a total of 93! Was it the Estate's intention, therefore, to clear both Achiltibuie and Badenscallie entirely? References in Richards & Clough (1989. 240) are ambiguous, and Rentals for 1850 and 1851 appear not to have survived for these particular townships. Oral tradition (see later, main text) suggests Achiltibuie east of the new dyke was to be cleared (ie Polglass and Achlochan), but on the evidence of the 1853 Rental this would have affected some 36 only of the Achiltibuie tenants — with Badenscallie and its pendicles, some 69 in all.

Acknowledgement

I am much indebted to many in Coigach and elsewhere in the north-west for their kindly interest and assistance over many years — mainly in the 1970s and the late 1980s/early 1990s:

Culnacraig:
Donald MacLeod
Dolina MacLeod
John Alec Campbell

Achnacarinan:
Angus MacLeod

Acheninver:
Sandy Miller

Achiltibuie:
Donnie Fraser
Mrs Abie Muir
William Muir

Polbain:
Alex MacLeod
Murdo MacLeod

Alltandhu:
Duncan MacLean

Achnahaird:
Mr & Mrs Alistair MacLeod (sen)
Angus MacLeod ('West')

Loggie:
Donnie MacLean

Kinlochewe:
Mr & Mrs Alec MacLean

Port a'chuple (Torridon):
Rory Beaton
Miss Mary Beaton

Fearnamore (Applecross):
Alex MacDonald
Miss MacDonald

Fanagmore (Laxford):
Alex MacAskill

Puzzled, apprehensive or even suspicious they may have been as we talked of earlier ways-of-life, but without exception they were unfailingly courteous, helpful and hospitable. Most will never know how invaluable their memories have been in helping document — from the people's point of view — the last decades of an ancient, fast-disappearing culture.

The late Earl of Cromartie kindly allowed access to Peter May's 1756 Survey of Coigach and other papers. I am grateful also for the advice and encouragement of Monica Clough and Malcolm Bangor-Jones whose knowledge of the documentary sources is wide-ranging; and to Ian Fraser for checking the Gaelic placenames and terminology, all of which originate from native speakers in Coigach. They, as well as William Muir and Angus 'West', were kind enough to read the typescript and to offer many valuable comments and suggestions. I make no claim to have gathered anything but a fraction of the material associated with everyday life and work whether in Culnacraig or more widely in Coigach. And such is the nature of oral tradition and personal experience that others will not always agree with what individual informants have recalled or suggested.

I much appreciate the continuing generosity of John and Diana Armstrong and family, and of Meg Fiddes-Watt; and as always I owe much to Vivien, David and Richard who have tramped the hillsides in search of past settlement and encouraged me to follow up clues and queries. Sadly I record the death of yet one more knowledgeable and ever-welcoming friend, William Muir, just as this volume goes to press.

The continuing support of Professor JB Caird and the graphics skills of Jim Ford (Geography Department, University of Dundee) in preparing maps and plans have been of considerable assistance; and Morag Holmes coped cleverly with a spidery manuscript to produce a clear and legible typescript.

Prints from the author's fieldwork negatives (1972-74) were kindly supplied by the Scottish

Ethnological Archive, and permission to reproduce illustrations has been granted by: the late Earl of Cromartie (14.6, 14.69, 14.70); the Royal Commission on the Ancient and Historical Monuments of Scotland (14.3, 14.22, 14.42); the National Museums of Scotland (14.2, 14.4, 14.8, 14.16-14.21, 14.23-14.27, 14.29-14.41, 14.43, 14.45, 14.53); the Trustees of the National Library of Scotland (14.9, 14.10); the Scottish Record Office (14.63, 14.66). All other photographic material is from the author's own collection.

References

Manuscript:

Scottish Record Office (SRO)

SC 25/22/54, 102, 119, 120	(Lybelled Summons 1792)
GD 128/36/8	(Cromartie Papers)
GD 305/1/64, 126, 129, 135, 146, 147, 163, 200, 203	
GD 305/2/85, 113-116, 119-122, 132, 136, 139, 142, 147, 150, 156, 157, 2050	
RHP 85395	
E 746/70, 72, 74, 189	(Forfeited Estate Papers)

National Library of Scotland (NLS)
    ms. 9646

Miscellaneous

Bangor-Jones, M. 'The Management of the Barony of Coigach by the Barons of Exchequer and Annexed Estate Commissioners, 1745-1784', ms. n.d. ?1988.
Fraser, D. 'Placenames of Coigach', ms. 2 vols. 1957. (Placename Survey, School of Scottish Studies, University of Edinburgh).
Fraser, J.N. Recollections recorded from Morag Shaw Mackenzie, 1982 (see Richards & Clough 1989. Appendix C 442-4).
Mitford ms., 'Coigach', 8 sections. n.d. ?1950s (see Note 5 above)

Printed:

Adam, R.J. (ed.) *John Home's Survey of Assynt.* (1775) 1960.
Baldwin, J.R. The Long Trek: Agricultural Change and the Great Northern Drove, in J.R. Baldwin (ed.) *Firthlands of Ross and Sutherland.* 1986.
Bangor-Jones, M. Land Assessments and Settlement History in Sutherland and Easter Ross, in J.R. Baldwin (ed.) *Firthlands of Ross and Sutherland.* 1986.
Close-Brooks, J. *Exploring Scotland's Heritage: The Highlands.* 1986.
Cromartie, Earl of. *A Highland History.* 1979.
Dunlop, J. *The British Fisheries Society, 1786-1893.* 1978.
Fraser Darling, F. *Wild Country.* 1938.
Fraser Darling, F. *Island Farm.* 1944.
Fraser Darling, F. *West Highland Survey.* 1955.
Inverness Journal 1808, 1809.
MacDonald, D.A. The Vikings in Gaelic Oral Tradition, in A. Fenton & H. Pálsson (eds.) *The Northern and Western Isles in the Viking World.* 1984.
MacRae, R. Parish of Lochbroom, in *OSA.* X (1792-3), XXI (1797-8). 1981.
Richards, E. & Clough, M. *Cromartie: Highland Life 1650-1914.* 1989. (referred to as R & C).
Ross, T. Parish of Lochbroom, in *NSA.* XIV. 1834.
Smith, A. *Jacobite Estates of the Forty-Five.* 1982.
Watson, W.J. *Place-Names of Ross and Cromarty.* (1904) 1976.
Watson, W.J. *The History of the Celtic Place-Names of Scotland.* (1926) 1973.

'LOCALS' AND 'INCOMERS': SOCIAL AND CULTURAL IDENTITY IN LATE TWENTIETH CENTURY COIGACH

Angus MacLeod & Geoff Payne

In addition to such well-recognised social divisions as class, race, religion and gender, less familiar forms of differentiation can be of equal or even greater utility in describing the social relations found within particular settings. A recent study of Coigach, the circumstances of which are specific, has shown the centrality of the divisions between 'locals' and 'incomers'.[1]

Such a local/incomer distinction is by no means unique: recent demographic and social change has underlined the wider relevance of this dichotomy in contemporary society. Since the 1960s people have been steadily moving out of Britain's big cities to sink new roots in the countryside. Between 1966 and 1981 London's population fell by more than 20%; in the 1980s another half million city dwellers headed for the countryside; and with job relocations, improvements in communications and transport, and the growing potential for computer-networking and telecrofting, this trend is likely to continue throughout the 1990s and beyond. While the arrival of large numbers of people in rural areas has coincided with widespread changes taking place in society, care must be taken in any attempt to isolate the underlying causes and consequences of in-migration. The inherent issues have become so complex as to require a different conceptual level of analysis to that found in earlier studies.

In previous work the local/incomer dichotomy has taken second place to other social divisions; particularly those associated with social class and housing in the commuter belt. The divisions between locals and incomers have been explained largely in terms of other dimensions.[2] This chapter will show that the division between the two groups is in fact a significant independent variable. In examining the local/incomer dimension from a more original perspective, examples will be given to show both how it is perceived and what it means to the people of Coigach, and more particularly the role of story-telling in maintaining a sense of 'local' identity. The choice of setting has facilitated the study of this dimension without it being obscured by other variables; the most pervasive social division can be explained solely in terms of 'locals' and 'incomers'.

COIGACH: SETTING, SERVICES AND WAY-OF-LIFE

The Coigach townships are spread over a rocky peninsula approximately twelve miles in length and five in breadth.[3] Still somewhat off the beaten track for most tourists, and with the nearest small town some 25 miles (40 kms) away, its resident population of about 260 live in relative geographical isolation.[4]

The settlement pattern is characteristic of such places throughout the north-west, as is the topography of the area. Less than 1% of the land surface can be classed as arable, and this has restricted the townships to the lower-lying coastal margins where the traditional landholding pattern of crofting persists. The function of crofts as agricultural producers, however, is of little economic significance today, with only a few vegetables for family consumption being grown. To own a cow is now the exception rather than the rule and the grazings (and infields) are predominantly under sheep, but less than 10 of the 105 or so permanent households run any significant number.

Typical of isolated settlements on the Atlantic margins, the area has limited services and facilities for recreation and leisure. Poor communication and transport networks leave it sufficiently cut-off from the outside world to make personal relations between its inhabitants crucial in everyday life. But although Coigach is rural and physically isolated, it is by no means depressed, declining or despondent. This is no 'Inishkillane', trapped in terminal decline and steeped in nostalgia for some lost age of Celtic innocence (Brody 1973).

The several settlements support two shops, two bars, a Post Office, a Church, a primary school and a village hall. In summer there is also a small hotel, a cafe, a camp-site and a few other 'tourist attractions'. Work is available in food-processing (there is a small plant originally financed by the Highlands and Islands Development Board), fish-farming (using capital from, among other sources, Scandinavia), the tourist trade, construction (there have been loans and grants to crofters), and basic services (eg. education, the mail, the road-gang). The Doctor, the Library and the Mobile Bank come once a week, and the older children go to secondary school in Ullapool each day by bus.

This current vitality has made it easier to avoid the romantic trap that has enmeshed some earlier writers of community studies (see Gibbon, 1973; Bell & Newby, 1971). Coigach is not an idyllic, self-contained, rural community. It is a geographically proximate grouping of relatively low-income households, set on a wet and windswept slope of hills. The way they earn their livelihoods, the way they spend their time, their connections with national institutions, the people themselves, are changing, just as in the rest of society.

Today's way of life is more varied than that of earlier times. In recent years a diversity of occupations unrelated to any local particularity and not providing any obvious social bond has come to prevail, making for differences rather than fostering common interest and cohesion. The dominant pattern is still one of manual work on a small scale, but the increased diversity of the economic base means that there is no collective work-oriented consciousness. The communal labour exchanges of the fank or the fishing are small-scale and occasional: the small-talk of work-tasks common to all in the daily round no longer applies. Instead, we have a local society in which many small groups can flourish, and where in many cases individuals move between one group and another from day to day, and during the day. At the same time, divisions do exist: for example, between crofters and fishermen, and between fishermen and fish-farmers. But the existing situation in Coigach, just as it cannot be explained in terms of well-recognised phenomena such as class, cannot be explained in terms of other simple oppositions like crofters and fishermen. The most important division existing in Coigach today is the one between 'locals' and 'incomers'.

BASES OF SOCIAL DIVISION:
LIFESTYLE, BIRTHPLACE, ACCULTURATION?

Coigach has witnessed in-migration for centuries, but it was not until the 1960s that this slow but steady stream began to take on the character of the heavy influx apparent in the 1980s [Fig. 15.1]:

CHANGING RATES OF INCOMERS
TO COIGACH:

1960-1989

YEAR	*NUMBER OF INCOMERS
1960-1969	12
1970-1979	36
1980-1989	72
Total: 1960-1989	**120**

Fig. 15.1 Incomers to Coigach, 1960-1989. *These figures represent only those incomers still living in Coigach and do not include either children born to incoming parents after their arrival, or incomers who have since left. Source: A. MacLeod, fieldnotes.

There is no doubt that this accelerating flow has been a source of change, and one which has not gone without remark by local people. They are now aware that 'their' community could soon be 'overrun' with outsiders, and this awareness has led to a division between the two groups. Living in a 'face-to-face' community it is inevitable that locals and incomers come into regular contact — at the school, at the shop, in the pub and so on. To the extent that frequent interaction between individuals of different backgrounds diminishes open conflict between them, this process is at work in Coigach. But at the same time, to the extent that conflict is caused or exacerbated by personal relations between locals and incomers, the difficulty of avoiding such contact renders continuing stress inevitable.

Elements of Social Cohesion:
Lifestyle, Clothing, Speech

Having said this, it is important to recognise that the two groups have a great deal in common and that there are no obvious characteristics that an outside observer could use to discriminate between them. Differences nowadays in normal speech, clothing and lifestyle are comparatively small for most Coigach people. The significance of family and kindred is in many ways the same for locals and incomers; households in both groups are made up of conjugal families; individuals in both groups share common expectations from kindred and obligations towards them. The division does not express itself in Coigach's formal organisations which are made up of both locals and incomers. Nor does it cut in any definite way through friendships, for it is certainly not the case that locals are only friendly with locals, and incomers with incomers. Many individuals from both groups have the same occupations and working conditions, and so on.

Over and against any differences between locals and incomers, there exists a range of 'community' and 'neighbouring' idioms whereby Coigach people can and do transform their sense of difference into one of social integrity. Through the practises of acknowledging, neighbouring and 'mucking in' (Phillips 1986), they experience and express their collective notions of being a community and belonging to it. The archetypal ideas of 'community' and 'neighbourliness' inform and pattern everyday practices that stress solidarity. Any visible evidence of the divisions between locals and incomers is therefore faint, but the reality of such a division nevertheless exists in the minds of Coigach people.

Concepts of Difference:
Birthplace & Upbringing

In reviewing fieldwork notes from weeks in which there were no major social events, it became apparent that there were a high number of references to locals and incomers in routine conversations. For example, in one seven day period in June 1989, 32 explicit references to the local/incomer dichotomy were recorded. The following quotes are taken from that week's fieldnotes:

> . . . I'm a local because I live here and I've lived here all my life.

> . . . If you live and work in Coigach, even if you are an incomer, and if you have a family here, then surely you are a local.

394

... I wouldn't think of them as real locals though. Maybe they are, but I don't think of them as locals.

... The only people who can call themselves local are the ones who were born here and brought up here.

These, and other quotes, bear testimony to the real social division that exists between locals and incomers. The two groups are often distinguished on the grounds that the latter were not born and bred in Coigach.[5] This criterion allows for locals to regard themselves as something akin to members of some sort of 'exclusive club' to which incomers cannot gain entry. It is designed to draw a definite dichotomous division in Coigach society, although in daily life other levels of division are also made.

Thus, in local conversational contexts Coigach people represent themselves to themselves, and to others, less in dualistic terms and more in qualified ways. They place themselves and their families along a 'scale of localness', ranging from 'real locals' at one end to recent incomers at the other. The term 'real local' infers the truism that there are 'degrees' of localness, as well as the division between locals and incomers. Some people, for example, regard themselves as being 'more' local than others because, as well as having been born and bred in the place, they can point to at least one parent satisfying the same criterion. If this were taken into account a simple table giving numbers of locals and incomers could be altered to look like this [Fig. 15.2]:

LOCAL/INCOMER STATUS OF ALL COIGACH RESIDENTS:

August 1989

Born and bred locals (with at least one local parent)	70
Born and bred locals (no local parents)	35
Incomers	156
Total population	**261**

Fig. 15.2   Status of Coigach Residents, August 1989, *not* differentiating between those with one or with two local parents. *Source:* A. MacLeod, fieldnotes.

By extension, a local with two born and bred parents can be regarded as more local than someone with only one, so the table can be altered yet again [Fig. 15.3]:

LOCAL/INCOMER STATUS OF ALL COIGACH RESIDENTS:

August 1989

Born and bred locals (with two local parents)	10
Born and bred locals (with one local parent)	60
Born and bred locals (no local parents)	35
Incomers	156
Total population	**261**

Fig. 15.3 Status of Coigach Residents, August 1989, **specifically** differentiating between those with one or with two local parents. *Source:* A. MacLeod, fieldnotes.

Potential complications of the table are endless. One could, for example, logically question the local status of grandparents, and so on. Yet such complications would be of little significance; so few people in Coigach today can claim 'pure' local grandparents that they are not important in differentiating locals from incomers.

Nevertheless, individuals who regard themselves as 'real locals' can, should any legitimation of their status be deemed necessary, remind others of their links to the locality through distant relatives and ancestors.[6] This shows that there may be more to being a local in Coigach than simply having been born and bred there. Many of the children who have been born in Coigach, but to incoming parents, are not thought of as being locals by the core of people belonging to old Coigach families. The term 'local', therefore, conjures up several related images in the minds of Coigach people — being rooted in the place; the identity that comes from belonging; bounded social horizons; and a sense of antiquity and continuity over time.

Concepts of Difference:
Length of Residence, Acculturation

It is notable how such an element as length of residence may or may not make a difference as to how an individual in Coigach is classified. Time spent in the locality does not pre-dictate localness if it does not go hand in hand with acculturation. Some incomers actually prefer to remain outsiders, and make no effort to integrate with the host community which, consequently, has never regarded them as anything other than outsiders. They maintain their incomer status through personal choice; unlike those who try hard to be accepted as locals but are not. For some find it impossible to gain the affection or goodwill of those in the receiving community — an essential prerequisite in any attempt to negotiate the boundary separating the two groups. This is not to say that one must continually remain on good terms with everyone; but the ability to 'fit-in' and maintain acceptable norms of behaviour is necessary.

Some find the negotiation of social boundaries easier than others and do not have to be born and bred in Coigach to be thought of as local in everyday situations. One can 'become' a local by virtue of marrying into the community, or by gaining the favour of the local population and 'mucking in', or by having lived there since childhood. But fulfilling such criteria is not always enough to gain the acceptance of the *whole* population. There are those who are regarded as being local by some Coigach people but not by others; and in certain social contexts but not in others.

Although there is a real division between locals and incomers, therefore, it is impossible to draw a neat dividing line between the two groups that would be accepted by all the people in Coigach all the time. The boundary between the two is open to manipulation, with some people constantly moving from one side to the other depending on situation and context.

BASES OF SOCIAL DIVISION:
EMPLOYMENT, CLASS, HOUSING, NATIONALITY?

There is, then, a recognised social division between locals and incomers in Coigach, but how is it to be explained? Is it merely a phenomenon used by Coigach people to deal with other, more fundamental, underlying issues in the community; or are the two categories important independent variables? To answer these questions some other social issues must be examined.

Employment

The changes taking place in Coigach today reflect a changing set of conditions in the country as a whole. The process of diversification in the labour market, for example, has considerably altered the social structure of the place. Changes in employment, income and welfare benefit have eroded much of the previous need for mutual aid between neighbours and relatives, and undermined the communal aspects of croft production (see Richards/ Baldwin, this volume). Gone are the days when most of the economically active men were crofter/fishermen at about the same economic level. Work now takes its character from the general economic life of the nation and makes for differences rather than fostering common bonds of interest and cohesion.

Yet unlike most communities, where work operates to differentiate between various categories of the population, the employment pattern in Coigach is not seen as a basis for division between locals and incomers. The increase in the number of locally available jobs has certainly attracted people to the area, but full employment means that there is very little competition with local people for these jobs. Rather than driving a wedge between the two groups, work actually serves to bring locals and incomers together. The local fish-farms, for example, employ incomers and local people. The same is true in the small food-processing factory, and both locals and incomers rely on inshore fishing as their main source of income. Local employment figures correspond with the higher numbers of incomers over locals in the total population [see Figs. 15.2; 15.3]; and the similar age and gender structure of both groups are also reflected in the labour market.

In many communities work operates as a divisive force primarily because it is class-linked — that is, people who work in different jobs associated with different prestige levels tend to choose people at their own level with whom to associate rather than to cross job-related class lines. In Coigach, however, personal esteem is more important than formal prestige, and class distinction in a formal sense is poorly developed.

Class

It would be theoretically possible to subdivide the population of Coigach on the basis of sociological convention into upper, middle, and lower classes. In both local and incomer camps there are individuals who could, theoretically, be placed on every rung of the class ladder.

Such a basis for stratification, however, would be largely unreal, unrecognised in the speech and behaviour of Coigach people. They do not see social class as a significant feature of interpersonal relations, and rarely show deference to people in class terms. They do not attribute status to people merely because they have a better job, or more money, or live in a bigger house. Class does not play a large or direct role in defining community lines, and Coigach people do not see it as an important organising principle with regard to the usually resident population.

They do, however, regard those who own holiday homes in the area as being on a different social level, and this is reflected in their use of the derogatory 'White Settler' label to describe them. (It is an interesting linguistic point that this label is rarely used to describe people who come to live long-term in Coigach, but is reserved for those who normally spend only a few weeks of the year in the place: MacLeod & Payne 1988).[7]

In other parts of the Scottish Highlands and Islands the term 'White Settler' has been widely adopted as a label for a colonial type of incomer stereotyped as English, affluent and arrogant. Such incomers are thought to have made their fortunes elsewhere before retiring to pleasant havens where they bid up house prices and adopt patronising attitudes to 'the natives'. This exploitative, elitist stereotype does scant justice to the majority of those who come to live in Coigach on a full-time basis, and their arrival needs to be evaluated on rather more than an impressionistic and anecdotal level. It is readily apparent, for example, that these incomers are not displacing local people by buying up houses and property; and they cannot generally buy the crofts upon which most are situated. In this respect the Highlands and Islands differ markedly from other rural peripheries in that access to the agricultural sector has been restricted by the institutional and legislative peculiarities of large estate management and crofting which prevent the operation of anything like an open market for croft land in which incomers could be expected to outbid locals. Crofting regulations ensure that local people retain considerable control over this crucial resource.

Housing

Housing is obviously a crucial issue, but in itself it causes no real social division between Coigach people. One local man neatly summed up the attitude of many of those in the receiving community when he said:

> You can't blame them [incomers] for wanting their own place to live. If they get a house then it's our own fault for selling it to them or letting them build it in the first place. Once they're in there's nothing you can do about it, so there's no point complaining.

Of the 105 permanent dwellings in Coigach (August 1989), 51 are the homes of incomers or incomer families. Several of these houses are rented from local people; others 'come with the job', e.g. fish-farm cottages, the school house, the nurse's cottage; and twelve are council houses. The total number of homes actually *owned* by incomers is less than 60% of the number of dwellings they *occupy* so they cannot be accused, as a group, of buying up all the available property in the area. The number of households in the locality is about the same as the number of permanently-occupied dwellings: the fieldwork discovered no 'hidden' households — i.e. those which would separate out if housing were available. Nor were there reports of young couples or others having to leave Coigach to obtain accommodation. Incomers do not have a monopoly on council accommodation. Several of the 19 council houses in Coigach are rented by local people and, should the situation arise, a local person would be given the opportunity to receive council accommodation before a prospective incomer. The availability of chalets, caravans and winter lets helps to ensure a balance of supply and demand.

What does cause resentment in Coigach is the fact that nearly 44% of the total stock of 187 habitable houses are holiday homes. Such resentment is understandable in the light of Highland Regional Council's Community Survey Report (1981) which commented that holiday homes are a problem where they constitute more than 20% of the local stock. Coigach people draw a distinction between 'cottages to let' owned predominantly by local people, and those houses that lie empty for the greater part of the year. The first are seen as tourist attractions that provide employment and income, especially during the busy summer months; the second are seen as expensive 'havens' for wealthy people who contribute little to the social and economic life of the place during the few weeks they spend there each year. It is these people, not the incomers, who are seen to boost house prices and severely restrict opportunities for 'ordinary folk' to contribute to Coigach life by coming to live and work in the area.

It is the relative isolation of Coigach that is one incentive for people to buy or build holiday homes in the area and may, therefore, be seen as a problem; but such isolation is also seen as an advantage in that it is a disincentive for commuters to set up 'base' there from which to travel to work. The presence of commuters in Coigach would undoubtedly lead to a far more rigid division than that presently found between locals and incomers who see the community as a central focus in their lives. Such incomers are not regarded as 'White Settlers', but as an important part of the community.

Nationality

The 'White Settler' stereotype is further discredited in that the majority of incomers to Coigach are not English (43.3%) but Scottish (54.2%) [Fig. 15.4]:

NATIONALITY AND PREVIOUS RESIDENCE OF INCOMERS (STILL RESIDENT) TO COIGACH:

1960-1989

NATIONALITY		PREVIOUS RESIDENCE	
Scottish	65	Highlands	11
		Lowland Scotland	51
English	52	England	52
Outside U.K.	3	Outside U.K.	6
Total	**120**	**Total**	**120**

Fig. 15.4 Nationality and previous residence of still-resident incomers to Coigach, 1960-1989. *Source:* A. MacLeod, fieldnotes.

Nor are all incomers to Coigach 'urban refugees'. Some have come to Coigach from other parts of the Scottish Highlands, and some from rural localities as far afield as Cornwall. Neither anti-English sentiment nor the rural/urban dichotomy, therefore, can adequately explain the division between locals and incomers. Nor is it the case, as protagonists of the 'White Settler' stereotype often imply, that the majority of incomers are retirees. Of the 69 adult (16+) incomers to Coigach between 1980 and 1989, only nine were aged over 60. The age structure of the incomers is similar to that of the receiving population, as is the percentage of males and females in either group.

THE ULTIMATE DISTINCTION: HISTORICAL AND CULTURAL IDENTITY?

If the division between locals and incomers cannot be fully or adequately explained in terms of the well-recognised indicators already discussed, how else may it be possible to distinguish between the two? Are there more distinctive, cultural factors?

Religion

There is certainly still a division, for instance, between those who are faithful attenders of Church and those who never go, but as less than a dozen people go to Church on a regular basis this is not a major division in the community, either in terms of numbers or the importance attached to it by most people in the locality. With the obvious impotence of such potentially divisive issues as religion, how else is it possible for Coigach people to distinguish culturally between locals and incomers? By language perhaps?

Gaelic

The use of Gaelic as a means of communication has declined and lost the meaning it once held for Coigach people. In the 1950s Gaelic was spoken a great deal: in the home; at work; in the pub etc. Now there are approximately 20 people in Coigach who can carry on a conversation in Gaelic, and it is heard infrequently — usually in relation to crofting matters. The youngest of these Gaelic speakers is in his early forties; and whilst there are several other fluent speakers under the age of 60, most are over 60. From the days when these people learnt Gaelic as a 'first language', the vast majority of those who regard themselves as locals today make no effort to learn it even as a 'second'. Proficiency in Gaelic is still regarded as a sure sign of localness, but its usage is no longer central to localness; there can be no overall distinction made between Gaelic-speaking locals and English-speaking incomers. There are some signs today of a slight upsurge of interest in

Gaelic — a few people, both locals and incomers, are trying to learn the language and some encourage their children to do so as well. Paradoxically, if this interest continues, Gaelic will become even less significant a tool for distinguishing between locals and incomers; but if it does not, and Gaelic dies, the loss is total.

A *Symbolic* Cultural Inheritance

Such cultural elements as language and religion, therefore, are no more relevant than place-of-birth, parentage, length of residence, nationality, employment, class or housing in differentiating adequately between locals and incomers.

Explanation is possible only in terms of the principal characters themselves, and in symbolic rather than structural terms.

The recent acceleration in the perennial phenomenon of in-migration has brought about many changes in the social organisation of Coigach, and local people perceive a threat to the traditional lifestyle and culture of the place. This has spurred an increased interest in their own identity on the part of those in the receiving community. Confronted by social change, they seek to replace the now-anachronistic *structural* bases of their community boundary with *symbolically-expressed cultural* bases before their community disintegrates as a distinctive entity:

> . . . they do so because . . . [they] find their identities as individuals through their occupancy of the community's social space; if outsiders trespass in that space then . . . [their] own sense of self is felt to be debased and defaced (Cohen 1985. 109).

In order to assert and preserve their own identity, therefore, they distinguish between their own culture and that seen to be confronting it. This distinction has been described as 'cultural totemism' or 'ethnognomony' (Schwartz 1975). The terms suggest that the associational category of 'local people' or 'community', and its refraction through self, marks what it is not, as well as what it is; that it emphasises traits and characteristics 'at once emblematic of the group's solidarity and of the group's contrasting identity in relation to the groups within its ambit of comparison' (Schwartz 1975. 109).

Such contrastive marking is exactly what makes the notion of 'social boundary' so central to an understanding of community. Coigach people emphasise their own and collective identity by using this notion to differentiate between those who they see as 'belonging' to the place and those who, by virtue of being outsiders, do not. The awareness and idiomatic expression of this differentiation is how Coigach people distinguish between locals and incomers.

A potential source of differentiation between the primary associational categories is the fact that many settlers have no knowledge of local history and culture. For local people, Coigach's past is bound up with their own personal history and identity; for the incomers it has no special significance

402

(MacLeod & Payne 1988). Having grown up in the place, local people know a great deal about local families and local ways. Incomers cannot share this unique relationship to Coigach and their lack of knowledge of kinship connections and the past, as well as posing difficulties when participating in local conversation and gossip, emphasises the cultural divide. But with the increasing number of incomers, and the amount of time some have spent in the locality, the divide has become more hazy and some of Coigach's cultural mainstays have weakened.

Let us look, nonetheless, at the nature and content of conversations recorded locally in Coigach, and more particularly at those (roughly one third of those recorded) which focus on the 'past' (for fuller details, see MacLeod & Payne 1988).

TALKING ABOUT THE PAST

Like most rural areas, Coigach receives hardly a reference in the major historical accounts of Scotland or in the more popular clan histories; nor is there an amateur local history. The reasons are obvious: there is no large family house to provide links to famous names, and the area has little strategic or financial significance to invite struggles for its control. One exception is the successful popular resistance to attempts to evict some of the tenant farmers during the Clearances, reference to which is to be found in several sources and to which we will return (Stevenson & Quinault 1974; Prebble 1963; Hunter 1976; Mackenzie 1914; Richards 1973; Grigor 1979; Richards & Clough 1989; Baldwin, this volume).

While there is so little *formal* local history, people do take an interest in the earlier parts of their own collective lives and there does seem to be a general awareness among 'locals' that first-hand experience and knowledge of one particular way-of-life is nearly at an end. The people now aged 60 and over, who have lived much of their lives locally, are the last generation who farmed the crofts in the traditional way: they include almost all of the fluent Gaelic speakers (MacLeod & Payne 1991). These people do sometimes speak sadly of what has been lost, but they seem no more concerned with the past than other men and women in their sixties and seventies elsewhere. The past is not the major focus of interest for them, nor do they constantly compare the present (to its detriment) with bygone days. Their interest in their own earlier lives is largely that it *is* their own lives. That the life-style was different makes it of sufficient interest to include sometimes in conversation.

'Historical' Themes and Local Reminiscence

Out of a total of 26 conversations containing references to the past (recorded over 27 working days and including nearly 50 speakers, 30 separate individuals), nine contained specific references to 'history', previous centuries or to global events. Three of these dealt with the World Wars; one with an old document about land tenure; two with local 18th century settlements, now in ruins; two with school days and what history was taught as a subject; and the ninth being one person reflecting on 200 years of social change in Coigach. The remaining conversations dealt with past events in the locality. Most were individual reminiscences, including four fairly technical reviews of how fishing and farming work methods had changed (including poaching salmon as a work method!) and how this had affected the talkers' lives. One was a recollection of visiting a particular house years ago, as a teenager; and one was a school-days memory of how different and better it had been then without so many visitors. In all, there were seven comparisons of the past with the present, mainly arising from reflections about the current New Year's celebrations. Three others dealt with anecdotes involving mutual friends or relatives, and the last was a remark about contemporary people's attitudes to the past or history.

It is interesting to see what historical references did *not* get included. There was no general British history, of this or any century, except the World Wars. There was no general Scottish history, or use of romantic tales of battle (unless one really stretches it to include a song or two). The content of the 26 extracts is overwhelmingly local, and every one of the deep past and the global events was given explicit local reference points.

With three or four exceptions, the specific evaluative comments, the tone of voice, the contexts in which the past was raised and the conversational responses, all tended to suggest interest rather than high levels of consciousness or a significant symbolic point of reference. What was striking, however, was the way that both the past, and every reference to history, was connected to the locality, and most of the time to some event in the present. To some extent, this is to be expected, because there has to be a trigger for the natural occurrence of the new topic. Nonetheless, the degree of connection goes beyond the initial introduction of topic. While some of the stories did look back nostalgically to better days, the general character was not dominated by a yearning for lost ways of life, which would have had little direct relevance for today.

Reinforcement of a Shared Identity

Instead, the past was commonly used as a device for sustaining shared identity among local people. For the most part, this was not done by parading their connections with the past in front of visitors and incomers. The past came up most when only the 'more local' people were present. Incomers with disparate backgrounds could neither participate, nor mobilise their own pasts in the same way when interacting with other incomers. Thus the emphasis was on what binds local people together, rather than what keeps incomers apart.

Put another way, nearly four-fifths of the conversations about the past occurred in locally-orientated groups, with no incomers or visitors. This could simply suggest that history is not greatly used as a conversational device among relative strangers, but that does not account for its lack of usage in the company of well-known incomers, or by incomers amongst themselves. It seems plausible to suggest, rather, that the more identifiably 'local' people tend to exploit their shared memories to re-establish and maintain their interpersonal links — and therein lies a particular significance. Incomers in particular are likely to be excluded because the essence of their identity is that they are *not* local, and so they are not encouraged to participate in the resource of common knowledge about the area's past. The constant re-creation of local identity could not be achieved if non-locals were allowed to play in the same game. The emphasis is nonetheless on who *is* included, rather than on an aggressive or conscious exclusion. It may be that incomers and visitors (and ethnographers in general!) can take naturally occurring discussions of the past as one indicator of their achieving growing acceptance into a rural settlement.

It is not surprising, then, that many of the mentions of the past are explicitly about *local* events and people. However, as indicated, the more strictly *historical* references were also linked to local events and history. The salience of history for Coigach is its capacity to sustain identity and to connect with the present; its 'localness', therefore, is paramount.

THE STORY OF THE CLEARANCES: A CULTURAL SYMBOL?

It has been suggested above that very few stories related specifically to known Scottish or local historical events, and also that very few stories reflected a significant cultural symbolism. One particular exception must be the story of mid 19th century resistance in Coigach to the Clearances.

Several recent publications (Richards 1973; Richards & Clough 1989 236-45; Baldwin, this volume) relate how the tenants of Coigach defied the authority of the landlord and the law by resisting eviction parties five times in twelve months (1852-53). Richards's account of the first attempt to serve the summons tells how the writs were burned after they had been seized from the officers of the law who had travelled from Ullapool to Coigach by boat. They were met by a large crowd of local people, mainly dressed in female fashion; they were humiliated and then sent packing. Prebble (1963), Mackenzie (1914), Stevenson & Quinault (1974) and Grigor (1979) seem to confine themselves to this event, describing the civil unrest and the writ-burning:

> The Marquis of Stafford informed forty of his tenants at Coigach that he required them out, as their land was to be put under sheep. The people threatened deforcement; the Lord Advocate was asked for soldiers; and in the meantime a party of sheriff officers was deforced, and their writs of removal were burned before them (Grigor 1979).

The number of tenants facing eviction varies from account to account (according to Eric Richards only 18 people were to be removed); so also do other details, not least of which is the part played by the Duchess of Sutherland. According to Alexander Mackenzie (1914) the Duchess interceded between her subordinates and the people and prevented the clearance: he claimed that the proceedings 'seem to have taken place without the knowledge of the noble proprietrix who, as soon as the true state of the case was laid before her, disallowed the violent proceedings of her underlings'. However, according to Richards (1988. 242-3), she urged full exertion of the law against the people.

In most of the written accounts, and in two local oral versions, the story has been radically condensed in its re-telling. First, the surviving tale is now by most standards a pretty good story, with drama and eventual triumph for the underdogs. Second, it is a story that is unique to the locality, of particular interest to people living there and in which the local people triumph. And third, as in the case when it was originally told to Payne, its text of locals versus outsiders can be turned to the modern context of locals and incomers.

We might therefore expect it to be a commonly-told tale, but while almost all local people to whom we have spoken seem to know it, at least in general terms, it does not assume a central place in the life of the people. It is not ritually told at some point of the year; there is no ceremony to mark it; MacLeod does not recall hearing it taught in the local school, or frequently recounted in his family upbringing, or told by more than three people. Payne, as an incomer, encountered the story on only two occasions in three years, apart from when he has raised the story himself.

Recent Versions of the Story

To demonstrate the quality of the story, two oral versions are given below. The first was written out in 1981 by a man in his eighties, who spoke to MacLeod of the incident and offered to write down a short historical account. What follows is a short extract from that account:

> ... At that period the Achiltibuie rents were leased by the Cromarty estate to two MacKenzie brothers, merchants in Ullapool. The MacKenzie merchants wished to break the lease so the estate decided to evict more Coigach crofters and summons were issued for that purpose. There were no roads here then. When the Sheriff's men came to Ullapool on their way to Coigach to serve the summons, a young lad named Gordon came quickly along the coast and told the people. A large crowd gathered on the beach below the hotel at Achiltibuie where the boat landed. A number of teenage girls and some teenage boys dressed as girls then caught hold of the Sheriff's men and stripped them, looking for the summons. They failed to find them on their bodies. Then they searched the boat. They found them nailed under the sole at the stern. The summons were taken and burnt there and then in a bonfire on the beach. Then one of the lassies was put sitting in the stern — the rudder was replaced and the beam put under her arm, and the boat carried shoulder high in triumph for about a quarter mile and dumped on top of a potato pit just below the hotel and left there. No doubt a drink or two would be taken to celebrate the victory

for the local cellar was only about fifty yards from the potato pit.

. . . My Grandmother, Margaret MacLeod, was sixteen years of age when she took part in the burning of the summonses.

The second version, taken from a video-interview, is a re-telling to MacLeod of the story as it was originally told to Payne:

Storyteller: . . . When the Red Coats arrived out the river [along the sea loch] . . . they said to the men in Ullapool, we will give 2/6 to any man (well it was called a silver shilling but I call it 2/6) to any man who will row us fresh, so we'd be fresh when we arrive in Coigach to land the eviction papers.

And this woman who came to Ullapool from Coigach said, 'If I am married to you boy, who will row me to my own people'. She walked into the water with her child and she persuaded him, she persuaded him and eventually she threw her child into the water and said, 'If you will go to the sea, to sail and take my people away, you can have my child back'. But, you know romanticism, knowing full well that her husband would jump out of the boat and save the child.

Interviewer: Oh. Aye . . .

Storyteller: But she told her oldest son to run over the hill to Coigach, which is only seven miles, today's 25 miles by road.

Interviewer: He came by the coast?

Storyteller: Aye, he ran over the Hill and he warned people . . . When they came . . . they dressed and they put the, the big black stockings on, you know what I mean the men, some of the men dressed up, the more weaklings of the men that looked like women, you know, and they waited on the beach, and the thing was if they went over high tide mark, it would be legal landing of a document you know, so they did was, they a . . . they went and met them on the beach . . .

You see the *Cailleachs* [old women], boy, with the hand like that, scooping the pebbles out of the beach, man, you know, and wallop! you know? and that's, that's the second-hand story, you know, and they just gie'd it to them. But when they thrashed the Red Coats on the beach . . . they got the bloody boat and dragged it up the beach and . . .

Interviewer: That was the women, aye?

Storyteller: Yes; yes, yes. Then the men came down, you see, because they were broken men. They were . . . the structure was broken after the, after the ['45] . . .

407

But anyway when, when they pulled the boat up over the sea-tide, they suddenly thought . . . that . . . if they pulled the boat up to burn it, that the eviction papers would be in the boat, and if the eviction papers were in the boat if they pulled the boat over the shore they would be doing what the Red Coats wanted . . . once it was landed . . . we're finished, you know? So they searched the whole boat and they found, you know the triangular draining board in the back of a coble boat, they lifted it and there was the eviction papers so they built a pyre below seaweed mark and they burnt that.

Interviewer: Aye.

Storyteller: And then they took the trousers and the fun the women had! Of taking the trousers off the Red Coats, six of them, taking the trousers off them, you know and the, the pants off them, you know long pants, and sending them marching home over to Ullapool, 25 miles, that was winter.

Interviewer: Oh, they made them walk back?

Storyteller: Aye, aye, aye . . . [You've heard] . . . the tune . . . The March of the, of the cold . . . Well, you know, testicles.

Interviewer: [laughs] Is that what its called?

Storyteller: Yes, aye, aye.

Interviewer: I must remember that.

Social and Cultural Significance

The story, then, is not just about the area; it has acquired numerous accretions of detail. In addition to the historical core (which broadly corresponds with other, some written, accounts), there is considerable local elaboration and embellishment of detail based on local reference, instance:

* the Achiltibuie woman who delays the Clearance party at Ullapool and sends her eldest son to warn his kin
* the 'legal landing' of the papers above the tide-mark
* the discovery of the papers concealed under the draining board at the back of the coble
* the burning of the boat between the tide-lines
* the local pipe-tune celebrating the trouserless march of the military back to Ullapool.

Furthermore, in addition to the many and various individual and personal responses which punctuate the tale, it embraces a number of wider elements seemingly unconnected with the actual event — reference to the '45 and local support for it, and references (not mentioned in these extracts) to the cod fisheries, to the advice of Irish fishermen and to a Pan-Celtic identity.

This all helps give the story some of its vitality, as well as establishing the same sort of inner world of meaning that the use of slang, technical terminology or Gaelic also creates — 'over the Hill', 'out the river'; details of the coble; 'cailleach' (and elsewhere, 'bodach', 'bochan'). In this it resembles the other historical stories told locally, and it nurtures a sense of local identity.

Within, however, is a deeper and stronger sense of identity. Some of the story's capacity to stimulate such a response must lie in the dramatic form, in the creative act of narrating it and in the outcome of the event; but it also contains idealised visions of contemporary issues. The local people *acted positively* rather than passively accepting their fate at the hands of outsiders. They *acted together* rather than as individuals. They were able to do so because of a warning sent by a female relative, acting out of *kinship obligation*.

The events of the past are used to re-state cultural values and norms of behaviour. Of course, this function of myth has been recognised by social scientists for a long time: Durkheim has been a fruitful source of ideas, not least for social anthropologists. What makes this story interesting is that it would appear to be a version of an event that 'actually happened', i.e. that it is recorded in written history, which conventionally is taken to mean that it actually happened. Oral tradition, therefore, has either kept alive details which were lost in the writing, or encouraged local and personal embellishments.

Second, the historicity of the event has been manipulated as a mechanism for sanitizing a potentially contentious statement. For whilst the second, video-taped version emphasises a sense of belonging as a Celt and a local, its first telling could be interpreted as a statement about incomers, stimulated by the unusual condition of someone moving house — signalling to them that they were outsiders, that they were part of a society which had exploited local people, and that differences could be felt between some white settlers and local people. This potentially contentious message was, however, rendered acceptable and indeed polite by the fact that it took the form of a description of a piece of 'history'. Thus there was no open antagonism, or start of a long term disagreement: rather, a boundary was laid out, which paradoxically provided the basis for future social relationships in the confined social space of a small settlement.

In other words, the story is much more than a description of events; it is not just one among several local tales but can be seen, on occasion at least, as a key symbolic tale. This confirms the more general view that the past and history are not casual conversational capital like the weather; nor yet a fixed, intrinsically interesting bank of knowledge. It is the selective use of history that makes it important for Coigach, and which contributes to the continuing sense of identity that sustains its indigenous people.

Notes

[1] This study was the outcome of MacLeod's research in Coigach for his Ph.D thesis, Plymouth University, 1992, supervised by Professor Payne.

[2] See Stacey 1960; Watson 1965; Merton 1968; Newby 1979; Ennew 1980; Strathern 1984; Stephenson 1984; Phillips 1986; Bryan 1987.

[3] In this study the term 'Coigach' refers to those townships grouped around the peninsula of Coigach, between outer Loch Broom and Enard Bay. It does not include the rest of the former Barony of Coigach. Because these townships are usually viewed collectively by their inhabitants and by other people as a single locality, they are taken to be a distinct social unit.

[4] The social organisation described in this paper is as it was during the fieldwork. There were 261 people living in Coigach in August 1989, but due to births and deaths, and in- and out-migration, the population figure has varied somewhat throughout the course of research and subsequently.

[5] In fact it is very rare for a baby to have been born in Coigach in recent decades. The nearest maternity unit is over sixty miles away and this means that expectant mothers usually travel to the east coast to have their babies delivered. Nevertheless, 'born and bred' is the phrase used by Coigach people to designate those who were raised from infancy in Coigach, and that is how it is used here.

[6] Such legitimation is only required in the event of one local vying with another in an attempt to prove him or herself 'more' local.

[7] Labels like 'local', 'incomer' and 'visitor' are all terms commonly used by people living in Coigach. The basic framework is as follows:

Local : Coigach-born and/or lived most of life in Coigach

Local non-resident: local, living away from Coigach

Locally-connected: non-local, married into local family, or with long local work-record

Incomer : non-local resident

Regular visitor : incomer for part of each year (e.g. school holidays)

'White settler' : incomer, usually well-off/middle class, with few local connections; rarely used to describe people who come to live in Coigach, but is reserved for those who normally spend only a few weeks of the year in their holiday home

'Bongley'/visitor : casual, non-local visitor or tourist

Individuals can pass through these statuses, e.g. from 'incomer' to 'locally-connected', over time. Equally, the line between 'us' and 'them' is constantly negotiated, and is re-drawn at various points within the above list according to what is currently taking place.

Acknowledgement

Fig. 15.5 is reproduced by courtesy of the Royal Commission on the Ancient and Historical Monuments of Scotland.

References

Bell, C. & Newby, H. *Community Studies.* 1971.

Brody, H. *Inishkillane: Change and Decline in the West of Ireland.* 1973.

Bryan, G. White Settlers — A Red Herring, in *The Scots Magazine.* July 1987.

Bryden, J. M. & Houston, G. *Agrarian Change in the Scottish Highlands.* 1976.

Cohen, A. P. (ed.) *Symbolising Boundaries: Identity and Diversity in British Cultures.* 1986.

Ennew, J. *The Western Isles Today.* 1980.

Gibbon, P. Arensberg and Kimball Revisited, in *Economy and Society.* vol. 2. 1973.

MacLeod, A. *Social Identity, Social Change and the Construction of Symbolic Boundaries in a West Highland Settlement.* Unpublished Ph.D thesis, University of Plymouth. 1992.

MacLeod, A. & Payne, G. *Talking About the Past: Social Identity in a Scottish Village.* B.S.A. Conference, Edinburgh. 1988. ms.

MacLeod, A. & Payne, G. *'When All's Said and Done': Identity Without Language in a Small Settlement.* Fasgnag Conference, Sabhal Mór Ostaig, Skye. 1991. ms.

Merton, R. K. Locals and Cosmopolitans, in *Social Theory and Social Structure.* 2nd Edition. 1968.

Newby, H. *Green and Pleasant Land.* 1979.

Phillips, S. K. Natives and Incomers: the symbolism of belonging in Muker Parish, North Yorkshire, in A. P. Cohen (ed.) *Symbolising Boundaries: Identity and Diversity in British Cultures.* 1986.

Stacey, M. *Tradition and Change:* A Study of Banbury. 1960.

Stephenson, J. B. *Ford: A Village in the West Highlands.* 1984.

Strathern, M. The Village as an Idea: constructs of village-ness in Elmdon, Essex, in A. P. Cohen (ed.) *Belonging: Identity and Social Organisation in British Rural Cultures.* 1982.

Fig. 15.5 Polglass, Coigach, 1993.

CONTRIBUTORS

JOHN R. BALDWIN has returned to Lothian Region Education Department and is currently seconded to develop Environmental Education.

MALCOLM BANGOR-JONES gained his PhD at the University of Dundee and is now a civil servant at the Scottish Office.

ELIZABETH BEATON has recently retired as an investigator with Historic Scotland and lives in Moray.

MARILYN BROWN is an investigator with the Royal Commission on the Ancient and Historical Monuments of Scotland, Edinburgh.

J. B. CAIRD has recently retired as Professor of Geography, University of Dundee.

MONICA CLOUGH formerly lectured at the University of Stirling and now lives in Drumnadrochit, Inverness-shire.

RICHARD COX gained his PhD at Glasgow University and now lives at Buchlyvie, Stirlingshire.

IAN A. FRASER lectures in the School of Scottish Studies, University of Edinburgh, and heads the Place-Name Survey.

AUBREY HALFORD-MACLEOD is retired from the Diplomatic Service and lives in Harris. He is a former Ambassador to Iceland.

EUAN W. MACKIE is Depute Director of the Hunterian Museum, University of Glasgow.

ANGUS MACLEOD gained his PhD at the University of Plymouth and is now living and working back home in Coigach.

JEAN MUNRO is an independent scholar living in Edinburgh who, as Jean Dunlop, made the definitive study of the British Fisheries Society.

R. W. MUNRO is also an independent scholar who, with his wife Jean Munro, has researched widely into West Highland history.

GEOFF PAYNE is Professor of Sociology at the University of Plymouth.

ERIC RICHARDS is Professor of History at the Flinders University of South Australia and, with Monica Clough, has carried out substantial research on the Cromartie Papers.

DOUGLAS P. WILLIS is Principal Teacher of Geography, Fortrose Academy, Easter Ross.